Human Resources Kit

FOR

DUMMIES®

3RD EDITION

by Max Messmer

WILEY

John Wiley & Sons, Inc.

Human Resources Kit For Dummies®, 3rd Edition

Published by
John Wiley & Sons, Inc.
111 River St.
Hoboken, NJ 07030-5774
www.wiley.com

WILEY

About the Author

Harold M. "Max" Messmer, Jr., is chairman and CEO of Robert Half International, the world's largest specialized staffing firm. He is one of the foremost experts on human resources and employment issues. Messmer's entire business is built on the premise that any company's success is based on the extent to which attracting and keeping outstanding talent is a top priority.

In 2011, Messmer received the prestigious Staffing Innovator Award from Staffing Industry Analysts and was named the Bay Area's Most Admired CEO in the large public company category by the *San Francisco Business Times.* In 2010, Messmer was inducted by the San Francisco–based Bay Area Council into its Bay Area Business Hall of Fame.

For the past 26 years, Messmer has served as CEO of Robert Half. He also has served on the boards of numerous major corporations. His community involvement includes service on the University of California, San Francisco (UCSF) Medical Center Executive Council and the Eisenhower Medical Center Board of Directors. He also is a past member of the board of overseers of the Hoover Institution at Stanford University.

Messmer, who began his career as a law firm associate and then partner, was valedictorian of his graduating class at Loyola University and graduated cum laude from the New York University (NYU) School of Law. In 2000, he received the prestigious Alumni Achievement Award from NYU's Law Alumni Association.

A frequent author, Messmer's other books in the *For Dummies* series include *Job Hunting For Dummies,* 2nd Edition; *Managing Your Career For Dummies;* and *Motivating Employees For Dummies.* He also has written countless articles on job seeking, employment, and management topics and is the author of the popular column "Resumania," distributed by Scripps Howard News Service.

Founded in 1948, Robert Half is a recognized leader in professional consulting and staffing services and is the parent company of Protiviti, a global consulting and internal audit firm. The company's specialized staffing divisions include Accountemps, Robert Half Finance & Accounting, and Robert Half Management Resources, for temporary, full-time, and senior-level project professionals, respectively, in the fields of accounting and finance; OfficeTeam, for highly skilled temporary administrative support personnel; Robert Half Technology, for information technology professionals; Robert Half Legal, for legal personnel; and The Creative Group, for interactive, design, marketing, advertising, and public relations professionals.

Robert Half International (NYSE: RHI) is a member of Standard & Poor's widely tracked S&P 500 Index. The company consistently appears on *Fortune* magazine's "World's Most Admired Companies" list, ranking number one in the staffing industry in 2012 (March 19, 2012).

Dedication

To my wife, Marcia, and my sons, Michael and Matthew, and their families, all of whom are my daily reminders that people are the most important source of inspiration — in life and in work.

Author's Acknowledgments

In preparing this third edition of *Human Resources Kit For Dummies,* I relied on the advice and assistance of a number of talented individuals whose contributions made this book possible. I want to thank Jeff Wuorio, Allen Scott, and Robert McCauley for their research and recommendations on the fast-changing world of human resources management. I also want to acknowledge the valuable insight of Reesa Staten, senior vice president of corporate communications at Robert Half, and Lynne Smith, director of talent management and staffing at Robert Half. I would be remiss if I didn't acknowledge those individuals who made the previous editions of *Human Resources Kit For Dummies* possible, most notably Joel Drucker, Barry Tarshis, and Lynn Taylor. In addition, I'm indebted to Stacy Kennedy, acquisitions editor at John Wiley & Sons, Inc., who saw the need to provide new insight on this important subject, and to the editors and reviewers whose efforts carried this third edition through to completion, Elizabeth Kuball and Debra Tenenbaum.

My sincere thanks also go to the highly respected law firm of Paul Hastings LLP, whose collaboration was essential to the whole project. Paul Hastings is a leading international law firm that serves many of the world's top financial institutions and Fortune Global 500 companies with 19 offices across Asia, Europe, and the United States. As legal issues continue to shape key HR practices, I believe our readers will benefit greatly from the insights provided by Kirby Wilcox, one of the firm's senior partners and a leading employment law expert, and Brit Seifert, an attorney with the firm's employment law department. I would also like to acknowledge with gratitude the law firm of O'Melveny & Myers, which was a valuable source of expert advice in the first two editions of this book.

A final acknowledgment goes to the founder of our company, the late Robert Half, who was a close friend. Bob established a corporate motto years ago: "Ethics First" — two words that continue to be the indispensable cornerstone of any successful business.

Publisher's Acknowledgments

We're proud of this book; please send us your comments at http://dummies.custhelp.com. For other comments, please contact our Customer Care Department within the U.S. at 877-762-2974, outside the U.S. at 317-572-3993, or fax 317-572-4002.

Some of the people who helped bring this book to market include the following:

Acquisitions, Editorial, and Vertical Websites

Project Editor: Elizabeth Kuball

(Previous Editions: Kelly Ewing, Tim Gallan)

Acquisitions Editor: Stacy Kennedy

Copy Editor: Elizabeth Kuball

Assistant Editor: David Lutton

Editorial Program Coordinator: Joe Niesen

Technical Editor: Debra Tenenbaum

Vertical Websites: Laura Moss-Hollister, Josh Frank

Senior Editorial Manager: Jennifer Ehrlich

Editorial Manager: Carmen Krikorian

Editorial Assistants: Rachelle S. Amick, Alexa Koschier

Art Coordinator: Alicia B. South

Cover Photos: © Alex Slobodkin / iStockphoto.com

Cartoons: Rich Tennant (www.the5thwave.com)

Composition Services

Project Coordinator: Katherine Crocker

Layout and Graphics: Carl Byers, Joyce Haughey, Corrie Niehaus

Proofreaders: Bonnie Mikkelson, Dwight Ramsey

Indexer: BIM Indexing & Proofreading Services

Publishing and Editorial for Consumer Dummies

Kathleen Nebenhaus, Vice President and Executive Publisher

David Palmer, Associate Publisher

Kristin Ferguson-Wagstaffe, Product Development Director

Publishing for Technology Dummies

Andy Cummings, Vice President and Publisher

Composition Services

Debbie Stailey, Director of Composition Services

Contents at a Glance

Introduction 1

Part I: Scoping Out the HR Role 7
Chapter 1: The World of Human Resources 9
Chapter 2: Setting the Stage: Key HR Trends 15
Chapter 3: HR Technology Systems and Social Tools 23

Part II: Putting the Right People in the Right Places ... 33
Chapter 4: A Bird's-Eye View: Launching a Workforce Plan 35
Chapter 5: Smart Start: Kicking Off the Hiring Process 55
Chapter 6: You, the Talent Scout: Recruiting for Your Team 63
Chapter 7: Narrowing Down the Field: Evaluating Applicants 85
Chapter 8: One on One: Getting the Most out of Interviewing 105
Chapter 9: The Home Stretch: Making the Final Decision 123

Part III: Keeping Your Best People 143
Chapter 10: Starting New Hires Off on the Right Foot 145
Chapter 11: Ensuring a Competitive Compensation Structure 163
Chapter 12: Creating the Right Benefits Package 183
Chapter 13: Creating an Employee-Friendly Work Environment 209

Part IV: Developing Your Employees 221
Chapter 14: Back to School: Tying Training to Business Goals 223
Chapter 15: Win-Win: Adding Value through Career Development 239
Chapter 16: Assessing Employee Performance 261

Part V: Law and Order 275
Chapter 17: Navigating the Legal Minefield of Hiring and Managing 277
Chapter 18: Handling Difficult Situations 293

Part VI: The Part of Tens 319
Chapter 19: Ten Keys to HR Success in the Future 321
Chapter 20: Ten Ways to Become a Great HR Professional 327
Chapter 21: Ten HR-Related Websites Worth Exploring 333

Appendix: About the CD 337

Index 347

Table of Contents

Introduction 1

    About This Book 1
    Conventions Used in This Book 3
    What You're Not to Read 3
    Foolish Assumptions 3
    How This Book Is Organized 4
        Part I: Scoping Out the HR Role 4
        Part II: Putting the Right People in the Right Places 4
        Part III: Keeping Your Best People 5
        Part IV: Developing Your Employees 5
        Part V: Law and Order 5
        Part VI: The Part of Tens 5
        Appendix 5
        The CD 5
    Icons Used in This Book 6
    Where to Go from Here 6

Part 1: Scoping Out the HR Role 7

Chapter 1: The World of Human Resources 9

    Grasping Key HR Responsibilities 10
    Building Your Team: Staffing Strategically 11
    Keeping Your Best People: The Art of Retention 12
    Training and Developing Employees 13
    Looking At the Legal Aspects of HR 13

Chapter 2: Setting the Stage: Key HR Trends 15

    Working As a Strategist, Not Just an Administrator 16
    Taking Technology to the Next Level 17
    Understanding the Specialist Economy 17
    Building In Workforce Flexibility 18
    Making Workforce Diversity Work for Your Organization 19
    Easing the Work/Life Conflict 20
    Managing Rising Healthcare Costs 21

Chapter 3: HR Technology Systems and Social Tools 23

    The Growth of HR-Related Technology 24
    Human Resources Information Systems 25
        Applicant tracking systems 26
        Employee profile systems 27

Time management systems 27
Benefits administration systems..27
Payroll administration systems 28
Employee self-service features..28
Talent Management Systems 29
Performance appraisal systems...29
Learning management systems..29
Succession management systems 30
Choosing the Systems That Are Right for You 30
Online Social Tools...32

Part II: Putting the Right People in the Right Places 33

Chapter 4: A Bird's-Eye View: Launching a Workforce Plan 35

Grasping the Big Picture...35
Ensuring that staffing needs are in sync with business needs 36
Bringing existing staff to their potential 38
Knowing when to begin staffing strategically 39
Finding the Right People for Open Positions...39
Inner peace: Filling jobs from within the organization 40
New horizons: Looking for staff outside the company 43
A Wide World of Talent: Understanding Worker Classification 44
Employees...45
Contingent workers 46
Independent contractors 46
Getting Permanent Benefit from Contingent Workers 47
Finding the right staffing source 49
Getting the most out of contingent workers 50
Keeping records and offering feedback to the staffing firm..........53
Looking at your legal responsibility...54

Chapter 5: Smart Start: Kicking Off the Hiring Process 55

Your Blueprint: Creating the Job Description 55
Look ahead, not behind 58
Set priorities 58
Consider educational requirements and qualifications.................59
Make sure that the job is doable 59
Be specific...60
Set a salary range...61
What's in a Job Title? 61
Besides Functional Skills, What Does It Take to Do the Job? 61

Chapter 6: You, the Talent Scout: Recruiting for Your Team 63

Putting Your Firm's Best Foot Forward 63
Kicking Off the Process...64

Getting the Word Out: How to Write a Great Job Posting 64
Investigating Candidate Sourcing Strategies...66
    Online job boards 66
    Your company website 68
    Social media and online networking...........................69
    Blind and classified ads..72
    Recruiters 72
    Campus recruiting 75
    Job fairs 77
    Employee referrals..78
    Open houses 79
    Professional associations 80
    Direct applications (walk-ins) 80
    Government employment services...............................80
Diversity Recruiting: Benefiting from a Diverse Workforce 81
Handling Helicopter Parents 82
Keeping Tabs on Your Progress 84

Chapter 7: Narrowing Down the Field: Evaluating Applicants 85
First Contact: The Résumé...85
    The evolution of the résumé 86
    Résumé roulette 88
Job Applications: Are They Obsolete?...92
Setting Up a System for Evaluating Candidates 94
Testing: Knowing What Works and What's Legal 97
    Finding the right test for your situation 98
    Staying out of test trouble 103
Phone Interviews: Narrowing Your List Further 104

Chapter 8: One on One: Getting the Most out of Interviewing 105
Interviewing: The Basics...106
The Five Deadly Sins of Job Interviewing 107
    Not devoting enough time to interviewing...............107
    Not being consistent from one interview to the next 107
    Talking too much 107
    Focusing on one positive attribute of a candidate
      and ignoring everything else 108
    Playing armchair (psycho)analyst.............................108
Setting the Stage 108
The Introduction: Warming Up 109
Q&A: Mastering the Art..110
    Have a focus 111
    Make every question count 111
    Pay attention 111
    Don't hesitate to probe 111
    Give candidates ample time to respond 112
    Suspend judgments 112

Take notes...112
Vary the style of questions..113
A Crash Course in Nondiscriminatory Questioning...........................115
National origin...116
Citizenship status..116
Address..116
Age...116
Family status..117
Religion...117
Health and physical condition.......................................117
Name..117
Language..118
Solid Questions to Ask and How to Interpret the Answers...................118
End Game: Closing on the Right Note.....................................122

Chapter 9: The Home Stretch: Making the Final Decision 123
Coming to Grips with the Decision-Making Process 124
Utilizing the Tools of the Trade..124
Past experience..124
Interview impressions...125
Test results...125
Firsthand observation..125
Selecting Your Candidate: You Need a System.......................................126
Setting up your own protocol...127
Factoring in the intangibles...128
Hiring Right...130
Anchor yourself to the hiring criteria..........................130
Take your time..130
Cross-verify whenever possible.....................................131
Get help, but avoid the "too many cooks" syndrome.................131
Don't force the issue..131
Avoid the "top of mind" syndrome................................131
Getting a Broader View...132
Checking hard-to-check references..............................132
Using your own network for checking.........................133
Online reference checking: Proceed with caution.....................134
Discovering the Truth about Background Checks 134
To do or not to do? That is the question!.....................136
So, what's the bottom line? 137
Making Offers They Can't Refuse..138
Don't delay...138
Put your offer on the table..138
Set a deadline...139
Stay connected...139
Know how to negotiate salary.......................................139
Know when to draw the line...140
Clarify acceptance details..140
Stay in touch..141

Part III: Keeping Your Best People 143

Chapter 10: Starting New Hires Off on the Right Foot 145
Onboarding: Going Beyond Orientation 146
Three Unproductive Approaches 147
Osmosis 147
"Just follow Joe around" 147
Watch the video 148
Doing It Right: A Little Empathy Goes a Long Way 149
The First Day: Easing Anxieties 149
The First Week: Revealing More about the Company and the Job 150
Provide the rules of the road 151
Keep orientation practical 152
Involve senior management 152
Hold large-group sessions in a suitable location 152
Make group presentations user-friendly 152
Provide an orientation agenda 153
Space things out 154
Give a clear sense of tasks and set concrete goals 154
Beyond Onboarding 156
Develop a checklist 156
Don't let your message die 156
Use mentoring to build a solid foundation 157
Feedback: How good is your program? 158
Employee Handbook and Separate Procedures Manual:
Yes, You Need Both 159
Knowing what to include 160
Playing it safe 161

Chapter 11: Ensuring a Competitive Compensation Structure 163
Your Role Defined 164
The Basic Language of Employee Compensation 164
The Foundation for an Effective Compensation System 165
Setting pay levels in your organization 167
Adopting a pay structure 168
Taking individuals into account 170
The payroll/sales ratio: What's an optimal balance? 172
In the states: Wage and hour laws 172
Exempt and Nonexempt: Why the Distinction Matters 173
Who's exempt and why? 173
The bottom line on overtime 175
Other legal considerations 175
What You Need to Know about Raises, Bonuses, and Incentives 176
Pay raises 177
Bonuses 178
Other incentives 178
What's fair versus what works? 181
What to Communicate about Your Policies 181

Chapter 12: Creating the Right Benefits Package **183**

What's a Benefit Anyway? 184
Key Trends in Benefits Management 184
    Demographic changes 184
    Cost containment 185
    Healthcare reform 185
    Home-based employees 185
    The watchful eye of Uncle Sam 186
The Basics of Benefits Coverage 186
    Social Security and Medicare 186
    Unemployment insurance 187
    Workers' compensation 188
A Healthy Approach to Insurance 188
    The flavors of health insurance 189
    Weighing the options 190
    Rising costs: Staying ahead of the game 191
Retirement Plans 193
    Defined benefit plans 194
    Defined contribution plans 195
    Employer contributions to retirement plans 195
    ERISA and other legal issues 197
The Rest of the Benefits Smorgasbord 198
    Dental insurance 198
    Vision care 198
    Family assistance 198
    Time off 199
    Leaves of absence 200
    Sick days 202
Employee Assistance Programs 203
Five Ways to Make Your Life Easier 205

Chapter 13: Creating an Employee-Friendly Work Environment 209

Goodbye, 9 to 5: Alternate Work Arrangements 210
    Paying attention to legal implications 210
    Looking at alternate work arrangement options 211
    Making alternate arrangements work 212
    Considering phased retirement options 214
    Getting managerial buy-in 214
Popular Perks 214
    On-site exercise facilities 215
    On-site childcare 215
    Tuition assistance or reimbursement 215
    Employee sabbaticals 215
Corporate Citizenship 217
Team Opportunities 218
Employee Surveys: Keeping Tabs on Company Morale 218
    Taking the pulse of your workforce 219
    Exit interviews 220

Part IV: Developing Your Employees 221

Chapter 14: Back to School: Tying Training to Business Goals 223
The Changing Face of Training 224
Creating the Right Environment for Training 225
Assessing Your Training Needs 227
    Employee focus groups 227
    Surveys and questionnaires 227
    Observation 228
Tying Training Needs to Strategic Goals 228
Evaluating Training Methods 229
    E-learning 229
    In-house classroom training 232
    Professional association conferences and public seminars 232
    Executive education seminars 233
    Mentoring 233
Knowing What Makes for a Good Training Program 235
    How receptive the students are 235
    The applicability of the subject matter 235
    The overall learning experience 236
    Reinforcement of classroom concepts 236
Using Employee Profiles to Manage Training 236
But Is It Working? Measuring Results 237

Chapter 15: Win-Win: Adding Value through Career Development 239
Understanding Why Career Development Matters 240
Seeing Mentoring As a Tool for Growth 240
    Why and how mentoring works 241
    Setting parameters 242
    Choosing the right partners 243
    Moving forward with the program 244
You Can't Do It All Yourself: Developing Strong Leaders 245
    Defining leadership qualities that will
        move your business forward 245
    Starting your program: Factors to consider 246
    Program options 247
    Measuring progress and success 248
The Future Is Now: Succession Planning 249
    Don't put it off! 249
    Putting together the plan 250
    Pinpointing succession candidates 251
    Selecting candidates outside the company 252
    Creating a flexible understanding with succession candidates ... 252
    Developing succession candidates 253
    Assessing succession outcomes 254

Saying Thank-You: Focusing on Employee Recognition 255
    Employee recognition programs defined 256
    Your employees benefit — how do you? 256
    Getting the fundamentals in place 257
    Administration and communication.. 259
    Handing out awards: The importance of publicity....................... 259
    Evaluating results 260

Chapter 16: Assessing Employee Performance **261**
    Reaping the Benefits of Performance Appraisals 262
    Deciding on a Performance Appraisal System.................................... 263
        Goal setting, or management by objectives 264
        Behaviorally anchored rating scale.. 265
        Critical incidents.. 266
        Multirater assessments.. 267
    Launching an Appraisal Program in Your Company............................ 267
        Enlist the support of senior management 267
        Choose performance measures with care................................... 268
        Develop a fair and practical tracking mechanism 268
        Develop a communication game plan 269
    Getting the Most Out of the Performance Appraisal Meeting 269
        Preparing for the meeting.. 270
        Conducting the session.. 270
        Giving constructive feedback.. 271
        Preparing for a negative reaction 272
        Choosing areas for further development.................................... 273
    Following Up on Performance Appraisals 274

Part V: Law and Order *275*

Chapter 17: Navigating the Legal Minefield
of Hiring and Managing **277**
    Legal Matters: The Big Picture... 278
    Keeping the Peace 279
    Discrimination... 279
    Disparate Impact 280
    The Equal Employment Opportunity Commission 281
    The Family of EEO and Other Employment Laws: A Closer Look 284
        ADEA: The Age Discrimination in Employment Act of 1967........ 284
        OWBA: Older Workers Benefit Protection Act (1990)................... 285
        AC-21: American Competitiveness
            in the 21st Century Act (2000).. 285
        ADA: Americans with Disabilities Act of 1990, as amended by the
            Americans with Disabilities Act Amendments Act of 2008....... 286
        COBRA: Consolidated Omnibus Budget
            Reconciliation Act (1986).. 286
        The Equal Pay Act of 1963 287

FMLA: Family and Medical Leave Act (1993)................................287
FLSA: Fair Labor Standards Act (1938) 288
FUTA: Federal Unemployment Tax Act (1939)........................288
HIPAA: Health Insurance Portability
    and Accountability Act (1996)..289
IRCA: Immigration Reform and Control Act of 1986....................289
Pregnancy Discrimination Act of 1978................................290
The Rehabilitation Act of 1973..290
Sarbanes-Oxley Act (2002)..290
Title VII of the Civil Rights Act (1964) 291
USA PATRIOT ACT (2001)..291
The WARN Act: Worker Adjustment and
    Retraining Notification Act (1988) 292

Chapter 18: Handling Difficult Situations. 293
Establishing an Ethical Culture..294
Fleshing Out the Meaning of At-Will Employment....................294
Staying Out of Court..295
Developing Progressive Disciplinary Procedures 296
Defusing Grievances..301
Settling Disputes: Alternative Dispute Resolution Programs 302
Firing Employees: It's Never Easy 303
    Avoiding common firing mistakes 305
    Delivering the news 306
    Putting in place a post-termination protocol....................306
    Asking the employee to sign a waiver of rights 307
Easing the Trauma of Layoffs..308
    Analyzing whether layoffs are the right strategy................309
    Knowing the federal and state law 309
    Easing the burden 310
    Hiring outplacement specialists 310
    Addressing the concerns of those who remain....................312
Protecting the Safety and Health of Your Employees..................313
Sexual Harassment: Keeping Your Workplace Free of It................313
    Spreading the word 315
    Creating a reporting process......................................316
    Investigating complaints..316
    Taking decisive action..316
Dealing with Workplace Violence......................................317

Part VI: The Part of Tens.. 319

Chapter 19: Ten Keys to HR Success in the Future. 321
Adopt a Strategic Approach to Staffing................................321
Understand the Strength of Traditional
    and New Strategies in Recruiting..................................322
Seek to Create a Healthy Culture......................................322

Get the Most out of Contingent Staffing.......................................323
Take a Proactive Approach to Regulatory Compliance........................323
Make Work/Life Balance a Priority..324
Keep Pace with Changing Demographics...324
Play It Safe When It Comes to HR Technology.................................325
View Training As an Ongoing Investment 326
Handle Discipline and Dismissal Carefully......................................326

Chapter 20: Ten Ways to Become a Great HR Professional 327

Develop a Business Orientation to HR Initiatives 327
Position Initiatives As Bottom-Line Benefits....................................328
Develop a Marketing Mindset 328
Share Your Expertise 328
Serve As the Model...329
Develop Your Communication Skills..329
Move Quickly — But Not Too Quickly 329
Create and Maintain a Flexible Workforce 330
Be Sensitive to the Needs and Agendas of Line Managers....................330
Stay on the Leading Edge 331

Chapter 21: Ten HR-Related Websites Worth Exploring...........333

American Society for Training & Development 333
Americans with Disabilities Act Document Center 334
Bureau of Labor Statistics 334
The elaws Advisors 334
Human Capital Institute 335
Occupational Safety & Health Administration...................................335
Society for Human Resource Management 335
U.S. Equal Employment Opportunity Commission 336
WorldatWork...336
Workforce Online..336

Appendix: About the CD 337

System Requirements 337
Using the CD 338
What You'll Find on the CD 338
    Software 338
    Documents..339
Troubleshooting 345
Customer Care...346

Index 347

Introduction

● ●

A company's ability to grow and stay on top of customer demand has always depended heavily on the quality of its people. Today, this relationship is even more relevant. In bottom-line terms, employees represent the intellectual capital that can make or break a firm's efforts to remain competitive. Businesses are now, more than ever, recognizing that a highly skilled and motivated workforce is pivotal to success.

About This Book

Managers and business owners with loyal teams that consistently delight customers and make money for the firm aren't hard to spot. They're the people who know how to attract and nurture these teams. In short, they're very good at managing human resources.

But recruiting and managing a first-rate staff is no small feat. In any job market, competition exists for the most desirable candidates, and, once hired, these top performers are only a competitor's phone call away from leaving you. Not only that, but the human resources (HR) function now encompasses everything from creating a strategic workforce plan to launching effective training initiatives, interpreting federal and state codes, and implementing policies and benefits that safeguard workers while protecting company interests. And the stakes are high. The legal and economic consequences of a major HR misstep can be enormous.

As a business owner or manager, you've probably already faced these and other challenges. You may not think of yourself as an "HR person," but you recognize that you need to hire the best people you can and motivate them to do their best work for you. In the past, you likely took on some aspects of finding and keeping top talent, with perhaps someone else on your team handling the details. Now, as your organization has grown, you're no doubt finding that your company's HR responsibilities have become more complicated. Whether you're a business owner who would like to make sure that you're up-to-date on employment regulations and HR best practices, or you're a manager who has been asked to take on HR-related duties, you're going to need a resource. Even if you attend outside courses in people management, you won't remember everything you hear. Ultimately, you need a straightforward yet comprehensive resource with information, insights, and tools to help align your company's HR practices and policies with the overall objectives of your business. That's why I decided to write *Human Resources Kit For Dummies*.

Some companies are lucky enough to have their own HR professional or even an entire HR department. Most of these HR specialists have developed their skills through years of education and on-the-job experience. In writing this book, my aim is not to pretend that I can magically turn you into a seasoned HR professional by the time you read the last page. I *do* believe, though, that I can give you a fair representation of the issues HR people deal with, how the best of them approach these challenges, and enough background to help you better oversee or handle the HR function for your organization — both today and as you continue to grow.

As you can see from the table of contents, human resources is a very broad and varied discipline. One book can't possibly tell you everything you need to know about this continually evolving subject area. So, don't worry — I won't overwhelm you with information. On the contrary, everything you read in this book and every tool available on the included CD directly relates to the operational issues most companies deal with daily.

What can you expect to gain from this book? For starters, you'll be better able to

- Evaluate your company's current HR policies and practices to ensure that they've kept pace with changes in the HR landscape.

- Understand the HR-related issues (changing demographics, for example) that are affecting the workplace of the future — and make the necessary long-term plans for success.

- Develop and implement an HR program that responds to the needs and resources of your firm.

- Understand the key regulatory issues that apply to many business owners and managers and, thus, put yourself in a better position to guard against costly legal disputes.

- Develop a strategic staffing mindset, ensuring that hiring and staffing practices and decisions are linked to long-term and short-term business objectives.

- Examine what today's most successful and progressive companies are doing with respect to such basic HR areas as recruiting, benefits, training, performance management, and staff retention.

- Gain insight into practices (flextime and telecommuting, for example) that have become basic components of today's "employee-friendly" workplace, determine which ones are right for your company, and administer them successfully and cost-effectively.

This book provides general guidelines on how to set up and implement successful HR practices, as well as actual tools — forms, templates, web links, and so on — that you can use right away. *Human Resources Kit For Dummies,* in other words, is not simply a book to read; it's a book to use.

Conventions Used in This Book

I don't use many conventions in this book, but I do use a few to help you find the information you need quickly and easily:

- ✔ When I introduce a new term, I *italicize* it and define it shortly thereafter (often in parentheses).

- ✔ I use monofont for all web and e-mail addresses.

Note: When this book was printed, some web addresses may have needed to break across two lines of text. If that happened, rest assured that we haven't put in any extra characters (such as hyphens) to indicate the break. So, when using one of these web addresses, just type in exactly what you see in this book, pretending as though the line break doesn't exist.

What You're Not to Read

You can skip sidebars (that's the text in gray boxes). Although the sidebars are interesting, they're not critical to your understanding of the subject at hand. You also can skip anything marked with the Technical Stuff icon (see "Icons Used in This Book," later, for more information).

Foolish Assumptions

In writing *Human Resources Kit For Dummies,* I had to make certain assumptions about you, the reader. Because I'm not sure exactly what your background and needs are, I wrote the book with two broad audiences in mind:

- ✔ Business owners who find that their growing companies are demanding a greater portion of their time and attention in managing one or more of the most common HR functions, such as hiring, benefits administration, performance evaluation, training, and regulatory issues

- ✔ Individuals in small to mid-size companies who have only a limited knowledge of HR functions but whose management has asked them to take on some or all of these roles

Although seasoned HR professionals may find much of the information a handy reference, my primary audience is people who are new to the field or are eager to discover new HR practices to gain competitive advantages for their companies.

First and foremost, I want to address you as a businessperson — someone who, after reading the book, is knowledgeable not only about the nuts and bolts of HR but also about how to approach the function with the goal of becoming a major player in helping to run your company.

Finally, when I use the term *senior management* at various points in this book, don't misconstrue it to refer exclusively to CEOs and other higher-ups at larger companies. Rather, I take it to also include the people I just mentioned — owners of small, growing companies and key managers in mid-size businesses, among others. The overriding point is, if you need a comprehensive overview of what HR involves, this book is designed to fit your needs, no matter what your day job is.

How This Book Is Organized

Human Resources Kit For Dummies is divided into six parts, each of which is further divided into chapters, totaling 21 chapters in all. It also includes a CD with forms, templates, and other tools that correspond to the topics covered in particular chapters. Every chapter contains not just information but also concrete advice on how to put this information to practical use.

Following is a brief description of what I cover in each part.

Part I: Scoping Out the HR Role

In this part, I introduce the fundamental responsibilities expected of someone in an HR role. Then I outline the key issues affecting the human resources field today. Throughout the book, I discuss various HR technology tools, but in this part, I talk about them as a group and explain how they can benefit even the smallest HR shop.

Part II: Putting the Right People in the Right Places

Here I get down to brass tacks. I focus specifically on the hiring process, beginning with the foundation that supports all your staffing activities. Successful staffing in today's workplace is a multistage process, with each phase linked to the others. I give you the background and tools you and your company's line managers need to recruit, interview, and select employees, or to engage contingent workers, who will be pivotal in growing your business.

Part III: Keeping Your Best People

This part covers policies that can either enhance or stand in the way of your ability to retain valued staff after you've attracted them to your organization. That effort starts on the first day a new employee walks in the front door. I then cover elements such as compensation, benefits, training, and establishing a culture that can give your company a reputation as a great place to work.

Part IV: Developing Your Employees

Here you discover how to offer training that's tied to your business goals, as well as career development opportunities that can help your people grow professionally. I also offer tips on the right way to measure employee performance.

Part V: Law and Order

This part addresses the legal challenges of hiring and managing your employees. I cover discrimination and a number of federal labor laws and guidelines. This part also includes a chapter on how to deal with difficult situations, such as grievances, layoffs, dismissals, and sexual harassment.

Part VI: The Part of Tens

The final chapters of this book provide you with useful supplementary information to help you build and maintain a productive, loyal workforce. Here, you find ten keys to HR success in the future, ten ways to become a great HR professional, and ten HR-related websites worth exploring.

Appendix

One last thing: I also include an About the CD appendix that covers — you guessed it — how to use the CD included with this book.

The CD

From sample job descriptions to sample employee policies, you get a variety of tools you need to implement state-of-the-art HR practices and procedures. Some of these forms are turnkey — ready to use immediately. Others are sample templates that you may want to adapt.

The collection of forms is pretty comprehensive, but your situation may be unique. When in doubt, the best practice is always to contact a knowledgeable and experienced lawyer who specializes in this area.

Icons Used in This Book

When I want you to pay close attention to a specific piece of information, I place little pictures, called *icons,* next to the text in the margin. Here's what the icons mean:

This icon flags what I consider to be good and practical advice.

I flag important conceptual information with this icon.

This icon indicates something that is particularly sensitive and could get you into legal trouble if not handled properly. Always contact an attorney if you're unsure if something is legally risky (regardless of whether it's flagged by a Warning icon).

This icon flags legal jargon and technical discussions.

Whenever I mention a document that you can reference on the CD, I use this icon.

Where to Go from Here

Every chapter in this book covers a topic of importance to the HR function. But you'll likely find that some chapters have greater relevance to your situation than others. If you're completely new to the HR role, for instance, you'll want to start with Part I to build your baseline knowledge. If you have some experience hiring and managing staff, you may instead choose to start with the later chapters to discover the finer points of these activities. You don't have to read this book from start to finish to get the most out of it. Look through the table of contents and index so you can find those chapters or sections that address the issues you currently face.

Part I

Scoping Out the HR Role

The 5th Wave   By Rich Tennant

"Very good answer! Now let me ask you another question..."

In this part . . .

I give you a 30,000-foot view of human resources. I lay out the fundamental categories of HR responsibilities and give you a quick summary of the steps involved in recruiting and retaining strong teams. I provide an overview of some of the most important trends in the HR field, such as the growing need to offer policies that support employees' desire to achieve work/life balance and the wider adoption of flexible staffing models. Another key trend, the continued effect of technology, is so rapidly changing the HR role that I devote an entire chapter to it.

Chapter 1

The World of Human Resources

In This Chapter
▶ Spelling out key HR responsibilities
▶ Staffing your organization
▶ Retaining your best workers
▶ Training and developing your workforce
▶ Understanding legal issues and challenges

A good deal of debate has traditionally existed over just how much responsibility (and how much time and money) a company needs to devote to the needs and priorities of employees as opposed to the needs and priorities of its business operations and customers.

To me, there has really never been much of a debate. I believe that a company's employees are not only integral to its success but also its heart and soul. Without them, there would *be* no business. No matter what products or services a company offers, the talents and abilities of every employee are what ultimately determine how well it performs. Whether you call them your employees, personnel, workforce, team, staff, or any other name, these special individuals differ from physical or financial assets of the company because they're all people — people with unique talents and needs.

Human resources (HR) is the field devoted to building strong teams of people and maximizing their value to an organization. But this is not a one-way proposition: As HR helps develop a company's people, their skills are enhanced in the service of their careers.

As a business owner or senior manager, operator of a nonprofit organization or educational institution, or representative of another type of employer, one of your primary jobs is to ensure the welfare and enhance the morale of your employees. Whether you turn over handling the details of this job to someone else or tackle them yourself, the role of HR management is a critical one. The effectiveness of the person(s) responsible for managing your employee base greatly affects the ongoing success of the business and your ability to differentiate yourself from the competition.

Grasping Key HR Responsibilities

Human resources management is the decisions, activities, and processes designed to support the needs and work performance of employees. The most common areas falling under HR management include

- ✔ **Staffing:** Strategically determining, recruiting, and hiring the human resources you need for your business

- ✔ **Basic workplace policies:** Orienting your staff on policies and procedures, such as general company compliance guidelines, schedules, safety, and security

- ✔ **Compensation and benefits:** Establishing legally compliant, effective — and attractive — wages and perks

- ✔ **Retention:** Continually assessing the quality of your workplace and HR programs to encourage people to stay with your organization

- ✔ **Training and developing employees**: Ensuring that your staff grows in knowledge and experience, and that their skill sets support the goals of the business, to help your organization expand and continue to meet the changing needs of customers

- ✔ **Regulatory issues:** Complying with the ever-increasing number of federal, state, and local regulations

After they reach a certain size, most employers find it more efficient to create an HR department — even if it consists of only one person. Because of the increasing complexity of HR issues, larger organizations have boosted the size of their departments and typically employ specialists in areas such as benefits administration, compensation, recruiting, and training. But smaller firms that don't have the resources for such specialization must ensure that the people who handle their HR functions are solid *generalists* — that is, they possess skills in several areas of HR rather than in one particular specialty. If your organization is on the smaller side and you want to meet the needs of your employees today, you'll need to know a lot about a lot of things — and the more you know, the better.

The human resources function in general has undergone enormous changes in the past 20 years. HR is a much more collaborative discipline, meaning that, instead of setting and enforcing policies in a vacuum, HR practitioners and line managers work cooperatively to set basic guidelines and carry out programs.

In this chapter, I give you a bird's-eye view of these key HR responsibilities.

Building Your Team: Staffing Strategically

One of the primary jobs of an HR professional is recruiting and hiring the very best people for the business. However, that means much more than hanging out a help wanted placard and signing up anyone who happens to come through the door.

Instead, much more thoughtful and comprehensive planning is needed. It all starts with developing an overall workforce plan. This involves putting your current employees in the right places to best address the organization's most critical tasks and also attracting additional people with the talent and attributes that complement both your short- and long-term business goals. Whew! There's a lot in that sentence, but that's because there's a lot involved in workforce planning. It's the foundation of everything else you do in regard to building strong teams. At its heart is strategic staffing — taking advantage of the strengths of your people and augmenting their ranks in a thoughtful, focused way rather than a haphazard one that doesn't jibe with the overall objectives of your business. (See Chapter 4 for more on strategic staffing.)

A carefully crafted job description — and job postings based on it — are critical to bringing the best people onboard. Both should focus on the actual demands of a job rather than past responsibilities that may no longer apply. Home in on the specifics of the job (for example, duties, relevant skills, and experience) to attract the best applicants possible. When you do this, you also diplomatically discourage others who may apply, whether they're qualified or not. (See Chapter 5 for more on writing a job description.)

From there, you have a broad array of potential candidate sources — all of which have pluses and minuses. These include Internet job boards, social media and online networking sites, and, of course, your own company website. Other sources include recruiting services, college campuses, job fairs, open houses, professional groups and associations, and government employment services. And don't forget employee referrals, an exceedingly fertile source. (See Chapter 6 for more on recruiting.)

Now comes the process of reviewing applicants and culling the field. You need to pick the most promising people to interview by reading between the lines in their résumés, looking for specifics about their experience and history of achievement and professional development. Then investigate other ways to further narrow your pool of candidates by using telephone interviews and online searches. (You'll also want watch the legal pitfalls here.) When it's time for the all-important in-person interviews, you need to bone up on job interview techniques and strategies, with a special emphasis on nondiscriminatory interview questions. (See Chapter 7 for more on evaluating applicants and Chapter 8 for tips on interviewing.)

As you near the final hiring decision, it's important to set up a system to help select the right candidate, including how to conduct lawful background and reference checks (see Chapter 9). Final considerations include ways to craft and present a job offer and, from there, techniques to negotiate salary, including setting parameters on how far you're willing to go with salary and benefits to be competitive and win over an attractive candidate.

Keeping Your Best People: The Art of Retention

Recruiting and hiring great employees is crucial but represents only one side of the workforce management coin. Keeping employees onboard is no less critical to the long-term growth of your business. Staff retention begins the minute new hires first walk through the door (see Chapter 10). One of your first responsibilities is to familiarize new employees with your firm's internal policies and procedures. You'll want to create an employee handbook that states policies applying to everyone in the company and, where appropriate, a separate manual that documents how people should perform their jobs.

You also need to know onboarding strategies to help new staff members get off to a strong start. It's important to make those first few days on the job as anxiety free as possible, while setting reasonable but concrete goals for the next several months and beyond. Consider a comprehensive checklist of items you need to cover so you don't overlook anything important. The onboarding process is also about following up on what employees learned at the initial orientation. Company values and best practices, for example, should continue to be stressed through the actions of role models such as supervisors and mentors, as well as through internal communications.

Every business needs an effective system to pay employees. Look into developing an overall compensation philosophy that can help establish pay levels and wage plans throughout the company (see Chapter 11). That thinking also should apply to raises, bonuses, and other forms of incentives. It's also important to understand the distinction between exempt and nonexempt employees and how that impacts overtime pay and other issues. Next, of course, are the benefits themselves (see Chapter 12). You need to understand the key components of health insurance, retirement packages, and workers' compensation, as well as encourage employee wellness and on-the-job safety.

An employee-friendly workplace means more than a sweet paycheck. It also takes in other elements that are important contributors to a motivated and satisfied workforce. Get to know the essentials of alternate work arrangements (for example, telecommuting arrangements and flexible work hours) and their value in retaining top performers (see Chapter 13). Consider, too, the importance of good corporate citizenship and workplace surveys — two components boosting employees' sense that they work in a business that does the right thing and values feedback from its people.

Training and Developing Employees

Keeping employees happy also means encouraging their professional development. Connecting employee training to your business goals makes the effort a win-win for the employee *and* the company (see Chapter 14). Investigate the variety of training options available — traditional classroom instruction, as well as a growing array of e-learning programs, which are often very cost-effective and convenient.

Whereas training programs typically are about hands-on task and skills improvement, career development emphasizes longer-term qualities and expertise that employees need to enrich their careers in general (see Chapter 15). Understand the role of mentoring relationships to foster personal growth, as well as leadership development and succession planning programs to identify and groom future leaders.

Employers need to offer feedback if they expect the people working for them to accomplish what's needed — and improve on their performance. That's why organizations create performance appraisal systems. These systems can confirm that employees have the skills and personal attributes required to do a particular job, address difficulties in the supervisor-employee relationship, and give underperforming employees the guidance they need to improve. Appraisal systems also provide an objective, legal basis for decisions about merit pay increases, promotions, and job responsibilities. (See Chapter 16 for details on establishing a performance appraisal system for your organization.)

Looking At the Legal Aspects of HR

There's no substitute for the guidance of an attorney, but HR professionals need to have a basic understanding of the many legal issues and challenges that come with hiring and managing employees — and with terminating the employee relationship.

Here and throughout this book, the legal-related information I provide is the result of a collaborative effort with the law firm of Paul Hastings LLP. All this information I present as useful guidelines and to increase your knowledge of employment-related law, but I strongly recommend consulting a knowledgeable and experienced lawyer regarding anything you encounter in your work that is legally complex.

First and foremost, you need to know how to avoid charges of discrimination and other employment-related legal claims. It's also important to understand the concept of disparate impact and steps you can take to keep your business as compliant with employment laws as possible. And, although your lawyers should take the lead in any formal legal actions or responses, you also need to be well acquainted with issues and situations covered by the Americans with Disabilities Act; the Family and Medical Leave Act; the Fair Labor Standards Act; and other important federal, state, and local laws that can impact your business.

A successful business takes an ethical approach to all its interactions with customers, as well as its employees. Driving every transaction is a culture that places integrity at the forefront. But problems do come up, no matter how conscious a business may be about ethics and fairness. You need to have strategies at the ready to address and resolve problems. These include defusing grievances, settling disputes, and developing thoughtful and effective disciplinary procedures across a variety of situations.

As an HR professional, you need to know how to sensitively but firmly handle what are undoubtedly the least pleasant aspects of your role. These include, but are not limited to, dismissals, layoffs, and sexual harassment or hostile work environment claims. (See Chapter 17 for a discussion of key HR-related laws and Chapter 18 for more on the specifics of termination and other difficult situations.)

Chapter 2

Setting the Stage: Key HR Trends

- -

In This Chapter

▶ Becoming an HR strategist

▶ Maximizing technology

▶ Seeing that this is an economy of specialists

▶ Being flexible with your workforce

▶ Reaping the benefits of a diverse workforce

▶ Helping your employees balance work with their personal lives

▶ Focusing on healthcare

- -

*P*icture yourself in the offices of a business 50 years ago. It could be a major corporation or a modestly sized startup (although they wouldn't have used the term *startup* back then). Another term you probably won't be able to find on any company directory or office door is *human resources*. After a few minutes of searching, you stop a passing employee and ask her for the department that handles job applications. The answer: "Personnel is down the hall, third door on the left."

This imaginary anecdote speaks volumes about the revolution that has occurred in the field of human resources. I realize that I'm going far back to paint this picture, but I do think it's helpful for someone new to HR to see the vast changes that have taken place in the field, as well as in the way companies of all sizes view the people who work for them. In one respect, this shift has been the result of more-comprehensive labor laws and improved working conditions. The more the government requires of a workplace, the more someone has to be charged with implementing whatever steps are mandated and making sure that they're maintained. But it also reflects how today's businesses value the people they employ.

This is not to suggest that companies around when John F. Kennedy was president didn't believe that their employees were important. What's different is the critical value that the best companies today place on each and every worker. When a company embraces the people it employs by doing everything possible to make their jobs better and more rewarding, it involves complexities and challenges that the personnel director from years ago probably never could've imagined.

Enter the modern field of human resources. It's a rapidly maturing, evolving discipline, one where significant changes over time have completely reinvented what it means to be an HR professional. As valuable as it is to know how HR has changed, it's just as important to know where it's headed. You need a clear sense of the trends that will continue to change the field in the future. The following sections offer a brief summary of key issues that are currently exerting the most influence on the HR function and are expected to continue to do so in the near future.

Working As a Strategist, Not Just an Administrator

Today's HR professionals are assuming an increasingly broad role in their companies, becoming strategic advisors to the senior management team.

This expectation creates many new opportunities for you. One key skill you need to develop is the ability to think strategically. "Argh!" you let out. "If I hear this term one more time, I'll be forced to take early retirement. I don't even know what it means." Good point. What does being a strategic thinker really mean?

Certainly, strategic thinkers spend plenty of time setting objectives and getting work done, but they also do much more. At heart, strategic business thinkers try to look ahead, attempting to anticipate which issues and information will be most relevant to a business in the medium or long term. They don't look at their work merely as a series of tasks or reactions to events. They also examine trends, issues, and opportunities — and, from there, shape what they identify into policies and recommendations.

How does the concept of strategic thinking apply to HR? In effect, strategic HR professionals now act as consultants to others in the business. They help set a path — a vision of how to ensure that HR effectively delivers on its mission. To achieve that in the most effective form possible, they develop a true understanding of the business they work for and the industry they work in. They also expand the range of people they talk to and listen to, drawing insights not just from departmental colleagues but also from finance, marketing, legal, manufacturing, sales, and other areas that can help them better understand what makes their companies tick. They then translate this intelligence into policies and recommendations for building and maintaining an organization's workforce.

Today's far more powerful analytic HR systems (see Chapter 3) also are driving the need for the HR job to become more strategic. Professionals will need the ability to interpret and use increasingly sophisticated and detailed data that is stored in these systems to drive decision making and behavioral changes.

This represents a great opportunity — the chance to be regarded not just as an HR person but also as a vital source of counsel and a central part of your firm's management team. Even taking just 15 minutes a day of solitary thinking and researching time can make a big difference. Consider this as time spent working *on* the business rather than just *in* the business. That's a valuable distinction.

Taking Technology to the Next Level

As in many fields, technology has had a dramatic effect on HR management. Software and technology applications that are focused on HR have grown in number and sophistication and continue to advance. These now include a variety of systems and programs designed to assist HR professionals with the broadened responsibilities and challenges they encounter on a daily basis. Also influential in the HR field has been the growth of social media. Online social tools are becoming widespread in many areas of HR, including training, where e-learning and, more recently, mobile learning are taking on prominent roles (see Chapter 14).

But there's more to the overall growth and maturation of HR technology. In one sense, it has revamped the concept of the varied skills and experience that now comprise a complete and effective background in HR. More and more, an HR professional who's not well versed with HR technology systems is becoming as hard to find as the writing pad and no. 2 pencil that were HR's stock in trade back in the day.

Because of the key role these systems and social tools play in the HR field today, I devote an entire chapter to them (see Chapter 3).

Understanding the Specialist Economy

HR has long had to address the issue of employee supply and demand: There are markets where candidates are plentiful and markets where they're scarce. Today, however, we're seeing a wrinkle in the supply-and-demand rubric: The supply of highly trained workers with specialized skills is limited, while the supply of those without college degrees and with more general skills is plentiful.

Specialization of labor is not new, of course — it dates back to the days of the auto industry and the concept of the division of labor — but the niche skills employers seek today are predominantly knowledge based. This is especially true in high-demand fields that require both education and specialization, such as information technology (IT), law, accounting and finance, transportation, marketing, and healthcare.

The current trend toward specialization has direct ramifications for HR professionals in their recruitment roles. As they size and design the workforces they need to move their companies forward, they're running into a shortage of educated workers with the specialized skills that are so important for companies attempting to compete in today's business world.

Building In Workforce Flexibility

Many years ago, the notion of assigning work to anyone other than full-time employees was viewed primarily as a stopgap measure. In those days, change came more slowly, it was easier to anticipate business cycles and, when necessary, companies could supplement their ongoing work efforts by adding a few extra personnel. Though the pace of business certainly had its volatile side, staffing needs were frequently predictable.

Today's business environment is drastically different. Advances in technology and communications, coupled with increased competition from all corners of the globe, have raised customer expectations about speed and quality. The new pace of business has triggered the need for companies to be more agile and responsive than ever before to changing circumstances. HR's approach to staffing needs also has had to change to keep up. Managers have become aware to a greater extent of the need to explore smart approaches and carefully assess their mix of employees.

More and more companies understand the importance of a flexible approach to staff management. Specifically, they're recognizing the appeal of having a variable-cost component in their otherwise fixed-cost labor structure.

At the heart of any flexible workforce arrangement is a core of capable full-time employees. Positions that are typically kept in-house include those involved in confidential matters, strategic planning, or business development, as well as jobs that require frequent interaction within an organization. Although full-time staff often is thought of as serving "static" roles within a company, that's not always the case. Companies may be able to fill some gaps by shifting the work responsibilities of current employees so that long-awaited promotions are granted, or team members receive opportunities to develop new expertise. Investing in cross-training can give firms greater flexibility in how they use their core employees. The more knowledgeable staff are about various aspects of the business or department, the more options managers have in deploying them to other areas or assignments as needs dictate.

The second vital component of a flexible staffing approach is the use of strategically selected contingent workers or independent contractors. The percentage of professionals in today's workplace who are working on a temporary or project basis is rising — and for a variety of reasons. Companies can bring in these individuals to supplement the core team whenever and for as long as necessary. They may be engaged to cover short-term needs or serve as technical experts when the skills required for a one-time, labor-intensive project — such as a systems conversion — don't exist in-house. The ability to call on contingent workers or independent contractors on an as-needed basis enables many companies to avoid the disruptive cycle of hiring and layoffs. Businesses increasingly use specialized staffing firms to recruit the talent they need for just the time they need it.

This trend also ties in directly with the specialist economy I discuss earlier in this chapter. Specialists at very high levels are choosing consulting and contract assignments over full-time work because of the flexibility they have to use their experience. This is a boon for companies, which are taking advantage of this in-depth knowledge and experience for key initiatives — work that in the past would've been assigned only to full-time staff.

To take full advantage of contingent workers at all levels, you need a strategy in place to help ensure that they're smoothly integrated into the work environment. (For a detailed discussion of contingent workers, see Chapter 4.)

Making Workforce Diversity Work for Your Organization

Diversity includes a lot more than minority representation. Trends such as delayed retirement, second careers, and increased longevity mean that the age spread of workers is also greater today than ever before. These professionals range from the Silent Generation (born before and during World War II) and Baby Boomers (born approximately between 1946 and 1964) to Gen Xers (born roughly between 1965 and 1980) and now Generation Y (often called Millennials), whose members were born in the early 1980s.

Diversity means that a wider range of people are bringing a greater variety of approaches, ideas, and lifestyle issues to the workplace. If, as they say, variety is the spice of life, then the workplace is getting more vibrant by the minute. To attract, retain, and maximize the contributions of all members of the changing workforce, HR policies must address these differences.

One example of how diversity is changing the way HR professionals function is the structure and administration of benefits packages. A one-size-fits-all plan is no longer commonplace. The trend today is toward cafeteria-style offerings, which give employees the opportunity to choose from a variety of benefits that best match their particular life and work circumstances.

To illustrate the value of cafeteria-style benefits, according to the U.S. Census Bureau, more people were 65 and over in 2010 than in any previous census. What's more, between 2000 and 2010, this segment of the population increased at a faster rate (15.1 percent) than the population as a whole (9.7

percent). With people living longer, an increasing number of employees are taking on the responsibility of caring for their aging parents or other relatives — a trend that's introduced a new term to the employee benefits vocabulary: *eldercare*. And, as the number of working women with young children continues to climb, childcare assistance is another highly requested benefit.

The intergenerational workforce also requires a new way of thinking about staff management. Each generation has unique priorities, perspectives, skill sets, and work styles. Each tends to respond to different kinds of motivation, seeks different types of support from managers, and reacts in different ways to company programs and policies.

As Baby Boomers begin to retire, companies will inevitably face a loss of these experienced workers. You'll need to ensure that your organization has a way to pass along their knowledge to the next generation of leaders. This responsibility carries profound implications for the kind of HR programs you build — from management skills training and flexible work arrangements to broader, strategic initiatives that help shape your firm's overall culture. Even after they officially retire, some Baby Boomers who have been focused on their careers for many years will ponder different directions. Highly skilled and experienced, they're finding ready acceptance working as project professionals and consultants at companies that benefit from their expertise applied to critical initiatives.

But your goal in an HR role is not just to adapt to or react to these changes. You also should take advantage of the ways diversity can enhance creativity and productivity. Many companies today are discovering that, when you're competing in the global marketplace, workforce diversity — especially at the managerial level — can be a significant competitive advantage. (See Chapter 6 for more on building diverse teams.)

Easing the Work/Life Conflict

Today's employees want flexibility. To attract and keep top performers, more and more companies are striving to be what's called *employee-friendly*. Essentially, this means that your scheduling and general operating policies take into reasonable account the personal needs of employees — in particular, their desire to balance job obligations with family responsibilities and outside interests. Being able to maintain more control over schedules has become a priority for most workers, especially parents and adults helping to care for their aging parents and in-laws.

Chief among the practices and policies that are typically found in companies actively pursuing work/life initiatives are flexible scheduling, telecommuting, and other off-site work arrangements; employee assistance programs; and benefits programs that enable employees to select the benefits (childcare or eldercare support, for example) relevant to their needs (see Chapter 13). Technology is a strong force enabling businesses to provide employees with flexibility, especially the ability to work remotely. Tools include Microsoft Office Communicator, for video calls, audio calls, sharing desktops, and instant messaging; Microsoft SharePoint, for collaboration; and voice over Internet protocol (VoIP) technology, which allows individuals to make and accept calls anywhere.

Policies supporting a healthier work/life balance do more than simply enhance a company's recruiting initiatives. They also can produce a number of bottom-line benefits, such as reduced absenteeism, fewer disability claims, and fewer workplace accidents. Less time spent commuting, reduced stress, fewer distractions, and the ability to more easily deal with personal issues such as child illness could be among the reasons for these benefits.

Managing Rising Healthcare Costs

The proper management of employee healthcare costs is a core business issue today. Average healthcare costs increased 6.9 percent from 2011 to 2012 and now total $20,728 per year, according to the 2012 Milliman Medical Index (www.milliman.com/mmi), which measures the total cost of healthcare for a typical family of four covered by a preferred provider plan. This includes annual employer contributions of $12,144. Of the $8,584 paid by employees per year, monthly premium contributions average $5,114, and co-pays, deductibles, and other out-of-pocket costs average $3,470.

Change seems to be the name of the game in managing healthcare costs. In June 2012, the U.S. Supreme Court upheld most provisions of the Patient Protection and Affordable Care Act, which brings fundamental changes to the healthcare landscape. As of this writing, the International Classification of Diseases diagnosis and procedure codes are being rewritten, and the digitization of health records is in full swing. No doubt, these will soon be joined or eclipsed by other issues and concerns.

Despite justifiable concern over the growing cost of keeping your employees healthy, healthcare isn't merely a line item to be managed. The overall health and well-being of *everyone* in your company is a key HR responsibility. As you work with benefits experts, insurance advisors, legal counsel, and others to create viable healthcare programs, you'll need to sort out how your healthcare plans are set up financially and also the factors within your firm's culture that promote — or don't promote — a healthy workforce. Addressing healthcare from this big-picture vantage point is a key example of the notion of the HR professional as a strategist. (I offer a closer look at company-provided healthcare and wellness efforts in Chapter 12.)

Chapter 3

HR Technology Systems and Social Tools

In This Chapter

▶ Keeping up with the growth of HR technology

▶ Understanding human resources information systems

▶ Using talent management systems

▶ Choosing the HR systems that are right for you

▶ Exploring online social tools

The amount of employee data stored by companies is growing every day. In simplest terms, what HR technology systems do is mine this data to help HR professionals and others build, deploy, and develop their workforces. Advances in these systems are bringing the capabilities of smaller, or even one-person, HR operations up to par with those that used to require scores of employees.

The other key area where technology is influencing the practice of HR is social media. In particular, social tools are playing an increasing role in HR's recruiting and training efforts, as well as communication with employees.

In this chapter, I offer a primer on how HR technology benefits an employer and what you need to know to get the most out of it.

Like anything technology related, the HR systems and social tools environment is ever changing. By the time you read this chapter, you can be assured that there will have been changes in which systems are offered, their capabilities, and even what they're called. Instead of shooting for an impossible roster with no spoilage date, I give you a feel for the direction HR is moving with respect to technology.

The Growth of HR-Related Technology

Not very long ago, tech applications within the HR field were largely focused on employee administration and recruitment, allowing for more efficient maintenance of employee records and automation of routine HR tasks and processes. That's still true to some degree, but HR technology systems, or platforms, have matured to become critical tools in a number of decision-making processes central to a business. They're making efforts such as talent development and measurement more accurate and easier to manage.

Meanwhile, social tools are having a wide-reaching impact on the HR function, as HR professionals increasingly turn to them to achieve efficiencies in responsibilities ranging from hiring and training to internal collaboration and process improvement. I cover social media's influence later in this chapter and in Chapter 6.

HR technology systems increase efficiencies and bring the following benefits:

✔ **More defined analysis:** Identifying trends and patterns within individual departments can be difficult if company records and data aren't specific enough. By virtue of their capacity for detailed record keeping, HR systems can make those sorts of important evaluations easier to break down and more accurate.

Many of the systems that are being implemented capture far more data than could be collected before. This capability is making analytics a more prevalent skill set for HR professionals. For example, having a learning management system to track training is useful, but why track training if you're not going to correlate it to job performance at annual review time? Another example of where analytics come in: the use of an applicant tracking system. Are there specific internal recruiters who have a better ratio of interviews to hires? HR professionals who can analyze the data that HR systems collect are becoming more and more valuable.

✔ **Better distribution of tasks:** Instead of you, as the HR professional, accepting responsibility for every HR-related function under the sun, technology can help spread the workload around more equitably. Different people can be assigned to complete different tasks within the system, with each receiving notification when there's a new issue to be addressed. In a sense, that invests others in the HR process — a connection that may not otherwise occur.

HR technology systems and smaller companies

In this chapter, I give you a comprehensive view of HR systems, even though not all of them will prove practical or affordable for companies of every size. (A firm with 50 employees, for example, probably won't find applicant tracking systems cost-effective.) I do this here — and with other HR tools and practices elsewhere in the book — because I feel it's part of the job for anyone in an HR role to have a current view of the entire landscape.

That said, it's only fair to point out that HR systems have become increasingly affordable as they become more modular. This scaling is made possible by cloud computing, which enables users to access applications or data stored on servers at a remote location (the *cloud*) through a web browser or mobile application. The arrangement not only reduces the hardware you have to maintain on-site but also allows you to purchase only the capabilities you need now, with the option of easily adding to them later. Gone are the days when bundles that came with tools you didn't want or need were your only option. Also, often you can choose one application from one vendor and another application from another vendor, giving you more shopping and service choices.

Besides the cloud, another option is a software as a service (SaaS) solution. Companies subscribe to the service, and the SaaS provider maintains the applications. An example is SuccessFactors for performance appraisals, development plans, and applicant tracking.

HR systems also can afford your business legal and financial protection. Consider the following:

- ✔ **Wage and hour claims:** In some cases involving wage and hour laws, time and attendance systems may provide you with the means to rebut or mitigate claims of failure to pay for all time worked, failure to provide compliant meal periods, and other claims.

- ✔ **Failure to hire:** Applicant tracking systems can help you implement a more consistent application and interview process. That can head off claims stemming from rejected job applicants.

- ✔ **Wrongful termination:** Similar to providing data on applicants who don't make the cut, empirical documentation of employee performance can defeat allegations of unjustified dismissal.

Human Resources Information Systems

An employee management system, often called a human resources information system (HRIS), is the traditional foundation of a company's HR technology. It serves as a central repository of employee data. Depending on whether some functions are outsourced or handled in-house, HRIS supports (and "contains") many of the functions I discuss in this section.

Applicant tracking systems

An applicant tracking system (ATS), sometimes called an e-recruiting system, offers a central location and database for an organization's recruiting efforts. Information can be gathered from internal applications, as well as from applicants on job boards. An ATS enables the review and management of applicant information and status. Other features may include the creation and administration of job requisitions, automated résumé ranking and evaluation, customized online applications, pre-evaluation questions, and response tracking. It also can generate interview requests to candidates via e-mail.

TIP

If you have more than 100 employees, you should be familiar with equal employment opportunity parameters. If you're considering applicant tracking systems, ask about features that automatically address Equal Employment Opportunity Commission (EEOC) compliance. That way, you stay as up-to-date as possible.

When you're ready to review résumés for a particular position, e-recruiting systems pre-evaluate them to identify appropriate experience, skills, education, and other credentials. The systems scan for keywords, work history, years of experience, and education. The technology identifies likely candidates and ranks them. Candidates who place poorly are weeded out from further consideration.

Some applicant tracking systems are integrated with e-mail solutions, such as Microsoft Outlook, to more easily handle résumés that are submitted this way. Some systems allow for the automatic scanning and upload of data from a candidate résumé into the ATS.

REMEMBER

Don't look to e-recruiting systems to take the human touch out of the hiring equation, however. They're designed to make your involvement more time efficient and more effective, but taking their results at face value in every case is risky.

Unfortunately, misstatements, omissions, and inconsistencies abound on résumés. In a Robert Half survey, 43 percent of managers polled said they believe job seekers include dishonest information on their résumés somewhat or very often. More than one in five workers in the same survey said they know someone who stretched the truth on these documents. It takes personal involvement to drill down to the truth.

When reviewing résumés, question vague descriptions of skills, such as *familiar with* and *was involved in* — potential signs that someone is trying to hide a lack of relevant work experience. Also, ask references to confirm basic information you see on a résumé, such as the candidate's employment history, job titles, responsibilities, and salary. You also can work with a reputable staffing firm that is skilled at identifying experienced job candidates for your business.

Employee profile systems

Employee profiles begin to take shape when job seekers submit online candidate profiles and are built from there by employee profile systems. Profiles include information on education, previous experience, professional training, and other skills. A manager can use data provided by the profiles in planning training for team members (see Chapter 14). The list of an employee's current skills within the profile is also very useful when you're evaluating internal candidates for promotions or other opportunities (see Chapter 4). Managers from other departments also typically have access to all employee profile information, allowing for talent management across the organization.

As records retention becomes more and more important in cases of legal action, keep in mind that any report generated by HR technology systems can be subject to legal review. If you're unable to produce them, your company can be in jeopardy. The bottom line: Establish appropriate record and information retention policies so that you have access to employee records when your organization needs them.

Time management systems

Although time management applications can be part of a larger software suite, technology packages specific to time management are an option. These systems not only track hours and attendance but also allow you to manage employee scheduling and produce invoices and other materials based in part on time allocated to a job or project. Some programs also let you identify and analyze labor costs according to employee, branch, department, and specific project. That can prove very helpful if, for instance, your business is considering redistributing workloads and responsibilities.

Advanced systems can automatically record employee hours when they log in to their accounts. In particular, time and attendance functions allow businesses to track and monitor employee work time from a remote location. This can prove especially effective for telecommuters, home-based workers, and remote sales and support staff.

Benefits administration systems

One of HR's biggest challenges is overseeing the administrative complexities of a business's benefits plan. From health insurance coverage to 401(k) plan registration, benefits as an overall HR field is growing larger and more complicated every day. (If you've ever had to juggle a six-month eligibility window for one program and several other time frames for others, you know all too well what I'm talking about.) Benefits administration systems (the term is sometimes shortened to *ben admin systems*) do the heavy lifting of determining which terms and conditions apply for certain benefits. Small wonder many small businesses choose to outsource this function instead of handling it in-house. Not only can internally handled benefits administration prove expensive, but it also can serve to distance you from the strategic planning and decision making in which HR is becoming increasingly involved.

This application can store information as to which employees applied for which benefits — and, by the same token, those employees who opted not to enroll. That makes for comprehensive record keeping, as well as valuable information for analysis as to the use and popularity of particular benefits programs and options.

Payroll administration systems

Back in the day, handling payroll was something that few people looked forward to, what with the headaches of handling pay scales and seeing to it that appropriate taxes and withholdings were addressed, let alone the simple responsibility of making sure that paychecks were accurate and out on time. Happily, technology has addressed this long-standing challenge with payroll administration systems. As the name implies, these systems automate a host of payroll functions and record keeping. In addition to compiling and maintaining up-to-date employee pay records, they also can see to a number of other payroll-related issues, among them paid time off, raises and bonuses, time sheets, and easy-to-access payroll information and pay stubs.

Employee self-service features

Systems designed with an employee interface give workers more ownership of their data by providing ready access to information such as their profiles, benefits, and payroll records. For instance, employees can see how many sick days and vacation days they've accrued, check on health insurance issues such as deductibles and co-pays, and review personal and dependent information. Employee self-service software typically isn't a separate system on its own but rather a feature or function of some of the systems mentioned in this chapter.

Employee input is another option. Certain programs allow employees to enter their own hours into a system for approval by management, as well as provide a simplified way to submit vacation requests. Perhaps even more valuable, employees can participate in open program enrollment and review benefits enrollment summaries, plan comparisons, documentation, and employer contributions to benefits. Employees also can make changes themselves to W-4 information, adjust direct deposit information, and handle various other tasks.

These features not only make employees feel more in control but also serve as an invaluable timesaver for HR. Instead of bombarding HR with phone calls and e-mails — many of which request the most elementary of information and guidance — employees can review the very same material by themselves and on their own time. That allows you to redirect energy to other responsibilities.

Talent Management Systems

Talent management system (TMS) is an umbrella term for a number of software applications supplied by a variety of vendors. A TMS, in general, however, is less about the administrative part of HR and more about developing and better utilizing an organization's people, its talent. The term does, however, mean different things to different companies. A TMS aids in a variety of decision-making processes by focusing on improving employee performance and helping managers plan for the future of their workforce. A TMS may include some of the following.

Performance appraisal systems

Here, a major HR task is, in part, automated. Performance appraisal systems are designed to measure as accurately as possible how well an employee is meeting the responsibilities and challenges of his particular position. A key advantage is the capacity to minimize any subjectivity in the overall review of an employee. For instance, the program includes comprehensive job descriptions/competencies that allow an accurate and empirical picture of whether an employee is, in fact, fulfilling the requirements of that particular job. That makes it easier to provide an accurate and helpful performance appraisal.

In a nutshell, many performance appraisal systems let managers view employee goals and objectives and, from there, enter information and feedback as to whether that person met those goals. At the same time, the employee is completing a similar form. From there, similarities and discrepancies can be identified.

Learning management systems

A learning management system (LMS) offers a centralized structure for a company's various training efforts. In effect, it streamlines employee access and content delivery, as well as the tracking and reporting of your educational programs. Another key function is to help you analyze what's working and what may need your attention with your learning initiatives. LMS technology gives you access to specifics about a person's progress and other data.

As with most HR technology, there are many LMS vendors to choose from. A good system allows you to administer and capture data tied to all aspects of your learning programs, including mobile platforms for employee learning on the go and social components, which involve learning from trainers or even peers through informal online channels such as blogs.

An LMS also can help you coordinate other efforts, such as mentoring and performance reviews, with your training efforts.

Succession management systems

In Chapter 15, I discuss the importance of developing a comprehensive succession plan for your business. Here, I jump the gun a bit to briefly discuss succession management systems.

Succession management applications can automate many of the tasks associated with succession planning. These can include laying out the necessary leadership and experience prerequisites for certain positions, as well as checklists that allow you to track when employees have reached specific benchmarks. Some applications also let you map out what-if scenarios — for instance, if a particular leader left the company unexpectedly, who (if anyone) in the developmental process would be best positioned to immediately assume those new responsibilities.

Succession software also can remove or, at the very least, mitigate some of the subjective forces that can negatively impact succession management. In Chapter 15, I point out the pitfalls of choosing someone as a successor just because he's likeable. Although that impulse is natural from an emotional standpoint, succession systems can provide empirical evidence that the potential successor, however amiable, simply hasn't had enough experience or instruction to emerge as the logical choice as successor.

Choosing the Systems That Are Right for You

When selecting HR systems, take the time to really shop. Speak with enough vendors to give you an adequate overview of the differences from product to product. And don't be shortsighted with the questions you ask. Does the proposed system have the capacity to grow as your business grows? What level and quality of support can you expect from your vendor? In short, which system best fits your specialized needs — now and in the future?

A key consideration in choosing any new system is integration: How well will it match up with any current systems you may be using? Whether going with an all-in-one or a-la-carte approach, it's important to start with the end result in mind. You need to have an idea what the finished solution is going to look like in order to understand the implementation phases — and so you know what you're going to be asking users to work with.

A key consideration in deciding whether to go with the a-la-carte approach is that a substantial integration effort often is required. A company already using PeopleSoft for payroll and benefits, for example, may want to implement SuccessFactors for recruiting. These systems have different user interfaces, system designs, and approval flows, all of which end-users have to learn and manage on a daily basis. That fragmentation needs to be weighed against the feature set of a certain application or vendor.

Sometimes vendors will have already taken care of integration (an example includes SuccessFactors, which is designed to "talk with" Jobvite for applicant tracking). But, generally, there is a core HRIS that stores the majority of the HR data and is considered the "system of record" for the other tools. Links must be established to any a-la-carte applications you want to add. For instance, when you hire a new employee, you may add her information to the core HRIS. It then must interface with your payroll administration system, benefits administration system, TMS, and so on in order for her data to carry over to those systems, as well. These integrations can become complex and should be factored into the decision process.

The bottom line: Having the "best of breed" application for every function won't work well for users unless the advantages of each product outweigh the fact that they're all different.

Given the speed with which technology changes, you may want to consider engaging a specialized HR applications consultant when deciding on a first system or a system upgrade for your organization. There are solid reasons to consider a consultant. First, technology is not a cosmetic issue. It's a vital part of your business and should be approached in that manner. If you lack some of the technical know-how to properly integrate HR systems with your primary business needs, an outsider can make a world of sense. Regardless of whether you hire a consultant, it pays to do some research on your own.

The International Association for Human Resource Information Management (IHRIM; www.ihrim.org) is a group of practitioners, vendors, consultants, students, and faculty that serves as a leading resource for information on HR information management systems.

Online Social Tools

Big HR systems are not the only areas of technology innovation in the HR field. HR professionals increasingly use social media to expand their networks and learn about promising new talent. In Chapter 6, I cover tools such as LinkedIn, Facebook (www.facebook.com), and Twitter (www.twitter.com) as candidate-sourcing options.

The real-time educational aspects of social media are especially useful for people new to an HR role. The best-known sites, as well as blogs and online communities, can help you stay abreast of changes in the field by enabling you to interact with HR professionals in your city, other states, and even other countries. You also can get news of helpful upcoming HR conferences or webinars you may want to attend.

Working with corporate communications and marketing, HR has always been a partner in employee communications. In fact, in a smaller shop, HR may be the sole source of employee messaging. Here again, social tools expand your possibilities. Many products now allow companies to create internal social networks. By using the newest editions of Microsoft SharePoint, for instance, employees can create individual profile pages much like they can on Facebook or LinkedIn, connect with colleagues, and post messages for others to see and respond to. These types of tools allow you to disseminate information on topics important to employees, such as benefits updates and organizational changes. Depending on their familiarity with new technology, employees may prefer social media over traditional communication channels.

Social media also allows companies to collect input from employees on the work environment like never before — whether good or bad. Some firms have created internal social tools that allow employees to post concerns and ask questions of company leaders. An example may be a worker who wants to know when company laptops will be upgraded; he can post the question on the firm's online bulletin board or ask the head of the IT group directly via her profile page.

Part II
Putting the Right People in the Right Places

The 5th Wave   By Rich Tennant

"According to this résumé you've done a lot of job hopping."

In this part . . .

After getting a big picture of what today's HR role is like, it's time to get down to the nuts and bolts of the hiring process, one of the key topics of this book. Part II takes you all the way from a threshold activity far too many managers skip — workforce planning — through posting your job opening, reviewing résumés, and narrowing the field of applicants to making your final selection.

Chapter 4

A Bird's-Eye View: Launching a Workforce Plan

In This Chapter

▶ Seeing why strategic staffing is the best approach

▶ Looking inside and outside the organization to fill open positions

▶ Understanding worker classification

▶ Considering the advantages of contingent workers

*N*ow that everyone knows you're going to be handling HR for the company, managers from seemingly everywhere bombard you: They want you to hire more people for them, and they want the folks right away. So, you'll need to waste no time in posting jobs, right?

Not so fast. Before you can begin the actual hiring process (as I describe in greater detail in Chapter 5), it's critical to first take a look at the organization as a whole. Your job starts not with unrelated, ad hoc efforts to close a perceived personnel gap, but with a comprehensive approach based on your overall business priorities. In short, you want to get a bird's-eye, or big-picture, view of your workforce needs and create a systematic, cost-effective plan to meet them. That's what this chapter is all about.

Note: This chapter involved collaboration with the law firm of Paul Hastings LLP, especially regarding the important matter of proper worker classification, which continues to be the basis of numerous lawsuits. Due to the complex nature of laws and regulations around hiring new employees, you may want to seek legal counsel as you add staff to your organization.

Grasping the Big Picture

The traditional hiring notion of finding the best people to fill job openings has been replaced by a much more dynamic concept. It's generally referred to as *strategic staffing*, which means putting together a combination of workers — both internal and external — that is strategically designed to meet the needs of your business and the realities of the labor market.

Rather than a knee-jerk reaction to fill a particular position, strategic staffing is a big-picture approach. It involves reviewing all jobs within an organization to determine how best to organize your people and resources to meet your needs in any business environment.

Ensuring that staffing needs are in sync with business needs

Strategic staffing begins with an effort to reassess your department's human resource requirements in the context of your firm's business priorities. It's a mindset rather than a process. The idea is to begin thinking in terms of need rather than job, long term rather than short term, and big picture rather than immediate opening. This approach ties directly to the changing role of the HR professional from administrator to strategist, which I discuss in Chapter 2. To succeed, you need a firm understanding of your company's major goals and priorities.

Table 4-1 shows the difference between the traditional approach to hiring and the strategic staffing model.

Table 4-1	Paradigms: Old and New
Old Staffing Paradigm	*Strategic Staffing*
Think job.	Think tasks and responsibilities that are keyed to business goals and enhance a company's ability to compete.
Create a set of job specs.	Determine which competencies and skills are necessary to produce outstanding performance in any particular function.
Find the person who best fits the job.	Determine which combination of talent can best handle the tasks and responsibilities that need to be carried out.
Look mainly for technical competence.	Find people who are more than simply technically qualified but who also can carry forward your company's mission and values.
Base the hiring decision primarily on the candidate interview.	View the candidate interview as only one of a series of tools designed to make the best hiring choice.
Hire only full-time employees.	Consider a blend of full-time employees and contingent workers to meet variable workload needs.

Looking at your company's overall priorities, your job is to determine their staffing implications. You need to make sure that any staffing decision clearly supports these business priorities. To do so, you must look beyond the purely functional requirements of the various positions in your company and focus instead on what skills and attributes workers need to perform those roles exceptionally well, as well as skills gaps that exist within your current workforce.

Unless you're a sole proprietor or run a very small business, you can't adopt a strategic staffing approach all by yourself. Make it a priority to reinforce the concept with other managers in your organization. You'll need their input to better understand company and departmental priorities — and they'll need your help in guiding them through the process and adopting this mindset as well.

Together, you'll need to identify everything that may affect the efficiency and profitability of your firm's operations — and not just in the short term, either. To get you started, here are some of the key questions that you and other people in your company should answer before you make your next move:

- ✔ What are your company's long-term strategic goals or those of departments seeking your assistance in hiring?

- ✔ What are the key competitive threats in your industry? In other words, what factors have the greatest bearing on your company's ability to compete successfully?

- ✔ What kind of culture currently exists in your company? And what kind of culture do you ultimately want to create? What are the values you want the company to stand for?

- ✔ What knowledge, skill sets, and general attributes are required to keep pace with business goals and, at the same time, remain true to your company values?

- ✔ How does the current level of knowledge, skill sets, and attributes among your present workforce match up with what will be necessary in the future?

- ✔ How reasonable is it for you to expect that, with the proper support and training, your current employees will be able to develop the skills they're going to need for your company to keep pace with the competition? In addition to on-the-job experience, would programs such as job rotation help reach these objectives?

- ✔ What combination of resources (rather than specific people) represents the best strategic approach to the staffing needs you face over the short term and the long term?

Change is the name of the game in business. Company priorities will undoubtedly shift over time as management seeks ways to keep the firm competitive. As a result, you should consider performing a needs assessment on an annual basis. That helps ensure that you're still on track with the assumptions and priorities that are guiding your staffing strategy.

Bringing existing staff to their potential

Strategic staffing is not just about hiring more employees. It involves making the best staffing choices available to address the core business needs you and other managers have identified.

For some needs, you may not have to hire at all. If budgets are tight and resources are limited, your job is to help company managers strategically — and honestly — evaluate projects and focus their teams' efforts on only those that grow revenues, increase efficiency, reduce expenses, or meet other company priorities.

If a line manager you support is thinking of filling an existing position, encourage him to consider how his group's most critical needs may have changed since the last time the job was open instead of immediately searching for a candidate to fill the vacant position. Is a full-time individual still required in this role? And should a potential replacement have the same skills and experience as her predecessor?

In some cases, employees may have full work schedules, but their expertise is not devoted to the right projects. Ask the hiring manager to analyze his work group's daily activities to better understand how current resources are allocated. Help him identify the frequency and timing of workload peaks and valleys and look for predictable patterns. Discuss any shifts in company priorities and what eventual effect these are likely to have on the work group in question. This discussion allows you to spot any shortfalls in human resources for upcoming initiatives.

Needs identified as crucial may be handled in other ways. Suggest the idea of creating project teams to focus on critical, but temporary, activities to the manager of a group who feels that there is a case for new staff. These groups could then be quickly disbanded or reassembled, depending on changing needs. Another option for managers is to look at current positions and consider combining the responsibilities of two less critical positions into one to free up a staff member who can help out elsewhere.

Encourage line managers to look at their group's projects and attempt to match staff members with assignments best suited to their talents, even if some tasks fall outside their traditional job duties. Better utilizing the skills and experience of each person can help teams operate more efficiently.

Also, discuss with line managers whether it makes sense to offer targeted training. Organizing a training session to help a team better utilize a common software program, for example, could be a cost-effective way to increase the group's efficiency.

Suggest to company managers that workload gaps they encounter may be a good opportunity to identify employee skills and competencies, as well as future leaders. Ask them: Can some employees take on more responsibility? As new projects arise, why not ask for volunteers to oversee these initiatives? Managers could then evaluate their performance and advancement potential.

Knowing when to begin staffing strategically

Strategic staffing requires that you don't wait until the need actually arises to refill a position suddenly vacated, respond to peak demand, or fill in for employees who are vacationing or on extended leave (by which time you're already in an emergency). Instead, work with your company's managers to help them forecast their needs well in advance. Help them budget for those staffing shortfalls.

To sum it up, strategic staffing is an ongoing process.

Finding the Right People for Open Positions

Redeploying full-time staff may partially address rising demands, but this step alone isn't likely to be the answer to all your company's staffing concerns. At some point, you'll need to replace people who leave your organization. And you'll also need access to fresh ideas and perspectives to help your company grow by bringing in new staff.

Inner peace: Filling jobs from within the organization

Before seeking outside talent, consider whether refilling positions or creating new ones by using internal resources may best serve your workforce plan. In other words, first consider promoting from within. Here are the key reasons:

- ✔ **Increased efficiency:** Filling jobs from within usually takes less time and is generally less costly (in the short term, at least) than hiring from the outside. You don't have to wade through reams of résumés. You can cut to the chase more quickly during the interview, and you don't have to worry about the reliability of your reference information. In addition, existing employees are a known quantity. You know what type of performance you can expect from them.

- ✔ **Higher morale:** Hiring from within sends a message to employees at all levels of your organization that good performance gets rewarded and that employees have a reason (apart from the regular paycheck) to work hard, be reliable, and focus on quality. It also demonstrates a commitment to career development and internal opportunities, which boosts retention. There's no better way to avoid excessive turnover at junior levels of an organization than to offer excellent advancement opportunities.

- ✔ **Shorter adjustment period:** Everything else being equal, an existing employee requires a lot less time to acclimate to the new job than an employee who's never been with your company. Not only are existing employees already familiar with company policies, but they're also probably aware of what the new job entails.

The drawbacks? Only two, really. The most obvious one is that limiting your search to internal candidates limits the pool, and you may end up promoting someone who's not up to the challenge of the job. The second drawback is that, whenever you recruit from within, you always run a risk that otherwise important and valuable employees who don't get the job may become resentful and even eventually decide to quit.

That's why it's essential to establish an atmosphere of trust when looking to existing employees for available positions. Make it clear that employees can be comfortable applying for open internal positions. No employee should be concerned about repercussions, such as a manager or supervisor being frustrated that she wants to change jobs when she's doing "just fine" in her current position. Additionally, if another candidate is selected for a position, the decision shouldn't be construed as a "black mark" against the employee who didn't get the job.

Boomerang employees:
Rehiring former staff members

Don't discount the idea of rehiring former staff members who left on good terms. You already know the person, so recruiting and hiring expenses can be low. And, when you rehire a former staffer, you already have a pretty good sense of what you're getting. In addition, the time and expense of bringing a returning employee up to speed are significantly less than with someone who's brand new to the company.

However, be as selective with former employees as you would be with any other hire. Focus on those with outstanding performance records, both with your company and in their endeavors since. If your company culture or values have changed since the employee left, make sure that he's still a suitable fit. And be sure that any issues that caused the former employee to leave the company have been resolved or are no longer present so he's more likely to remain with the organization this time around.

If an employee doesn't get an internal job after applying, provide the employee with feedback. This provides an opportunity for development within her current job so she'll be ready for another future internal opportunity when it opens up.

Creating a successful internal hiring process

Key procedures you need to put in place to set up a successful internal hiring process include establishing a way to communicate job opportunities to your employees and a procedure they can use to submit applications. Go out of your way to ensure that everyone understands the scope and basic duties of the job, as well as the hiring criteria you're using. You also must make sure that, whatever system you use to alert employees to job opportunities in the company, everyone gets a fair shot at the opening. This is an important aspect of creating a culture of equal employment opportunity.

Developing an employee skills inventory

If you see yourself hiring internally at some point down the road, a dynamic employee skills inventory that you plan for in advance can be a great help when the time comes. This inventory is exactly what the name implies: a portfolio of the human capital in your company — a catalog of the individual skills, attributes, credentials, and areas of knowledge that currently exist.

See the CD for a Blank Skills Inventory Form and Sample Skills Inventory Form.

Your skills inventory doesn't have to be set up as a stand-alone database; in fact, it shouldn't be. The database you use to store your employee profiles (see Chapter 14) can be used to pull together this information when you need it. That way, if you keep your employee profiles up-to-date, your organization-wide skills inventory will be based on the most current information each time you pull it.

The idea itself is not that new — most companies have traditionally maintained a personnel file or job history file for each employee. The difference lies in how the information is categorized. Conventional job histories tend to focus on accomplishments. An employee skills inventory focuses on the skills and attributes that led to those accomplishments — and that could be called upon once again.

You may assume that this practice is one that is suitable only for big companies. And you may assume, too, that the process is more bother than it's worth. Neither assumption is necessarily true.

Even if your company is relatively small, it still may be worth the time and effort to develop the capability of pulling an employee skills inventory. The chief benefit is that, instead of picking your way through reams of folders to compile a list of people who may be logical candidates for an opening in your company, you simply search your employee profile database using specific categories.

Some of the categories you may want to pull from the employee profile include the following:

- ✔ **Skills/knowledge areas:** Business-related functions or activities in which the employee has either special knowledge or a proven record of proficiency.

- ✔ **Second-language skills:** Anything other than English. Emphasize that familiarity with another language is not enough; the candidate must be fluent if he is going to assist customers or work with suppliers who communicate in that language.

- ✔ **Special preferences:** Requests the employee has made about her own career aspirations, other jobs in the company she'd like to pursue, or areas of the country (or world) to which she may be interested in relocating.

- ✔ **Educational background:** Schools, degrees, and subjects in which the employee majored and minored.

- ✔ **Job history at your company:** Include the title, department, organizational unit, and actual job duties the employee has performed.

- ✔ **Previous job history:** Include the same general information as for the preceding category but for the employee's prior employers.

- ✔ **Training courses and seminars:** List the program, topics covered, and, if applicable, the number of days spent in training.

✔ **Test results:** Key results, if applicable, of any company-sanctioned tests or other types of measurement activities that the employee has formally undergone during his or her tenure at the company.

✔ **Licenses, credentials, and affiliations:** Obviously, all these categories should be work related and logically linked to the tasks and responsibilities of the job. (A warehouse employee who's going to operate a forklift, for example, doesn't need a certificate from a stunt-driving school, and the person you hire to supervise the kitchen of your company cafeteria doesn't need to belong to an international wine society.)

REMEMBER

The preceding list is meant to be a set of recommendations, nothing more. You can incorporate into your own employee skills inventory anything that you consider relevant. Just be careful that, as you develop your inventory (and the employee profile that drives that inventory), you don't inadvertently violate any equal employment opportunity (EEO) laws. If you have any question about any category, check with legal counsel.

The more in touch you are with the existing talents, skills, and attributes of your people, the easier time you'll have getting the most out of their expertise. To paraphrase an old saying, many companies today spend so much time looking for the diamonds on the horizon that they often overlook the "pearls" in their midst. Your employee profiles and skills inventory is a valuable jewel case.

New horizons: Looking for staff outside the company

For all its virtues, a staffing strategy that's built almost entirely around promoting from within isn't always the best way to go — especially if your company has never taken the time and effort to develop a well-structured career development program (see Chapter 15).

Bringing in new talent to assist you (or other company managers) in running the business is a large part of your responsibility in your HR role. Likewise, it's a major concern of this book. Here are the basic arguments for looking outside the company to locate talent:

✔ **A broader selection of talent:** Basic mathematics shows that if your search is confined solely to your current employees, the pool of likely candidates will be a lot smaller than if you're looking outside the company. This constraint may not be a problem for certain jobs, but for critical positions, you may not want to limit your options.

✔ **The "new blood" factor:** Bringing in outside talent can go a long way toward diminishing the "We've always done it that way syndrome," sometimes known as *organizational inbreeding*. Recruiting from outside the company is usually helpful for companies that have held on to the status quo for too long. Hiring from the outside helps to foster creativity, innovation, and a new way of thinking.

✔ **The diversity factor:** Workforce diversity (or the effort to allow and encourage diversity in the workplace) enables a business to draw on the resources, expertise, and creativity of people from the widest possible range of backgrounds: gender, age, color, national origin, ethnicity, and other factors. It also makes good business sense (see Chapter 6).

A Wide World of Talent: Understanding Worker Classification

When looking outside the company for staff, you have a number of options.

If core team members are fully occupied, and you have new tasks that must be handled on an ongoing basis, it probably makes the most sense to hire additional full-time or part-time employees. Much of the advice in this book concerns this option — hiring and managing a core team of employees — and I address the best ways to go about this in upcoming chapters.

If, however, upcoming projects are of limited duration or you need specialized skills unavailable internally, then a mix of full-time employees and contingent workers may be your best bet. Think back to the concept of strategic staffing at the beginning of this chapter. I talk about considering a blend of talent to meet variable workload needs. Now, I delve a bit deeper into what this means from a practical standpoint.

There's a wide world of talent out there, and you don't have to approach tapping into it the same way for every individual or job. There are different ways you can engage workers that depend on your particular needs at the time you're recruiting. But you have to know what you're doing when you engage workers who are not employees of your company in the traditional sense.

The relationship of various workers to your company is of key concern to federal and state governments, in particular the agencies responsible for collecting payroll taxes. Confusion around these relationships is driving a growing number of lawsuits, and it's critical that you understand the differences. Here is a fundamental look at worker classifications. (For more information on the way these classifications affect salary, payroll taxes, and benefits administration, see Chapters 11 and 12.)

There are three factors determining how workers will serve a business:

- ✔ Their relationship to the company in need of their services (the capacity in which they work)
- ✔ The duration of their engagement (short term or long term)
- ✔ The schedule they work (part time or full time)

Of these three, relationship is most important from a legal standpoint. There are three basic types of worker relationships:

- ✔ **Employees:** Workers are employed directly by the company for which work is performed.
- ✔ **Contingent workers:** Workers are provided by a staffing firm to the company for which work is performed and are employees of the staffing firm.
- ✔ **Independent contractors:** Workers submit their own invoices for services provided. They are neither employees of the company for which the work is performed nor employees of a staffing firm

Factoring in duration and schedule, workers in all three relationship categories could be full time, part time, short term, or long term.

You can't be too careful when it comes to the area of working with independent contractors. There is a significant risk that the Internal Revenue Service (IRS) may not agree with your interpretation of an independent contractor or contingent worker and may declare that the proper classification of the worker is as an employee. Likewise, the employee himself may claim that he never should've been treated as an independent contractor but, instead, should've been treated as an employee, entitled to the various financial and other benefits associated with an employer/employee relationship. You must understand the specific distinctions between independent contractors and employees. Seek the advice of a knowledgeable and experienced lawyer.

See the Worker Classification Quick Reference Table on the CD for a printout you can keep handy that explains the major differences between employees, contingent workers, and independent contractors.

Employees

Companies hiring *employees* are required to pay whatever payroll taxes are required by law and must also withhold applicable state, federal, and local taxes. Employees can be either full time or part time, and they may be hired either on a short-term basis or on an ongoing, indefinite basis. Regular part-time employees enjoy many of the same benefits (usually on a prorated scale) and the same federal and state protections as full-time employees.

Contingent workers

Contingent workers are employees of a staffing firm, which, for a fee, assigns them to client companies to augment the client's employees or provide skills and knowledge not available internally to the client. This category includes temporary to full-time staffing but not independent contractors. Staffing firms employing contingent workers are required to pay whatever payroll taxes are required by law and must withhold applicable state, federal, and local taxes. As with all three of the worker relationships, contingent workers can be either full time or part time and either short term or long term.

Correctly defining contingent workers can be tricky for someone beginning in an HR role (or anyone, for that matter) because there are no uniform, commonly understood terms used to describe them. In fact, contingent workers often are described collectively and interchangeably as temporary, contract, interim, leased, or project-based workers; consultants; or other designations. For the purposes of this book, I use the term *contingent* when referring to workers in this category (again, excluding independent contractors).

Contingent workers represent the fastest growing segment of the workforce, and the tasks they perform are no longer primarily administrative or clerical. Indeed, the world of contingent workers now includes doctors, teachers, and lawyers — even CEOs. For this reason, I discuss contingent workers in more detail in the next section of this chapter.

Independent contractors

Strictly defined, an *independent contractor* controls the methods and means of performing her tasks and is responsible to the company she's working with only for the results. The company engaging the independent contractor has no tax liability and almost no other administrative responsibility other than paying the invoice and reporting payments on 1099 forms.

Exercise extreme caution before you accept that any individual working with your organization is truly an independent contractor. The independent contractor work model has come under attack in recent years. Companies relying on services provided by independent contractors are subject to being targeted for audit, investigation, and even litigation for not treating those contractors as employees. In particular, federal and state government agencies have stepped up investigation and enforcement of worker classification. Consult a knowledgeable and experienced attorney for help in this sensitive area.

For clarity with regard to worker classification, I consistently use the term *contingent workers* throughout this book whenever I refer to individuals employed by a staffing firm and assigned to a client company — even when the workers are professional-level specialists, an increasingly likely scenario in today's business world.

Getting Permanent Benefit from Contingent Workers

Contingent workers have become a significant part of today's workforce, and there are sound reasons for this growth. More and more talented people are drawn to contingent work because of the flexibility and opportunities these arrangements provide. It enables them to pursue personal and professional goals and, at the same time, explore a variety of industries. Contingent assignments allow job seekers to try out work in different firms and office cultures, and, in fact, many times a contingent engagement may become a full-time employment opportunity.

Increasingly, professionals who want a flexible work schedule along with the diversity of working in different offices and work environments are attracted to this arrangement as a long-term work style. This group includes working parents who want more time to devote to their children, Baby Boomers acting as caregivers to elderly parents, and people at retirement age who still want to be active but perhaps not on a full-time basis. For these and many others, project work fills the bill.

The use of contingent workers is not new, of course. What's new is not only the enormous growth in their numbers but also the level of experience and expertise that you and the line managers you work with can bring into your company on a contingent basis. A company can now engage a highly skilled professional in virtually any specialty: finance, sales, marketing, operations, information technology, law, medicine, and human resources, among others. And in contrast to the past, the specialist who joins your firm is often part of the contingent workforce by choice rather than necessity.

New thinking about contingent working arrangements is evident not only among these workers themselves but also among the businesses that engage them. Firms are increasingly attracted by the labor cost flexibility they can gain though a combination of full-time or part-time employees and contingent workers. This trend was reflected in a mid-2011 survey by the McKinsey Global Institute: When employers polled were asked how their workforces would change in the next five years, 58 percent said they would hire more temporary and part-time workers.

The flexibility of variable-cost labor provides an advantage to companies that seek greater control over their human resources budgets and appreciate having access to skilled talent when and for as long as they need that talent. In fact, as companies continually rebalance their workforces to remain profitable in both good and difficult times, many are discovering that a *year-round* mix of core employees and contingent workers is their best bet for ultimate flexibility.

Here are some of the advantages of using contingent workers in your work-force mix:

✔ It allows departments to adjust staffing levels to the ebb and flow of business cycles, thus helping keep overhead costs under control.

✔ It eases the work burden on employees who may already be spread too thin because of business demands or duties added to their roles from prior layoffs or downsizing.

✔ It offers departments a way to handle special projects — or special problems — that lie beyond the expertise of current staff members.

✔ It gives the company an opportunity to engage — on a short-term basis — high-level specialists it can't afford to bring onboard for the long term.

✔ It creates job stability for a core group of full-time workers in highly cyclical businesses. Otherwise, those sorts of businesses would need to subject their workforces to constant nerve-racking cycles of hiring and layoffs as the demands of the business fluctuate.

✔ It provides what amounts to a trial period for potential new employees. If, as your needs evolve, you decide to consider converting a contingent worker to employee status, you have the advantage of already knowing some of the individual's capabilities and personal attributes.

The more proactive and systematic you and line managers are in approaching your staffing needs, the bigger the payoff.

Here are some threshold questions as you consider the use of contingent workers:

✔ **What specific tasks do you need someone to perform and over what time period?** The shorter the time period, the more inclined you should be to seek contingent help.

✔ **What skills or expertise are necessary to perform those tasks?** Generally speaking, the use of contingent workers enables you to tap into a knowledge base that's far broader than you can find in your current staff.

✔ **Can people who are on the company's payroll perform those tasks — without affecting other aspects of their job performance and without creating excessive overtime costs?** Balancing basic responsibilities with additional tasks isn't easy. To answer this question, departmental managers will likely look to you and your HR colleagues, because you're probably more familiar with the skills and workloads of people in all parts of the company.

✔ **Can the department and company afford the extra cost involved to engage highly skilled supplemental staff?** Think overall value, not just immediate expense.

Finding the right staffing source

You can engage many types of contingent workers on your own without going through a staffing firm. You also can run a marathon in a pair of sandals. But here's the question: Why put you and the overloaded line managers you're working with through the extra effort? If help is required, managers are probably in a time bind already. Why add to everyone's miseries by involving everyone in such labor-intensive details as recruiting, interviewing, hiring, payroll, and other responsibilities?

The case for using a staffing firm to help execute a contingency staffing strategy is fairly airtight. Firms that specialize in providing contingent workers already have a pool of experienced people they can assign to your company. They understand the complex legalities (including tax-related issues) of contingency staffing. They handle all the paperwork.

True, the cost is a little more than the average pay rate for people in that particular specialty. But the staffing firm handles preliminary evaluation of the candidate and government-mandated benefits and assumes responsibilities as the employer of record. (See Chapter 7 for more on general pre-employment evaluation.)

Your company has a number of options, as staffing firms expand their services in efforts to remain competitive. But with so many options available, making the right choice can be a problem.

Reputation is important. The best job candidates — and these are the people you want access to — work for the best staffing firms. Specialization is a key factor in attracting skilled talent, so look for staffing firms that focus on the types of positions you're looking to fill or individuals with the types of skill sets or experience you need.

Checking things out

To help you on your way, the following checklist offers several questions you may want to ask whenever you're checking out staffing firms:

- ✔ Does the firm specialize in the areas where you need help?
- ✔ How long has the firm been in business?
- ✔ Does the company have locations in other cities where you have operations?
- ✔ How does the service recruit and retain a highly skilled set of candidates?
- ✔ How does it evaluate and select its workers?
- ✔ How broad and deep is its candidate base?
- ✔ How does the service match needs with skills?

    ✔ Does the service guarantee its contingent workers? Does it provide
      replacements?

    ✔ Is a contact person available after hours?

The Staffing Firm Evaluation Checklist on the CD can serve as a quick reference when evaluating staffing firms.

One last thing: Make sure that you nail down all the costs ahead of time.
Clarify this information with the departmental supervisor who's going to be
managing the worker(s). A reputable firm is always willing to communicate
its fee structure in writing.

Asking the staffing firm's manager to visit your business

Have the staffing firm's representatives come to your office and give them a
tour of your facilities. Introduce them to the managers and supervisors who
are going to be coordinating the work of the contingent workers. And, most
important of all, make sure that you've worked with line managers to provide
the staffing firm with a detailed, written description of the jobs involved,
including the required skills and anticipated length of the assignment.

Another good idea is to tell the firm whether your company is thinking
of turning the assignment into a full-time or part-time employee position.
Remember that some contingent workers have more interest in landing a full-
time job than others do, and you want to make sure that you bring in people
whose personal goals are consistent with the nature of the assignment.

The more familiar a staffing firm is with your business — how it operates, who
your employees are, the needs of various departments — the greater its ability to provide you with the right workers.

Getting the most out of contingent workers

I'm going to take a slight detour now from workforce planning. I want to give
you some hints on how to blend contingent workers into your team.
It requires a certain amount of preparation at the departmental level to
make sure that you're getting the most out of these professionals. Here are
some ideas:

    ✔ **Brief your staff.** You're inviting trouble if you don't communicate
      beforehand to your staff the rationale behind your strategy of engaging
      contingent workers for a project. Failing to do so can cause trouble on
      two fronts:

- It leads to needless confusion or even tension among your full-time employees, who may wonder why the individual has been engaged, what his role is to be, and what may be amiss that caused the need for a contingent worker in the first place. That kind of speculation can lead to morale and productivity problems.

- It creates unnecessary pressure for the contingent staff who must work with or near a group of people who are puzzled by his mere presence.

Here's a better approach: Instead of merely announcing that a contingent worker has been engaged, involve employees weeks earlier in the staffing process to help you clarify the scope of the department or project team's workload. In many instances, staff members can offer input about specific tasks that require attention or skills that are needed. Or they may provide creative solutions, such as reassigning certain activities among themselves and carving out a particular function for the supplemental worker. This way, beforehand, as a team and under the supervision of a manager, the entire workgroup can be clear about the scope and nature of the individual's engagement, how long the assignment is going to last, and how the situation is going to affect each of them (if at all).

✔ **Set up a plan.** You need to have a clear idea — before the contingent worker arrives — about the scope of the project, when it should be completed and, as appropriate, matters related to quality. Just make sure that your expectations and those of other managers are realistic, particularly regarding the difficulty of the task. Also, factor in the reality that even seasoned contingent workers need time to acclimate themselves to a new working environment. Again, other staff members can provide valuable input in clarifying the scope of work and the amount of time it takes to get specific tasks done.

✔ **Get the workplace ready.** Ready means a number of things: You've communicated with the manager to whom the individual will report and arranged an adequate workspace. Materials and supplies the worker needs are already there upon her arrival. The equipment must be free of glitches: Computers have the latest versions of software used by your company, the Internet connection is secure and fast, any necessary logon IDs and passwords are provided, and other details have been addressed. Adjusting to a new workplace is one of the constant challenges that contingent workers face. Don't give them additional hoops to jump through.

✔ **Make safety a priority.** Be sure to provide appropriate safety and health training, particularly for workers in manufacturing or other nonoffice settings.

✔ **Create a friendly atmosphere.** The more at home a company can make contingent workers feel, the more productive they're likely to be. You don't have to go to extreme lengths — no need for a big welcome sign or a desk covered with roses. At the very least, however, make sure that the receptionist has been alerted ahead of time. Either you or someone in the department to which the worker has been assigned should conduct a mini-orientation: a quick tour of the immediate work area and location of restrooms, fire exits, lunchroom, vending machines, and any tools that will be needed for the job. Take time to explain lunch-hour policies, security procedures, office protocols, parking, and so on.

✔ **Be explicit about the tasks.** One of the concerns that contingent workers who have unsatisfying work experiences voice most often is that they're not given enough direction at the start of the assignment. Here's a general rule: The lengthier and more complex the assignment is, the more time you or a line manager needs to spend on orientation and explaining the nature of the assignment. Putting the instructions in writing is particularly useful.

✔ **Provide adequate supervision.** Regardless of how busy your company is, make sure that you stay connected with the work of the contingent workers you engage. They're working under your direction. Check in with line managers and make sure that they're communicating well with contingent staff. Bear in mind that some people consider admitting that they don't know how to do something a sign of incompetence — and, thus, waste an enormous amount of time trying to figure out for themselves a problem that you or another staff member can solve in seconds. The manager and others within the department should encourage contingent workers to ask questions when they don't understand something.

✔ **Intervene early.** As important as it is for managers to provide clear direction to contingent staff, sometimes the work simply isn't getting done properly. Let managers on your team know that if they're not pleased with the quality of a contingent worker's contributions, they should contact you or the staffing firm immediately.

✔ **Don't settle.** A reputable staffing firm won't argue with you if the person who's been sent to your firm isn't doing a good job. The firm simply sends a replacement and handles communication directly with the individual (he's their employee, after all) regarding termination of the assignment. For everyone's sake, however, try to be as specific as you can when expressing displeasure. If you do a good job of telling the firm where the individual fell short, you're more likely to get a suitable replacement.

What most contingent workers need to know

One of the best things you and the line managers you work with can do to ensure that contingent workers are as productive as possible is to anticipate their information needs. Here's a list of the questions they're likely to have the first day they show up for work:

✔ What's the job?

✔ What are your policies and procedures?

✔ What does your company do?

✔ What's the office culture like?

✔ What's the dress code?

✔ Who's the boss?

✔ Where do I go if I run into a problem?

To save time, consider preparing a one-sheet flier that covers the preceding issues and provides space for notes. You should share this information with your staffing firm before the assignment, too, so it also can prepare the contingent workers who will be assigned to your company.

Keeping records and offering feedback to the staffing firm

When contingent workers finish their assignments, make a record of what you thought of their performance. Depending on whether your experience was positive or negative, you may want to ask the staffing firm for a particular person again — or ask that she never return!

Sharing your assessment with the staffing firm helps the firm do a better job of meeting your company's needs. (*Note:* Many staffing firms offer evaluation forms after an assignment to solicit this type of feedback.) As you go through this exercise, you and line managers who have used contingent staff should ask yourselves whether he

✔ Met your expectations

✔ Finished the job on time and professionally

✔ Required little, some, or too much daily instruction

✔ Fit well into the workplace

Additionally, ask yourselves:

✔ What could the contingent worker have done differently? Done better?

✔ Would you hire this person as a full-time or part-time employee? If no, why not?

Be aware that your assessment is not to be used as a performance evaluation. Your records should be treated as internal documents only and shared only with internal staff and with the staffing firm. Under no circumstances should you share what may be perceived as a formal performance evaluation with a contingent worker. Why? Doing so is one of the criteria the courts use to determine whether the worker was really working on a contingent basis or directly for you. If you're sued, and the decision goes the wrong way, you could be liable for back payroll taxes and other expenses.

This is not to say that you can't offer words of encouragement ("Good job!") to a contingent worker or point out when she hasn't met your expectations during the course of the assignment ("I need you to improve your performance"). Just don't formalize the encounter or offer anything in writing.

At the end of the assignment, ask for feedback from contingent workers about your company or department and its procedures and approaches. They can usually offer unbiased opinions that are invaluable. And there's a good chance they'll be more forthcoming with an HR practitioner than they may be with the managers they've been working with each day. If problems arose with the project, the individual's comments may help you prevent similar situations in the future.

Looking at your legal responsibility

Apart from whatever strategic benefits the use of contingent workers offers, their growing presence in the workplace introduces some thorny legal issues as well. One key question: To what extent are companies that hire temporary or project workers directly (instead of relying on staffing firms) obliged to provide these workers with the same benefits and protections that regular employees receive?

Equal coverage

The Equal Employment Opportunity Commission (EEOC) believes that discrimination is discrimination — regardless of whether the victim of discrimination is working for you as an employee on a full-time, part-time, or interim basis. The bottom line is that contingent workers have many of the same fundamental rights with respect to EEO legislation as do regular employees — and this fact holds true for all forms of discrimination, including sexual harassment.

Workplace injuries

Even if a staffing service employs someone working for your company on a contingent basis, your firm may be responsible for that individual's health, safety, and security while on the job at your company. Check with your staffing firm to determine whether your workers' compensation package adequately protects you. And remember: You can always face a lawsuit from anyone who's injured while working on your premises.

Chapter 5

Smart Start: Kicking Off the Hiring Process

....

In This Chapter

▶ Understanding the central role of job descriptions

▶ Establishing job titles

▶ Determining the soft skills the job demands

....

For those needs in your workforce plan that you've determined are best addressed by hiring additional full-time employees, it's time to find this talent! This chapter kicks off a group of chapters in this book where I take you step by step through one of your major roles in HR: the hiring process.

Nearly everything else you do with respect to HR policies and practices becomes easier if you're making good hiring decisions. If you don't have to spend the bulk of your time each day putting out personnel fires, you can concentrate on the big picture: where you or your senior management want your business to go in the years ahead, and what needs to happen on the HR side to get you there.

That's the benefit of good hiring decisions. A bad hiring decision (which brings an ill-suited person to your company) produces just the opposite result. You spend more time as a firefighter and less time as a manager and strategic planner.

Your Blueprint: Creating the Job Description

Throughout the hiring process, you'll need a set of criteria as you attempt to find, attract, and make a job offer to the best candidates. Among other things, these criteria define the duties to be performed in each position you hope to fill, as well as the credentials and qualities candidates should possess to perform well in those positions.

The many purposes of job descriptions

There are a number of reasons to create job descriptions, and a description's content can vary greatly depending upon its intended uses. For example, a company may create job descriptions primarily

✔ To establish performance expectations

✔ To help with recruiting and hiring

✔ To highlight the essential functions of a position in the event the company needs to accommodate an individual with a covered disability under federal or state law

✔ To differentiate between jobs that are exempt versus nonexempt from legal overtime and other requirements

In this book, I focus on how job descriptions are essential tools for the purposes of effective recruiting, hiring, and performance management. At the same time, to ensure that your job descriptions are written in a way that carries out your reasons for having them, you may want to consult a lawyer before finalizing and using them.

The *job description* is where your hiring criteria are first formally set forth. But this doesn't mean just any garden-variety job description will do. The job description you'll construct will be airtight. And it'll have to be. Why? Because the job description will eventually drive the job ad, the candidate selection process, and a new employee's first performance appraisal.

In general, I use the terms *responsibility, role,* and *function* to reference a particular position's higher-level features within an organization, and the terms *duties* and *tasks* to describe the actual day-to-day activities of a particular position.

A well-thought-out job description

✔ Accurately outlines the applicable hiring criteria

✔ Ensures that everyone who has a say in the hiring decision is on the same page with respect to what the job entails

✔ Ensures that candidates have a clear idea of what the position requires if they're hired and what performance success looks like

✔ Serves as a benchmark for performance after you hire the candidate

✔ Serves as a reference tool during the evaluation process

Think of the job description as your blueprint. Do a good job of constructing it, and all the subsequent pieces of the hiring process will more easily fall into place.

The following important elements may be included in a well-written job description:

✔ The job or position title (and job code number, if applicable).

✔ The department within the organization in which the position exists.

✔ The reporting structure for the position, both up and/or down, as applicable. For example, the title of the person(s) to whom the position reports and any position(s) and/or numbers of employees over whom this position has supervisory responsibility.

✔ A brief summary (one to three sentences) of the position and its over-arching responsibility, function, or role within the organization and how it interrelates to other functions within the organization.

✔ A list of the position's essential or key job duties (see the "Accurately describing job duties" sidebar, later in this chapter). You also could include a list of the less important or marginal job duties identified as such, the estimated time to be spent on each duty (which should total to 100 percent), and the frequency of performing each (daily, weekly, periodically).

✔ Whether the job is exempt or nonexempt.

✔ Whether regular and prompt attendance is required.

✔ A qualifying statement that the list of job duties is not exhaustive and may be revised from time to time as per business needs.

✔ The qualifications for the position (meaning, the specific knowledge, skills, employment, or other experiences, training, language, or aptitudes required for the job).

✔ The educational requirements for the job, if any, such as degrees and licensing.

✔ Qualities or attributes that contribute to superior performance in the position.

✔ If appropriate, a statement of the physical demands of the position (for example, lifting or mobility requirements).

✔ A statement that the position also includes "such other duties as assigned" to protect your company's ability to add duties as needed.

✔ A statement that your company is an equal employment opportunity employer.

Legal and other considerations for job description elements

One item it's important to clarify (in the job description and in general) is whether the position is nonexempt or exempt. Generally speaking, nonexempt workers are "not exempt" from state and federal overtime compensation requirements, and, as a result, they're entitled to overtime pay. Exempt workers are "exempt" from state and federal overtime pay requirements. Exempt workers must perform certain job duties to qualify as "exempt." Consequently, how a job description describes certain job duties may be relevant if there is litigation involving whether an exempt-classified employee was misclassified. (For more on this topic, see Chapter 11.) You should consult with a knowledgeable and experienced lawyer for assistance with evaluating your employee classifications.

A requirement that regular and prompt attendance is expected is also an important item to include in a job description — unless the position is one that can be performed elsewhere or without adhering to scheduled work hours.

Look ahead, not behind

You may look at this section and think, "This is a piece of cake. I already have on hand the job descriptions we've always used for the positions I want to fill." I advise you to consider this: The tasks and responsibilities that constitute most people's jobs today are a far cry from what they were as recently as a few years ago. What's happened in most companies is that tasks and responsibilities that were formerly regarded as jobs unto themselves are now consolidated with other functions. The overall result is that many existing job descriptions are pretty much obsolete.

Jobs today are generally broader in scope than those of the past. Job descriptions, therefore, now need to take into account the expanded skill sets that employees need to handle greater responsibilities. Focus on what the job should look like now and in the near future (18 to 24 months out), based on your company's current needs and long-term objectives.

Set priorities

An effective job description consists of more than simply a laundry list of the duties that the job entails. It reflects a sense of priorities. In other words, it identifies those duties that are primary or essential, and if secondary or marginal duties are listed, it differentiates between the two.

Aside from establishing the priority of job duties from a business needs perspective, this distinction can be legally significant. The Americans with Disabilities Act (and many analogous state laws) protects disabled employees who are able to perform "essential" (which has a special legal definition) job duties, with or without a reasonable accommodation. Courts and agencies like the Equal Employment Opportunity Commission (EEOC) investigating a charge of disability discrimination will consider which duties the employer treated as primary or essential in determining whether they're "essential" within the meaning of the statute. Although the employer's characterization of a duty as "essential" is not conclusive, it is evidence of which duties are most important.

Consider educational requirements and qualifications

Educational requirements like degrees and licenses are formal acknowledgments that a candidate has completed a specific field of study or passed a particular test. Credentials like these, or qualifications like certain work experiences or fluency in particular languages, are absolute necessities in some jobs. The person who delivers pizza for you, for example, must have a driver's license; the appropriate medical boards must license the surgeon you hire. Be thoughtful about the credentials for your position to ensure that they accurately reflect the needs of the position.

Don't go crazy with requiring credentials, however. Sure, every manager wants someone with an MBA and maybe a PhD and probably some sort of industry certification, too. But unless these are actually required for the job, they shouldn't make it into the job description or be used as hiring criteria.

Educational requirements or qualifications may discriminate by eliminating candidates with protected characteristics. An attorney can help you address this area.

Make sure that the job is doable

The job you describe must truly be realistic. Some job descriptions work beautifully until the person you hire actually tries to perform the job. One factor to consider is the compatibility of a job's various duties. Some people who are very creative may be less adept at tasks that require considerable attention to detail. By the same token, some people who are at their best when they're working by themselves on complex, analytical tasks may be content to work independently and not as part of a tightknit team. The lesson here is to make sure that when you're lumping several tasks into the same job description that you're not creating a job very few, if any, people could fill.

Accurately describing job duties

Job descriptions, although not essential, can be very helpful. But it is important that a job description accurately reflect the current job duties of the position you want to fill. If a description hasn't been updated in a while, the duties it includes may not match the duties actually performed by the employee who previously held the job. Hiring mistakes can result from job descriptions that fail to accurately capture the essence of a job. Good matches can be less likely as you proceed through job posting, narrowing down applicants, and interviewing. Poorly drafted job descriptions also can be used against your business in litigation — instigated either by a job applicant or by an employee you've hired.

At the same time, be careful not to understate or overstate any of a position's job duties. Embellishing the duties of a job to make an employee feel better isn't helpful. If, for example, a job description is to be used as a performance management tool, then exaggerating the responsibilities may create unrealistic expectations to which you cannot reasonably hold the employee.

Apart from everything else, a job description reflects your company's hiring practices and terms and conditions of employment — which are areas subject to federal and state laws prohibiting your company from unlawful discrimination. As such, any references to race, color, religion, sex, national origin, age, physical or mental disability, genetic information, or other status protected by state or local law can expose your company to a possible discrimination suit. In rare cases, an employer can rely on certain protected statuses in hiring (or in other employment practices) when doing so is a bona fide occupational qualification (BFOQ). One frequently cited example is recruiting only women for a position as a live-in counselor in a female residence hall. Rarely will a discriminatory hiring criterion qualify as a BFOQ, however, and BFOQs are very difficult for an employer to prove. So, before you include such criteria in a job description, it's smart to consult an experienced and knowledgeable lawyer.

Be specific

You don't need to be William Shakespeare to write a solid job description, but you definitely need to appreciate the nuances of the language. For example, use clear and concise language and, when possible, words with a single meaning. And you want to make sure that the words you choose actually spell out what the job entails. "Good communication skills," for example is too general; more specific would be: "Ability to communicate technical information to nontechnical audiences."

Set a salary range

Before you start the recruiting process (see Chapter 6) and look at options for how and where you'll find the ideal candidate for the job you're designing, you should establish a salary range for the position. In Chapters 11 and 12, I discuss the details of salary and benefits and what constitutes an effective compensation structure. Your ideal candidate could come at a hefty price, so know market compensation for people with the skills you seek.

What's in a Job Title?

Be thoughtful about what you're calling the job in its title. An inaccurate or overblown job title can create false expectations and lead to resentment, disappointment, or worse. Now that the majority of positions in most companies involve multitasking, some job titles are probably outdated. If your receptionist left, for example, does *receptionist* accurately describe the job she was doing, and is that the title you should still use for your opening? Or is *office manager* now more accurate for the position as it has evolved?

Besides Functional Skills, What Does It Take to Do the Job?

Every job has a set of technical requirements, but a job description is not complete without those broad but telling aspects of a candidate known as *soft skills, interpersonal abilities,* or simply *qualities and attributes.*

These include an aptitude for communicating with people of all levels, abilities, and backgrounds; the capacity to work well in teams (as both a leader and a team member); and other factors, such as a strong sense of ethics and a talent for efficient and creative problem solving. Candidates who are weak in these areas — even while having solid hard skills and work experience — may prove unable to grow as your company goes through the inevitable changes that are part of today's business world.

As another example, say your company is in the business of selling home security systems. One way to market your service is to solicit potential customers by phone. The basic job of a telemarketer is, of course, to generate leads by calling people on the phone. Some telemarketers, however, are clearly much better at this than others. They have a knack for engaging the interest of the people they call. They don't allow repeated rejections to wear down their spirits. In other words, they have certain attributes that contribute to superior performance.

Some consulting companies specialize in helping businesses identify these *success drivers* (sometimes called *competency models*) for key functions or positions. The following suggestions can help you gain insights on success drivers for your firm's positions:

✔ **Interview your own top performers.** Assuming you have a group of people who perform the same job — and assuming one or two of those people are clearly the "stars" of the group — sitting down with your key people or their immediate supervisors to determine what makes them so successful at what they do is certainly worth your time.

Try to answer the following questions:

- What special skills, if any, do these outstanding performers possess that others don't?

- What type of personality traits do they share?

- What common attitudes and values do they bring to their jobs?

✔ **Talk to your customers.** One of the best — and easiest — ways to find out which employees in your company can provide the basis for determining your desired soft skills is to talk to people with whom your staff interact on a regular basis: your customers. Find out which employees your customers enjoy dealing with the most, and, more important, what those employees do to routinely win the affection of these customers.

Hiring decisions that rely on subjective criteria are particularly susceptible to being challenged as discriminatory. Applicants may argue that unconscious stereotypes can be injected into the decision via subjective criteria. If subjective criteria are used, be sure that your company's hiring decision makers can articulate a clear and reasonably specific factual basis for assessing whether a candidate possesses that criteria. For example, to support a conclusion as to whether a candidate "exercises initiative," ask her to describe times when she has spearheaded work projects, and record how she responds to that question. Base your conclusion about whether she exercises initiative on those responses.

See the CD for a Blank Job Description Form and Sample Job Descriptions that you can use as a starting point and modify to align with your particular jobs.

Chapter 6

You, the Talent Scout: Recruiting for Your Team

....

In This Chapter

▶ Promoting your firm

▶ Writing an effective job posting

▶ Exploring various recruiting sources

▶ Understanding the benefits of diversity recruiting

▶ Getting to know helicopter parents

▶ Tracking your progress

....

The recruiting stage of the hiring process is a lot like fishing: Your success depends not only on how well you fish but also where you drop your line and what bait you use. You can go fishing for qualified candidates in any number of ways; no one fishing expedition meets the needs of every company in every situation. Some strategies involve more time and cost than others. But in your quest to attract the best possible employees, the extra effort is usually worth it.

Putting Your Firm's Best Foot Forward

To attract the best and brightest, you'll need to convince potential recruits that yours is a great company to work for.

You need to represent your company as professionally as possible. When the time comes to choose the person or people who will attend a job fair or visit a college campus on your company's behalf, forget about seniority and look instead for individuals who have good people skills and consistently generate positive energy. Pay attention, too, to the impression your company website sends and the experience applicants have when they call your company for information or show up for interviews. Make it clear to everyone in your business who may interact with a candidate how important it is to be warm and courteous. After all, today's job seeker may be tomorrow's desired employee or even a potential customer.

At a time when a candidate can spread news of his or her poor experience at your company like wildfire via social media, your reputation can be affected overnight. And the last thing you need when you're searching for top talent is a bad reputation.

But recruiting for your firm doesn't mean exaggerating the company's positive qualities either. If you misrepresent your business's scope or capabilities, you'll feed false expectations for employees who decide to join you. That can lead to job dissatisfaction after they're onboard. Clearly communicate what the company is, as well as what it wants to become, and why you need capable, committed employees to help the business reach its goals.

Kicking Off the Process

You should always have a general idea before you start any recruiting effort of how you intend to conduct and manage the process. A good way to begin is to set a deadline for when, ideally, you want to see the position filled. After the deadline is in place, you can establish a sequence of steps, each with its own deadline. You may decide, for example, that you're going to look inside your company for a certain period of time — say, two weeks — and if unsuccessful, you'll post the opening or seek the services of an outside staffing firm.

No one plan is right for everyone, so keep your options open at all times. Don't become so locked into one strategy that you become unable to see that it's not working for you.

Be systematic. If you don't tackle the purely administrative side of recruiting early on in the process, you're asking for trouble. Before you start the search, set up a protocol — a predetermined, systematic procedure — for how you intend to process applications, résumés, and cover letters. Try to set aside a certain amount of time each day to focus on the recruiting effort.

If you're using an outside recruiter, make sure that someone in the company — either you or the hiring manager — has a direct line to the individual who's handling the search. If you're seeking candidates online, you'll need secure systems in place for taking in, evaluating, sorting, and tracking the many résumés you'll attract.

Getting the Word Out: How to Write a Great Job Posting

Obviously, you won't have candidates beating down your door to apply for a position you want to fill if they don't know about it. You have to get the word out in the form of a job posting.

Writing a good job posting is a critical step in the hiring process, but the task is often more difficult than many people think. You're not trying to win a literary prize, but you are trying to attract job candidates — and the right candidates at that.

Keep in mind the following two considerations in writing a job posting:

✔ **Help your firm stand out.** As I describe at the beginning of this chapter, when you're recruiting, you're also putting out the word that your company is a great place to work. In effect, you're advertising a product — your company. Every aspect of your posting must result in a favorable impression of your organization.

✔ **Focus on quality, not quantity.** Your goal is not only to generate responses from qualified applicants but also to eliminate candidates who are clearly unqualified. You're better off getting only 5 responses, each from someone who clearly deserves an interview, than 100 responses from people you'd never dream of hiring.

Your next step is to actually write the posting. If you've done a good job of preparing the job description (see Chapter 5 for more about developing a quality job description), then you've very nearly accomplished this task. In fact, you should think of the posting a brief synopsis of the job description, albeit with a little flair added to get your job noticed. Here are some elements you'll want to include:

✔ **Headline:** The headline almost always is the job title.

✔ **Job information:** A line or two about the general duties and responsibilities of the job.

✔ **Company information:** Always include a few words describing what your company does.

✔ **Qualifications and hiring criteria:** Specify the level of education and experience and relevant attributes and skills (per your success drivers or competency model) required to do the job.

✔ **Response method:** Let applicants know the best way to get in touch with you. Also, let them know certain ground rules, such as whether you prefer to receive online responses as an attachment or embedded in the e-mail itself. Though most companies have moved almost exclusively to electronic response methods, firms must still provide a mailing address or toll-free phone number to meet Americans with Disabilities Act requirements specifically geared toward applying for jobs.

Bear in mind, too, the following key points:

✔ You want to convey some sense of your workplace environment and values with a few phrases (for example, *fast-paced, ethical,* or *client-centered*).

✔ Use the active voice and action words throughout the posting. Make it move, not just sit passively on the screen or page.

✔ Create a buzz, a sense of enthusiasm; pique applicants' interest. An uninspired posting will almost certainly draw uninspired candidates.

When crafting a job posting for an online job board, try to write it in a way that results in a higher ranking on popular job boards; this is called *search engine optimization* (SEO). You want your posting to appear near the top of the job board's search results, and SEO allows you to improve your posting's visibility. SEO is becoming more important with the growing number of job-board aggregators that are emerging (see "Online job boards," later in this chapter).

See the Sample Job Ads on the CD for examples that take into consideration the preceding criteria.

Investigating Candidate Sourcing Strategies

After writing an effective posting, the next step is figuring out where to place it to attract the most qualified applicants, a process often called *sourcing* in the HR world. Following are some key strategies used by recruiters and hiring managers. You'll note that a growing number of them are technology driven.

Establish a system to keep track of your recruiting success by using any of these sources. How many candidates did each source produce? How qualified and skilled was each applicant? These metrics can help you determine the return on your investment in a variety of recruiting channels.

Online job boards

Job boards are extremely popular with job seekers. These websites, used by employers to advertise jobs, may be the best way for a company to reach a large number of candidates quickly. Literally thousands of job boards cover virtually every industry, profession, educational background, experience level, ethnic group, and much more.

Two of the best-known traditional job boards are CareerBuilder (www.careerbuilder.com) and Monster (www.monster.com). These and similar sites cover a wide range of industries and locations. Complementing them are niche job boards, which more closely target their audiences by focusing, for example, on a particular profession or field. Dice (www.dice.com), for example, is a popular job search site for information technology profession-als. LawCrossing (www.lawcrossing.com) focuses on legal positions, and eFinancialCareers (www.efinancialcareers.com) is dedicated to jobs for financial services professionals.

Another type of job board is an *aggregator,* such as Indeed (www.indeed.com), Simply Hired (www.simplyhired.com), and many others. These services pull together job listings from thousands of sites across the web, including traditional job boards, newspaper and classified listings, profes-sional associations, social networks, content sites, and company career sites. Then they distribute those jobs on their websites, as well as on social networks, blogs, and other website partners. Clients can gain premium placement across aggregators' networks through pay-per-click advertising, whereby advertisers pay each time their posting is clicked. Some aggregators are more specifically targeted, including jobs from company websites only, for example.

These are just a few of the job boards existing today. You can be confident that, by the time you're reading this, many others will have joined their ranks — or replaced them.

Part of job boards' appeal is their ability to help you locate qualified candi-dates at extremely low costs. More candidates for less money? Sounds like a hiring manager's dream. But hang on. It also can become a nightmare if not managed properly. For starters, it has the potential to dramatically increase the number of responses to your ads. Many HR managers report that they have great difficulty even keeping track of submissions. Even small compa-nies can receive hundreds of résumés from a single posting, depending on the position and job market.

Online job boards come with a number of legal implications that you need to understand and properly manage. You must consider an alphabet soup of laws affecting the handling of online job ads and candidate responses. Any time you post a job opening, make sure that you don't imply that can-didates can apply for the job electronically only. Title VII of the Civil Rights Act of 1964 (Title VII), the Americans with Disabilities Act (ADA), and the Age Discrimination in Employment Act (ADEA) stipulate that employers can't discriminate in any aspect of the employment process. This rule, of course, includes interactions via the Internet. In other words, you must make sure that you offer avenues to candidates who do not own computers or have access to e-mail to apply for an open job. This requirement is particularly important given the fact that some candidates may not only send you résumés electroni-cally but may also direct you to web pages that extensively showcase their accomplishments and qualifications. Keep in mind that those without access to such online tools deserve an equal chance to be considered for a position as those who do have access.

Being responsive to job applicants is simply good business practice. As I discuss earlier in this chapter, anyone who comes in contact with your company forms a perception that can influence the firm's reputation. A simple, straightforward message sent to all applicants is a good way to showcase your organization's professionalism. For a good example of an Acknowledgement of Receipt of Résumé or Job Application, see the CD.

Your company website

There was a time when ambitious candidates would try to study up on the company they were applying to by requesting company literature — annual reports, sales material, marketing brochures — or by visiting a library to conduct various forms of research.

The Internet has rendered this form of old-school sleuthing virtually obsolete. Just as you and the hiring managers you're supporting are now able to find out more about candidates who may be applying, job seekers can uncover in-depth information about your company. Although the savvy ones review a variety of sources — articles, discussion groups, industry analyst reports — your website is a great place to communicate your unique culture and most appealing characteristics.

Well executed, your website can give job seekers a glimpse into the employee experience — what it's like to work in your company. Today, even the smallest of companies have websites describing what they do and, often, the advantages of working for them. Your website gives you an opportunity to explain why your company is an employer of choice. If properly outfitted, your website also can receive applications directly from interested job seekers and potentially use this information to create employee profiles that will be used later as new hires join your organization (see Chapters 4 and 14). The implications of these changes for HR professionals are twofold:

- ✔ **With information now so much more accessible than ever, you want to make sure (to the extent that you can) that your company's website accurately showcases your firm's strengths and range of capabilities.** After all, you want the best people to be drawn to your company. A website that's outdated, difficult to navigate, or lacking relevant information can reduce your chances of attracting top-notch candidates.

- ✔ **Because of all the available information about companies, don't be surprised at how well prepared candidates are today when you get to the interview process.** You'll also need to be prepared and raise your expectations for the discussion. The topics you cover can relate more specifically to business priorities and issues affecting your industry and company. (I discuss interviewing in detail in Chapter 8.)

Social media and online networking

It may sound obvious, but it's worth pointing out: Job seekers go where the jobs are. Because of the sheer number of openings they list, job boards and aggregators (see "Online job boards," earlier in this chapter) and company websites (see the preceding section) are among the first stops on a typical candidate's itinerary. But social media is not far behind. Many job candidates have an incredibly large online network of friends they contact for insight on various jobs and companies. Even people who didn't grow up using computers engage in active social networking. Because of this, a social media and online networking strategy is an essential part of your overall recruitment program.

The first step in building a social media presence for your company is to understand how various media differ. In addition to stand-alone job boards, some social networks — LinkedIn (www.linkedin.com) being the prime example — feature job-seeking services directly through their platforms. Others benefit from outside firms that enable these features. TweetMyJobs (www.tweetmyjobs.com), for instance, integrates with a job seeker's existing profile on Twitter (www.twitter.com) or Facebook (www.facebook.com), allowing her to identify open roles that have been posted to these social networks. BranchOut (www.branchout.com), which is integrated with Facebook, and BeKnown (www.beknown.com) are two similar services. Aggregators such as SimplyHired and Indeed, also piggyback on a person's social media profiles, enabling him to identify contacts who are somehow connected to open roles that have been posted.

There are many advantages to listing your job openings on social networks, either directly or through a third party. Perhaps the most important benefit is the ability to reach a very wide audience. The most popular social networks have millions of users — sometimes hundreds of millions of users — and information can be shared among individuals very quickly. Before you realize it, your job ad may reach someone who otherwise wouldn't have known about it (or your company).

You also may be able to communicate your vacancy to highly targeted groups of professionals. Communities of like-minded individuals exist within every social network. For example, LinkedIn features groups for people who share the same profession, job title, alma mater, or interests.

One of the defining characteristics of social media is that they encourage interaction. The whole point is to talk to other members — virtually, of course — and share links, photos, videos, news, and other tidbits. As a result, you can take an active role in recruiting. Sending a message or tweet or changing your status ("Looking for a new A/P supervisor") quickly lets everyone you're connected to know about your opening and encourages them to share the news with their own connections. You also can easily search people's profiles (especially on LinkedIn) and identify professionals with certain skill sets. Many sites offer tools to help you do this. This can be an effective way of locating *passive job candidates* (those not active in the job market but who would consider a job change if the right opportunity came along).

At the same time, job seekers can contact you directly and ask questions about the company or position, enabling you to address concerns they may have and highlight aspects of your organization that may appeal to potential employees. Of course, candidates also can identify people who work *for you* — and reach out to them for candid thoughts on the company. Do employees know how to respond or whom to forward requests to? Do you want them to respond at all? You may want to prepare your workers for these types of inquiries by providing training or drafting social media guidelines that outline acceptable behavior. Also, recognize the potential benefit of giving workers the freedom to share their experiences with the firm with their online networks. You may find that, with the right guidance, your employees can aid your recruiting efforts and help spread the word about why your company is a great place to work. Sincere and unfiltered insight into the organization, provided by actual employees, can be a powerful draw for job seekers.

It's becoming more and more expected that all companies have a presence on social media. Those who don't may be seen as being behind the times, especially by workers who've embraced social media or younger people who've grown up with it. In some ways, an organization's Facebook page or Twitter feed is becoming the new web page. In fact, some companies have a Facebook page only and no traditional company website at all.

An additional advantage of establishing a presence on LinkedIn, Twitter, Facebook, or any other social platform is that you can build a large community of people who are actively engaged with your company — including potential hires. By sharing news about your firm, fostering interaction among your followers and fans, and addressing inquiries from users, you can create a virtual "open house," where interested job candidates are able to learn about the business, its culture, and its people. When it comes time to make your next hire, you can tap a group of individuals who are already familiar with your company and invested in it. It's important to realize, however, that this takes time and effort. Users expect regular postings and open communication from the brands they follow, as well as a high level of interaction with real people inside those firms. If you aren't willing or able to make that type of commitment, you may not be ready to launch your online open house just yet.

Keep in mind that social media also include review services where individuals can rate your company across various categories; Yelp (www.yelp.com) is perhaps the best-known example. Of particular interest to those in a recruiting role may be Glassdoor (www.glassdoor.com), which provides company reviews from the employee's perspective. Visitors can access candid feedback about an organization's culture, management, and pay practices and even learn the questions potential hires can expect to be asked during a job interview. Such reviews can bolster — or greatly harm — your firm's reputation among in-demand candidates. My advice: Monitor what's being said about your company on these sites, and be prepared to counter a comment or claim you disagree with.

Technology moves very quickly, and I can't offer you specific advice in this area, but you may want to think about whether you need a social media presence. Yes, there's a lot to consider — which social networks you'll join, who will run the sites, what resources will be needed to maintain an active presence — but it's worth addressing these types of questions now if you haven't done so already.

As with all technology-based tools, keep in mind that, although social networking sites such as LinkedIn can be useful in recruiting, they are no substitute for the value of in-person networks and reputable recruiters. Anyone in an HR role who has unlimited time and resources can identify job candidates online. Recruiting professionals meet with the candidates they place to determine their suitability for various jobs and often provide skills testing and select reference checking. This is time you don't have to spend on these activities. The best firms also fill a consultative role, helping you develop an effective overall staffing strategy. No technology, no matter how popular, is a cure-all for your recruiting challenges. It can be an important part of your efforts, but it can't entirely replace all other recruiting methods.

The wide world of social networks

Facebook, LinkedIn, Twitter, and Google+ (http://plus.google.com) are among the largest and best-known social networks. But you may not want to limit yourself to these services only. New ones are constantly emerging and offering new takes on the online social experience. Pinterest (www.pinterest.com) is a photo-sharing platform that launched in 2010 and has quickly amassed millions of users. It may seem to have limited use for hiring managers, but think again: Some job seekers have begun to post their résumés to the site.

Also, keep in mind that the services that are most popular in the United States are not necessarily household names elsewhere in the world. If you're recruiting for overseas positions, the following sites may be of greater use to you: Xing (www.xing.com), popular in Germany; Viadeo (www.viadeo.com), prevalent in China and France; and Orkut (www.orkut.com), well known in Brazil, India, and Japan.

The point here is that the world of social media and online networking is changing rapidly, and you have to stay current with emerging trends to take full advantage of this recruiting source.

Blind and classified ads

Some companies choose to place *blind ads* — online postings that don't identify the company and typically direct replies to an unidentifiable e-mail address. The only problem with blind ads is that they're a turnoff to many potential candidates — particularly those who are already employed but looking. Unless you have a compelling reason to do otherwise, avoid blind ads.

Few jobs openings are posted in print publications these days, but classified ads may be worth considering in certain situations. Newspapers and specialty magazines can help you reach highly targeted groups of job candidates — those in a particular field or among a certain demographic, for example.

Recruiters

Recruiters can be an invaluable part of your candidate search arsenal. Yes, they cost money, but if you know how to maximize their services, recruiters can more than pay for themselves. Using outside recruiters has several key advantages:

- ✔ Outside recruiters generally have access to a large pool of applicants. After all, it's their job to continually locate quality candidates.

- ✔ They handle such cumbersome administrative details of recruiting as placing ads, evaluating skills, and conducting preliminary interviews.

  In the course of their evaluation process, the best recruiters check selected references from their candidates' past employers to gather skill proficiency information and job performance history. Employers should perform their own reference checks as well. This is because a preliminary check may or may not reveal all the information you want to consider in making your final decision as to whether to bring an individual into your company.

- ✔ Recruiters often are a valuable source of staffing advice. A recruiter who knows her stuff often can help you identify whether you need a contingent worker, full- or part-time employee, or a generalist or specialist. Recruiters also can provide feedback on what the market looks like right now to find the applicant you need. They can be particularly helpful in identifying passive candidates who may be interested in working for your firm.

Who does what?

If you at times have difficulty determining what makes a headhunter different from a recruiter and an employment agency different from a search firm or staffing firm, you're not alone. The names can be confusing. All these sources fulfill the same basic function, although the service approaches differ from firm to firm: They find job candidates for client firms for a fee. The difference between the various specialists in this large and growing industry is primarily how they charge and on which segment of the labor market they focus.

In describing how these players differ, it's only fair to point out that not everyone uses these terms in the same way.

Employment agencies and staffing firms

You engage these companies to find job candidates for specific positions. What they all have in common is that you pay them a fee — but only after they find you someone you eventually hire. These firms recruit candidates in virtually every industry, and companies call on them to fill positions at all levels of the corporate ladder. If you want to hire a full-time employee, they typically charge you a percentage of the new employee's first year's salary. It can vary, depending on the level of the position you're filling and the skills required.

Employment agencies and staffing firms typically differ in the types of positions they help you fill. In most cases, employment agencies are generalists and focus on entry-level and midlevel jobs in a range of industries, whereas staffing or contingency search firms focus on mid- to upper-level positions. Specialized staffing firms can find you the people you need in a shorter amount of time than the generalists because their candidate pools are focused on a particular field or profession — finance or marketing, for example. In another usage, a staffing firm can refer to a firm that provides contingent workers, whereas a recruiting firm places full-time employees. Again, usages vary.

Executive search firms or headhunters

Executive search firms or headhunters focus on higher-level executives, up to and including CEOs. Unlike employment agencies, most search firms charge a retainer regardless of whether they produce results. You also can expect to pay, in addition to expenses, a commission of 25 percent — or even one-third or more — of the executive's annual salary if the firm is successful in its search.

Why, then, go to an executive search specialist? The main value comes into play if you're seeking someone for a high-level job that's most likely to be filled by an executive who's already working for another company. A good search specialist usually has the contacts and the expertise to handle very targeted, high-level searches.

The most general term for firms or representatives from firms that find job candidates for client companies for a fee is *recruiter,* and that's the way I describe these roles in this book. (Implied is that these firms and individuals are *outside* recruiters, not internal recruiters who are employees of a company, often residing in the HR department at larger businesses.)

Should you use recruiters?

Most companies that rely on outside recruiters to fill positions do so for one of two reasons:

- They don't have the time or the expertise to recruit effectively on their own.
- Their recruiting efforts to date haven't yielded results.

True, using an outside recruiter involves an extra cost, but bear in mind that, handling all aspects of recruiting yourself may not be the best use of your time in your HR role. Evaluating résumés, in particular, has become exceptionally labor intensive because of the amount of applications received from Internet postings. Perhaps most important, recruiters typically have wide networks they can tap on your behalf.

Finding the "right" recruiter

You choose a recruiter the same way you choose any professional services specialist. You take a look at what services are available. You ask colleagues for recommendations. You talk to different recruiters. And you leave it up to the recruiters to convince you why they're the best way to go. Ultimately, you want a recruiter you feel confident will be able to effectively articulate your company's mission, values, and culture to job prospects.

The following list provides some reminders that can help you make a wise choice:

- **Check them out personally.** However busy you may be, make visiting any recruiter who may be representing your company part of your business. Make sure that you feel comfortable about the way the recruiter runs and maintains its office. (A good question to ask yourself as you visit a recruiter: Would I, as a job candidate, like to work with this recruiter?) Don't hesitate to ask for references.

- **Be explicit about your needs.** The cardinal rule in dealing with recruiters is to be as candid and as specific as possible about your needs. Make sure that the firm understands your business, your company culture, and what exactly you're looking for in a candidate. Extra bonus: A savvy recruiter often can tell you, simply by looking at the job description, how likely you are to find someone to fill the position.

- **Clarify fee arrangements.** Make sure that you have a clear understanding — before you enter into a business agreement — of how your recruiter charges. Make sure that any arrangement you agree on is in writing. If you don't understand something, ask for clarification; a reputable firm is always happy to explain its fee structure.

✔ **Ask about replacement guarantees.** Most of the leading recruitment firms offer a replacement guarantee if a new employee doesn't work out after a reasonable period of time. Just make sure that you understand the conditions under which the guarantee applies.

✔ **Express your concerns openly.** Speak up if you're unhappy about any aspect of the arrangement you've struck with a recruiter. Tell the recruiter exactly what your concerns are. If you don't feel comfortable expressing your concerns with the recruiter you've chosen, you're probably dealing with the wrong company.

WARNING!

As in any field, recruiting has its bad apples. Fortunately, the industry has done a very good job in recent decades of policing itself. Still, you need to be wary of any recruiter that

✔ Is evasive about providing a list of satisfied clients it has worked with or unwilling to provide information about its procedures.

✔ Is reluctant to provide progress reports or vague about fees and billing arrangements ("Don't worry about it — we're friends").

✔ Charges applicants for services (résumé preparation, testing fees, and so on).

✔ Has no business track record or has a record of legitimate consumer complaints.

Campus recruiting

College campuses have long been fertile hunting ground for companies in search of entry-level talent. Smaller firms without well-organized college recruiting programs have always been at something of a disadvantage. If you're one of the "smaller guys," here are some tips on how to level the playing field:

✔ **Get to know the folks in the career center.** Campus recruiting is usually coordinated by the college career center. As long as your company has a reasonably good reputation, the people in the career center will be receptive to your recruiting overtures and are likely to steer good candidates your way. A big part of their job, after all, is getting good jobs for their graduates. The best way to build a strong relationship with career center personnel is to pay them a personal visit — or better still, invite them to your company to see what you have to offer. The career center is also the place to gain access to campus job fairs (see the next section).

What to watch out for when recruiting on campus

Consider the following points before taking part in any campus recruiting activities:

✔ **Hit your message points.** Make sure that you (and other company representatives you bring with you) are well prepped to cover the key benefits of working at your company. What does your firm provide in terms of a career? What training opportunities do you offer?

✔ **Make sure that you know your job openings.** A sure way to annoy students you're trying to impress is to come unprepared to discuss the jobs you currently have open.

✔ **Be prepared to be asked about your policies.** Don't be surprised if you're closely queried on policies, including diversity, domestic partner benefits, green practices, or any number of social issues. You may

want to spend a little time with your corporate communications department clarifying the best way to answer these questions.

✔ **Get a good night's sleep.** Placement offices tend to stack interviews, often every 30 minutes. You may wind up interviewing 16 students in a single day. That's why students often complain that interviewers frequently seem like they're just going through the motions. (**Note:** Savvy students are aware of this problem and vie for appointments in the morning.)

✔ **Keep your energy up.** Burning out after a day of interviews is all too easy to do. After all, you have to repeat the same information over and over, and you have to be just as enthusiastic at 4:30 p.m. as you were at 9:00 a.m.

✔ **Get to know the students better in small groups.** You can target students pursuing a major or majors in the field in which you're seeking talent by contacting student organizations. This can take the form of cosponsoring study hours, community events, or other small activities with the student group where you can provide snacks, network, and sometimes even make a presentation about your company.

✔ **Focus on topics that students will be interested in.** When speaking to students at job fairs or student events, limit the time you touch on generalities about your company and instead focus on students' interest areas, such as opportunities for advancement in your firm or what to expect in the recruiting process. They don't want just a rehash of what they can read on your website.

✔ **Be prepared to promote your company.** The image projected by you (or anyone else in your company who goes on a campus recruiting mission) goes a long way toward determining how successful you are at attracting a school's top candidates. Make things simple for yourself. Put together a PowerPoint presentation that you can use repeatedly on your laptop, but don't stop there. Students want to hear your company's story in your own words. How did you build your own career there? They want real-life examples and testimonials.

- ✓ **Speak their language.** By speaking "their" language, I don't mean you need to actually talk like a student — unless you're cool enough to get away with it and not sound ridiculous. You just need to *think* like a student. Words like *opportunity, growth,* and *learn* will strike exactly the right chord. Yes, money still talks for most college students today, but students also want to know the nature of the job and the culture of the company.

- ✓ **Promote volunteerism.** If your company is active in the community, don't forget to mention it. According to results from Deloitte's 2011 Volunteer IMPACT Survey, 70 percent of Millennials strongly favor companies that are committed to the community.

- ✓ **Follow through.** For certain positions, recruiting on campus can be very competitive with other companies, so you'll need to be a lot more than a dog-and-pony show. Students expect a short turnaround time in the recruiting process. Let them know when you'll be back on campus. And needless to say, follow through on your promise to be there.

Job fairs

Job fairs are recruiting events that bring together employers and job seekers in one location. They're not only held on college campuses but also sponsored by professional associations and community organizations or non-campus educational institutions such as state teachers associations. The sponsoring group rents a meeting or exhibition space, invites potential employers to set up recruiting and/or information booths and tables, and handles all the administrative and publicity arrangements. Sometimes the sponsors charge admission fees to defray expenses. Most job fairs are held on a single day or over a weekend, but some fairs can run as long as a week.

Generally, job fairs focus on a particular industry or professional group — computer engineers, teachers, or recent college graduates. Properly run job fairs resemble trade shows or conventions and have the same lively atmosphere and buzz.

The main downside of job fairs is their competitive aspect. Because job fairs are usually regional and industry specific — IT professionals in Boston, for example — they tend to attract firms from your region who are looking for the same folks you're looking for. You may well end up with your company's booth located just down the aisle from your main local competitor. This proximity means that potential job applicants can directly compare your company with your nearest competitors simply by walking across the room.

This isn't a problem, of course, as long as you've made every effort to make the strongest impression possible. Here are some suggestions:

✔ **Put your best foot forward.** Whether you're going to be greeting applicants at a booth or a table, you want to make sure that the general impression you're conveying is one of quality and professionalism. The promotional information you distribute doesn't necessarily have to be expensively designed and printed — and you don't have to invest vast sums in elaborate posters or audiovisuals. Just make sure that everything you do with respect to your booth or table is neat, substantive, and well organized.

✔ **Send good company ambassadors.** The people staffing your booth or table should not only be able to handle all questions attendees are likely to ask about your company but also be enthusiastic and personable — the kind of people potential employees will enjoy meeting and, possibly, would enjoy working with. Remember, too, that having senior people as part of your recruiting team tells applicants that your company takes potential candidates and the job fair seriously.

✔ **Keep the paperwork down.** Instead of requiring applicants to fill out lengthy applications, put together a simple form that takes only a minute or two to complete. You'll have the opportunity later in the recruiting process to gather more detailed information.

Your diversity outreach efforts also can be a way to make recruiting an ongoing process. Booths at ethnic and cultural community fairs or events, for example, can serve both marketing and recruiting purposes.

Employee referrals

Employee referrals used to be considered a somewhat risky practice — an invitation to nepotism and favoritism. But today employee referrals are considered one of the most reliable recruiting sources. Few employees would risk their own reputation by recommending a friend or relative who may turn out to be a source of embarrassment.

No surprise, then, that more and more companies today have instituted employee referral programs, with rewards (extra vacation days, trips, cash bonuses, or other goodies) for employees who recommend a person you eventually hire and who stays with the company for a specific period. Employee referrals can be especially effective in helping to locate candidates for critical or hard-to-fill positions.

As with other elements of your recruiting program, keep in mind that your employee referral program can pose legal issues in the areas of discrimination and wage and hour law. Consult an experienced attorney for assistance with analyzing the legal risks of your recruiting program.

Before you launch a program, make sure that you consider all the ramifications and establish a systematic process for administering it. Here are some questions you need to answer:

- ✔ Is everyone eligible to receive a referral award, or are certain positions not eligible, such as executives, officers, board members, recruiters, and hiring managers for their own position?

- ✔ What incentives are you going to offer to the employee who refers someone? Are you going to vary the incentives based on the importance of the job?

- ✔ How long does any referred employee need to remain with your company before the person who makes the referral becomes eligible for the incentive? (The norm in most companies is three to six months.)

- ✔ What procedure must any employee who's making a referral follow?

After you set up an employee referral program, don't keep it a secret. Publicize it every way you can — through posters, e-mails, and newsletters, for example. Your objective is to generate as many quality referrals as possible, and reminders always help. Finally, make sure that everyone knows when an employee receives a bonus for a referral.

Open houses

Open houses are most commonly held by companies in industries that experience high turnover and, thus, have an almost constant need for new employees: mass market retailing or fast food restaurants are examples. But open houses also can be an effective recruiting strategy for companies that are about to expand into a new region.

Conducting a successful open house hinges on several important factors. One key, certainly, is getting the word out by using a variety of media (social media, fliers, store posters, notices to local schools and colleges, commercials on local cable TV and radio outlets, and banner ads on your company website) to stir up interest. Yet another strategy is to set up an effective, well-organized, and nondiscriminatory process that not only makes applicants feel welcome but also enables you to determine when individuals are clearly unsuitable.

Some other considerations:

- ✔ **Choose the place carefully.** You can hold open houses at either your own premises or at some outside location, such as a hotel ballroom or conference room. Each has pros and cons. Holding the event on company premises gives attendees a firsthand look at what you have to offer, but your facilities — because of their location, configuration, or security considerations — may not lend themselves to this kind of an event.

✔ **Think about timing.** Open houses are typically held after working hours and on weekends to attract potential applicants who are currently employed. Before you select the date, double-check to make sure that your open house doesn't conflict with other events that can hold down attendance, such as a popular sporting event or religious holiday.

✔ **Be friendly and informal.** Not everyone who attends your open house will be a potential candidate, but they'll all come away from the event with an impression that they'll pass along to friends, relatives, and acquaintances. Make sure that the impression you make is as favorable as possible.

Professional associations

Most professional associations have some sort of job referral service, publish an e-newsletter listing available positions, or maintain a résumé bank. The Internet, of course, has made this process even easier, in essence creating an online community that lets members exchange information and ideas. Any of these avenues can be a good starting point for a focused candidate search, especially if you're looking for a technical or professional specialty. And advertising your opening on these services may be free for members. These associations also give you a chance to meet potential candidates, formally or informally — at meetings, conventions, and networking events — where you can circulate or perhaps host an information booth.

Direct applications (walk-ins)

Some people view walk-in applicants as a nuisance. But think about it: Anyone who has the energy and the gumption to make a cold, face-to-face appearance is someone whose résumé probably deserves a review. So, at the very least, have a policy in place to deal with such applicants. Invite the person to fill out an application or either leave behind or send you a résumé, along with a cover letter.

Government employment services

Since the Great Depression of the 1930s, every state has operated a public employment service in conjunction with the Department of Labor. Employer-paid unemployment taxes fund these offices — in other words, you foot the bill. These agencies exist primarily to offer services to job seekers. They register the unemployed, determine and pay unemployment benefits, offer counseling and training, and provide labor market information.

In the past, state employment agencies have generally been considered a source for unskilled labor and lower-level clerical and industrial jobs. This perception, however, is not necessarily accurate anymore. Technicians and professionals are registering with these agencies, too, and, as is true of many other aspects of the government, their operations are becoming less bureaucratic and more client oriented. Your local agency is always worth a try — after all, you pay for it.

The downside: Although all government agencies are subject to federal standards and guidelines, the quality and usefulness of the services they offer can vary widely from state to state.

Diversity Recruiting: Benefiting from a Diverse Workforce

In recent years, the term *diversity* has entered the business lexicon in a big way. Countless articles, papers, studies, and books talk about how diverse the workplace is becoming. Everyone knows that white males no longer dominate the workplace. But did you know that, over the course of this decade, the share of minorities in the labor force will expand more than ever before, according to the Bureau of Labor Statistics? By 2020, minorities will make up nearly 40 percent of the workforce. Of course, workplace diversity entails more than the presence of racial or ethnic minorities. It also covers culture, gender, sexual orientation, disability, mobility, and many other characteristics.

Chapter 17 summarizes the laws that have been enacted to bar discrimination in hiring and other employment-related practices. These laws often are changed or updated, such as the addition of the Internet Applicant Final Rule of 2006, which requires federal contractors to collect and maintain data for use in enforcing nondiscrimination laws, and the Genetic Information Nondiscrimination Act, prohibiting consideration of a person's genetic information in the terms and conditions of employment.

But the need to nurture a diverse workplace is not limited to ensuring legal compliance. As I touch on in Chapters 1 and 2, an organization is not well served by employing only people who come from the same mold. Building a diverse workforce can enhance creativity and productivity. If everyone in your company thinks alike, you miss the opportunity for innovative ideas that often come from individuals from diverse cultures and backgrounds — input that can help you improve your products and level of customer service.

Diversity recruiting means *seeking out* people who can bring a greater variety of ideas and approaches to the workplace. By ensuring that your HR policies embrace the importance of diversity, your company can attract, retain, and maximize the contributions of all members of the changing workforce.

And it's not all about the people who bring new ideas with them. Exposure to diverse employee groups gives everyone on your team the chance to benefit from different ideas, cultures, and perspectives that can expand their thinking and attitudes. Additionally, being known for maintaining a diverse workforce can prove attractive to potential job candidates.

When recruiting, consider whether your company reflects the demographic makeup of the communities in which you do business or the markets you serve. To address this, connect with local organizations, including churches, cultural and social institutions, and colleges. They can be great sources for building a diverse base of applicants.

As a reminder, don't overlook employee referrals, which I mention earlier in this chapter. They, too, can prove a valuable resource for diversity recruiting. Your internal staff also serves as an effective marketing tool by telling others that they know what a great place your company is to work.

Also, consider diversity training. Make sure that employees and managers understand and value the importance of diversity.

Last, although diversity is important, employees should understand that hiring decisions are based on finding the best candidate and not meeting diversity quotas. Making the recruiting process more transparent can help ease the minds of skeptical employees.

It may be prudent for certain employers to hire members of protected groups as part of an affirmative action plan. If your company doesn't have an affirmative action plan, a decision to hire a person based on his or her protected status may produce a *reverse discrimination* claim by an applicant outside that protected group.

Handling Helicopter Parents

What do hiring managers have in common with youth sports coaches, high school teachers, and college administrators? All these professionals are likely to encounter *helicopter parents* (parents who are hyperinvolved in their kids' lives, holding their hands through every stage of growing up, whether the kids want them to or not). These moms and dads are always "hovering," rarely out of reach in case guidance, advice, or a terse phone call is needed to help their kids along.

Helicopter parents may have called sports coaches to argue that their kids deserved more playing time, enrolled their children in endless summer camps and academic prep courses, or lobbied with college admissions counselors for a spot at a preferred school. If you've ever met a mom who calls her son every day at college to make sure that he's eating well and doing his laundry, you've come across a helicopter parent.

It should come as no surprise then that, as their sons and daughters enter the workforce, helicopter parents are nearby to help them land the jobs of their dreams. Helicopter parents have been known to submit their kids' résumés, attempt to negotiate salary and benefits, and even show up to sit in on job interviews. No kidding.

As surprising as this phenomenon may be to you, helicopter parents are a reality that today's hiring managers face. And there are several ways to address the issue:

- State in your application materials or job posting that issues such as compensation and benefits can be discussed only with an applicant. You may even stipulate that parents are not allowed to sit in on job interviews.

- Even though you want to discourage too-close parental involvement in your hiring process, recognize, too, that a parent who thinks yours is a good company to work for will likely have an impact on the child's opinion of your workplace. To that end, some companies send the same recruitment package to parents that they send to the applicants themselves.

- If parents appear at a job fair to present you with a résumé, diplomatically inform them that, although you appreciate their involvement, you'll likely get a better impression of their son or daughter if he or she is the one submitting the résumé.

- If parents call you multiple times or attempt to go above your head, remain polite and keep your cool. Offering a curt response will only add to your headaches. Parents who feel dismissed or disrespected — whether for legitimate reasons or not — are apt to let others know about their poor experience with your firm. In the age of social media, you don't want to give anyone cause to complain about you or your company.

- Assertive parents who insert themselves into the hiring process should give you reason to pause: Is the applicant mature and self-sufficient enough to conduct a job search on his own? If hired, will the parent continue to contact you and interfere? Will the applicant be able to perform the duties of the job if she had the help of a parent to write a résumé or cover letter? These are reasonable questions to ponder. But don't rule out a promising applicant simply because of a parent's actions. Consider following up with the candidate to gain more insight. He may offer an apology or reassurances that the third-party intrusions will end. You may even find that the embarrassed applicant didn't know a parent had interceded.

"Do you mind if I bring my mom to the interview?"

Parents care about their children and want to ensure that they're as successful as possible. But in a son's or daughter's job search, parental involvement can be seen as inappropriate and unprofessional. In a Robert Half survey, executives were asked to recount the most unusual or surprising behavior they had heard of or witnessed from the parent of a job seeker. Here are some of the most memorable responses:

✔ "A parent called a politician to push me to hire his son."

✔ "Someone stopped an employer at a grocery store to ask that person to hire her child."

✔ "A parent called to ask about a job applicant's work schedule and salary."

✔ "A parent called during the interview to try to push me to hire her daughter."

✔ "A parent called to find out why we did not hire her son and why we felt he was not qualified."

Keeping Tabs on Your Progress

Monitor your recruiting efforts on a daily basis, and evaluate your progress not only in terms of the number of inquiries you receive but also in terms of their quality. *Quality*, in this context, refers to responses from applicants who not only meet but also exceed your basic requirements. Depending on your sense of urgency, be prepared to intensify your efforts if you come up empty in the initial stages of the process.

Be flexible. If the initial response to your recruiting efforts produces poor results, you need to be prepared to revisit the job description or even explore the possibility of restructuring the job in an effort to attract more (or better) candidates.

Companies known for their ability to attract and hire good employees are always recruiting — even if they have no current openings. If recruiting is, indeed, an ongoing process, and if you're the person in your company responsible for recruiting talent, you're always looking for people who can contribute to your organization's success, even if those people are working somewhere else now and you have no immediate need for them. At the very least, you want to keep an active database of names and résumés of people you've met or who've sent in letters or contacted you online expressing interest in your firm — assuming, of course, that they have the qualities you're looking for.

Chapter 7

Narrowing Down the Field: Evaluating Applicants

. . . .

In This Chapter

▶ Dissecting the résumé

▶ Knowing how to use a job application

▶ Setting up a candidate evaluation system

▶ Understanding the ins and outs of pre-employment testing

▶ Conducting phone interviews

. . . .

*J*ust about everyone agrees that the job interview is the most important phase of the hiring process. But what many otherwise savvy businesspeople often forget is that one of the keys to effective interviewing is effectively evaluating who should be interviewed in the first place.

If you don't have an efficient evaluation process in place, two things are likely to happen, neither of them good for you or your business. First, you may inadvertently weed out candidates who clearly deserve a second look. Just as unfortunate, your evaluation process may fail to accomplish its fundamental purpose: making sure that you're not wasting your time and effort on candidates who are clearly unqualified for the position you're seeking to fill. This chapter can help you avoid this common — but avoidable — hiring pitfall.

First Contact: The Résumé

The résumé is typically the first time you hear from potential employees and your "fishing expedition" (the recruiting stage of the hiring process) begins to pay off. If you still think of a piece of paper when you think of a résumé, you need to update your perspective. In this section, I bring you up-to-date on what's been happening with résumés (in case you don't already know).

The evolution of the résumé

Legend has it that Leonardo da Vinci created history's first résumé. (He wrote a letter in 1482 to the Duke of Milan outlining his skills and ways he could be of use in fortifying the duke's territories.)

How far we've come. Résumés are received electronically today as Microsoft Word documents, PDFs, or HTML files — rarely as paper documents sent by mail. In fact, you may receive a link to a candidate's LinkedIn (www.linkedin.com) profile or other online biography and no "résumé" at all. Most employers, however, do request a résumé after receiving a link to an online profile, but, in the not-so-distant future, the profile may be all that's exchanged.

Candidates who cut and paste résumés into e-mails or within various fields in an online form instead of uploading a formatted document are usually advised to pay close attention to how it looks before hitting Send or Submit. Some online forms can change the format of what's pasted into them. Candidates who take the time to correct any formatting issues may deserve extra points from you as you review submissions.

When you're hiring, don't be surprised to see some of the following in addition to the conventional printed résumé. Although none of the following approaches is widespread yet, many job seekers are exploring options beyond the traditional résumé in an attempt to stand out from the crowd:

✔ **Video résumés:** A video résumé is a one- to two-minute video that allows the candidate to discuss her achievements and credentials while also giving potential employers a sense of who she is and how she presents herself. Video résumés have been around since the days of VHS tapes, but they've enjoyed a bit of a resurgence in the last few years thanks to the growing use of webcams and YouTube.

✔ **Social network-enabled services:** This category includes a whole host of services that have a common thread: They piggyback on a job seeker's social networks, scanning the person's connections and biographical or professional data to create a profile that is relevant and appealing to hiring managers. Each service offers slightly different features. For example, Identified (www.identified.com) assigns a numeric value to a person's connections and job experience for easy evaluation. BranchOut (www.branchout.com) helps users identify connections at target companies through Facebook (www.facebook.com). The point to keep in mind here is that this is a rapidly changing area that is now just beginning to emerge as a job-hunt tool.

✔ **Infographic résumés:** With this format, a person's skills, experience, and professional accomplishments are displayed primarily with colorful illustrations, charts, graphs, or other visuals. The advantage is that the information can be understood at a glance. The downside is that, with much less text, you're likely to get fewer details about a candidate's qualifications. Although infographic résumés are perhaps used most often by design professionals to show off their creative talents, individuals in other fields — such as IT — rely on infographic résumés to streamline the information they present. (Vizualize.me [www.vizualize.me] and Re.vu [www.re.vu] are two of the many firms that exist today to help job seekers create infographic résumés. These websites and others feature examples of infographic résumés.)

✔ **Twitter résumés:** The rise of Twitter (www.twitter.com) has led some applicants to promote themselves in 140 characters or less. As you can imagine, this doesn't allow a lot of room for exposition. So, a Twitter résumé — or *twesume* — is usually just a concise summary of the person's professional biography and objective. For example: "Marketing whiz with ten years of experience seeks boundary-pushing firm. Offering enthusiasm and a long list of happy clients." Twesumes also typically include a link to the candidate's online résumé, blog, or networking site profile page, as well as the hashtag *#twesume,* making it easy for employers to search for these tweets.

✔ **Slideshow résumés:** Posted on places such as LinkedIn or document-sharing sites like SlideShare (www.slideshare.net), slideshow résumés are an interactive way to review a candidate's work history and qualifications. The hiring manager pushes a button, and a new slide appears to highlight a particular achievement or attribute.

✔ **QR code links:** You know those peculiar-looking square barcodes that have popped up on ads everywhere? They're called QR codes (short for *quick response codes*). Some job candidates have begun putting them on their résumés and linking them to work samples; others place QR codes on the backs of their business cards to direct employers and recruiters to their online résumés. There are a now a variety of websites that make QR code generation a relatively quick and painless process.

It remains to be seen if any of these résumé trends will gain more steam or fizzle out. And candidates assume some risk by attempting to use them. Hiring managers are likely to be confused if all they receive is a QR code, for example. Likewise, your résumé-scanning software may not be able to evaluate an infographic résumé for keywords or relevancy. Although the traditional résumé still dominates, it pays to be aware of these trends. Throughout the book, when I talk about a résumé, you can assume this refers to the entire gamut mentioned here. By and large, the same advice applies.

Using résumé-scanning technology

Résumé-scanning applications that are a component of applicant-tracking systems are commonplace at large companies that routinely have to evaluate tens of thousands of résumés every year. At the other end of the spectrum, the smallest companies typically don't receive résumés in numbers that can't be reasonably handled by an HR manager simply reading through them.

In a nutshell, the programs are designed to scan for keywords, work history, years of experience, and education. The technology identifies likely candidates and ranks them. Candidates who place poorly are removed from further consideration. See Chapter 3 for more on applicant-tracking systems and other tech tools for managers in an HR role.

Some companies have begun asking applicants to provide their usernames and passwords so the prospective employer can access their Facebook, Twitter, or similar online accounts. The goal: to evaluate a potential hire's connections and activity for any red flags. Don't follow in these organizations' footsteps! The practice has been widely condemned (even by Facebook itself) as overreaching and a threat to the candidates' personal privacy. In fact, there has been significant legislative activity in this area. Be sure to check the law in the states in which your company does business regarding the status and type of protections provided to applicants and employees for their electronic accounts. (See Chapter 9 for more on the risks of learning about candidates through their social profiles.)

Résumé roulette

Based on résumés alone, you'd think all your candidates are such outstanding prospects that you could hire them sight unseen. And no wonder. Anyone who does any research at all into how to look for a job knows how to write a résumé that puts him in the best light. And those who don't know how to write a great résumé can now hire people who do know.

Why, then, take résumés seriously? Because résumés, regardless of how perfect or imperfect they are, can still reveal a wealth of information about the candidate — after you crack the code.

Mastering the basics

Here's what you probably know already: Basically, job candidates submit only two types of résumés:

✔ **Chronological,** where all work-related information appears in a timeline sequence

✔ **Functional,** where the information appears in various categories (skills, achievements, qualifications, and so on)

In the past, the general rule was that candidates trying to hide something, such as gaps in their work history, wrote functional résumés. But because a well-rounded background (in conjunction with one's specialty area) can prove an asset, the functional résumé is now more accepted. The key point to keep in mind: Don't automatically become suspicious about either type of résumé.

Some applicants use a combination of the two formats, presenting a capsule of what they believe are their most important qualifications and accomplishments, together with a chronological work history.

Before diving into that pile of résumés, consider the following observations:

✔ No job applicant in her right mind is going to put derogatory or unflattering information in her own résumé.

✔ Many résumés are professionally prepared, designed to create a winning, but not necessarily accurate, impression.

✔ Résumé evaluation is tedious, no matter what. You may need to sift through the stack several times. Have plenty of aspirin, coffee, or tea handy.

✔ If you don't do any résumé evaluation at all (or delegate it to the wrong person), you're likely to miss that diamond in the rough — that ideal employee who unfortunately has poor résumé-drafting skills.

Reading between the lines

Now that more and more people are using outside specialists or software applications to prepare their résumés, getting an accurate picture of a candidate's strengths simply by reading his résumé is more difficult than ever. Even so, here are some of the résumé characteristics that generally (although not always) describe a candidate worth interviewing:

✔ **Lots of details:** Although applicants are generally advised to avoid wordiness, the more detailed they are in their descriptions of what they did and accomplished in previous jobs, the more reliable (as a rule) the information is.

✔ **A history of stability and advancement:** The applicant's work history should show a steady progression into greater responsibility and more important positions. But don't go by job titles alone; look at what the candidate actually did and what skills she acquired. Assess how important the work was to the company involved. Generally, too, you should be wary of candidates who have bounced from one company to the next (although this is much more common today than it used to be, and it may very well be a judgment call on your part depending upon common practices within your particular industry). Again, though, you should be open to the possibility that she had good reasons for her career moves.

✔ **A strong, well-written cover letter:** Some applicants don't send cover letters with their résumés, assuming they've been rendered obsolete by online technology. A savvy job seeker (in other words, someone you may want to have on your team) will still manage to prepare and send the modern equivalent of a cover letter, perhaps in the body of an e-mail message. Nearly eight in ten company managers interviewed for a 2012 Robert Half survey indicated that it's common to receive cover letters even when applicants submit résumés electronically. Someone who takes the time and effort to do this shows a sincere interest in your firm.

Watching out for red flags

Résumé writing is a good example of the law of unintended consequences. Sometimes what's not in a résumé or what's done through carelessness or a mistake can reveal quite a bit about a candidate. Here are some things to watch out for:

✔ **Sloppy overall appearance:** This is a fairly reliable sign that the candidate is lacking in professionalism and/or business experience.

✔ **Unexplained chronological gaps:** Breaks in employment history may mean one of two things: The candidate was unemployed during these gaps, or the candidate is deliberately concealing certain information. A well-designed application form or probing interview questions can uncover hidden downtime — for example, if a candidate says he left one job and started another in the same year but actually left the first job in February and didn't start his next one until late December. But before jumping to conclusions, check to see whether periods of schooling or military service cover the time period. Also, bear in mind that, depending on economic conditions, talented people may have been out of work for periods of time through no fault of their own.

You must tread very carefully in this area. Inquiries into employment gaps may cause the applicant to reveal information that lawfully may not be considered in a hiring (or other employment-related) decision, such as family or medical information. Also, there has been legislative activity to prohibit discrimination based on unemployed status. On this latter point, you should check the laws applicable to your worksites — for example, by consulting a knowledgeable attorney — to determine if such prohibitions exist. If so, such laws will directly impact the extent to which you can consider periods of unemployment, if at all, in making hiring decisions.

✔ **Static career pattern:** A sequence of jobs that doesn't include increasing responsibility may indicate a problem — the person wasn't deemed fit for a promotion or demonstrated a lack of ambition. That said, sometimes solid performers who enjoy just doing their job and don't necessarily have a career progression history still can add tremendous value as part of your team. Don't reject a résumé on this criterion alone. It's something to review and assess but not judge.

✔ **Typos and misspellings:** Generally speaking, typos in cover letters and résumés may signify carelessness or a cavalier attitude. In a Robert Half survey, 76 percent of executives said that they wouldn't hire a candidate who submits a résumé with even one or two typographical errors. Although not all jobs require candidates to have strong spelling skills, most do call for attention to detail. Not proofreading a résumé (or not having someone else do it) may be a sign a candidate isn't conscientious.

✔ **Vaguely worded job summaries:** Perhaps the applicant didn't quite understand what his job was. Or perhaps the job responsibilities didn't match the title. Before you go any farther, you probably want to find out what a "coordinator of special projects" actually does. You want to see job summaries that indicate how crucial the job is to her company's success.

✔ **Weasel wording:** Phrasing such as *participated in, familiar with,* and *in association* can indicate the applicant may not have the actual experience he's claiming. Did the applicant actually work on that vital project, or did he merely run errands for someone who did? A sentence doesn't need to be untruthful to be misleading.

✔ **Job hopping:** Cradle-to-grave employment is by no means the norm today, but a series of many jobs held for short periods of time may signal an unstable or problem employee or a chronic job hopper. Be sure to look at the whole employment history. People do leave jobs for good reasons and should be prepared — and willing — to tell you about it.

✔ **Overemphasis on hobbies or interests outside of work:** This kind of emphasis may indicate an applicant who's trying to pad his résumé because he doesn't have enough relevant experience. He instead adds details about outside interests to make it seem longer. Again, though, don't overreact. An applicant with a broad array of outside interests doesn't necessarily mean an employee who isn't just as enthusiastic about his job.

The CD includes a Sample Résumés document. You can see an example of a well-written résumé, as well as one that should give you reason to pause.

Job Applications: Are They Obsolete?

Applications no longer figure as prominently in the hiring process as they once did, except perhaps for jobs that are outside of a formal office environment, such as a food services order taker. One reason is that the typical résumé today contains most, if not all, of the information normally asked for on most job applications.

A bigger reason, however, is equal employment opportunity (EEO) legislation. EEO laws prohibit many inquiries that routinely appeared on job applications years ago — items relating to gender, age, marital status, and even birthplace. Some states and localities also have specific regulations restricting the type of information that lawfully may be considered — and, therefore, asked about — in hiring.

If you take care to observe these policies, though, one big advantage of a job application over a résumé is that its uniformity simplifies the task of keeping a file on unhired candidates you want to consider for future job openings. In addition, if you design the application form to match your business needs, it generally works better than a résumé as an evaluation device. That's because the same information appears in the same place, regardless of the candidate, allowing you to quickly assess important qualifications.

You can find a Sample Employment Application on the CD. Many business-supply companies offer inexpensive preprinted application forms. Their services are worth investigating. If you decide to create your own, however, give yourself some time to think about how much information you really need.

As a general rule, less is more when it comes to employment applications. In addition, you want to make absolutely sure that the questions you ask are not discriminatory and are in line with federal and state laws. Don't shoot yourself in the foot by including questions in the application that relate to any of the following areas protected under federal law — and be sure to check whether state or local laws governing your operations protect additional characteristics (for example, sexual orientation, gender identity, or marital or familial status):

- Race
- Color
- Ancestry or national origin (although you can ask whether a candidate is eligible to work in the United States)
- Sex
- Religion
- Age

✔ Physical or mental disability (although you can ask if the applicant can perform essential job duties, such as lifting certain amounts, either with or without a reasonable accommodation)

✔ Genetic information

✔ Veteran status or military service

✔ Height or weight (unless directly related to job performance)

The following list describes other things you shouldn't ask for during the preliminary stages of the hiring process:

✔ You can't ask the applicant to provide a photograph before employment.

✔ You can ask an applicant's name but not a maiden name or a spouse's maiden name. Why? Such a question may be interpreted as another way of asking about marital status.

✔ You can ask an applicant's address but not whether she owns or rents or how long she's lived there.

✔ Most education qualifications are fair game, but don't ask for high school or college graduation dates or dates of attendance. It's a dead tip-off for age.

Final rule: If you don't need it, don't ask for it.

Have legal counsel review your company's job applications. Among other things, you want to be absolutely sure that the forms are not in any way discriminatory.

You should require applicants to sign the application and affirm the accuracy of the information they furnish, even if they do so through an online application process with boxes to check attesting to the accuracy of the information. This step doesn't necessarily guarantee that the information is true, but it gives you some protection if, after you hire an applicant, he doesn't work out, and you discover that he misrepresented something on the job application. Misrepresentations in the application process, when discovered, can provide an independent basis for an adverse job action, like demotion or discharge.

The CD contains an Applicant Self-Identification Form for use by federal government contractors and subcontractors. In general, employers with contracts with the federal government, or who are subcontractors to such contracts, are subject to equal employment opportunity requirements, including affirmative action obligations, under several federal laws. Among these requirements, firms are required to maintain and analyze data on certain protected categories of applicants. To ensure that you're aware of the laws and requirements related to federal contractors or subcontractors, consult a lawyer or vendor who is knowledgeable in this complicated area.

How the Internet is changing the definition of a job applicant

Although submitting and processing résumés and applications online is a boon for both employers and job hunters, employment non-discrimination laws have complicated the process of record keeping and compliance.

The Internet Applicant final rule of 2006, issued by the Office of Federal Contract Compliance Programs, addresses record keeping by federal contractors doing more than $10,000 in government business in one year. The law requires these firms to collect and maintain specific records about hiring done by using the Internet or related technologies, such as e-mail, applicant tracking systems, and a variety of databases containing information on job seekers.

These requirements don't currently apply to companies that are not federal contractors, but given the continuing growth of the Internet, HR professionals should keep abreast of new developments in this area. In the near future, similar rules may apply to public and private companies as well.

Employers using or considering technology to evaluate or sort job applicants may want to anticipate these and other requirements by creating an Internet hiring policy. At a minimum, you may want to ensure that your job descriptions are very clear regarding applicant qualifications. Later in this chapter, I talk more about the kinds of questions that are appropriate and inappropriate when interviewing applicants.

Setting Up a System for Evaluating Candidates

No set rules exist for evaluating job applicants — other than common sense (and the legal considerations noted earlier). The important thing is to have some kind of system or protocol in place before résumés begin to arrive.

No matter who does the evaluating — an HR specialist, line manager, or business owner — the process should include a set of hard criteria to use as the basis for decisions. Otherwise, there's a good chance you'll end up making choices based on factors that may have no bearing on desired work performance, such as courses taken at a university you admire or a particularly impressive skill that would be virtually useless in tackling the responsibilities of your job opening.

You need to keep in mind the following three questions at all times:

✔ **What are the prerequisites for the position?** These should track with the qualifications listed in the job description, as long as your description is current, targeted, and carefully thought through (see Chapter 5).

✔ **What are the special requirements of your organization, such as certifications or special education?** If you own a public accounting firm, for example, you would most likely only consider applicants with a valid certified public accountant (CPA) credential.

✔ **What qualifications and attributes are critical to high performance in this particular position?** Think of the key qualities of your best people (see Chapter 5). If your business depends on telemarketing, for instance, some people will be better than others at engaging the interest of the people they call. What attributes make them better? One is certainly an ability to not allow repeated rejections to wear down their spirits. There may be other characteristics as well. Identify those attributes that you feel will produce superior performance. Look for these attributes in prospective employees.

If you haven't answered these three questions, you're not ready to start the candidate evaluation process.

Here's an overview of the candidate evaluation process:

1. **Scan applications or résumés first for basic qualifications.**

   If you do a good job of communicating the job's qualifications to your recruiter or in the posting (based on the job description), you shouldn't get too many replies or résumés from unqualified candidates. Keep in mind, however, that some applicants apply to virtually any job opening, regardless of whether they're qualified. Their attitude is, "Hey, you never know." For example, if you're seeking to hire a medical technician who will be working on equipment that requires a license, and your job posting expressly says that such a license is required, eliminate applicants whose applications or résumés don't indicate they have that license.

2. **Evaluate résumés based on your hiring criteria.**

   After you eliminate unqualified candidates, you can focus on more specific hiring criteria, such as solid organizational skills, supervisory experience, or a good driving record. Here again, your task is considerably easier if you do a thorough job of identifying these requirements at the time you put together the job description. But no matter how much time you spent identifying criteria, don't rush this step. Some résumés clearly reflect the skills and experience you're looking for; others may come close but just don't do the trick.

   Begin the résumé evaluation process by setting a high standard (for example, the résumé must meet a certain high percentage of the criteria). But if your reject pile is growing, and you haven't cleared anyone, you may need to review your criteria to see where you may be able to be more flexible.

3. Set up a process to flag and identify top candidates.

At this point, you probably want to separate the wheat from the chaff, which means establishing a separate file for every applicant who passes the initial evaluation process. Some HR professionals like to develop a *flow sheet* (a document that you attach to the outside of a folder that lists the steps in the evaluation process with spaces for the date and initials of the person completing the step). A flow sheet isn't really complicated — it's just a form that enables you to tell at a glance what stage of the evaluation process the candidate has reached.

Rather than this manual method, many HR organizations use an applicant tracking system (see Chapter 3). These software applications can post job openings on various websites, automate résumé scanning, generate response letters, and perform other functions.

4. Extend an invitation.

Your next move depends on how many applicants remain. If you have only a few, you may want to invite them all to come in for an interview. If you have more applicants than you can handle, you may want to add yet another level of evaluation. Possibilities for the latter include a phone conversation or a visit to your office so they can complete your company's own application form. (See the section "Phone Interviews: Narrowing Your List Further," later in this chapter.)

Earlier in this chapter, I discuss the declining use of job applications. However, they still can be effective as an evaluation tool. Some application forms are *weighted,* meaning that you give each element in the form a certain value, putting more emphasis or weight on qualifications you feel may more heavily influence later performance on the job. In other words, weighting the application questions can help you figure out how likely a person with a certain type of experience or skill is to be the right employee for this particular job.

The trick, of course, is figuring out how to weigh the criteria. The basic idea is to determine how accurately a specific criterion may predict superior job performance. The problem, however, is that no one has developed any sort of weighting scale flexible enough to cover everything that can affect job performance. Educational levels, for example, may closely link to success in a certain job in a company filled with people with advanced degrees. In that case, you would assign it a higher weighting value relative to other criteria. But education credentials may not be as important in a company focused on tasks that don't require advanced degrees. And if you assign values to work experience, licenses held, and so on, you have to be careful that the criteria you're using relate to actual job performance. Again, if you don't really need the skill, you shouldn't list it as a criterion.

Is the entire process scientific? Hardly. But a weighted system can weed out obviously unqualified employees and give you at least a preliminary idea of who the top candidates are for the job.

One way to add validity to a weighted application form is to do your own tracking. Score applicants for a while and then recheck the scores of those you hire. You're looking for relationships between good performance and objective qualifications. The criteria used in an interview to assess how well an applicant might fit a job should be the same criteria used for the performance evaluation of the person in that job. If you can determine the attributes and qualifications that make successful employees, you may find that you can structure a weighted application form that indicates when these qualities are present in a candidate. This procedure is useful if you do a lot of hiring; if you hire only a few people a year, on the other hand, you may just create more work for yourself.

For those candidates who do not make it past your initial evaluation, the CD includes a Rejection Letter — politely worded, of course.

Testing: Knowing What Works and What's Legal

Pre-employment testing is probably the most controversial of all evaluation options in use today. Everybody agrees with the basic rationale that test results often can alert you to attributes and potential problems that you can't infer from a résumé and that don't necessarily surface during an interview. No one, however, has proved in a scientifically conclusive way that testing leads to foolproof or even better hires. In addition, many types of tests are subject to legal restrictions.

So, why test? Because if you use them correctly and in the right situations, many tests can help you evaluate job candidates. Correctly and fairly administered, tests objectively measure basic skills (such as software proficiency), assess acquired knowledge and qualifications, and gauge aptitude for certain jobs. The quality and sophistication of tests have improved markedly in recent years, and many organizations, including some of the largest in the nation, are returning to certain types of testing as a valuable predictive tool.

Businesses often conduct some types of evaluative tests prior to selecting candidates for an interview. These are the kinds of tests I describe in this section. Some companies also administer more comprehensive, extensive, and costly tests and checks *after* the candidate's first or second interview, when managers are closer to making a final decision (background checks, for example); I discuss these in Chapter 9. Still other employers test professionals after making a conditional offer of employment.

Pre-employment testing raises myriad legal issues that can be extremely complicated to work through. If you do test candidates, keep in mind that individuals can't be singled out to be tested. Tests must be applied consistently to all candidates for a position or, in some cases, for all positions within a particular department or business unit. For example, if you require a forklift ability test for a forklift operator, all applicants for this job must take the same test. Bottom line: Any testing policy for a specific situation (and not company-wide) should be clear, documented, and consistently practiced — as well as directly related to the employment in question.

In general, employee hiring or selection tests must have a direct relationship to the employment in question. If a hiring test results in an adverse impact on a protected group (for example, women, African Americans, and so on), it's the employer's burden to show that the test is job related and consistent with business needs. (See Chapter 17 for a discussion of employment-related legal issues.) One way to make this clear, especially with scored tests, is to show that the testing procedures have been validated by scientifically acceptable methodology.

The Uniform Guidelines on Employee Selection Procedures, adopted by a collaboration of federal agencies (including the Equal Employment Opportunity Commission [EEOC] and Department of Labor) and set forth in federal regulations, apply (by their own terms) to employee-selection devices. The guidelines set forth detailed criteria for validating selection devices and seek to ensure that testing results in decisions based upon meaningful differences in qualifications. The safest course is to consult with an attorney before implementing a hiring test of any kind.

The EEOC has published a helpful fact sheet, entitled "Employment Tests and Selection Procedures," which includes employer best practices for testing and selection. You can view it on the EEOC's website at www.eeoc.gov/policy/docs/factemployment_procedures.html.

Finding the right test for your situation

Tests are tools meant to measure specific aspects or qualities of applicants' skills, knowledge, experience, intellect, or — more controversially — personality or psychological makeup. Figure out what you want to find out about a candidate and then choose the appropriate test.

Selecting the right test for your situation probably won't be a problem because choices abound. Dozens of commercial test publishers collectively produce thousands of tests. You can find out about these tests by looking in two reference books — *Tests in Print* and *Mental Measurements Yearbook*, both published by the Buros Center for Testing (www.buros.org).

Other sources are regional government or nonprofit employment agencies, which may even conduct some of the testing for you. The business centers of local colleges also may provide test materials or at least point you in the right direction (or connect you with an expert who can lead you through the testing thicket). When engaging a staffing firm, the recruiter often handles testing in such areas as computer software skills.

Employment tests come in all shapes and sizes. The following sections provide a rundown of what they are, what they do, and how to use them.

Proficiency tests

What do they do? Measure how skillful an applicant is at a particular task (word processing, for example) or how knowledgeable he is in a particular field.

Why would you use them? Proficiency tests measure skills that applicants need for successful job performance. These are useful if a baseline of a particular skill (usually trade related) is essential.

How reliable are they? Generally quite good. This sort of testing has a good track record of validity in the business and industrial world.

Aptitude and ability tests

What do they do? Measure an applicant's capability to learn and perform a particular job and her capability to learn job-related skills or tasks. These tests fall into the following three basic categories:

- ✔ **Mental abilities:** Often called *cognitive tests,* these measure intelligence, verbal reasoning, perceptual speed, and so on. A classic example is the SAT, taken each year by college hopefuls.

- ✔ **Mechanical abilities:** These tests gauge ability to recognize and visualize a mechanical relationship. For instance, applicants may be asked to distinguish between pulley and lever systems.

- ✔ **Psychomotor abilities:** These test an individual's skill and/or ability to make certain body movements or use certain senses.

Why would you use them? Aptitude and ability tests show a readiness to learn or perform a certain task. Whether you use them alone or in batteries of tests, they help many organizations, including governments, select the most likely applicants for specific jobs.

How reliable are they? Generally excellent to adequate so long as they don't violate antidiscrimination laws. (Again, you need to make sure that hiring decisions based on the results of such tests [or any tests] do not work to the disadvantage of groups covered by EEO legislation.)

Physical ability

Definition: An individual's health and physical condition or ability to perform certain tasks.

When important: For jobs that require physical abilities (for example, the ability to lift packages of a certain weight if this is vital to job performance).

How to measure: Any number of testing methodologies can test an individual's physical ability to perform a job.

Requiring a physical or medical examination before employment is illegal under federal law. Employers may test for physical agility or ability if it's a legitimate job requirement under federal law, but they may do so only after they have extended a conditional offer of employment to the candidate. Also, you must consistently administer the same test to other successful candidates conditionally offered employment for the same position. Before you decide that some physical attribute or ability is necessary for the job, however, keep in mind that a number of fire departments around the country have been successfully sued because of their physical tests. Likewise, physical or medical examinations may be unlawful under applicable state law.

How reliable are they? Depends on who administers the exam, but they can be quite effective.

Personality and psychological tests

What do they do? Measure certain personality characteristics, such as assertiveness, resiliency, temperament, or stability. This group of tests also includes interest inventories, which claim to show how close an individual's interests match those of a particular occupational group. These tests are generally lengthy and sometimes involve elaborate and complex scoring keys to predict different personality profiles and traits. There are a number of aptitude/style indicators available, ranging from the Myers-Briggs Type Indicator and NEO Personality Inventory to the Hogan Personality Inventory. Many more are available online.

Be careful when selecting a personality indicator (or any other kind of test) to make sure that the one you choose is both legal and appropriate for hiring. Personality testing is rarely lawful and subject to rigorous requirements even when it is permitted. You should consult an attorney experienced in this area before considering implementing or using such testing.

Why would you use them? This sort of testing is designed to uncover personality traits that make good employees — or those that make bad employees. Because personality is a component of job performance, finding out all you can about an applicant's personality can help predict his performance.

How reliable are they? Depends on who you ask. These types of tests were originally designed to diagnose mental disorders, and even for that purpose — and in the hands of trained professionals — they often leave much to be desired. A primary problem is that the results aren't always crystal clear and sometimes need professional interpretation. If this kind of information is necessary to your evaluation process — for example, you're looking for people who can fit into a certain work team or have certain personality traits that are important to the job — you may feel compelled to use personality tests. Be aware, however, that the subjective nature of the evaluation process creates a legal risk for any company that chooses to use them in the selection process. Consider consulting a lawyer.

Drug tests

What do they do? Measure the presence in an applicant's body of illegal drugs or controlled substances.

Why would you use them? Substance abuse by employees can mean attendance and productivity problems, impaired performance, safety concerns, and potential employee theft, among other issues. Pre-employment drug testing to check candidates for current substance abuse can be lawful under certain circumstances — sometimes including only after a conditional offer of employment has been extended to the candidate — though you must always check federal and state law before implementing such a program.

For some positions, pre-employment drug tests are mandatory. Certain classes of employees — school bus drivers, for example — must submit to testing for drugs and alcohol under the law. In fact, pre-employment drug testing has become so common in some industries that it causes hardly a ripple. Keep in mind, however, that you must give all applicants advance written notice that you intend to test for drugs and obtain their consent. Generally, you can't observe the test itself (employers often contract with third-party testing facilities to administer such testing), and you must hold test results confidential. Other requirements include giving candidates notice of a positive result and, sometimes, the opportunity to challenge the result or submit to retesting. Also, you can test only for what you say you're testing for. Finally, individuals with past drug addictions, and individuals currently in rehabilitation for such issues, are protected under the Americans with Disabilities Act (ADA) and possibly state laws.

Myriad laws in this area, including privacy concerns, ADA concerns, and federal contractor testing rules, among others, make this a legal minefield. Check with a lawyer before you start any applicant or current employee testing.

How reliable are they? If conducted by a competent, reputable lab, very accurate. Shrewd and/or experienced abusers can sometimes slip by, however, either by abstaining long enough to eliminate drug traces from the system or by using other substances to mask drug traces.

Integrity tests

What do they do? Measure an individual's personal honesty and sense of integrity. These tests generally include questions on situations of ethical choice. For instance, what should an employee do if she sees a co-worker stealing? Or they include questions that can reveal personal standards of behavior — whether the candidate can follow simple procedures and keep company information confidential.

Why would you use them? An employer needs to determine how an applicant may behave in a position of trust — handling cash or safeguarding property, for example. A test of this nature is designed to identify people who may be too unreliable to trust with the company cookie jar. Most employers understand that honest people make the best employees. Keep in mind, however, that integrity tests must be job related. You can't ask questions about an applicant's level of debt or credit rating (a violation of the Fair Credit Reporting Act). Tests must remain free of bias based on race, sex, age, or any other protected trait.

As is the case with personality and psychological testing, these tests are very risky legally, with many privacy issues to consider. Talk to a lawyer before using this form of testing.

How reliable are they? Depends on the exact test. Research has shown that some of these tests can produce reliable, unbiased information, while others aren't very accurate at all.

Polygraph (lie-detector) tests

What do they do? Measure stress-related physiological changes, such as blood pressure, sweating, and body temperature, to detect untrue statements.

Why would you use them? Employers need to ensure that people who are being hired for jobs with critical security implications are telling the truth about their backgrounds.

How reliable are they? Depends on who you ask. The skill of the person administering the test also matters. Most experts agree that a competent polygraph operator usually can detect falsehoods from an average individual, provided that person hasn't taken any number of drugs that can modify the reactions the machine measures. The problem is the sociopath with no concept of right or wrong who slides right by. The legal community mistrusts polygraphs enough that their results are inadmissible as evidence in any U.S. court. Be aware that the passage of the Employee Polygraph Protection Act of 1988 prohibits private employers — except under certain conditions — from conducting polygraph tests either on employees or on job applicants. (The same holds true, incidentally, for other devices that purport to measure honesty, such as voice stress analyzers.) Under this law, you can't even ask an applicant to take a polygraph test.

Some states ban the use of polygraph tests in employment decisions, including in hiring. You should consult a lawyer with experience in this area before using or relying on the results of any polygraph test.

Googling candidates: Yes or no?

A job applicant's personal information is no longer the sole purview of a résumé. A few clicks of a mouse can uncover scads of information about anyone who may want to join your company.

In recent years, employers have increasingly turned to general Internet searches to see what the web has to say about an applicant. Although that can be as straightforward as a general search, employers also can see who applicants' Facebook friends are or, by the same token, what buyers think about a particular applicant on eBay.

That may seem like a fertile way to dig up dirt that some job applicants would prefer to remain buried, but there are serious caveats for the companies and HR personnel doing this sleuthing. For one thing, the anonymity of the Internet can prove anything but reliable — anyone can post pretty much anything about you, regardless of whether it's accurate or completely contrived. There's no guarantee that the information you uncover is accurate or insightful.

Separately, legal risks abound with cyber-sleuthing. When you start exploring a candidate beyond the information contained in his résumé or professional profile or bio, you risk legal claims like invasion of privacy and discrimination, or even Fair Credit Reporting Act and similar state law violations. If you want to incorporate web-based searches of applicants into your overall evaluation procedures, work with a lawyer to develop lawful policies, procedures, and guidelines for the gathering and use of Internet-based information. In other words, find your online sleuthing limits and honor them — for the protection of your company.

Staying out of test trouble

The following tips may keep you out of hot water:

- ✔ Before adopting or implementing any employee selection testing, get legal advice. As mentioned earlier, pre-employment testing implicates numerous federal and state law regulations.

- ✔ Establish what traits or information the test is designed to evaluate and make sure that a relationship exists between these traits and the hiring criteria.

- ✔ Carefully check the credentials and reputation of any test vendor. Ask to see validation data.

- ✔ If you use a test, double-check that the test isn't biased either in its objective criteria or unintentionally by disproportionately impacting a protected group.

- ✔ Verify that the test is certified by an established, reputable group, and validated in accordance with the Uniform Guidelines on Employee Selection Procedures from the EEOC.

✔ Network. Talk to colleagues, associates, and people in other companies who use testing. Ask if their testing has been successful.

✔ Local colleges or other organizations sometimes offer skills assessment assistance or programs. Check them out.

A final word of advice on testing: Remember that your company is ultimately responsible for any testing that you conduct. EEOC guidelines treat online testing in the same manner as paper-and-pencil tests. Given that this is legally a very complex area, consult with an attorney before implementing a hiring test of any kind. Also, be sure to carefully manage the data you collect through these tests. Limit the number of people with access to this information to the fewest possible in order to protect the confidentiality of the candidates you test.

For more on testing and other pre-employment evaluation measures, see Chapter 9.

Phone Interviews: Narrowing Your List Further

After you've sorted through résumés and selected the most promising candidates, conducting a telephone interview can help you narrow the list of individuals to call in for an interview. Before calling a candidate, review résumés and cover letters carefully, noting questions to ask. You'll likely see a pattern emerge among applicants who are a good fit for your firm.

See the Sample Phone Interview Questions for Hiring Managers on the CD for a list of questions to ask.

Estimate how long you'll need to effectively conduct a telephone interview with job applicants. It typically can take from 15 to 30 minutes — 15 minutes for a basic preliminary evaluation, 30 minutes if you want to ask deeper questions for a more comprehensive evaluation and assessment. The key is to be consistent with your questions so you can fairly compare job hopefuls.

If the candidate isn't available, and you need to leave a message, suggest a time frame (such as in the morning or between 2 p.m. and 5 p.m.) when she should return your call the next day. This request can be a good test of initiative — candidates who fail to return the call or who don't make a reasonable effort to contact you to make alternative arrangements demonstrate either a lack of interest or halfhearted commitment.

Chapter 8

One on One: Getting the Most out of Interviewing

. . . .

In This Chapter

▶ Getting an overview of today's interviewing playing field

▶ Discovering five leading pitfalls of job interviewing

▶ Setting the stage for an interview

▶ Beginning the interview

▶ Mastering the fine art of Q&A

▶ Nondiscriminatory questioning: Knowing what you can ask and what you can't

▶ Asking hard-hitting questions (and interpreting the answers)

▶ Ending the interview gracefully

. . . .

Conducting an interview looks easier than it is. And that's the problem. The vast majority of managers and small-business owners seem to think that, because they've seen Oprah do it a million times on TV, they pretty much know all there is about interviewing. As a result, most hiring managers take this step in the hiring process for granted. They don't invest the time, effort, and concentration that effective job interviewing requires. And, above all, they don't prepare enough. Instead, they wing it. (I guess you could say they're "ducking" their responsibilities.)

The results of this misguided mindset speak for themselves. More often than not, little correlation exists between the positive reports that emerge from the typical job interview and the job performance of the candidates who receive those glowing assessments. That's the bad news. The good news is that this correlation goes up dramatically whenever interviewing becomes a structured, well-planned process — one that's well integrated into a company's overall staffing practices.

This chapter takes an in-depth look at interviewing, with a focus on the things you need to know and do to get the most out of the interviewing process.

Interviewing: The Basics

Job interviews enable you to perform the following four tasks that, combined with other steps, are essential to making a sound hiring decision:

- ✔ Obtain firsthand information about the candidate's background, work experience, and skill level. This helps clarify what you discovered from the candidate's résumé, candidate profile, or previous interviews.

- ✔ Get a general sense of the candidate's overall intelligence, aptitude, enthusiasm, and attitudes, with particular respect to how those attributes match up to the requirements of the job.

- ✔ Gain insight — as much as possible — into the candidate's basic personality traits, her motivation to tackle the responsibilities of the job, her desire to become a part of the company, and her ability to integrate into the current work team.

- ✔ Estimate the candidate's ability to adapt to your company's work environment.

That's pretty much it. What occurs during a job interview doesn't tell you — not directly, at any rate — how effectively candidates may perform on the job if, indeed, you hire them. Nor does the image of the candidate that emerges during the interview necessarily represent an accurate image of who the candidate really is and how he's likely to react in actual job situations.

Today's interview-savvy candidates

The people you'll be interviewing today are savvier than ever about interviews. Here are two things today's candidates know that their parents may not have:

- ✔ **They know how to excel in an interview.** More and more candidates these days are well schooled in the art of making you believe, by virtue of their interview performance, that they're the answer to all your hiring prayers. Unless you're disciplined and vigilant, you may fall in love with the wrong candidate who has all the right answers.

- ✔ **They know about antidiscrimination laws.** Now that more people are well versed in antidiscrimination legislation, candidates who don't get the job are more likely than ever to claim, justifiably or not, that your company's interviewing practices are discriminatory. Your best protection is to make sure that you and everybody else conducting job interviews steer clear of any subject or any line of questioning that may leave your company open to a discrimination claim.

The Five Deadly Sins of Job Interviewing

This section takes a look at some of the all-too-common practices that create a surefire recipe for hiring mistakes.

Not devoting enough time to interviewing

Failing to give the interviewing process the time and effort it deserves is, by far, the main reason interviews fail to reveal useful information about a person. You can probably understand why managers frequently neglect to take the necessary steps to prepare for interviews, conduct them diligently, and evaluate the results in a thoughtful manner: They're busy. Everybody's busy. Time is at a premium. But your job is to make every interview you conduct count. Encourage line managers who make their own hiring decisions to do the same.

Not being consistent from one interview to the next

One major difference between interviewers who have a knack for picking winners and those who don't is nothing more complicated than simple discipline. Skillful interviewers think through the process and tend to follow the same method every time — albeit with variations that they tailor to individual situations. Unsuccessful interviewers tend to wing it, creating a different routine for each interview and entering unprepared. The hidden danger of a lack of planning: You deprive yourself of the one thing you need the most as you're comparing candidates: an objective standard on which to base your conclusions. Without structure, you have no way of knowing whether the impressions you gather from the interview would be different if your approach and other aspects of the interview were consistent for each candidate. If you wing it, you're also not giving the candidate a very good impression of your company.

Talking too much

If you're talking more than 20 percent of the time during a job interview, you're talking too much. Savvy candidates are usually adept at getting their interviewers to do most of the talking. They've figured out that the more interviewers talk, the easier they, the candidates, can determine what answers are going to carry the most weight. Probing through active listening (for example, letting the candidate's comments spark related questions) is a critical interviewing skill because it allows you to gain valuable information you'd miss if you did most of the talking. You can — and should — react, comment on, and build on the answers that candidates give in job interviews. Just bear in mind: The only thing you discover about a candidate during any session where you're doing most of the talking is that the candidate knows how to listen.

Focusing on one positive attribute of a candidate and ignoring everything else

This situation describes the *halo effect*, a term managers often use to describe a situation in which the interviewer becomes so enraptured by one particular aspect of the candidate — appearance, credentials, interests, — that it colors all his other judgments. Then again, interviewers are only human, and so are you. You can't always help yourself from placing too much significance on one part of the candidate's overall presentation. At the very least, however, be aware of your halo-effect tendencies and do your best to keep them in check.

Playing armchair (psycho)analyst

The ability to read people can be an enormously valuable skill for anyone who interviews job candidates. But unless you're formally trained as a psychologist or psychiatrist, leave your couch at home and try not to seek out the subconscious meaning behind everything the candidate says and does. If you have strong evidence that ties certain psychological factors to a person's ability to handle a particular job, great. Bring in an outside professional to help you develop questions that can capitalize on that knowledge.

Setting the Stage

Your ability to get the most out of the interviews you conduct invariably depends on how well prepared you are. Here's a checklist of things you should do before you ask the first interview question:

✔ **Thoroughly familiarize yourself with the job description, especially its hiring criteria.** Do so even if you draw up the criteria yourself.

✔ **Review everything the candidate has submitted to date.** That includes a résumé, cover letter, online profile, and so on. Note any areas needing clarification or explanation, such as quirky job titles, gaps in work history, or hobbies that may reveal aspects of the candidate's personality that can have a bearing on job performance.

✔ **Set up a general structure for the interview.** Create a basic schedule for the interview so that, as the meeting progresses, you reserve enough time to cover all the key areas you want to address. Having a rough schedule to adhere to will help you begin and end the session on time, allowing you to be more efficient and showing that you respect the candidate's time.

A phone screen is a great use of time to provide the candidate an opportunity to answer general questions you have and for you to determine if he's worth the time investment to bring on-site for an interview. (See Chapter 7 for more on phone interviews.)

✔ **Write down the questions you intend to ask.** Base your questions on the areas of the candidate's background that deserve the most attention (based on the job description and your hiring criteria). Keep the list in front of you throughout the interview.

✔ **Hold the interview in a room that's private and reasonably comfortable.** Clear your desk, close the door, and either set your phone so all calls go to voicemail or have your calls forwarded somewhere else.

Try not to schedule job interviews in the middle of the day. The reason: You're not likely to be as relaxed and as focused as you need to be, and you may have a tough time fighting off interruptions and distractions. The ideal time to interview candidates is early morning, before the workday starts. You're fresher then, and so is the candidate. If you have no choice, give yourself a buffer of at least half an hour before the interview so that you can switch gears and prepare for the interview in the right manner.

The Pre-Interview Checklist for Hiring Managers, found on the CD, can serve as a handy reference when preparing for an upcoming interview.

The Introduction: Warming Up

Your priority in meeting a candidate face to face for the first time is to put her at ease. Disregard any advice anyone has given you about doing things to create stress just to see how the individual responds. Those techniques are rarely productive, and they put both you and your company in a bad light. Instead, view the first minutes of the meeting as an opportunity to build rapport with the candidate. The more comfortable she is, the more engaging the interview will be, and the more you'll find out about her.

If you're seated at your desk as the candidate walks in, a common courtesy is to stand and meet the individual halfway, shake hands, and let him know that you're happy to meet him (basic stuff but easy to forget). You don't need to cut to the chase right away with penetrating questions. Skilled job interviewers usually begin with small talk — a general comment about the weather, transportation difficulties, and so on — but they keep it to a minimum.

Multiple, panel, and video interviews

Companies today use more than just the traditional one-on-one, in-person interview format. It's not unusual, for example, for more than one company employee to interview a candidate to provide a variety of opinions on the individual, especially if she will play a key role in the organization. In fact, sometimes these meetings are carried out simultaneously through the use of an interviewing panel made up of the hiring manager plus other members of the management team or work group, usually no more than three to five people.

Panel interviews are beneficial when you want to quickly get a promising candidate through multiple interviews in a timely manner. It's best for the hiring manager to conduct one-on-one preliminary interviews with applicants first, choosing only a few finalists for panel interviews. This saves panelists time and ensures that the hiring manager is presenting only those candidates she may ultimately hire. Panel interviews are most successful when the hiring manager distributes job criteria to the interview team in advance, along with some suggested questions to ask the candidate. This ensures that panel members will be able to compare candidates in a consistent fashion, using like criteria.

For the most part, panel interviews are the exception to the norm because candidates can feel overwhelmed by a panel approach. If the interview is intimidating, the job seeker may not provide candid information and could even decide the position isn't right for her.

Given the expense of bringing far-flung candidates in for face-to-face interviews, more companies are conducting video interviews by using Skype and similar technology. Approach a video interview with the same level of professionalism as you would any other. Conduct the interview from an uncluttered setting, such as a conference room. Additionally, make sure that you're comfortable with the technology. If you're new to the system, try it out first with your company colleagues or friends. Any technical problems that crop up during the interview will reflect badly on both you and your business.

The same guidelines for appropriate questioning and comments that apply to the formal interview apply to casual discussions and chitchat. (See "A Crash Course in Nondiscriminatory Questioning," later in this chapter.)

After the small talk is out of the way, your next step is to give the candidate a very basic overview of what you're expecting to get from the interview and how long you estimate it to last. Be careful not to give too much information, though. Saying too much about the skills and characteristics you're looking for turns a savvy interviewee into a "parrot" who can repeat the same key words she just heard. Don't give away the keys to the kingdom!

Q&A: Mastering the Art

The Q&A is the main part of the interview. How you phrase questions, when you ask them, how you follow up — each of these aspects of interviewing can go a long way toward affecting the quality and value of the answers you get.

The following sections describe the key practices that differentiate people who've mastered the art of questioning from those who haven't.

For an Interview Q&A Form, see the CD.

Have a focus

Even before you start to ask questions, you want to have a reasonably specific idea of what information or insights you're expecting to gain from the interview based on your research and the hiring criteria you develop in your job description. You may uncover two or three items on the candidate's résumé that warrant clarification. Or you may have a specific question, based on the notes you take during earlier candidate evaluation, about one particular aspect of the candidate's personality. Whatever the need, decide ahead of time what you want to know more about and build your interview strategy around that goal.

Make every question count

Every question you ask during a job interview must have a specific purpose. That purpose may be to elicit specific information, produce some insight into the candidate's personality, past performance, or simply put the candidate at ease. The general rule: If the question has no strategic significance, think twice before asking it. Again, tie questions to the criteria defined in the job description.

Pay attention

Listening attentively is difficult under the best of circumstances, but it's often an even tougher challenge during a job interview. That's because it's tempting to draw conclusions before the candidate has completed the answer. Yet another habit is to begin rehearsing in your mind the next question you intend to ask while the candidate is still answering the earlier question. Fight these tendencies. Consider writing down your questions before the interview begins and then direct the full measure of your concentration to the candidate and what he's saying.

Don't hesitate to probe

Whenever a candidate offers an answer that doesn't address the specific information you're seeking, nothing's wrong with asking additional questions to draw out more specific answers. If a candidate talks about the money she saved her department, ask how much and what, specifically, she did to accomplish that. Too many interviewers let candidates off the hook in the interest of being nice. That practice, however, can prove counterproductive — she may give you valuable background on specific abilities if your questions are more penetrating.

Give candidates ample time to respond

The fact that a candidate doesn't respond immediately to a question you ask doesn't mean that you need to rush in with another question to fill the silence. Give the candidate time to come up with a thoughtful answer. If the silence persists for more than, say, ten seconds, ask the candidate if she wants you to clarify the question. Otherwise, don't rush things. Use the silence to observe the candidate and to take stock of where you are in the interview. Remember that the interview is a time for you to listen, not talk.

Tread carefully whenever you come across a candidate who seems flat and disinterested during the job interview. If a candidate can't demonstrate any real enthusiasm during the interview, don't expect him to muster any fire in the belly after you hire him.

Suspend judgments

Reserving judgment isn't easy, but try to keep your attention on the answers you're getting instead of making interpretations or judgments. You'll have plenty of time after the interview to evaluate what you see and hear. What you don't want to do is prejudice yourself in the beginning of the interview so that you fail to accurately process information that comes later.

Take notes

Memories can do tricky things, leading people to ignore what actually happens during an interview and to rely instead on general impressions. Taking notes helps you avoid this common pitfall. Just make sure that you do so unobtrusively so the candidate doesn't feel like she has to pause for you to keep pace. Keep all notes factual and within ethical and nondiscriminatory boundaries. Also, give yourself a few moments after the interview to review your notes and clarify them or put them into some kind of order.

Vary the style of questions

You can usually divide questions into five categories, based on the kinds of answers you're trying to elicit.

Closed-ended

Definition: Questions that call for a simple, informational answer — often a yes or no.

Examples: "How many years did you work for the circus?" "Did you enjoy it?" "What cities did you tour?"

When to use them: Closed-ended questions work best if you're trying to elicit specific information or set the stage for more complex questions.

Pitfalls to avoid: Asking too many of them in rapid-fire succession and failing to tie them back to the job criteria, thus making candidates feel as though they're being interrogated.

Open-ended

Definition: Questions that require thought and oblige the candidate to reveal attitudes or opinions. One type of open-ended question is the *behavioral interview question*. With a behavioral question, candidates are asked to relate past on-the-job experiences to situations they are likely to encounter in the position being discussed.

Examples: "Can you describe how you handle tight deadlines on the job?" "Can you give me an illustration of how you improved productivity at your last job?"

When to use them: Most of the time but interspersed with closed-ended questions.

Pitfalls to avoid: Not being specific enough as you phrase the question and not interceding if the candidate's answer starts to veer off track.

Hypothetical

Definition: Questions that invite the candidate to resolve an imaginary situation or react to a given situation.

Examples: "If you were the purchasing manager, how would you go about selecting a new automated purchase order system for the company?" "If you were to take over this department, what's the first thing you'd do to improve productivity?"

When to use them: Useful if framed in the context of actual job situations.

Pitfall to avoid: Putting too much stock in the candidate's hypothetical answer. You're usually better off asking questions that force a candidate to use an actual experience as the basis for an answer.

Leading

Definition: Questions asked in such a way that the answer you're looking for is obvious.

Examples: "You know a lot about team building, don't you?" "You wouldn't dream of falsifying your expense accounts, would you?"

When to use them: Rarely, if ever. You're not likely to get an honest answer — just the answer you want to hear. And you run the risk of appearing unprofessional.

Off-the-wall

Definition: Questions that, on the surface, may seem bizarre but may actually be revealing in the answers they elicit.

Examples: "What literary character do you most closely identify with?" "If you could be reincarnated as a car, which one would you choose?"

When to use them: Some businesses have used these kinds of questions to determine whether a candidate is a fit for the company culture or to see if the interviewee can think outside the box, but most firms should approach them with a good deal of caution. A candidate's response to an off-the-wall challenge may highlight his creativity and offer insight into his thought process. But you also can come off as unprofessional, if not out and out weird, if you don't handle these questions carefully.

Pitfalls to avoid: Overuse. If you decide to ask an off-the-wall question, just do it once. A series of weird questions may send your candidate scrambling for the door before the interview is over.

Recording an interview can be risky. In fact, some states make this practice illegal. If you want to record an interview (and most interviews are *not* recorded), check first with a knowledgeable and experienced lawyer for any legal restrictions. Even if recording the interview is legal, there may still be reasons to consider the usefulness of doing so. Most people resent being recorded secretly, so the interviewer should tell the candidate that the interview is being taped to ensure an accurate record for the protection of both parties. However, even if the fact of the recording is disclosed, most people are less forthcoming and candid if they're aware that they're being recorded.

A Crash Course in Nondiscriminatory Questioning

As I mention earlier in this chapter (see the sidebar "Today's interview-savvy candidates"), the questions you or others in your company ask during a job interview can result in legal problems for the company if you fail to follow certain guidelines. Even the most innocent of questions can result in a discrimination suit at some point.

Antidiscrimination and consumer protection legislation passed since the 1960s restricts the type and scope of pre-employment questions that you can ask. Moreover, court decisions and administrative rulings have refined what you can and can't ask, and, to make matters even more confusing, standards can vary from state to state — and even from city to city.

Here are some current pitfalls:

- **Be sensitive to age discrimination issues.** Remember that any question that may indicate the candidate's age may be interpreted as discriminatory. In other words, don't ask a question such as "When did you graduate from high school?"

- **Beware of double-edged questions.** Caution all the interviewers in your company to keep their innocent curiosity (as evidenced in a question such as "What kind of a name is that?") from exposing your company to charges of discrimination.

- **Don't confuse before and after.** Questions considered illegal before hiring may be acceptable after the individual is on the payroll. Age is a good example. You can't ask a person's age before hiring, but after hiring, the information may be needed for health insurance or pension forms.

For more detailed information on how to avoid discrimination when you're asking interview questions, see the Employment Inquiries Fact Sheet on the CD.

The following sections provide a rundown of which questions are permitted before hiring and which are not. Check with your attorney for any local restrictions or new rulings and keep in mind that all questions must directly relate to a bona fide job requirement.

Even questions that seem okay to ask under the following guidelines may be discriminatory if they're asked in circumstances that suggest a discriminatory intent — for example, if you ask only female employees who reveal that they have children if they have any reason they couldn't work overtime or on the weekend.

Keep your questions focused on the job requirements and away from the candidate's personal life.

During the interview, you can use the Nondiscriminatory Interview Question Reference Sheet on the CD to help you avoid potentially problematic questions.

National origin

Questions okay to ask: None.

Risky ground: Questions related to the candidate's national origin, ancestry, or native language or that of family members. That also applies to the applicant and the applicant's parents' places of birth.

Discriminatory: "What sort of an accent is that?" "Where were you born?" "Where were your parents born?"

Citizenship status

Questions okay to ask: "If hired, will you be able to prove that you have the right to remain and work in the United States?"

Risky ground: Questions that may oblige a candidate to indicate national origin.

Discriminatory: "Are you a U.S. citizen?"

Address

Questions okay to ask: "Where do you live?" "How long have you lived here?"

Risky ground: Questions about housing aimed at revealing financial status. (May be considered discriminatory against minorities.)

Discriminatory: "Are you renting, or do you own your home?"

Age

Questions okay to ask: None.

Risky ground: Questions regarding age when age is not a bona fide job requirement.

Discriminatory: "How old are you?" "In what year were you born?" "When did you graduate from high school?"

Family status

Questions okay to ask: "Can you relocate?" (If relevant to the job.)

Risky ground: All questions regarding marital or family status.

Discriminatory: "Are you pregnant?" "When are you due?" (Even if the candidate is obviously pregnant.)

Religion

Questions okay to ask: "Can you work overtime on days other than Monday through Friday?"

Risky ground: Any question whose answers may indicate religious beliefs or affiliation.

Discriminatory: "What religious holidays do you observe?"

Health and physical condition

Questions okay to ask: "Can you perform the expected job functions with or without reasonable accommodation?"

Risky ground: Questions that aren't directly related to a bona fide job requirement and, in addition, aren't being asked of all candidates.

Discriminatory: "Do you have a hearing impairment?" "Have you ever filed a workers' compensation claim?"

Name

Questions okay to ask: "Have you ever used another name or nickname?"

Risky ground: Questions about whether the applicant has ever changed her name or about the candidate's maiden name.

Discriminatory: "What kind of name is that?"

Language

Questions okay to ask: "What language do you speak, read, and/or write?" (Permissible if relevant to the job.)

Risky ground: Questions that reveal the applicant's national origin or ancestry.

Discriminatory: "What language do you speak at home?" "Is English your first language?"

Solid Questions to Ask and How to Interpret the Answers

What makes an interview question "good"? A good question does two things:

- ✔ It gives you the specific information you need to make a sound hiring decision.
- ✔ It helps you gain insight into how the candidate's mind and emotions work and her experience and style.

Avoid timeworn, clichéd questions, such as "What are your strengths and weaknesses?" or "Where do you see yourself in the next five years?" Instead, develop a list of questions designed to elicit responses that will be most help-ful in evaluating a candidate's suitability for your position and organization.

You can ask hundreds of such questions, but here are some to get you started, along with ideas on what to look for in the answers:

- ✔ **"What interests you about this job and what skills and strengths can you bring to it?"** Nothing tricky here, but it's a solid question all the same. Note that the question is not "What are your skills and strengths?" but "What skills and strengths can you bring to the job?" The answer is yet another way to gauge how much interest the applicant has in the job and how well prepared she is for the interview. Stronger candidates should be able to correlate their skills with specific job requirements: "I think my experience as a foreign correspondent will be of great help in marketing products to overseas customers." They will answer the ques-tion in the context of contributions they can make to the company.

- ✔ **"Can you tell me a little about your current job?"** Strong candidates should be able to give you a short and precise summary of duties and responsibilities. How they answer this question can help you determine their passion and enthusiasm for their work and their sense of personal accountability. Be wary of applicants who bad-mouth or blame their employers. If they're not loyal to the people they work for now, how can you expect them to be loyal to you? ("They wouldn't let me bring my pet iguana to work. Can you believe it?")

✔ **"In a way that anyone could understand, can you describe a professional achievement that you're proud of?"** This question is especially good when you're interviewing someone for a technical position, such as a systems analyst or tax accountant. The answer shows the applicant's ability to explain what she does so that anyone can understand it. Does she avoid jargon in her description? Does she get her points across clearly? Failure to do so may be a sign that she can't step out of her world sufficiently to work with people in other departments, which is a growing necessity in many organizations today.

✔ **"How have you changed the nature of your current job?"** A convincing answer here shows adaptability and a willingness to take the bull by the horns, if necessary. An individual who chose to do a job differently from other people also may show creativity and resourcefulness. The question gives candidates a chance to talk about such contributions as greater efficiencies or cost savings. If a candidate says he didn't change the nature of the job, that response can tell you something as well.

✔ **"What was the most difficult decision you ever had to make on the job?"** Notice the intentionally vague aspect of this question. It's not hypothetical; it's real. What you're looking for is the person's decision-making style and how it fits into your company culture. Someone who admits that firing a subordinate was difficult demonstrates compassion. Those who successfully decided to approach a co-worker over a conflict may turn out to be great team players. Individuals who admit to a mistake exhibit honesty and open-mindedness.

Also, note how people went about making the decision. Seeking the advice of others, for example, may mean that they're team centered. This question is an especially important one if you're interviewing a candidate for a middle- or senior-level management position.

✔ **"Why did you decide to pursue a new job?"** This question is just a different way of asking, "What are you looking for in a job?" Some candidates come so well rehearsed that they're never at a loss for an answer. Sometimes by phrasing the question in a different way, you can cause them to go off script.

✔ **"I see that you've been unemployed for the past few months. Why did you leave your last job, and what have you been doing since then?"** This question is important, but don't let it seem accusatory. Especially in challenging economic times, it's not unusual for highly competent people to find themselves unemployed through no fault of their own and unable to prevent gaps in their employment history. Pursuing the issue in a neutral, diplomatic way is important. Try to get specific, factual answers that you can verify later. Candidates with a spotty employment history, at the very least, should be able to account for all extended periods of unemployment and demonstrate whether they used that time productively — getting an advanced degree, for example.

At the same time — and as noted in Chapter 7 — the reasons for employment gaps may pertain to legally protected information that you, the employer, may not consider in making hiring or any other employment-related decision. For example, an applicant who was unemployed due to cancer very likely has a protected disability under the Americans with Disabilities Act and similar state laws. Probing into the reasons underlying employment gaps can unearth information that you, the employer, may not want to be injected into the application/hiring process. You must be careful when approaching this issue.

✓ **"Who was your best boss ever and why? Who was the worst, and, looking back, what could you have done to make that relationship better?"** These two questions are more penetrating than you may think. Among other things, the answers give you insight into how the candidate views and responds to supervision. A reflective, responsive answer to the second part of the question may indicate a loyal employee capable of rising above an unpleasant supervisory situation and/or learning from past mistakes, both highly desirable qualities. A bitter, critical answer may indicate someone who holds grudges or simply can't get along with certain kinds of people. Yes, personality clashes occur all the time, but in today's team-oriented workplace, you want employees who try to minimize these clashes and not use them as excuses.

✓ **"Are you more comfortable and successful working alone with information or working with other people?"** The ideal answer here is "both." People who say they like working with information are obviously a good choice for technical positions, but it may be a red flag if they don't also enjoy communicating and collaborating with other individuals — increasingly a function of even highly technical jobs. An excellent candidate may say that the different perspectives within a group produce more innovative ideas than one person working alone can, but without information a team can't get very far.

✓ **"What sorts of things do you think your current/past company could do to be more successful?"** This one is a great big-picture question. You're probing to find out whether the candidate has a clear understanding of his current or past employer's missions and goals and whether he has worked with those goals in mind. Candidates who can't answer this question well are demonstrating a lack of depth and interest, which can quite likely carry over into your organization. Sometimes the answer to this question also reveals hidden bitterness or anger at an employer. But make clear to the candidate that you're not looking for proprietary or confidential information.

✓ **"Can you describe a typical day at work in your last job?"** Strong candidates can give you specific details that you can verify later, but the main point of this question is to see how the applicant's current (or most recent) routine compares with the requirements of the job in question. How interviewees describe their duties can prove highly revealing. Do you sense any real enthusiasm or interest? Do the details match the information you already have? You're looking for enthusiasm and some indication that the applicant connects his current duties with company goals.

- ✔ **"What sort of work environment do you prefer? What brings out your best performance?"** Probe for specifics. You want to find out whether this person is going to fit into your company. If your corporate culture is collegial and team centered, you don't want someone who answers, "I like to be left alone to do my work." You also may uncover unrealistic expectations or potential future clashes ("My plan is to spend a couple months in the mailroom and then apply for the presidency of the company"). People rarely, if ever, work at their best in all situations. Candidates who say otherwise aren't being honest with themselves or with you.

- ✔ **"How do you handle conflict? Can you give me an example of how you handled a workplace disagreement in the past?"** You want candidates who try to be reasonable but nonetheless stand up for what's right. Unfortunately, most candidates say the right things, which is why you want some specifics. Be suspicious if the answer is too predictable. Some people may be naturally easygoing, but candidates who say that they never get into conflict situations are either dishonest or delusional.

- ✔ **"How would you respond if you were placed in a situation that you felt presented a conflict of interest or was unethical? Have you ever had this experience in previous positions?"** No rational candidate is going to say that sometimes it's okay to be unethical. But how individuals approach this question and any anecdotes they share can offer valuable insights as to how they may respond if faced with such a situation.

- ✔ **"What are your compensation expectations?"** There's no "trick" to this question. You simply want to get a sense early on if the candidate's desired pay is in line with what you've budgeted for the open position. This can prevent you from continuing to move through the hiring process a promising candidate whose salary expectations far exceed your own.

In addition to an opportunity to showcase their qualifications, savvy candidates use the interview to find out as much as they can about the position and company, so don't be surprised if they come prepared with questions of their own. Don't interpret questions as disruptive to your agenda. They're a show of interest and professionalism. In fact, you can address many of their concerns by proactively promoting your company during the interview. Just as candidates try to show how their skills are a match with the position, you also can point out programs and policies that fit the needs of promising applicants and highlight the aspects of the corporate culture that make your firm a great place to work.

End Game: Closing on the Right Note

With only a few minutes to go, you can bring the session to a graceful close by following these steps:

1. **Offer the candidate a broad-brushstroke summary of the interview.**

   Sum up what the candidate has said about her fit for the position, reasons for wanting the job, and so on. This summary demonstrates that you were a sincere listener and that you care about the candidate as a person. That leaves a good impression. It also gives the candidate an opportunity to clarify any misunderstandings.

2. **Let the candidate ask questions.**

3. **Let the candidate know what comes next.**

   Advise the candidate how and when you're going to contact him and whether any further steps need to be taken — for example, forms or tests. This practice not only is a common courtesy but also creates a good impression.

   Also, let him know you'll be in touch regardless of the hiring decision. Not all companies say, "Thanks, but no thanks" to rejected applicants, but it's a sign of respect and consideration.

4. **End the interview on a formal but sincere note.**

   Thank the candidate for her time and repeat your commitment to follow up. Either stand or shake hands again. This action formally ends the session and provides a signal for the candidate to leave. Walk the applicant out of the office to the elevator lobby or front door.

And one last suggestion: As soon as possible after the candidate's departure, take a moment to collect your thoughts and write down your impressions and a summary of your notes. You don't need to make any definitive decisions at this point, but recording your impressions while they're still fresh in your mind will help you immeasurably if the final choice boils down to several candidates, all of whose qualifications are comparable. Along these lines, collect all feedback from other interviewers who met with the candidate the same day that they met with him. This allows you to gather feedback while it's still fresh and when it's most relevant.

The CD contains a Candidate Interview Evaluation Form, which you can use to record your impressions of job candidates.

Chapter 9

The Home Stretch: Making the Final Decision

In This Chapter

▶ Remaining objective when evaluating candidates

▶ Knowing what factors to consider

▶ Developing a disciplined and logical system for selecting the best candidate

▶ Avoiding poor hiring decisions

▶ Checking references

▶ Deciding about background checks

▶ Presenting and negotiating the offer

*N*ow comes the moment of truth in the hiring process: choosing who will get the job. Because hiring mistakes can be costly, a lot is riding on your ability to select the best people for your available positions. If you find yourself constantly second-guessing your hiring decisions, you may want to take a close look at the process you're using to make your final choices. This chapter can help you get this process started.

Much of the information in this chapter is the result of a collaborative effort with the law firm of Paul Hastings LLP. Don't be your own lawyer. Legally complex (and potentially costly) issues require a case-by-case evaluation by your own attorney. Not only do laws limit what factors can and can't be considered in making hiring decisions, but also negligent hiring lawsuits are common. For example, employers have been held liable for hiring someone with a history of violent or criminal acts. Also, labor law is constantly changing, which makes consulting with an attorney all the more essential. I discuss this and other issues regarding background checks later in this chapter.

Coming to Grips with the Decision-Making Process

Stripped to its essentials, the decision-making process in the final stages of hiring isn't really that different from selecting the right school for your child or deciding on a new home. You look at your options, weigh the pros and cons of each, and then make a choice.

Of course, hiring involves people, not a school or home. Managers differ in their basic approaches to selecting new hires. Some rely entirely on their own judgment and assessments. Others are highly systematic and may also seek guidance from others.

You can never be absolutely certain that the decision you make is going to give you all that you expect. You can improve your chances significantly, however, if you manage the decision-making process in a reasonably disciplined way.

Remain objective in evaluating candidates. Don't let your personal biases steer your focus away from your hiring criteria (the halo and cloning effects I describe later in this chapter). Consistently focus on the key hiring criteria you established at the outset of the process when you were identifying your needs and drawing up a job description that pinpoints the combination of skills, attributes, and credentials that a particular position requires.

Utilizing the Tools of the Trade

Here are some of the factors on which different HR managers base their hiring decisions and what you need to keep in mind as you're considering each one. I discuss them in more detail later in this chapter.

Past experience

A long-time truism in successful hiring is the concept that the best indicator of a candidate's future potential is past performance. If a candidate was hardworking, highly motivated, and team oriented in his last job, the same is likely to hold true in the new job. Similarly, the candidate who consistently lacked enthusiasm and drive in his last position isn't likely to turn things around in his next one. People do change, of course, but only in fairy tales do frogs turn into princes.

The only caveat to this usually reliable principle: The conditions that prevailed in the candidate's last job need to closely parallel the conditions in the job she's seeking. Otherwise, you have no real basis for comparison. No two business environments are identical. For all you know, certain systems or people in place in the candidate's previous job may have been instrumental in her success (or failure) — and you can rarely replicate such factors in your company (and may not, in fact, even want to).

Interview impressions

Impressions you pick up during an interview almost always carry a great deal of weight in hiring decisions — and understandably. Managers naturally place more trust in what they actually see and hear than in information from third-party sources. The problem with interview impressions is that they're just that — impressions. You're listening to answers and observing behavior, but your own preconceived perceptions and experiences almost always influence your judgments.

This doesn't mean that you should disregard your interview impressions — only that you keep them in their proper perspective with test results, references, and other information you've collected to evaluate a prospective hire.

Test results

Some people regard test results as the only truly reliable predictor of future success. The argument goes as follows: Test results are quantifiable. In most tests, results aren't subject to personal interpretation. With a large enough sample, you can compare test scores to job performance ratings and, eventually, use test scores as a predictor of future performance.

The only problem: Some candidates simply don't test well. They freeze up, which affects their ultimate scores. Other candidates may be clever enough to figure out what most tests are actually testing for and tailor their responses accordingly. So, if you're going to use test results in your decision-making process, ensure the validity of the tests (whether they do, indeed, predict the quality of future job performance) and their legality (whether they comply with all state and federal laws and don't result in discrimination). (See Chapter 17 and "Discovering the Truth about Background Checks," later in this chapter.)

Firsthand observation

Call it the proof-in-the-pudding principle. Watching candidates actually perform some of the tasks for which you're considering hiring them is clearly the most reliable way to judge their competence. That's why more and more companies these days start out an applicant as a contingent, or temporary, worker, with the idea that, if the person works out, he may eventually become a full-time employee.

In the past, some companies have instituted probationary periods to gain firsthand knowledge about candidates. Today, firms should stay away from the term *probation* because it may create an implied contract of employment. Some courts assume that after a worker is no longer on probation, the employer must have good cause to terminate her.

Selecting Your Candidate: You Need a System

The easiest way to make a hiring decision is to weigh the options and simply go with what your intuition tells you to do. Easy — but risky. Gut decisions, whether they originate from one person or a group of people, are almost always biased in the following respect: Their roots tend to be firmly planted in wishful thinking. These decisions often are a reflection of what you'd ideally like to see happen as opposed to what's most likely to happen based on the evidence.

Decision makers in companies with good track records of making successful hires don't give themselves the luxury of relying solely on intuition. They use — and generally trust — their intuition, but they don't focus on intuition as the sole basis for their judgments. The following list describes what these decision makers rely on.

- ✔ **They have in place some sort of system** — a well thought-out protocol for assessing the strengths and weaknesses of candidates and applying those assessments to the hiring criteria. These decision makers always make it a point, for example, to precede any face-to-face interview with a phone conversation. And they've established a set of steps that they routinely follow after they've interviewed a candidate.

- ✔ **The system that they use, regardless of how simple or elaborate, is weighted** — that is, it presupposes that certain skills and attributes influence job performance more than others do, and it takes those differences into account. They know, for example, that the personal qualities that underlie effective performance in sales aren't necessarily the same ones that underlie effective performance in, say, administrative jobs.

- ✔ **They constantly monitor and evaluate the effectiveness of the system** — always with an eye toward sharpening their own ability and the ability of others to link any data they obtain during the recruiting and interviewing process to the on-the-job performance of new hires. If a particular type of testing mechanism is used in the selection process, the validity of the test (how closely the test results correlate with successful on-the-job performance) is monitored on a regular basis.

Setting up your own protocol

Some companies invest a great deal of money in developing elaborate selection procedures, the express purpose of which is to make the candidate evaluation process more objective and accurate. Whether you want to go that route is up to you, but the following sections describe the fundamental steps you must go through with all such processes, regardless of cost.

1. **Isolate key hiring criteria.**

   By this point in the hiring process, you should know what combination of skills and attributes a candidate needs to perform the job well and fit your company's pace and culture. If you don't, refer to Chapters 4 and 5.

2. **Set priorities.**

   You can safely assume that some of your hiring criteria are more important than others. To take these differences into account, and, depending on the nature of the particular position at issue, some employers may want to set up a scale that reflects the relative importance of any particular skill or attribute. For example, one way to ensure reasonable accuracy in assigning these values is by asking the following question: If the candidate didn't have this skill or quality, how would it affect her job performance? The greater the effect, the higher the value placed on that skill or quality.

3. **Evaluate candidates on the basis of the weighted scale you established in Step 2.**

   This segment of the process is the tricky part. Instead of simply looking at the candidate as a whole, you examine each of the criteria you set up, and you rate the candidate on the basis of how he measures up in that particular category.

   This weighted system of evaluation takes into account the performance priorities unique to each of the key hiring criteria. It helps ensure that the requirements of the job reasonably align with the strengths and weaknesses of the candidate.

Say, for example, that one of the candidate's strengths is the ability to work as part of a team. The candidate's rating on that particular attribute may be a 5 on a 5-point scale, but the relative importance of teamwork to the task at hand may be anywhere from 1 to 5, which means that the overall ranking may end up as low as 5 (5×1) or as high as 25 (5×5).

All in all, a weighted system gives you an opportunity to see how well candidates measure up against one another and how closely their skills and attributes match the job requirements. You must be careful, however. The effectiveness of this system depends on two crucial factors: the validity of your hiring criteria and the objectivity of the judgments that underlie any ratings you assign to various candidates.

Tables 9-1 and 9-2 demonstrate how a weighted evaluation system works. Notice that the candidate under evaluation in Table 9-1 is relatively weak in two hiring criteria — previous experience and computer skills — but is much stronger in the criteria that carry more weight. The candidate's aggregate score, therefore, is higher than that of a candidate who meets only the technical requirements of the job.

Table 9-1	How Candidate 1 Shapes Up		
Performance Category	Weighted Importance (1–5)	Candidate Rating (1–5)	Score
Previous customer experience	3	1	3
Computer skills	2	2	4
Communication skills	5	4	20
Reliability/work ethic	5	4	20
Ability to cope with stress	4	4	16
Empathy	4	4	16
Total			79

Table 9-2	How Candidate 2 Shapes Up		
Performance Category	Weighted Importance (1–5)	Candidate Rating (1–5)	Score
Previous customer experience	3	5	15
Computer skills	2	5	10
Communication skills	5	2	10
Reliability/work ethic	5	3	15
Ability to cope with stress	4	4	16
Empathy	4	1	4
Total			70

Factoring in the intangibles

The really tough part of any evaluation process is attaching numerical ratings to the *intangibles*, those attributes that are difficult to measure. The following sections cover those intangible factors that you commonly find in the criteria for most jobs, along with suggestions on how to tell whether the candidate measures up.

Industriousness and motivation

Definition: Candidates' work ethic — how hard they're willing to work and how important they feel it is to perform to the best of their ability.

When important: All the time.

How to measure: Verifiable accomplishments in their last jobs. Evaluation by past employers and co-workers. Track record of successful jobs that goes back to college or even earlier.

Intelligence and problem-solving ability

Definition: Mental alertness, thinking ability, capability to process abstract information.

When important: Any job that requires the ability to make decisions (and not just follow instructions).

How to measure: Evidence of good decision-making ability in previous jobs. Also through testing. (Make sure, however, that the tests aren't in any way discriminatory. See Chapter 7 and "Discovering the Truth about Background Checks," later in this chapter.)

Temperament and ability to cope with job demands

Definition: General demeanor — whether the candidate is calm or hot-headed.

When important: In any job where the stress level is high or in any work environment where people must interact and rely on one another.

How to measure: The best way to measure these criteria is to ask during the interview about workplace pressure in candidates' previous jobs and how they feel they performed.

Creativity and resourcefulness

Definition: The ability to think outside the box — to come up with innovative solutions to problems.

When important: In jobs that require imagination or problem-solving skills that don't rely on set procedures.

How to measure: Examples of previous work (graphic design work, writing samples, and so on). Specific examples of situations in which the candidate has devised an innovative solution to a problem. Previous accomplishments or awards.

Capacity for teamwork

Definition: The ability to work collaboratively with others and share responsibility for achieving the same goal.

When important: Any task with a strong need for employees to work closely and collaboratively.

How to measure: Previous work experience. (Did candidates work on their own or with groups?) Team successes mentioned during the interview. Evidence of ability to work within project team rules, protocols, and work practices. Support for co-workers. Willingness to ask for (and offer) help.

Hiring Right

Bad hiring decisions rarely happen by accident. In retrospect, you can usually discover that you didn't do something you should have. This section covers the key principles to follow in order to hire the right person.

Anchor yourself to the hiring criteria

The hiring criteria that you establish from the beginning should serve as your strict guide throughout the evaluation process. If, in looking ahead, you decide to change the criteria, fine. Just make sure that you aren't changing criteria simply because you're enamored with one particular prospect and decide to change the ground rules to accommodate that candidate.

Anchoring yourself to hiring criteria helps to prevent three of the most common pitfalls in hiring:

- ✔ **The halo effect:** Becoming so enraptured by one particular aspect of the candidate — appearance, credentials, or interests, for instance — that you let that aspect influence all your other judgments

- ✔ **The cloning effect:** Hiring someone in your image even though someone with your particular mix of skills and attributes clearly isn't qualified for that particular job

- ✔ **How much you "like" the candidate**

Take your time

The more pressure you're under, the greater the likelihood of rushing the decision and ending up with someone who not only isn't your best choice but you're probably going to end up firing — with all the disruption that firing someone entails. Keep in mind the main pitfall of acting out of urgency: You overestimate the qualities of candidates who may be only marginally qualified to fill the job. If you're worried about finding someone right away, see whether you can bring in a temporary replacement to keep projects on track as you continue the search.

Cross-verify whenever possible

Whatever else they may disagree on, most hiring experts contend that you can never have enough information from enough different sources. So, try not to rely solely on any one source, whether interview impressions, résumé data, reference checks, or testing. Cast a wide net and pay careful attention to discrepancies.

Get help, but avoid the "too many cooks" syndrome

A smart practice — particularly when filling a key position — is to get input from others before you make a final choice. Involving too many people in the final decision, however, is a mistake. If too many people have a say, the likely outcome is a compromise choice. Instead of getting the best employee, you end up with the candidate who's the least objectionable to everyone. Try to restrict your circle of decision makers to three to five people who understand the job, your company's culture, and the personality and working style of the potential hire's manager. As I discuss in Chapter 8, you can gain these additional perspectives on candidates by holding multiple and panel interviews. When it comes time for the final decision, these same people can help you choose the best applicant.

Don't force the issue

The recruiting process sometimes uncovers a "dream" employee — except for one problem: The candidate's skills and attributes don't match the hiring criteria of a particular job. The best thing to do if you find yourself in this situation is to see whether you can find another job in the company that better suits this particular candidate. The worst thing that you can do is try to put a good worker in the wrong job.

Avoid the "top of mind" syndrome

Do your best to stay alert to any extraneous factors that may distort the selection process. Employers tend to choose some candidates over others, for example, not because those candidates are more qualified but because they're interviewed later in the hiring process and are fresher in the minds of the interviewer. The best way to avoid this pitfall is to keep your focus on the hiring criteria, no matter what.

Getting a Broader View

References and other third-party observations are useful and necessary components of the hiring process. Selected references from past employers help you separate those with good employment records from others who have a less-positive job performance history. Not taking these steps can increase your risk of making a hiring mistake and putting your organization at a disadvantage. If you succeed in matching up the candidate and the credentials she has presented to you, however, there's a much better chance that she'll prove to be a productive and valuable member of your team. It's best if you conduct reference checks or other checks personally if you'll be the one working with the employee.

Checking hard-to-check references

Getting a candid reference from an employer is tougher than ever these days. Because employers know that both saying too much and saying too little can have legal consequences, they're increasingly wary of being specific about past employees and their work histories. Although companies have been sued for not disclosing enough information about former workers, others have paid enormous settlements because they provided negative references — whether true or false.

Because of these difficulties, rushing through the reference-checking process — or bypassing it altogether — to make a quick hire may be tempting. But getting reliable information from former supervisors and peers is an important task to complete before selecting someone as an employee of your company.

Here are some tips on approaching this often-difficult process. Like much of the advice in this book, these tips apply to you directly if you're the hiring manager; if you're not, they're for you to communicate to line managers who are spearheading the hiring process in your organization.

✔ **Let the candidate know that you check references.** Be clear with candidates from the outset that your company will be checking their references. Checking references is perfectly legal as long as the information being verified is job related and doesn't violate discrimination laws. Informing applicants that you're checking usually helps ensure that the answers they give you during the interview are truthful, especially when you start the interview by saying, "If we're interested in you, and you're interested in us, we'll be checking your references."

✔ **Don't delegate it.** If the employee will report directly to you, *you* should check the references. No matter how thorough a delegate or deputy may be, the hiring manager will have corollary questions that may not occur to others. Also, calling someone at your same level may establish greater camaraderie that will prompt a more honest and detailed reference. If that weren't enough, checking references yourself is a great way to gain insight from a former supervisor on how best to manage the individual. If you lack the time to do the complete job, then compromise by assigning just part of the reference checking to capable co-workers in your group. Handle one, preferably two, yourself.

✔ **Use responses from the interview.** Asking candidates during the job interview what their former employers are likely to say about them can provide you with a good starting point for getting the former employer to talk openly. You can start out by saying something such as, "Joe tells me that you think he's the greatest thing since sliced bread," and have the employer take it from there. You may not get a totally frank answer, but you can get valuable comments and insights. After all, the candidate must assume that you're going to check out his answers.

✔ **For the best responses, pick up the phone.** Don't put much stock in written references presented to you by candidates. They're of limited value. Many are prepared at the time of termination and, because firing a person is a sensitive task, the employer may have focused on the positive and few, if any, negatives. (How many bad letters of reference have you ever seen?) E-mailing companies is usually ineffective as well. References aren't likely to be as candid or as detailed in writing as they would be verbally, if they respond at all. Companies that do respond aren't likely to be very timely, increasing the likelihood that you'll lose a good potential employee. The best way to communicate with references is via phone. Calling gives you an opportunity to ask spontaneous questions based upon what was said in response to one of your primary questions. You can often detect enthusiasm, or lack of it, if you pay attention to tone of voice.

The CD includes Sample Reference Check Questions you can use when contacting a candidate's references.

Using your own network for checking

You don't need to limit your search for reference information to only those people the applicant suggests. You may find people in your own circle of professional acquaintances or friends with firsthand knowledge of the candidate who probably aren't as reluctant as a former employer may be to level with you. Also, ask the candidate's references for names of other individuals you may contact for information.

Try to be fair, however. If you get information that puts the candidate in a bad light, try to get verification from one or two other sources, just to make sure that what you're hearing isn't sour grapes from one specific individual.

Online reference checking: Proceed with caution

Advances in technology and more sophisticated online search capabilities have increased the popularity of reference checking via the Internet. The practice will undoubtedly grow as more record holders create databases that employers can easily access. (See also "Discovering the Truth about Background Checks," in the next section of this chapter.)

Everyone knows about the practice of searching for a person's name online to see what comes up. Social media offer other means of accessing information online. These include such services as Twitter (www.twitter.com), Facebook (www.facebook.com), and LinkedIn (www.linkedin.com), all of which feature at least some public content about most users. Some employers also access blogs and personal websites. My message here: Proceed carefully. Although this approach can reduce costs and sometimes yield faster results, you also must understand that much of the information on a candidate you discover can be either erroneous or irrelevant. A person's *digital footprint* also can reveal facts that are illegal to consider in a hiring decision, and your company's review of online information can raise privacy concerns. The same legal constraints that govern interviewing apply to reference checking. Online reference checking should be viewed as a complement to, not a replacement for, traditional methods. A web search is no substitute for personal assessments of the work quality and professionalism of candidates that carefully selected individuals can offer. Inaccuracies exist in many online data records, and some forms of investigation require written permission from the applicant and are subject to other legal limitations.

Discovering the Truth about Background Checks

Many companies, increasingly aware of the pitfalls of failing to adequately evaluate applicants before bringing them onboard, are conducting formal background checks on candidates. *Background checks* take reference checks a step farther, and businesses use them because they feel they're a way to gain more assurance that the people they hire are what they represent themselves to be. In other words, where reference checks allow you to verify with former employers a potential hire's accomplishments and personal attributes (see the preceding section), background checks attempt to delve into additional aspects of a candidate's activities and behavior.

Background checks can take many forms, depending on the position and what the employer considers most important in evaluating job candidates. The principal measures in use today include

- ✔ Criminal background checks
- ✔ Social Security number verification
- ✔ Education records/academic degree verification
- ✔ Certification and license verification
- ✔ Credit checks
- ✔ Driving histories
- ✔ Medical exams
- ✔ Drug tests
- ✔ Workers' compensation reports

A growing number of online services advertise their ability to perform background checks for businesses in a very short time frame. These services can be tempting — especially to smaller businesses that lack the budgets to conduct checks on their own.

But there's one problem: Even though many of the firms offering these services make it sound easy and inexpensive, performing a meaningful background check is, in fact, rarely free of complications. Many of these providers present an overly simplistic picture of what these searches entail and downplay the potential for obtaining incomplete or inaccurate reports and test results.

Many factors contribute to the complexity of background checks:

- ✔ **No central information source:** It may come as a surprise to you that no single, national source of information exists for most types of background checks. Criminal records, for example, are generally maintained by individual states or counties, many of which do not store them electronically.

- ✔ **Possibility of flawed data:** Another issue is reliability. Even the most comprehensive checks yield flawed or incomplete records with greater frequency than some employers realize.

- ✔ **Need for retesting:** The frequency with which you conduct background checks must also be a factor in deciding whether to use these methods for evaluating prospective new hires. Academic credentials must be verified only once, but a drug test or criminal background check can become out-of-date almost as soon as it's conducted.

✔ **Legal restrictions:** Further adding to the complexity of conducting background checks on job candidates are federal laws governing them, as well as state laws that can vary considerably from one to another. For example, if your company uses an outside agency to furnish background information, you may be required, under federal law and the laws of some states, to provide applicants certain disclosures and get their permission before the background check can take place. As a result, you may want to consider seeking legal advice before you even request some types of checks.

✔ **Technology not keeping up:** Although technology makes background checks easier to some degree, obtaining reliable information can be much more difficult than most people recognize. The apparent ease of accessing information online obscures the fact that the quality and completeness of the underlying information may not have kept pace with the technology. Many records simply aren't available electronically and are accessible via paper-based systems only. And many of the databases that do exist aren't updated frequently.

The CD includes the following forms that may be useful during the background-check process. The cover sheet that accompanies each form provides more information about it.

✔ Employment Inquiry Release

✔ Consent to Criminal Background Check

✔ Background Check Permission (Comprehensive) for Prospective Employee

✔ Disclosure and Authorization Regarding Procurement of Consumer Report for Employment Purposes

✔ Disclosure and Authorization Regarding Procurement of Investigative Consumer Report for Employment Purposes

✔ A Summary of Your Rights Under the Fair Credit Reporting Act

✔ Confirmation of Receipt of the Summary of Your Rights Under the Fair Credit Reporting Act and the Copy of Consumer or Investigative Report

✔ Letter Giving Notice of Planned Adverse Action Based on Information in Consumer Report or Investigative Consumer Report (Fair Credit Reporting Act)

✔ Disclosure of the Adverse Action Based on Information in a Consumer or Investigative Report

To do or not to do? That is the question!

As you can see, conducting background checks is frequently not a simple matter. But that doesn't mean that they aren't useful tools when pursued appropriately. Whether to conduct a background check depends most on the nature of your business and the position for which you're hiring. In limited cases, you don't have a choice because federal and state laws require background checks for certain jobs. But for most positions, the employer determines the need for investigation.

You need to weigh many questions, including the following:

- ✔ Is the job highly visible, such as a senior executive or someone who will be in the public spotlight?
- ✔ Does the position involve working with children or the public?
- ✔ Do you have a specific suspicion or concern about a candidate?

The list goes on, but the point is that no formulas or universal criteria dictate whether background checks are necessary or appropriate for a position or an organization. Unless the law requires a check, only you can determine what's right for your business. Similarly, you shouldn't assume that staffing companies perform background checks. Most staffing firms don't routinely conduct background checks. If a background check is required, the staffing company will likely have you work directly with a firm that specializes in this area. Although staffing companies are very good at what they do, they don't specialize in this type of investigation. Given the complexities, you want a firm that *does* specialize in background checks.

The logistical and legal complexities alone shouldn't determine whether you conduct a background check. Although risk is involved (in addition to the time and expense) when businesses conduct checks and obtain erroneous information, businesses also can invite problems if they fail to adequately evaluate candidates. The decision is yours to make.

So, what's the bottom line?

Because of their complexity, background checks require unique expertise. If, after weighing all the factors, you decide to conduct a background check on a job applicant, employ the services of a third-party investigative agency. Not only is it difficult for a nonexpert to conduct a thorough search, but you'll also likely need assistance in navigating the legal restrictions, which aren't always obvious or commonly known. Laws, for example, govern how information obtained during a background check can and can't be used in your hiring decision — and whether certain information may be collected in the first place. The best choice is to retain a firm that specializes in performing these services.

The point is that you should go in with your eyes open. If performed properly, background checks can be much more complex than many people realize. Conducting rudimentary searches on your own just to "cover all bases" is unlikely to yield accurate and useful information. That's why your decision to conduct a background check should be based on the unique needs of the position and your business. It also should be consistently applied to all positions that fall into this category.

Making Offers They Can't Refuse

After you make your final choice of whom to hire, you may think that you and the other decision makers can just sit back and relax. Not just yet, I'm afraid. You still must make the offer official, and you still need to remember that if you fail to handle this phase of the hiring process carefully, one of two things can happen: You can lose the candidate, or, even if the candidate comes aboard, you can start the relationship off on the wrong note. The following sections tell you what to keep in mind.

Don't delay

After you make up your mind about a candidate, make the offer immediately. *Remember:* Even a day or two delay can cost you the employee of choice. If your company has procedures that can slow down the process — for example, no one gets hired unless the president interviews him personally — look for ways to streamline the process.

Put your offer on the table

At this stage in the process, you have no reason to be coy. Call the person you want to hire and give her all the details about pay, benefits, and anything extra. If you don't have these details nailed down yet, you're not ready to make the offer.

You should establish a salary range for the position even before you begin recruiting (see Chapter 5). This parameter can help you stay within your budget should you need to negotiate. (In Chapters 11 and 12, I discuss the details of salary and benefits and what constitutes an effective compensation structure.)

Most companies make job offers verbally by phone and then follow up with an official letter or e-mail. Making the offer by phone rather than waiting to get the candidate back into your office will avoid having too much time elapse between the interview and the offer. Make sure that you have a standard job offer letter as a template that you can customize and that you clear the template with legal counsel.

See the Offer Letter to a Prospective Employee on the CD.

After you and the candidate speak or meet again in person, remind the individual of the benefits of joining your firm. Don't just discuss the financial aspects of the offer. You also should highlight other positives, such as a supportive work environment and exposure to a variety of assignments.

Set a deadline

Give candidates a reasonable amount of time to decide whether to accept the offer. What's "reasonable" generally depends on the type of job. The time frame for an entry-level job may be a few days, but for a middle- or senior-level candidate in a competitive market or for a position that involves relocation, a week isn't excessive.

Stay connected

While a candidate is considering an offer, you or the hiring manager should stay in touch with him, or have individuals from the interview team contact him if you're using multiple or panel interviews. The purpose is for you to reinforce your enthusiasm about the candidate potentially joining your team.

Know how to negotiate salary

After receiving a candidate's response to your offer, be prepared to negotiate. Job seekers today have access to an abundance of information on salary negotiation through websites and books, so most will enter the meeting knowledgeable on the topic. To reach a fair deal, you need to be equally prepared.

Decide how far you're willing to go

The first step is not unlike that in any other form of bargaining. If the candidate suggests a higher figure than you've offered, you can choose to raise the amount of your proposal or stick to your guns. If the candidate keeps pushing, whether you want to exceed the established range generally depends on two factors: how badly you want the person and the policies and precedents in your company.

Ask yourself three questions before you start promising the moon:

- ✔ **Are other, equally qualified candidates available if the applicant says no?** If the answer is yes, the leverage to make accommodations rests with the company.

- ✔ **Has the job been particularly hard to fill, or are market conditions making finding and recruiting suitable candidates difficult?** If the answer is yes, the leverage rests with the candidate.

> ✔ **Will a stronger offer be significantly out of line with existing pay levels for comparable positions in your company or hiring manager's department?** As I discuss in Chapter 11, the lack of a reasonable degree of internal equity in compensation levels diminishes the spirit of teamwork and fairness.

Recognize that if you decide to go beyond the firm's pay scale to win a stellar candidate, you risk poor morale among existing staff should they learn that a new hire in the same role is being paid at a higher rate. And the best-kept secrets often do get out. In addition, paying above scale may create a legal issue if the pay isn't equitably distributed among the members of your workforce.

Think creatively

If you're not able to match a candidate's salary request, consider expanding other components of the package. Applicants often are willing to compromise on base compensation if concessions are made in other areas.

Flexible scheduling is one candidate-pleasing option that will cost you little to nothing. Providing additional time off or opportunities to telecommute may also be acceptable to a candidate in lieu of higher wages. Also, consider a signing bonus (see the nearby sidebar) or a performance-based bonus after a specified time period (see Chapter 11).

Know when to draw the line

Some HR experts insist that you shouldn't push too hard if a candidate isn't interested. Probing a bit in order to find out why he's being hesitant isn't a bad idea, though. Try to identify the source of the problem and make reasonable accommodations.

But don't get so caught up in negotiations that you lose sight of what's appropriate for your organization. Sometimes you just have to walk away. If your attempts to woo a reluctant candidate fall short, the best thing to do in many cases is to cut your losses and look somewhere else. It may well be that the candidate knows something about himself that you don't know, so don't push too hard. The goal at this point should be to end the process so that the candidate leaves with a feeling of being treated fairly and with dignity.

Clarify acceptance details

If a promising candidate accepts your final offer, congratulate yourself! You're helping to build a strong team for your business. But before you break out the champagne, you still need to take care of some details.

Signing bonuses

A *signing bonus* is a sum of money that is offered as an extra inducement to the candidate to join the company. According to a 2011 WorldatWork survey, 54 percent of organizations polled offer signing bonuses. How much do they usually consist of? It varies widely by position, job market, and skills that are sought, but respondents to the WorldatWork survey indicated that supervisors, middle managers, and professionals most frequently receive signing bonuses of between $5,000 and $9,999. Of course, signing bonuses vary depending upon market conditions and many other factors.

The signing bonus is exactly what it seems: an upfront cash payment that you give to an employee at the start of employment, independent of salary. The benefit to employees? Cash in their pockets. The benefit to employers? In a tight labor market, it may help you secure the employee you want without distorting your salary structure. If you use signing bonuses, however, it's a good idea to make them contingent upon a specified period of employment. For example, the new manager will receive a signing bonus of $10,000 as long as he is employed with your company for a period of at least one year. Just make sure the offer specifies that the new hire must repay the signing bonus, on a prorated basis, if he leaves the company before 12 months have passed.

Some companies are now asking candidates to sign a duplicate copy of the job offer letter as an indication of acceptance. The signature confirms that the candidate understands the basic terms of the offer. If you're making a job offer contingent on reference checks, a physical examination, drug and alcohol testing, or background checks, make sure that the offer letter says as much and the candidate understands and accepts this restriction.

Stay in touch

Even after a candidate accepts your offer, and you agree on a starting date, keeping in touch with the new employee is still a good idea. If the new hire is employed, her current company may be using the time before she starts with your firm to convince her to stay put. The more you can stay connected through regular communication, the more excited the person will be about working for your organization and the more confident she'll be in her decision.

Two to three weeks is the customary time between an acceptance and start date. Most people who are changing jobs give a standard two-week notice to their former employer. For those who want to take a few days off before starting their new job, a three-week interval is not unusual. Use the transition period to mail off all those informational brochures and employment forms and to schedule a lunch or two, if appropriate. You want to subtly help the new employee transfer loyalty from his old employer to you and to make dismissing any other offers that may surface from prior interviews easier for the person you now want on your team.

Employment contracts: Should you or shouldn't you?

Once a rarity, written employment contracts are increasingly prevalent in the United States — as protection for both employers and new employees. An *employment contract* is an agreement between an employer and an employee stating the level of compensation and other benefits the employee will receive in exchange for specific work performed.

These contracts are usually (but not always) made for executive or senior-level positions. In highly competitive industries and in those that handle issues of intellectual property, employment contracts can help employers by contractually

prohibiting employees at any level from working for a competitor and revealing trade secrets. You have to be careful, however, that you don't word the contract in such a way that guarantees employment.

An employment contract doesn't need to be a 20-page legal document. It can take the form of a one-page letter that specifies the job title, duties, responsibilities and obligations, conditions of employment, and, most important, severance arrangements if things don't work out.

See the sample Employment Agreement on the CD.

It's important that there's no sense of wasted lag time between acceptance of a job offer and the candidate actually starting work. Take advantage of this time to get a head start on certain tasks and to begin cementing what you hope will be a positive and long-lasting relationship. Provide her with a copy of an employee handbook (or make an online version available). Stay in touch and ask if any additional questions or concerns have cropped up prior to the first day of work. The more you can accomplish during this time, the greater the sense of connection and involvement the new employee will have. That makes a solid start all the more likely. At the same time, if you plan to have nonexempt employees perform any tasks to prepare for their first day of work, it would be a good idea to check with a lawyer to see if the tasks you're assigning are compensable.

The CD contains an Employee Self-Identification Form for use by federal government contractors and subcontractors. If you fall into this category, you'll need to provide the form to new hires after they've been offered the job. Also included is an Employee Self-Identification Form for use by non-contractor employers with 100 or more employees that are required to file an annual EEO-1 Report.

Part III
Keeping Your Best People

The 5th Wave   By Rich Tennant

TOOTLE TOY CO

"Of course we offer a generous vacation plan. If we didn't let employees have time off to have kids, who'd we sell toys to?"

In this part . . .

Successfully bringing new employees onboard isn't the end of the road for someone in an HR role. Far from it. Now you need to offer them ways to enhance their productivity, tools to boost their skills, and incentives to remain loyal to your company. You need to do all you can to keep your best people, and, in this part, I give you the tools to do it.

Chapter 10

Starting New Hires Off on the Right Foot

. . . .

In This Chapter

▶ Taking a broader view of orientation

▶ Avoiding common mistakes

▶ Empathizing with new employees

▶ Easing anxieties on the first day

▶ Revealing more about the company and job

▶ Following up on an employee's onboarding experience

▶ Understanding the role of the employee handbook and procedures manual

. . . .

One of the running themes of Clint Eastwood's classic *Dirty Harry* movie series is that the main character, San Francisco police inspector Harry Callahan, has a new partner in each film. Someone always warns each partner that when you work with Callahan, you stand a good chance of getting killed or injured. Callahan himself makes clear from the beginning that the newcomer must watch him in action to learn the ropes. By mid-movie, after a series of adventures, both Callahan and his partner are working effectively as a team.

Although working in corporate America is a lot less treacherous than the plot of a police drama, your new employees are similar to Dirty Harry's new partners in one key respect: They're uncertain of what's expected of them, apprehensive of what's going to happen, unsure of what to do — and looking to the HR department and others for answers.

The initial weeks or months on the job are especially pivotal for newcomers in establishing attitudes about their duties, their colleagues, and your company. Activities planned for this early period must not only provide job-related information but also foster a clear understanding of your firm's philosophy and core values.

You're likely familiar with many of the logistical aspects of helping a new hire adjust to a company, ranging from completing forms and learning about office technology to parking and security procedures. But the big-picture goal of this chapter is to help you create a rigorous, ongoing process that truly helps new employees thrive. In this chapter, you discover ways to ensure that newcomers thoroughly grasp their responsibilities, become productive, and feel that they're part of the team.

Onboarding: Going Beyond Orientation

Historically, the process to help recently hired employees acclimate to a new environment has been known as *orientation*. It usually started with an introduction to the work area, building, or factory facilities on the first day of work, followed by a formal or informal presentation of company policies, operating procedures, and other administrative details.

Today, however, orientation is not a stand-alone event but part of a bigger process, often called *onboarding*. Some view onboarding as just a new buzzword for orientation, but it's actually your opportunity to do far more to ensure that new employees become productive and satisfied members of your staff. The process also is known by other names among HR professionals, such as *alignment, assimilation, integration,* and *transition.* Though you can probably spend a few hours talking with other HR colleagues parsing each term's differences, what they all have in common is an attempt to go beyond, while still including, the old concept of employee orientation.

An effective onboarding program consists of supplemental efforts taken early in a new employee's tenure to help him build a better understanding of your organization's culture, his job responsibilities, and how they tie into company and departmental priorities. This more holistic approach to orientation is consistent with your strategic HR role. Onboarding goes beyond mere practicality and acknowledges that what new employees learn in their first few weeks has long-term effects on their ability to tackle the challenges of today's faster-paced business environment. In other words, starting out on the right foot is even more important than employers ever thought.

Depending on your company's size and the complexity of the work, an onboarding program can last from several weeks to several months. It covers matters related to training, scheduled milestones, mentoring programs, and interactive meetings where employees can ask questions about corporate or departmental initiatives.

Above all, onboarding is an opportunity. Virtually all new employees are enthralled with the experience they're about to have. This period is the time to capitalize on that excitement and begin building strong bonds between new hires and the organization.

Although you set up overall onboarding events and policies, the line manager handles specific job-related parts of the process. But here, too, you're responsible for offering advice and guidance to supervisors, especially those who are new to management. You play an important role as a resource for both the manager and the new employee. The policies and procedures you establish about how to onboard new employees greatly shape how managers and employees interact with one another. Your place is to ensure that managers understand these guidelines and the importance of adhering to them. And you'll also want to make yourself available throughout the new employee's early days to address any concerns or questions.

Three Unproductive Approaches

The key to successful onboarding is to get the right results. No one formula works for everyone. Every company and every new employee is different. Some ways do exist, however, that are clearly *un*productive. The following sections cover three examples that unfortunately occur all too often.

Osmosis

How the method works: No formal orientation or adjustment process exists for new employees. You leave each employee alone to learn the ropes simply by observing and asking questions on a spontaneous, as-needed basis.

Faulty rationale: If employees are smart enough to get hired, they can probably figure out for themselves what they need to know about the job, the company, and the facilities.

Why this method doesn't work: Relying on osmosis fails to take into account how difficult it is for new employees to grasp the nuances of a company and simultaneously learn what's expected in a new job. Worse yet, this method conveys a general attitude of indifference that can very easily carry over into employee performance. Another problem is that new employees are often shy about asking questions, which means that they don't get the answers or guidance they need until after they begin to make costly mistakes.

"Just follow Joe around"

How the method works: "Joe" can be "Jill," "Frank," "Melanie" or anybody who has been with your company for more than a few years. The idea is to pair the newly hired employee with one of your tenured staff members — but without giving the experienced employee specific instructions on how to manage the process.

Faulty rationale: If you have the newcomers simply follow around more tenured employees for a couple days, they pick up the basics. This approach is simple and inexpensive.

Why this method doesn't work: Joe and the newcomer may have nothing whatsoever in common, making communication strained. By the time the first day of shadowing is over, you may have a veteran employee convinced that the firm is now scraping the bottom of the barrel and a newcomer who wonders whatever possessed him to join this company in the first place. Another problem is that Joe's idea of communicating may be for the newcomer simply to watch as Joe does his job. Joe may have little or no insight into the new hire's role or the expectations of the person's manager. In addition, the newcomer may pick up more than just Joe's skills — for example, any negative feelings or opinions Joe may have toward the company. Without clear instructions and careful selection of which person the new hire follows around, you may unwittingly be undermining your efforts.

Watch the video

How the method works: You hire a hotshot production company to produce slick video content that tells new employees everything they need to know about your company in a 12- to 15-minute session. The program consists of seating new employees in front of a monitor and having them watch the presentation. You don't even serve popcorn. Or worse yet, you e-mail new employees the link to the video on your intranet, telling them to watch it on their computers whenever they have the time.

Faulty rationale: Everybody loves videos, right? Besides, you don't need to waste any time with person-to-person contact or training.

Why this method doesn't work: Videos, no matter how cutting edge the presentation, can't answer questions. You have no guarantee that the newcomer is actually paying attention and not daydreaming. Nor do videos offer concrete insights into that specific individual's job. By simply using a piece of technology with little or no input from you and other key managers, you also run the risk of employees assuming that you view helping new employees adapt to the company as little more than a formality, like getting your driver's license renewed. That's not a good message to send.

Doing It Right: A Little Empathy Goes a Long Way

You don't need a PhD in clinical psychology to appreciate what's going on inside the heads of new employees the first day that they walk through the door. The first few days and weeks on a new job can be exciting — and often just as intimidating. As the new kid on the block, the most recent addition to your staff will encounter unfamiliar people, policies, and procedures. Everything from your first-day welcome to the remainder of your onboarding process should address those concerns.

Think about what *you* would want and need if you were going through the process of joining a new company. Your concerns or areas of interest would likely include new employee anxieties, job tasks and goal setting, company operations and culture, as well as basic policies and procedures. These topics are areas to focus on regardless of how formally or informally you want to approach the onboarding process. Encourage your line managers to pay attention to them as well.

After the number of new employees joining your company reaches a certain threshold — and you must determine when the company gets to this point — you'll probably want to formalize your approach, creating a series of onboarding activities that you repeat whenever a new employee or group of new employees joins your company. The following sections should help ensure that any program you develop is as effective as possible.

Your onboarding program can be as elaborate as a weeks-long combination training and boot camp or as simple as a series of scheduled one-on-one conversations between the new employee and a manager or HR staffer, or something in between. Whatever form you take, you want to give it structure. You need to provide a schedule, and everyone involved needs clearly defined roles. You want the individual elements of the program *weighted* — in other words, a logical and strategic connection between the importance of a particular issue or topic and how much time you devote to that issue or topic must exist.

The First Day: Easing Anxieties

Even though new employees have likely been on your company premises previously during the interview phase, their experiences on the first day of work will leave a lasting impression. It begins from the very minute they walk into the building or onto the jobsite. You need to offer a first-day welcome to begin the process of making them feel at home. Following are tips for you — or the individuals' bosses if you're not supervising the new hires — to remember:

✓ Alert the receptionist or security guard (if you have one) that a new employee is arriving and make sure that this person greets the newcomer warmly.

✓ Arrange for someone (you, if possible) to personally escort the new hire to her workstation or office.

✓ Have an agenda for the first couple days so the newcomer knows what to expect. It may include, for example, meetings you've set up for the new hire, training sessions he may need to attend, and even group lunches meant to help welcome him to the team.

✓ Personally introduce the newcomer to other members of the team.

✓ Show the new employee where she can find company employees' names, job titles, phone numbers, and e-mail addresses. If that's online, provide the newcomer with access to it.

✓ Encourage current employees who haven't formally met the new hire to introduce themselves and offer to help in any way they can.

✓ At some point during the day, meet with the employee to take up where the last interview left off. Let her know how glad you are to have her onboard and that you'll be providing a comprehensive introduction to the company and the job over the next few days.

✓ Schedule a lunch with the new employee and her manager on the first day.

The First Week: Revealing More about the Company and the Job

You probably gave the new employee plenty of information about your company while recruiting and interviewing. Even so, the first few days on the job are the best time to reinforce that information and build a sense of connection with the company. In a survey by Robert Half, 35 percent of executives whose firms offer an onboarding program said the greatest benefit is that it helps employees better understand the company's values, guidelines, and expectations.

At the very least, a new employee should know the following:

✓ Your company's basic products or services

✓ The size and general organization of the company

✓ An overview of your industry — and where your company fits into the overall picture (including who the chief competition is)

✓ Your company's mission statement (if you have one) and values

✓ Department goals and strategic objectives

Provide the rules of the road

If your company has an employee handbook and procedures manual, make sure that the employee gets copies on his first day and give him time to look them over, just to make sure that he has no misunderstandings. If the handbook is online, provide him with appropriate access. (See "Employee Handbook and Separate Procedures Manual: Yes, You Need Both," near the end of this chapter.)

Make sure, in particular, that new employees are aware of policies regarding their immediate work areas (that is, whether you allow personal photographs, digital music players, and other items that could, to some, be distracting from work priorities). If your company has unusual rules in this regard, take the time to explain the rationale — for example, "The last employee we had liked to play Wagner operas at full blast."

Don't take anything for granted, particularly about basic considerations such as where employees park, how they sign in, and, for nonexempt employees, how they clock in and out for work shifts and meal periods — and the importance of them doing so properly. Make sure that the newcomer knows whom to call — and how — for questions and emergencies. Provide keypad door codes and advise employees of any security procedures.

Other locations that you should show new employees as soon as possible include the following:

- ✓ Company bulletin boards or other display areas or walls on which important legal notices (like equal employment opportunity [EEO] posters) and employee information are posted

- ✓ Restrooms, break rooms, lunch areas, and employee lounges

- ✓ Fire exits, evacuation points, and emergency assembly areas

- ✓ Immediate supervisor's desk

- ✓ Human resources representative's desk

- ✓ Departmental facilities (such as the copy room and supply cabinets)

- ✓ Health facilities, nurse's office (if one exists), and first-aid kit

- ✓ Security office

If your company has specific security procedures or policies regarding personal phone calls or e-mail, make sure that you communicate these policies on the first day of work.

See the CD for an example of an Onboarding Checklist.

Keep orientation practical

Because new employees join your company at varying intervals, scheduling formal sessions can present a problem. On the one hand, an orientation event should be conducted as soon as possible. Of course, if you're frequently adding new employees, holding a formal session on each new hire's first or second day may be impractical. The best option is a combined approach — a formal event that takes place on a weekly or monthly basis (depending on how many employees you're hiring), preceded by an informal, first-day, personalized orientation that covers the mandatory administrative and operational aspects of the job. (See "The First Day: Easing Anxieties," earlier in this chapter.)

Involve senior management

Formal orientation sessions should always include an appearance (and, ideally, a brief message of welcome) from some key member of senior management — the higher up in the organization, the better. (If you're the business owner, this is you!) Some companies launch these sessions with a video message from the head of the company — which is acceptable as long as the video is of high quality and up-to-date. Generally speaking, however, having key company managers appear during a session gives more credibility and importance to the entire process.

Hold large-group sessions in a suitable location

If you're running large-group orientation sessions with video or oral presentations, you need a room large enough to accommodate the audience comfortably. Unattractive, cramped surroundings sabotage your ability to communicate and send the wrong message to new employees. An attractive environment tells new employees that the company is organized and professional and cares about its workers. If you don't have suitable facilities for holding these sessions on premises, consider renting a hotel conference room for the purpose.

Make group presentations user-friendly

Keep in mind that the orientation event is often the first formally structured experience an employee has on the inside of the company. With that in mind, you want everything that occurs that day to be consistent with the message that you conveyed during the recruitment process. To put it simply, everything should reflect how the company presents itself to the business world.

You can convey information in several ways: verbally, in written form (such as in a workbook), or through audiovisual materials. Each does a different job. The following list gives you a look at which option works best with varying types of information:

- ✔ **Verbal information:** This type of information is okay for the simple and most obvious stuff — the location of the lunchroom and restrooms, how to use the door keypad, the best places to eat lunch in the area, and so on.

- ✔ **Audiovisual presentation:** This type of presentation is most effective if you're seeking to create an emotional effect, as in the case of the company mission and goals.

- ✔ **Written documentation:** Use written documentation for anything complex or legally mandated, such as the company's compliance with equal employment opportunity legislation or the Americans with Disabilities Act. (See Chapter 17 for a complete discussion of these and other laws and the associated documentation.)

Deciding on the mix of oral, audiovisual, and written information to include in an orientation event depends primarily on how often you need to conduct a session and how many employees you're working with at any given time. You don't need to go overboard. Unless you're typically hiring large groups of new employees at the same time, a company video is a luxury you can probably do without. Rely instead on a PowerPoint presentation or something similar. Whatever you do, make sure that you provide new employees with information on key policies and benefits in writing. (If you contract out your benefits administration, vendors usually provide brochures, forms, and other materials.) One last point: Have everything ready before new employees walk in the door.

Provide an orientation agenda

A written agenda for orientation events serves three main purposes:

- ✔ It eases a new employee's anxiety by mapping out what's going to happen during the day.

- ✔ It enables you to adhere to a formal structure.

- ✔ It shows newcomers that you take the matter of orientation quite seriously as opposed to feeling you can just wing it.

By creating a well-organized and businesslike agenda, you also let employees see how your company likes to conduct business. The document doesn't have to be fancy. A single sheet of paper works fine.

Space things out

One consistent criticism shared by new employees is that they have to handle too much information at one time. So, try to space things out. Break up orientation sessions during the first week or move parts of them into the second or third week to give your new team members a chance to absorb what they're learning. Another benefit of this approach is that subsequent information is likely to make more sense to employees after they have several days of experience under their belts.

Here's a sample agenda for a one-day orientation program:

9:00 a.m.	Welcome by I. M. Helpful of Human Resources
9:15 a.m.	Remarks by Ray Joinus, president
9:45 a.m.	Coffee break with Mr. Joinus
10:00 a.m.	Company overview by Bill Smiley, HR manager
10:45 a.m.	Walking tour of key facilities led by Ms. Helpful
11:15 a.m.	Benefits briefing and completion of forms
12:00 p.m.	Lunch
1:00 p.m.	Distribution of company handbook and procedures manual
2:15 p.m.	Tour of office with manager
3:00 p.m.	Security office: ID photos and parking permits
3:30 p.m.	Work area familiarization with manager

Give a clear sense of tasks and set concrete goals

At some point during the first week of work, newly hired employees need to sit down with their supervisors for an in-depth discussion about job responsibilities and goal setting. The role of the HR practitioner is to ensure not only that this meeting happens but also that the manager is well prepared and understands its importance. The new employee should come away from this discussion with a crystal-clear understanding of expectations, tasks, and priorities. In the process, the employee and supervisor will clarify the job's objectives and, most important, work together to set specific, concrete goals for the newcomer.

The following list provides several suggestions for this meeting:

- Tell new employees about how the department operates, including expectations about quality standards.

- Make sure that the employee understands the nature of the job, its importance, and how it fits into broader corporate objectives.

- Define the factors that will shape the new employee's evaluation.

- Together, set short- and long-term goals. Involving employees in defining their objectives makes it more likely that they'll work hard to achieve them. Goals should include not only specific job tasks and results but also training and development activities.

- Build a timetable for reaching goals over the next 30 to 60 days, as well as longer-range objectives.

- Discuss a development plan for any training that can address skills gaps pinpointed during the hiring process.

Cascading goals: Aligning individual goals with corporate strategy

In the most successful organizations, employees don't set their goals in a vacuum. HR professionals ensure that line managers fully understand the company's strategic goals and are properly prepared to help their employees create individual objectives that support this higher-level vision. Sometimes called *cascading goals,* this approach allows the broader perspectives of senior management to cascade, like falling water, into more specific goals at all levels of the company.

In the case of a food company, for example, senior management might share a new direction, such as "Connect more with the desires of local families." This vision, in turn, takes on several meanings as it cascades through the organization and to individuals in each department. For product development, the focus may be on creating more family-friendly food items. For marketing, it may mean researching the attitudes of local families toward eating. This method also allows employees to set their objectives in line with their managers' goals, all

of which are part of the cascade throughout the organization. Simply stated, cascading goals put everyone on the same page.

The net result of cascading goals is improved company performance. When employees are aware of what they're being evaluated for and what's expected, they tend to do a better job. And when they're encouraged to create goals that are in sync with something larger, workers tend to feel more of a sense of purpose and importance, which leads to increased morale and productivity.

Employee objectives must be periodically revised as time goes on to ensure that they remain aligned with current company strategies and departmental priorities. It's counterproductive for an employee to be focused on a set of tasks that aren't quite in sync with a new overall company direction. You, line managers, and employees all need to keep goals cascading and attuned to the visions articulated by senior management.

Beyond Onboarding

A key part of the onboarding process is thorough follow-up. You or supervising line managers should meet with employees at predetermined points: two weeks after the first day on the job, a month after, two months after, or at intervals that work best for each job's complexity and take into account any changes in responsibilities. These meetings allow you to check in with new team members to find out how things are going for them. How well do they understand the company and their roles? Do they have any questions that haven't been answered? How has communication been with their managers? Do they feel prepared for their new roles? In particular, ask about the value of job-specific training programs the company has provided. Are they helpful? Do they address the right areas? Are they worth the time being spent on them? What future developmental experiences would employees like to see?

These follow-up meetings also are good times to hear new team members' assessment of the onboarding process thus far. (See the section "Feedback: How good is your program?," later in this chapter.)

Develop a checklist

To make sure that you're covering all bases during an employee's first 90 days on the job, create a checklist of everything he needs to know — every place he needs to see, every form he needs to fill out, and everyone he needs to meet. If possible, sort everything by time and priority. Make both the new employee and his manager responsible for completing all items, signing the checklist, and submitting the completed checklist.

When you get the signed checklist back, scan and insert it into the employee profile. It could prove invaluable in showing that the employee was informed right off the bat about key personnel issues if he brings a later claim against the company, such as a breach of contract claim, wage and hour lawsuit, or discrimination claim.

Don't let your message die

The company values and best practices you stressed during the orientation period should come through loud and clear month after month — through the actions of role models such as supervisors and mentors, as well as through internal communications, such as employee publications and your company intranet. In ongoing training activities, continue to make it plain that values such as respect for colleagues, commitment to quality service, and doing what's right rather than what's easy or convenient aren't just first-day lip service but integral to your philosophy of doing business.

Use mentoring to build a solid foundation

Mentoring programs have become a popular way for firms to assist new employees during the initial months on the job. By being paired with appropriate *mentors* (more experienced employees who act as a new hire's guide to your workplace) newcomers gain valuable, real-world experience and skills that are difficult to transmit in classroom settings or workshops.

Mentoring relationships are a key part of the onboarding process, although they often continue beyond an employee's initial period with the company as well. These pairings augment other elements of onboarding, helping to fill in the gaps that even the best-thought-out programs invariably overlook. After all, no matter how many steps you take to ensure a smooth adjustment to the company's culture, a few areas invariably require additional clarification. And a mentor and an employee can discuss certain "unofficial" topics in a way that isn't possible in a structured setting or with an immediate supervisor.

The one-on-one nature of the mentoring relationship can help a new hire integrate quickly into your firm's culture and become a productive member of the staff. Mentors can show new employees the ropes, introduce them to individuals in other work areas, and serve as a sounding board for thoughts, ideas, and concerns. Good mentor-protégé relationships also nurture an inviting culture, demonstrating to newcomers the benefits of an open environment where people are constantly sharing knowledge, generating ideas, and mutually committed to building a successful company.

But keep in mind that mentoring is not a one-way street. Individuals who become mentors stand to gain as well. For example, serving as a mentor can help even the most accomplished long-term employee improve her management skills. In addition, new employees often bring with them fresh perspectives and enthusiasm that can benefit a tenured mentor in return.

Mentoring also is a valuable recruiting and retention tool. When evaluating a firm as a potential employer, many job candidates consider a formal mentoring program an attractive asset. It indicates that the company is committed to the professional development of all its employees.

Mentors are different from supervisors. They don't typically oversee the new employee's day-to-day work performance. Their true function is to act as an additional source of support during an employee's early period with your company (although, again, these relationships can continue indefinitely).

Sometimes you'll hear the term *coaching* used in place of mentoring. In the field of HR, however, coaching and mentoring have different, but related, meanings. In general, coaching is more performance oriented and focuses on changing particular behaviors through specific skill improvement. A coach, who can be either external or internal to the company, helps an employee improve in specific areas. Mentoring, on the other hand, typically implies a more long-term relationship. It occurs most often between a senior or more experienced company representative who is quite familiar with an organization's overall structure, policies, and culture and a less experienced individual. Mentoring is often, but not always, a one-on-one relationship. (For an extended discussion of the distinction between the two and a broader discussion of mentoring as a career development tool, see Chapter 15.)

Feedback: How good is your program?

Whether through surveys or meetings, you need to get feedback on your onboarding program so you can make improvements for future new hires. Here are some questions that can form the basis of any feedback mechanism you develop for new employees immediately after the initial orientation:

- What elements of the initial orientation event(s) were most useful?
- What elements were least useful?
- What information should be included in future programs?
- How well did the session relate to your job?

But, of course, your work isn't done after you've received initial feedback. I also suggest you gather assessments from employees several months after they're hired. When they've been part of your organization for a while, they'll likely have a broader perspective about what helped them effectively adjust to the company and what was less valuable — and perhaps offer suggestions for improvement.

Here are additional questions you can ask employees several months into the job:

- What were the things you most wanted to know when you first joined the company?
- Has your experience so far been in line with the information about the firm that you received during the hiring process?
- Were those issues and concerns adequately covered during your first month on the job?
- Were you given enough time to acclimate yourself?
- Were other employees helpful when you asked questions?
- Were the printed and online materials you received useful? What could be improved?
- What do you know about your job and this company now that you would have benefited from knowing during the first few days you were on the job?

Employee Handbook and Separate Procedures Manual: Yes, You Need Both

Even if your company has only a handful of employees, keeping your basic policies and procedures well documented is always a good practice. Whatever effort may be required to get basic company information in print or on your intranet can save you time and headaches down the road.

The following list gives advice for creating an employee handbook and separate procedures manual:

- **Separate company policies from job-specific procedures.** Your employee handbook should consist of policies that apply to everyone in the company (general hours, payroll, vacation time, and so on). Set forth in a separate manual or other format those procedures that relate specifically to how people do their individual jobs. Keep these distinctions separate. You may want to develop separate procedures manuals — if you want to take this extra step — for specific job procedures.

- **Keep it simple.** Employee manuals don't need to be literary works, but they do need to be clear and concise. Use plain English and try to avoid overly formal, bureaucratic wording and phrasing. You may want to consider hiring a professional writer to polish your final draft.

- **Pay attention to legalities.** Here's some scary news: Anything that you put in writing about your company's policies or procedures automatically becomes a legal document. That means someone may use it against you in a wrongful dismissal suit. Numerous cases have occurred in which discharged employees received large settlements because they proved in court that either they were following procedures published in the company handbook or the company itself didn't comply with these procedures. Also, some laws require that if a company has a handbook or manual of policies, certain policies — with certain key elements addressed — must be included (for example, the federal Family and Medical Leave Act).

Play things safe. Make sure that a knowledgeable and experienced lawyer reviews the employee handbook and any procedures manuals before you publish them — and then ensure that your company's day-to-day practices match its written policies and procedures.

- **Control the distribution.** Every employee who receives an employee handbook should sign a document that acknowledges her receipt of the handbook and that she has read and understands its contents. In the document, she also should attest that she is required to work under its policies and that she knows the handbook is not a contract of employment in any way. Finally, the document the employee signs should include that the company, in its discretion, may change its policies in the future from time to time — and such changes will apply to her. Put the signed form in the worker's employee profile. You may need it in the event of a disciplinary proceeding or lawsuit.

You don't want the manual to circulate outside the company — and the manual needs to contain a clear statement to this effect. Some companies require departing employees to turn in their company handbooks before they leave. You may want to consider this policy as well, especially if your handbook details your operational procedures, contains trade secrets, or includes confidential or proprietary information.

Knowing what to include

Most employee handbooks follow the same general format. What differs from one company to the next are the specifics.

The following list gives you a look at a typical table of contents for an employee handbook:

- Welcome statement from the CEO
- EEO policy statement (including prohibition on sexual and other forms of discrimination and harassment and the procedure for reporting such conduct)
- Company history and overview
- Employment at-will (if applicable)
- Company mission statement and values
- Essential company rules, such as work hours; attendance, timekeeping, and payroll practices; business ethics; and dress and grooming standards
- Other company policies such as a code of ethics, harassment policies, open door policies, and vacation guidelines
- Performance appraisal procedures
- Standards of conduct and disciplinary procedures (have a lawyer carefully review this section)
- Health, safety, and security rules and procedures, including fire exit maps
- Employee benefit information, including available health and dental insurance coverage, pension, and deferred-income and retirement programs, paid time off benefits (including company holidays, vacation time, and sick days), leaves of absence, and eligibility requirements
- Technology policies, such as e-mail policies and social networking policies
- Parking and transportation information, including maps
- State-specific supplemental information, which usually is required by law

What about other languages?

In today's diverse, multilingual workplace, you may want to produce your employee handbook in languages other than English. Such a practice is a good idea, especially if English is a second language to many of your workers. But be warned: You need a professional translator to do the work, not a staff member who took language courses in high school. It's a legal document.

This sample table of contents is just that: a sample. The employee handbook you end up with will be one of your own design. Laws are constantly evolving, especially those involving the use of social media by companies and employees. For a full understanding of what's right for your handbook, consult with a knowledgeable attorney.

See the Employee Handbook Table of Contents on the CD for another sample. Also included is an Employee Handbook and At-Will Employee Status Acknowledgement.

Also, be sure to keep the big picture in mind. Don't just adopt policies because I refer to them in this book or on the accompanying CD. Think about the rules you want to govern your workplace. This isn't a mechanical exercise — it's an exercise in creating the rules you want to apply to your employment relationship with your workers.

Playing it safe

Whatever else your employee handbook does, make sure that it doesn't do any of the following:

- ✔ Make promises you can't keep.

- ✔ Publish procedures you don't follow or can't enforce.

- ✔ Say anything that someone may construe as discriminatory.

- ✔ Use the phrase *termination for just cause.* If this phrase is used, be sure you're prepared to give up at-will employment and specify exactly what you mean by *just cause.* (See Chapter 18 for more information.)

One last piece of advice: Always include a disclaimer that emphasizes that the handbook is a general source of information and not for anyone to construe as a binding employment contract, and that employment contracts can be created only with a written document signed by authorized company representatives.

Chapter 11

Ensuring a Competitive Compensation Structure

In This Chapter

▶ Knowing HR's role in compensation

▶ Understanding compensation terms

▶ Creating an underlying compensation philosophy

▶ Recognizing the legal implications of exempt versus nonexempt employee classifications

▶ Using raises, bonuses, and incentives effectively

▶ Communicating compensation policies

The quality of your business's compensation and benefits packages plays a major role in your ability to recruit and retain employees. You don't need an advanced degree in economics to figure out the kind of financial hole you could put your company in if you're not paying attention to this side of your business.

In this chapter, I discuss compensation concepts. In Chapter 12, I cover benefits.

The following information is as legally accurate and comprehensive as I can present in this format. I prepared the material in collaboration with the esteemed law firm of Paul Hastings LLP. However, you should still seek the sound advice of your own lawyer when making decisions of this kind. Your attorney can assist you in setting up policies and wage structures that can help keep you out of legal trouble.

Your Role Defined

Your goal is not to know everything that anyone can know about employee compensation. As you take on the task of managing your company's HR function, though, you do need to remain aware of changes taking place in this critical area. Although many traditional salary practices — automatic pay increases for time on the job, for example — are disappearing in favor of a wide range of other options, the basic challenges in developing a wage system remain.

So, what is HR's responsibility in building a compensation plan? Generally, in your HR role (if you're not also the owner of the company), you don't need to decide how much a particular individual should be paid. Your responsibility, instead, is to alert senior management to the options available for building a compensation system. It's your job to make sure that your compensation and benefits are competitive enough to keep your top employees from being wooed away by companies that claim to offer more attractive packages.

You need to be both consistent and flexible with regard to compensation. The two may sound contradictory, but they actually go hand in hand. Consistency means that you have a logical plan and structure to everything you do in the area of compensation and benefits. That way, you don't inadvertently create employee discord by giving the impression that you're showing favoritism or acting capriciously. Flexibility means that you're doing your best — within reason — to adapt to the individual needs and desires of your employees.

The intended end result of balancing these two factors is a wage and salary structure that not only gives your employees equitable compensation but also focuses on the market realities of your industry and business.

The Basic Language of Employee Compensation

Unless you specialize in employee compensation, terminology can get confusing. So, to start you out, the following list offers a quick rundown of key terms in the field, along with their definitions:

- **Base wage or salary:** The base wage or salary is simply the salary or wage — before deductions and other incentives — that employees receive for the work they do. (If you want to get really technical, you generally use *wages* as an umbrella label for all forms of pay, including hourly rates, day rates, commissions, and salaries. More specifically, salary typically describes the pay arrangements of employees who receive their compensation as a flat weekly, biweekly, or monthly amount, regardless of how many hours they work.)

✔ **Benefits:** Benefits are items that you offer to employees in addition to their base wage or salary. Examples include health insurance and retirement plans. (Chapter 12 covers benefits.)

✔ **Bonuses and incentives:** Generally speaking, any payment made to reward performance, attendance, productivity, tenure, a specific result, or other work-related behavior is an incentive. Bonuses are just one form of incentive. Additional forms of incentives include prizes, awards, and special sales incentives.

✔ **Commission:** This term refers to a percentage of the sales price of a service or product that salespeople receive in addition to (or in lieu of) base wages. Commission arrangements include the following:

- Straight commission with no salary.

- Commission combined with a base salary.

- A draw. Technically, a draw against future commissions, it's an arrangement in which the salesperson receives a set amount on a regular basis, regardless of how much commission is actually earned during that period. If your salesperson never hits his stride, he'll accumulate a large negative draw, which may be difficult to pay back.

✔ **Compensation:** You use this term to define everything employees receive in exchange for their work, including base pay, bonuses, and incentive pay, as well as benefits.

✔ **Exempt and nonexempt workers:** These labels apply to those who are covered (nonexempt) or not covered (exempt) by various federal and state overtime rules and other rules related to compensation (such as reporting time pay) and noncompensation (such as meals and vacation) matters.

This is a very complicated area. Consult a knowledgeable and experienced attorney before labeling an employee exempt from these obligations.

✔ **Raises:** This term refers to increases in base wages or salary, as opposed to one-time or periodic payments.

The Foundation for an Effective Compensation System

Creating an effective compensation system requires a constant eye toward the long-term needs and goals of your business. Your objective is a well-thought-out set of practices that helps ensure the following results:

✔ Employees receive a fair and equitable wage for the work they perform.

✔ Payroll costs are in line with the overall financial health of your company.

✔ The basic philosophy of compensation is clearly understood by your employees and has the strong support of managers and employees alike.

✔ The pay scale for various jobs in the company reflects the relative importance of the job and the skills required.

✔ Pay scales are competitive enough with those of other employers in your region and industry so that you're not constantly seeing competitors hire your top employees away.

✔ Compensation policies are in line with state and federal laws involving minimum wages and exempt or nonexempt classifications.

✔ Compensation policies are keeping pace with the changing nature of today's labor market — particularly in recruiting and retaining your company's top performers.

The first step in creating a compensation system is embracing a compensation philosophy — a set of criteria that becomes the basis for wage and salary discussions. Here are some questions you may want to ask yourself as you formulate this philosophy:

✔ Are you going to make your basic salaries simply competitive with the going rate for employers in your area and/or in your industry or higher?

✔ Are you going to establish a structured pay scale for specific jobs in your company, or are you going to tie salaries to individuals, basing pay on the qualities and potential of the person filling the job?

✔ To what extent are the monetary rewards you offer your employees going to take the form of salary, performance bonuses, or benefits?

✔ Are salaries based on employee performance or on other factors, such as how long staff members stay with you or what skills or credentials they bring to the job?

✔ Are you going to award bonuses on the basis of individual performance, tie bonuses to company results, or use a combination of the two?

Keep in mind that no specific answers are right or wrong for every situation. What's important is that your compensation philosophy takes into account your company's mission and goals. If your goal is to become the dominant company in your industry within five years, you'll probably need to offer generous wage-and-benefit packages to attract the people who can fuel your growth. And you may need to pay highly talented employees a little more than market value today so you can reap the benefit of their contributions three or four years from now. If your goal is to improve productivity, you most likely want to tie compensation to performance and productivity. You start with your goals and work forward from there.

Setting pay levels in your organization

One of the main tasks in any effort to create an equitable and effective wage and compensation system is to develop a consistent protocol for setting pay levels for every job in your organization. In setting the actual pay scale for specific jobs, you have several options.

The more essential a job is to the fundamental mission of your company, the higher its job value and, thus, its pay range is likely to be. Job value is determined by using one or more of the following job valuation methods.

Job ranking and leveling

How this approach works: You make a list of all the jobs in your company, from the most senior to entry-level employees. Then you group the jobs by major function — management, administrative, production, and so on. Working on your own or with other managers, you rank jobs by the degree to which they generate revenue or support revenue-producing functions. Eventually, you produce a ranking or hierarchy of positions. In the process, you create a measure of internal equity. As a result, employees feel that they're being treated fairly. Keep in mind that you're not rating individuals — you're rating the relative importance of each job with respect to your company's revenue goals.

The rationale: In large companies, you may want to use a reasonably structured approach to decide what pay range to apply to each job. The more systematic you are as you develop that structure, the more effective the system is likely to be.

The downside: Creating and maintaining a structure of this nature takes a lot of time and effort.

Market data and pay trends: "The going rate"

How this approach works: You look at what other companies in your industry (and region) pay people for comparable jobs and set your pay structure accordingly. You can obtain this data from government and industry websites and publications. Robert Half publishes a variety of salary guides focusing on professional disciplines such as accounting and finance, law, technology, advertising and marketing, and the administrative field. You can access the salary guides at www.rhi.com/salaryguides.

Rationale: The laws of supply and demand directly affect salary levels. Benchmarking salaries (and benefits) is important to ensure that you're paying people competitively.

The downside: Comparing apples to apples can sometimes be difficult in today's job market. Many new jobs that companies are creating are actually combinations of jobs in the traditional sense of the word. As such, they can prove difficult to price, because you can only go by how other companies pay. Still, it's a good starting point.

Management fit

How this approach works: The owner arbitrarily decides how much each position is paid.

Rationale: A business owner has the right to pay people whatever he deems appropriate.

The downside: After people are on the job, inconsistent wage differentials often breed resentment and discontent. Lack of a reasonable degree of internal equity diminishes the spirit of teamwork and fairness. Without any sort of rationale, employees can only wonder why some people are paid more than others.

Collective bargaining

How this approach works: In unionized companies, formal bargaining between management and labor representatives sets wage levels for specific groups of workers. These are based on market rates and the employer's resources available to pay wages.

The rationale: Workers should have a strong say (and agree as a group) on how much a company will pay them.

The downside: Acrimony arises if management and labor fail to see eye to eye. In addition, someone else — the union — plays a key role in your business decisions. Also, in this system, employees who perform exceptionally well can feel shortchanged because less proficient colleagues in similar positions receive the same pay.

Adopting a pay structure

One major trend in wage systems in recent years is to base pay on what workers can do — the skills, knowledge, and talents they bring to the company — and not the nature of the positions they fill. To do so, the company adopts a pay structure that best supports the compensation philosophy and job valuation method used. In this section, I fill you in on some of the ways businesses design their pay structures.

Variable pay system

Variable pay systems link a percentage of a position's pay to defined performance and accomplishment targets.

How the system usually works: You establish a base pay rate and define group and individual objectives as a variable salary component. Some systems set base pay at about 80 percent of the possible compensation under the variable system. You can base proportions of the variable component on the attainment of departmental or company objectives and on individual achievement.

Advantages:

✔ It imposes a direct relationship between pay and production.

✔ It guarantees employees a stable base income, while providing incentives for superior performance.

Disadvantages:

✔ If employees can't meet performance targets, it can lead to morale problems in an economic downturn.

✔ It can result in unequal pay among workers doing essentially the same jobs.

✔ Administering it can be exceptionally labor intensive.

Broadbanding

With *broadbanding*, you reduce a lengthy series of narrowly defined base-pay categories to a few broad ranges.

How the system usually works: You boil down a cluster of related jobs into one pay *band*. For example, you currently have six different job titles and pay groups for your administrative staff (office assistant, office manager, receptionist, executive assistant, administrative assistant, and senior administrative assistant), with base salaries ranging from $22,000 to $52,000 a year, depending on job title. Under broadbanding, you eliminate all job titles and salary ranges and combine everything into one band — administrative staff — with the same overall pay range as before but with no hard-wired connection between specific salaries and job titles.

Keep in mind that the actual salaries you pay don't change. You may still have one person earning, say, $40,000 and another earning $25,000. On the other hand, managers now have the option of basing pay on factors that derive from job performance or some other criteria, as opposed to job title.

Managers also have the option of moving employees around as the work requires — according to the employees' skills — without needing to worry about job titles.

Advantages:

- ✔ Gives managers flexibility in setting base salaries and work assignments
- ✔ Eliminates bureaucratic barriers to transfers and employee development (such as job titles)
- ✔ Eliminates unnecessary distinctions between similar jobs
- ✔ Lets managers reward superior performance more easily

Disadvantages:

- ✔ May prove disconcerting to long-time employees who may see broad-banding as a threat to their status.
- ✔ Can result in inconsistent compensation decisions across departments.
- ✔ Unless guidelines are clearly established, management can be open to charges of favoritism or discrimination.
- ✔ It may be more difficult to document the exempt/nonexempt status of jobs at specific points in time.
- ✔ In unionized industries, you can implement the system only through collective bargaining.

Skill-based and competency-based pay

Under a *skill-based pay system,* you set pay scales by skill level and not by job title. Although skill-based pay is still an option, few companies use this approach today, partly because, if a firm's required skill sets change rapidly, it must continuously reinvent the system.

Competency-based pay systems base compensation on an employee's traits or characteristics rather than on specific skills. This method is used by only a few employers today because it's very tricky to develop and administer.

Taking individuals into account

You pay people, not positions. So, sooner or later, you must program into your salary decisions those factors that relate solely to the individual who is to perform the job. The following list describes the key "people factors" you may want to consider in finalizing your compensation system.

✔ **Experience and education:** To a certain extent (and in particular occupations more than others), you see a fairly reliable correlation between employee productivity and their education level and experience. Be careful, however, not to take this principle too far. More education and greater experience don't always translate into better work. People who are overqualified for positions, for example, can prove less productive than individuals with less experience or less education. The key here is to make sure that a logical connection exists between the employee's education and experience and the basic requirements of the job.

✔ **Past job performance:** In theory, at least, you should pay more to workers who can demonstrate that they produce more. The challenge is putting this simple idea into practice. To do so effectively, you need to address the following questions:

- What barometers are you using to measure job performance, and how do they tie in to your strategic objectives? If you're evaluating customer service specialists, for example, are you interested in quantity — the number of inquiries handled in a specific time frame — or are you more concerned about the satisfaction level reported in customer surveys? If you're evaluating the performance of technical service personnel, are you going to key pay levels to technical proficiency or their ability to interact with others?

- Who's responsible for measuring performance? Is it the employee's immediate supervisor, or do you use a team-based approach to performance evaluation? What recourse do employees have who take issue with your evaluations? If they don't think the performance criteria are fair, can they take their case to someone other than their supervisor?

- Are the performance criteria you're using to reward performance discriminatory in any way? In other words, does any aspect of your company's job performance criteria favor one gender over another, individuals under 40 years of age compared to those 40 and older, or one ethnic group over another?

✔ **Seniority:** Length of service has long been a factor in the pay scales in most industries — unionized industries in particular. The rationale is that loyalty is valued and should be rewarded. The downside: No strong evidence suggests that seniority and productivity in any way directly correlate.

✔ **Potential:** Some companies justify higher pay for certain individuals because they consistently demonstrate the potential to become exceptional producers or managers. This consideration is generally why comparatively unskilled, inexperienced college graduates may receive extra compensation if they enter management trainee programs.

The payroll/sales ratio: What's an optimal balance?

Regardless of the compensation system you set up, you must make sure that your company can afford to carry the costs. No optimal ratio exists between payroll costs and revenues, but whatever you decide needs to be a structure you can handle comfortably. Employees should feel that their salaries are reasonably well insulated from the ups and downs of your business. Given a choice, most employees may be willing to take home a little less on a yearly basis (within reason) in exchange for the reassurance that they're going to receive their pay regularly throughout the year.

Most business consultants tell you that the key issue in determining an appropriate cost/revenue ratio is how much of a profit margin you realize on your products or services. Companies that operate on relatively high margins (50 percent or higher) can absorb higher payroll costs than can companies operating on smaller margins. For insight into the average payroll/sales ratio for firms in your industry, visit the U.S. Census Bureau's website, which features various business and economic measurements based on the latest Economic Census: `www.census.gov/econ/census/ratios.htm`.

In the states: Wage and hour laws

The states have varying policies governing the determination and payment of wages. In general, state laws require employers to pay wages

- At prescribed intervals, such as weekly, biweekly, semimonthly, or monthly (so-called *pay frequency*)
- Within prescribed periods of time after the close of each interval, such as no later than seven days (so-called *pay timeliness*)

The wage and hour laws of many states also restrict the types of deductions that employers may take from an employee's paycheck. Although it's typically lawful to automatically deduct taxes (withholding taxes, Social Security, unemployment taxes, and state disability insurance payments) that are forwarded to a government, other deductions often may be barred outright or allowed only with a signed authorization from the employee. Deductions subject to an outright bar can include, depending upon the state, product breakage and cash shortages. Deductions subject to prior employee authorization can include (again, depending upon the state) medical insurance premiums, life insurance premiums, 401(k) contributions, or other deductions for employee-paid benefits.

Wage and hour laws can be very tricky to comply with, and federal laws may or may not correspond with the requirements of state laws. This is an area where employers are wise to consult with an experienced and knowledgeable attorney.

Exempt and Nonexempt: Why the Distinction Matters

The three main purposes of the Fair Labor Standards Act (FLSA), enacted in 1938 and amended several times since then, are to

- ✔ Establish a minimum wage.

- ✔ Provide overtime (typically at time and a half the regular rate of pay) for work in excess of a weekly standard (typically 40 hours).

- ✔ Set minimum standards for child labor.

Included in the FLSA are special rules for determining whether a position is eligible for exemption from the FLSA's overtime and minimum wage standards. Thus was born a key distinction between exempt and nonexempt workers.

Compliance with wage and hour laws can be very complicated. Employers should consult with an attorney who is knowledgeable and who has experience with such laws. Don't try to soldier through this heavily regulated area without such advice.

Who's exempt and why?

The rules that distinguish exempt and nonexempt employees focus on their job duties and forms of pay. *Exempt employees* are those who perform, as their primary duty, specified tasks and who, depending upon the particular exemption, exercise discretion and independent judgment. Typically, exempt employees receive a fixed salary, without regard to the quantity or quality of their work. In some instances, especially in the entertainment industry, exempt employees may receive a fee, rather than a salary. Also, certain kinds of computer professionals can receive an hourly rate of pay equal to at least $27.63 and receive an overtime exemption. So, salary is a common test of exempt status, but it's by no means exclusive.

Nonexempt employees are those who do not meet the exemption requirements. They may receive pay in any form (for example, an hourly rate, a piece rate, a salary, or a commission), but employers must reduce that pay to an hourly rate for each workweek in which they work overtime. Employers must make this conversion, because overtime typically is a rate per hour and because that rate typically must include (or blend) all forms of pay for work performed.

The rules for distinguishing exempt from nonexempt employees are technical and fact based. It is not safe to base exempt status on job title or job description, salary level, job complexity, access to confidential information, or safety sensitivity.

In addition, the burden is on the employer, not the employee, to justify exempt status. Moreover, the back pay, interest, and other damages that can flow from misclassifying your employees can be large, going back two or three years. Keep in mind that individual states can, and often do, create higher standards for exempt status than those imposed by the FLSA. Some states impose higher damages or penalties for misclassification, and some states look back more than two or three years. For these reasons, you should consult an attorney when drawing lines between your exempt and nonexempt employees.

An employee can't waive her right to overtime. So, even a signed agreement saying an employee won't receive overtime is meaningless. The employee can later claim that nonexempt status.

Keep in mind the following guidelines as you're classifying workers:

- ✔ **Analyze jobs to determine actual duties.** Focus on day-to-day activities and correlate them with the requirements of the law. Compare what the employee actually does with the formal job description. Lawsuits can arise as a result of conflict between the two.

- ✔ **Correct problems when you find them.** Don't wait for a lawsuit to drop in your lap or a government inspector — municipal, state, or federal — to walk in the door. Bear in mind, though, that a voluntary reclassification of positions can, in and of itself, trigger a lawsuit by those who claim that the reclassification has exposed prior noncompliance.

- ✔ **Keep accurate records.** You need to keep accurate time records for all nonexempt employees. If a dispute arises as to whether an employee worked overtime, the employee probably will win unless the company can produce an employee-completed time sheet showing otherwise.

- ✔ **Don't allow employees to work "off the clock."** There is no point to going from the frying pan to the fire — going from improperly classifying someone as exempt to underpaying her as nonexempt. Remember this basic rule: If you knew or should have known that a nonexempt employee was working, you must pay for that time, even if the employee didn't write it down. You can impose discipline for working unauthorized hours, but this is tricky because, if you resort to discipline, you must do so in a way that doesn't discourage anyone from writing down the hours for which she's entitled to pay.

The bottom line on overtime

Overtime often is an integral part of today's nonexempt jobs. Employees in many industries depend on the extra money they make in overtime wages to support their standard of living. No one disputes that relying on overtime work certainly makes sense in many situations. The question you need to ask yourself is whether overtime is the best option for your company in any given situation.

Responding to temporarily increased demand by putting existing workers on overtime can be less expensive than hiring new employees. Of course, cost savings from using overtime are true only for a short period of time. A steady diet of overtime to increase production can have negative long-term consequences. Excessive, long-term overtime can increase the rate of on-the-job accidents, erode employee morale, and cause family pressures. Also, a steady diet of overtime may suggest, at some point, the possibility that adding staff actually will decrease your compensation burden because a new hire may cost less than the recurring overtime.

You're best off viewing overtime as a stopgap strategy, reserving it for short-term situations, such as when people call in sick or take vacations or when the workload increases in the short term. If the need becomes constant, consider adding a new employee or filling the gap by using contingent workers (see Chapter 4).

Other legal considerations

The following list gives you a brief look at federal laws that address discrimination, as well as how much you pay your workers. Don't forget to check your local and state regulations, too.

- **The Equal Pay Act of 1963:** This law prohibits unequal pay to men and women doing the same job, assuming that the jobs require equal skill, effort, and responsibility and that employees perform the jobs under similar conditions. Most states have similar statutes. The law permits a few exceptions, such as seniority, merit pay, or productivity, so check with a lawyer.

- **Civil Rights Acts of 1964:** Title VII of this law prohibits wage (and other employment) discrimination on the basis of race, sex, color, creed, religion, or national origin. The U.S. Equal Employment Opportunity Commission (EEOC) enforces this law.

- **Age Discrimination in Employment Act of 1967:** As amended in 1978, this law bans wage (and other employment) discrimination for employees ages 40 or older, including pay increases, bonuses, and benefits. One of the most common violations is the denial of pay increases to people nearing retirement to avoid increasing retirement benefits that are based on salary. The EEOC enforces this law, too.

✔ **The Americans with Disabilities Act of 1990:** This law prohibits discrimination in compensation (and other employment terms and conditions), including access to insurance, against qualified applicants and workers on the basis of disability.

✔ **The Davis-Bacon Act of 1931, the Copeland Act of 1934, the Walsh-Healey Act of 1936, and the Anti-Kickback Act of 1948:** These four laws focus, in different ways, on the compensation policies of companies with federal contracts. Each law has its own wrinkle, but the basic purpose is to ensure that employers pay prevailing wages and overtime while prohibiting excessive wage deductions and under-the-table payments by employees to obtain work.

✔ **The Wage Garnishment Law:** This law prohibits employers from firing workers whose wages, for whatever reason, are subject to garnishment by creditors or a spouse. In most cases, it also limits garnishments to no more than 25 percent of an employee's take-home pay.

For more information on the first four laws in the preceding list, see Chapter 17.

What You Need to Know about Raises, Bonuses, and Incentives

Offering competitive compensation is key to attracting top talent to your organization. But after employees are onboard, salary levels don't stay competitive for long. As employees develop new skills and increase their knowledge of your business, they become increasingly valuable. Their value in the marketplace increases as well, meaning that they become attractive targets for other companies. To keep your best and brightest, you need to figure out fair (and affordable) ways to augment what you pay them. Most companies enhance their compensation through raises, bonuses, and incentives designed to give their best workers a reason to stay.

Effective bonus and incentive programs are

✔ **Results-oriented:** Employees must accomplish something to receive a bonus.

✔ **Fair:** The rules for bonuses are clear and enforced equitably.

✔ **Competitive:** The program rewards extra effort and superior performance.

Pay raises

Some pay systems link raises to *tenure* (time spent in that grade or position). Other systems tie raises to performance. The most common types of raises include

- **Seniority step-ups:** These types of raises usually depend solely on an employee's length of service. They're pretty much automatic. Such raises are a common feature of union contracts.

- **Merit raises:** These raises are increases for superior performance, usually based on a formal performance evaluation system. However, they're sometimes driven by other considerations, such as attainment of an educational or training objective.

- **Productivity increases:** These raises generally involve increasing pay after employees exceed a certain norm — a production quota, for example. These systems usually apply to production or assembly workers or to clerical workers performing repetitive tasks.

You should always key merit pay to a fair and consistent performance evaluation system (see Chapter 16). The key decision you often must make (or help others make) is whether you're going to peg performance standards to company performance or to departmental performance. Company-wide merit pay systems are the traditional rule. However, managers in many firms have discretion to make individual salary increases that are outside the range if they feel someone's salary isn't competitive with market conditions or a strong performer is at risk of being lured away. This increasingly popular method of allocating annual raises works something like this:

> Mary Allen has 20 employees in her department. The company allocates her sufficient funds to give each employee a 4 percent increase, based on the group's total current salary dollar. She may decide to give a 4 percent boost to the majority of the team because that's management's general guidance. But she may decide to give superior performers more than 4 percent and underperformers less — or even no raise at all. For example, 12 employees may receive 4 percent; 4 employees, 6 percent; and 4 employees, only 2 percent.

Set up merit pay systems with the following principles in mind:

- You need to have a workable employee appraisal system in place. Managers and supervisors must know how to implement it.

- Individual differences in performance must be large enough that you can measure them. They also must be significant enough to warrant additional pay.

- ✔ Merit pay increases must be large enough to be of value to the employee.

- ✔ Senior management must commit to an honest and equitable administration of the system.

- ✔ Employees must accept the principle of distinctions in pay based on performance. Merit pay systems are especially contentious in highly unionized industries, where raises based on job title and seniority are more the norm.

Bonuses

Bonuses are one-shot payments that you always key to results — the company's, the employee's, or those of the employee's department. They come in a variety of flavors:

- ✔ **Annual and biannual bonuses:** These bonuses are one-time payments to all eligible employees, based on the company's results, individual performance, or a combination thereof.

- ✔ **Spot bonuses:** Spot bonuses are awarded in direct response to a single instance of superior employee performance (a particularly successful suggestion, for example). Employees receive the bonus on the spot — that is, at the time of, or immediately thereafter, the action that warranted the bonus.

- ✔ **Retention bonuses:** You make such payments to persuade key people to stay with your company. These bonuses are common in industries that employ hard-to-recruit specialists. They're also effective in retaining top managers or star performers.

- ✔ **Team bonuses:** These bonuses are awarded to group members for the collective success of their team.

 Employers must be aware that the amount of a bonus may — depending on certain circumstances — need to be included in determining an employee's regular rate of pay, which is the amount of pay upon which overtime pay is calculated. Mistakes can violate federal or state wage and hour laws. A knowledgeable attorney can help you navigate this tricky area.

Other incentives

The following sections outline some other common incentive programs, besides bonus programs.

In Chapter 12, where I cover employee benefits, I discuss a number of retirement plan options you can offer your staff. I mention some of them in this section as well because these plans can be viewed as incentives or retirement plan benefits, depending on how the employee intends to use them.

Profit-sharing plans

Profit-sharing plans enable the company to set aside a percentage of its profits for distribution to employees. If profits go up, the employees get more money. You can vary these programs by allocating profit sharing on a department or business-unit basis. Employees who stand to share in the company's profits have an extra incentive to work hard and be more aware of avoiding waste and inefficiency. After all, it's their business, too.

Profit-sharing plans fall into one of two categories:

- ✔ **Cash plans:** Payments are distributed quarterly or annually.
- ✔ **Deferred plans:** The company invests the profit-sharing payment in a fund and then pays out an employee's share if she retires or leaves the company.

Deferred plans offer significant tax advantages to both the company and employees. On the downside, deferred plans can have less effect on productivity. In some cases, the worker doesn't actually see the profit-sharing money, except as a figure on paper, until retirement.

Certain employer-deferred compensation plans and arrangements are subject to complex tax laws, notably Internal Revenue Code Section 409A. You should exercise caution before locking in any contractual obligations and consult a tax attorney for counsel.

Stock

Stock in the company is an incentive that publicly traded firms (or firms planning to go public) may choose to offer their employees. *Stock option plans* give employees at publicly held companies the right to purchase shares in the company at a time of their own choosing, but at a price that is set at the time the option is awarded. Employees are under no obligation to exercise that option. However, if the stock price goes up, employees can buy the stock at the cheaper price and either hold on to it or sell it for the current value, thereby earning a profit.

Stock options also have given small, growing companies a way to attract top talent without having to pay high salaries. In the 1990s, these plans became commonplace in fast-growth industries such as technology.

If your company is thinking about offering stock options as part of your overall benefits package, there are certain aspects of the process everyone must be aware of. If you're a privately held company, for example, your employees need to recognize that a stock option plan isn't likely to mean anything to them unless your company goes public or is acquired. If you're publicly held, you need to make sure that you have an organized plan and mechanisms in place that will not dilute the value of the stock to non-employee stockholders. Bear in mind, too, that these programs must comply with tax laws and with Securities and Exchange Commission (SEC) regulations.

Another major legal factor to take into account is that stock options must now be counted as a corporate expense for accounting purposes, a change in law that has led many companies to offer fewer or no stock options to employees than they had in previous years. Get thorough legal, tax, and accounting advice before you put together any sort of stock option plan.

Here are some other considerations you need to bear in mind about stock option plans:

- ✔ Most stock option plans include some form of *vesting*. That means options may not be exercised until an employee has been with the company for a specified period of time. Vesting is a retention strategy.

- ✔ Most stock option plans set an expiration date, a point beyond which employees can no longer exercise options.

- ✔ Most plans require the approval of current shareholders.

- ✔ The plan you adopt may obligate you to provide periodic financial information and reports to option holders.

- ✔ If you offer stock options to nonexempt employees, be sure to consult an attorney to make sure that these options qualify for exclusion as wages used to calculate overtime.

Many companies that have eliminated stock options are instead offering *restricted stock* to their employees. Restricted stock is ownership in a company with rights to vote and receive dividends without the right to transfer or sell the shares until they're vested. After the vesting conditions have been satisfied, the shares may be held, transferred, or sold as an employee desires, subject to applicable securities laws and payment of withholding taxes and applicable commissions.

What's the difference between stock options and restricted stock? Basically, when a stock option vests, employees don't own any company stock until they exercise the option and purchase the stock. After a restricted stock vests, however, employees automatically own the stock and can keep or sell it at their discretion. Although they need to pay withholding taxes, they don't have to pay an exercise price as they would with stock options. As a recipient of restricted stock, they also are immediately eligible to receive any dividends declared by the company.

What's fair versus what works?

The easiest way to start a mutiny among your staff is to institute policies for raises, bonuses, or other incentives that people don't understand and that neither managers nor employees buy into. The following list offers guidelines to help you avoid this all-too-common pitfall:

- ✔ **Set clear rules.** Whether you're dealing with an incentive system or a merit-raise program, everyone must understand the rules that govern the rewards program. Key information includes who's eligible for the program, what they must do to receive the reward, who decides on those who benefit, and the size of the reward.

- ✔ **Set specific targets or goals you can quantify.** If you're going to establish incentives, make sure that you set a specific target: "125 percent of our annual sales quota," for example, or "more than 500 pieces per day." Specific numbers eliminate arguments and misunderstandings.

- ✔ **Make the goal worthwhile.** If the incentives aren't attractive, they're not really incentives. So, gear the reward to the group whose performance you're seeking to enhance. Think about setting up different rewards for varying levels of achievement — for example, a 4 percent increase for an average performer and an 8 percent increase for a top-notch employee.

- ✔ **Don't ask for the impossible.** Such terms as *killer goals* may sound highly motivational, but you may only discourage employees if they think they're simply unattainable. Not only can that dampen their motivation and effort, but it also costs you credibility. That's not to say there's anything wrong with "stretch" goals, but they should be attainable.

- ✔ **Don't make promises you can't keep.** Never promise a bonus or incentive you're not sure you can afford.

What to Communicate about Your Policies

Many companies unfortunately spend a lot of time and effort designing a pay system, only to leave it to the paycheck alone to communicate the philosophy and administration behind that policy. Silence is not necessarily golden in promoting compensation policies. In particular, you need to thoroughly brief managers and supervisors on your company's pay systems so that they can effectively explain, administer, and support your policies. Managers and supervisors need the following information:

- ✔ Your company's pay philosophy.

- ✔ How to conduct a performance appraisal, if your company has such a system. (Many smaller companies may not have a formal system for performance appraisals.) I cover this topic extensively in Chapter 16.

✔ How to handle and refer employee pay complaints.

✔ The legal implications of all compensation policies.

You also need to advise employees of the company's pay policies and how those policies affect them individually. You need to communicate and fully explain any changes in these policies promptly. Employees need to know

✔ The job's rating system, how it works, and how it affects them

✔ How the performance appraisal and incentive systems work

✔ How they can raise their own income through performance and promotion

✔ How to voice complaints or concerns

You must keep your compensation system competitive and up-to-date. The key steps in doing so are as follows:

✔ Obtain and review competitive data at regular intervals.

✔ Review — and adjust if necessary — salary ranges at least annually.

✔ Look over job descriptions regularly and make adjustments based on disparities between actual work performance and the formal description.

✔ Evaluate the performance appraisal system. One common problem is that too many employees get superior ratings.

✔ Review salary systems in terms of your company's financial condition to determine whether the system is in line with the company's financial health and is tax effective and efficient.

✔ Periodically measure and rate productivity, and determine whether any links exist between productivity increases (or declines) and pay policies.

Chapter 12

Creating the Right Benefits Package

In This Chapter

▶ Understanding what benefits are

▶ Identifying trends in benefits

▶ Grasping the basics of benefits coverage

▶ Controlling health-insurance costs while still meeting employee needs

▶ Rethinking retirement planning

▶ Considering other benefits offerings

▶ Creating employee assistance programs

▶ Making benefits administration less stressful

*Y*ou have a lot to think about these days when you're managing benefits for your team — administrative details and government regulation, not to mention pressure to reconcile employee desires with the financial realities of your business. However, a comprehensive package of employee benefits is a critical component in recruiting and retaining talented teams. It is by no means an inexpensive undertaking, but the payoff is more than worth the cost. As I discuss in this chapter, there are a variety of strategies available to address the rising expense of employee benefits.

Much of the complexity in benefits planning and administration today is due to the changing face of the workplace. Today's diverse workforce has many needs, and this diversity extends to the benefits workers want. Add to this a wide range of laws and healthcare and retirement plan options, and you quickly see how complicated it can be to create and implement effective benefits programs.

As challenging as all these factors seem at first glance, you have opportunity here as well. After you get your arms around this area of human resources, you can do a great deal of good for your employees and your company. And, best of all, if you know what you're doing in building and promoting a competitive benefits package, you can greatly strengthen your company's ability to attract and retain top talent.

What's a Benefit Anyway?

Strictly speaking, you can define a *benefit* as any form of compensation that isn't part of an employee's basic pay — and that isn't tied directly to either job requirements or performance.

Specific employee benefits today take a multitude of forms ranging from multiple-option healthcare coverage and tuition reimbursement to childcare and eldercare assistance. There are even such benefits as in-house concierge services, health club memberships, and on-site auto repair and detailing services. Exactly which benefits you offer and how much of your payroll expense goes to pay for them are decisions your company's financial health and business philosophy must determine. Your job in taking on the HR function is to make sure that both your company and its employees are getting the best bang for their benefits bucks.

Key Trends in Benefits Management

The world of benefits administration is changing rapidly. The following sections provide you with a quick glimpse of four key trends.

Demographic changes

Shifts in the U.S. workplace in the past 25 years have affected both the number and the nature of the offerings you now find in the typical benefits package. Trends such as delayed retirement, second careers, and increased longevity mean that the age continuum of workers is greater than ever before. As a result, it's now common to see four generations working side by side in the workplace. This shift, as well as the growth of dual-income couples, same-sex couples, and single-parent households, coupled with alternative work arrangements such as telecommuting, has drastically changed the profile of a typical employee and his expectations of a company benefits program.

Most large companies are well aware of the incredible diversity shaping today's workplace and in response have long offered flexible, or *cafeteria,* benefits (which give employees a "menu" of choices) rather than the traditional one-size-fits-all approach. The plus side to this trend is that employees are clearly happier when they can tailor their benefits package to their specific needs. The downside is that the more choices you give your employees, the more complex your benefits plan becomes to administer.

Cost containment

To offset the rising cost of employee benefits, more companies these days are asking employees to assume a larger portion of the overall benefits tab. For example, in the all-important realm of healthcare costs, the typical employee's contribution has risen considerably. Workers nationwide are expected to pay an average of $2,764 in healthcare premium costs in 2012, a 40 percent increase from five years earlier, according to the 2012 Towers Watson/National Business Group on Health Employer Survey on Purchasing Value in Health Care. To ease the sting of increased employee payments, progressive companies have introduced so-called *lifestyle benefits* — relatively inexpensive rewards or services, such as allowing employees to use the mailroom, that make life a little easier for their teams but avoid substantial costs.

Healthcare reform

President Barack Obama signed the Patient Protection and Affordable Care Act into law on March 23, 2010. The law requires most adults to maintain "minimal essential [healthcare] coverage" either through an employer or government-sponsored insurance plan or individual coverage or pay a penalty (referred to as the "individual coverage mandate"). After being contested in court, the act was largely upheld by the U.S. Supreme Court.

Home-based employees

As the telecommuter population increases, a new need has surfaced — benefits geared specifically for people who divide their work time between the office and home, or who work exclusively at home. The biggest can of worms you face in this situation is how to structure a work-related injury- or illness-insurance program that accounts for the possibility that on-the-job injuries can now occur in an employee's home.

The likely resolution? Hybrid policies that combine traditional workers' compensation policies with disability insurance. Additionally, you may want to consider a written agreement between the employer and telecommuter covering who's responsible for what in the home. Work-related injuries in a home office, for example, are covered provided the home office is in at least as safe a condition as the conventional office. Some companies require a home safety inspection as part of the deal. The agreement also should cover what happens if any employer-provided equipment, such as a laptop, requires repair or replacement.

The watchful eye of Uncle Sam

In recent years, Congress and state legislative bodies have taken a more active role than ever in regulating many basic benefits policies, especially health insurance and 401(k) retirement and pension plans. In large part, increasing government involvement is a response to the well-publicized financial misconduct within some companies that triggered the failure of their pension plans. The most worrisome possibility consists of potential lawsuits from employees who may claim that the company's healthcare provider failed to provide adequate medical care. Amid this environment, corporations need to be proactive in communicating the ins and outs of their benefits plans to employees.

The Basics of Benefits Coverage

Offering most employee benefits is voluntary: You're under no legal obligation to provide them. Three notable exceptions to this rule are Social Security and Medicare, unemployment insurance, and workers' compensation. The following sections take a brief look at each program.

Social Security and Medicare

Purpose: The Social Security system was originally designed to provide basic retirement income for all workers who have contributed to the plan and to provide healthcare benefits to Americans who are age 65 or older or who become disabled. You and your employees may be eligible to begin receiving payments as early as age 62, but keep in mind that the benefit will be reduced permanently if it's taken this early. On the other hand, if an individual delays applying for this benefit past the age of eligibility, the benefit will increase.

In 2003, the age of eligibility for full retirement began to increase gradually. People born between 1943 and 1954 must be 66 to quality for a complete retirement benefit. By the year 2025, the retirement age for full benefits will be 67.

Another key part of Social Security is Medicare, a federal health-insurance program for people 65 and over. Beginning in 2006, the government passed laws reducing the cost of prescription drugs for those covered by Medicare.

How the system works: Payroll taxes finance Social Security and Medicare. Your employees typically contribute 7.65 percent of their gross take-home pay to fund both programs. Federal law obligates your company to match that amount. (Self-employed workers pay 15.3 percent.) The first 6.2 percent of the tax that goes to the Social Security fund is assessed only up to a specific income ceiling — $110,100 in 2012. Any income over that limit isn't subject to Social Security tax. No ceiling exists, at present, on the 1.45 percent Medicare tax. These rules are subject to change.

Check out *Social Security For Dummies,* by Jonathan Peterson (Wiley), for much more information on the complex rules surrounding Social Security.

Unemployment insurance

Purpose: Unemployment insurance provides basic income for eligible workers who become unemployed through no fault of their own.

How the system works: Individual states run the unemployment insurance program, which was established as part of the 1935 Social Security Act. The federal guidelines are rather loose. Except in a handful of states (Alaska, Pennsylvania, and New Jersey) that expect employees to pay a small percentage of the cost, employers pay for their workers' unemployment insurance. The cost to employers is generally based on the company's *experience rating* (how frequently its former employees receive payments through the program). The more people you lay off, the greater your potential assessment becomes.

The experience-rating method of calculating employer unemployment costs is yet another reason for your company to avoid cycles of new hires in flush times and layoffs whenever demand sags. It's also a good reason to use contingent workers during times of reduced business or to handle normal workload peaks and valleys. In addition, it's important for a company to regularly pay unemployment insurance taxes. This fact may seem obvious, but in recent years, a number of companies have behaved illegally.

Workers' compensation

Purpose: Workers' compensation provides protection for workers who suffer injuries or become ill on the job, regardless of whether the employee or the employer was negligent. It pays medical bills, provides disability payments (income replacement) for permanent injuries, and distributes lump-sum death benefits.

How the system works: Workers' compensation is an insurance program. Some states permit private insurance — if your company can demonstrate financial capability to state authorities, you may choose to be self-insured. Other states require you to contribute to one state-managed fund; still others permit a mixture of state and private insurance. Generally, however, contributory systems are experience rated: The number of claims that employees file against your company determines your rates. Good workplace health and safety practices, therefore, pay off.

Some employers, especially those with large numbers of off-site workers or telecommuters, have integrated workers' compensation programs into health-insurance programs. Keep in mind, though, that certain laws — federal and state — can make such a combination difficult to manage. As with other areas related to employees who work away from a specific office, thoroughly explore this option with an attorney.

If you include the 50 states, the District of Columbia, Puerto Rico, and the Virgin Islands, at least 53 separate workers' compensation programs currently exist. You need to consult with your lawyer, insurance carrier, and state officials to determine your own liability. Workers' compensation, with very limited exceptions, is a no-fault system: No matter who's to blame for the illness or injury, it still covers the employee. If your company operates in more than one state, you must adjust your workers' compensation policies according to local rules. If you run into legal problems, you most likely must retain lawyers licensed to practice in the state in which the problem arises.

A Healthy Approach to Insurance

Health insurance is today's most expensive employee benefit. Without a doubt, it's also the most difficult benefit to administer, not just because of its cost but also because of the many options available and the challenges companies face balancing two seemingly contradictory objectives: keeping costs down while at the same time meeting employee needs.

The flavors of health insurance

The number of individual healthcare plans available today is enough to fill a book — a book that, given the changing world of healthcare, would no doubt be out of date quite quickly. Following is a bit of information on the three most prevalent healthcare plan options. Bear in mind that these options (in fact, the entire structure of employer-provided healthcare) may change rapidly, given the pressure on companies to control healthcare costs.

Fee-for-service plans

Fee-for-service plans are insurance programs that reimburse members for defined benefits, regardless of which practitioner or hospital delivers the service. Under some fee-for-service arrangements, members pay the bills themselves and then submit their claims to the carrier for reimbursement. Under other plans, the physicians or hospitals assume the responsibility for filing and collecting on claims.

Fee-for-service plans have two fundamental parts: the base plan and major medical. The base plan covers certain "defined" services, usually in connection with hospitalization — an appendectomy, for example, but not routine mole removal. Major medical — an option — covers such services as routine doctors' visits and certain tests.

Health maintenance organizations

Health maintenance organizations (HMOs) offer a wide range of medical services but limit your choices (both in medical practitioners and facilities) to those specialists or organizations that are part of the HMO network. Each person whom the plan covers must choose a primary physician (sometimes known as the *gatekeeper*), who decides whether a member needs to seek specialty services within the network or services outside the network. As long as employees stay within the network (that is, they use only those facilities and medical practitioners who are part of the HMO network), the only additional cost to them if they undergo any procedure that the plan covers is a modest co-payment. HMOs differ in their out-of-network policies. Some are highly restrictive. Others allow members to seek care outside the network but only with the approval of the gatekeeper; members who use approved services outside the network may assume additional costs (up to a predefined deductible) for each out-of-network visit.

Preferred provider organizations

Preferred provider organizations (PPOs) are similar to HMOs but with several key differences:

✔ Employees have a wider range of choices as to whom they can see if they experience a medical problem.

✔ PPOs typically require no gatekeeper — members can go outside the network as long as they're willing to assume the costs, up to the agreed-upon deductible.

✔ The cost to employees for participating in a PPO is usually more than the cost to participate in a comparable HMO plan.

Weighing the options

In recent years, many companies have altered the options they offer. The traditional fee-for-service plans are still available, but most companies today make it most advantageous for employees to choose HMOs and PPOs, which are also known as *managed-care programs*. HMOs and PPOs provide the same benefits as the traditional fee-for-service plans but set limits on which practitioners and which facilities that employees on the plan can use to receive maximum benefits. Some managed-care programs provide no benefits at all if employees go outside the approved networks.

When deciding which type of plan to carry for your employees, you need to take into account the following factors:

✔ **Extent of coverage:** The procedures that health-insurance plans cover can vary widely, but most plans offer the same basic coverage. This coverage includes emergency trips to the hospital, illness-related visits to doctors, most routine tests, most surgical procedures (but not cosmetic surgery), and hospitalization. What varies widely, however, are any "extras" — the extent to which coverage includes, for example, chiropractic care or home nursing, or whether it accommodates long-term needs such as hospitalization for mental illness.

✔ **Quality of care:** The quality of medical services that members of managed-care programs receive has become an issue today for an obvious reason. Employees covered by these plans are obliged to use only those physicians or facilities designated by the plan's administrators. Therefore, you must make sure that any managed-care program you choose has high standards and a quality reputation. In addition, check to see whether the National Committee for Quality Assurance (www.ncqa.org) certifies that program.

✔ **Cost:** In shopping for your company's health insurance, keep in mind that you always get exactly what you pay for, regardless of the particular option you choose. Insurers generally base their pricing on three factors:

- The number of people the plan covers

- The demographics of your workforce (average age, number of children, and so on)

- The amount of deductibles and co-payments

The higher the deductible and the more money that members pay for each doctor's visit, the less expensive the premium.

- ✔ **Ease of administration:** A key factor in your choice of insurance carriers is the ease with which you can administer the program. The best plans, for example, offer an easy-to-use website and a 24-hour toll-free number that lets individuals swiftly modify benefit plans or levels. Some plans, on the other hand, curtail costs by shifting much of the administrative burden to you.

Although you can save some money by using in-house resources to handle administration, servicing your benefits can require a major commitment of staff time and financial resources. If you decide to assume this responsibility, make sure that you have the administrative ability.

On the CD, you find a Certificate of Group Health Plan Coverage. This form helps employees document their prior health coverage when enrolling in a new employer's health plan. Insurance companies are required by the federal Health Insurance Portability and Accountability Act (HIPAA) to provide health-plan participants with a certificate when coverage ends. You, as the employer, should ensure that employees receive such notices.

Rising costs: Staying ahead of the game

The good news about contemporary healthcare is that society takes its well-being very seriously. People of all ages are leading healthier and longer lives. But a major part of taking better care of themselves means more trips to doctors for examinations, more preventative procedures and, when necessary, surgery. All these factors point to a pragmatic financial reality: Healthcare costs will continue rising. The numbers bear this out. The Towers Watson/National Business Group on Health study estimated that employer healthcare costs per employee were expected to increase by 5.9 percent to $11,664 in 2012.

That rise isn't a mere blip. Although costs have stabilized in recent years, the study also reported healthcare costs have risen by no less than 5.4 percent every year for the prior ten years. The message here appears to be: Don't expect the cost of keeping employees healthy to level off any time soon.

You're right in the thick of this dialogue. In many ways, issues related to healthcare strike right to the core of a company's responsibility for its employees. And there's no question that, depending on culture, history, and financial resources, different companies approach the matter of healthcare in different ways. Some see increased government involvement as an answer to rising costs. Others point to a benefit realignment in which employees bear most of the responsibility for healthcare costs and provider choices. You need to keep up with all these developments but also understand what companies are currently doing to contain healthcare costs.

Five ways to minimize healthcare costs

Even though it's true that you pretty much get what you pay for in a healthcare plan, you can adopt a few strategies that will help you save money without compromising the quality of your employees' medical care. Here are four guidelines to keep in mind:

✔ **Affiliate with the largest group possible.** When it comes to health-insurance premiums, safety lies in numbers. The larger the group of companies with which you affiliate, the more competitive the rates you're likely to pay. Shopping around pays off.

✔ **Raise the deductible.** Increasing the deductible amount employees are responsible for covering on a typical fee-for-service plan can save you anywhere from 10 percent to 50 percent on premiums, depending on the size of the deductible. Bear in mind, however, that in some states the deductible can't exceed $1,000.

✔ **Consider consumer-directed health plans (CDHPs).** CDHPs are a relatively new experiment in determining ways companies may be able to reduce healthcare costs. CDHPs usually consist of a high-deductible medical insurance plan coupled with *health savings accounts* (HSAs). HSAs were created by the Medicare bill signed by President Bush in 2003 and are designed to help individuals save for future qualified medical and retiree health expenses on a tax-free basis. To offer HSAs to employees, you first need to institute an HSA-eligible, high-deductible health plan.

✔ **Manage drug benefits.** Many companies have eliminated co-pay arrangements for prescription drugs, opting instead for plans that require coinsurance and/or deductibles on a cost-sharing basis. One cost-cutting aspect is to provide preferred coverage for generic drugs. Some plans offer reduced costs to participants who elect home delivery by mail for long-term prescription needs instead of purchasing these items each time at a local pharmacy.

✔ **Consider working with a benefits consultant.** Bringing in an outside benefits expert to analyze your company's healthcare needs and recommend the best approach to health insurance may cost you money in the short run, but the recommendations can more than offset the initial expense. Another option is to find a local insurance agent who specializes in medical insurance and ask that person to recommend the best program. Just make sure that the programs recommended to you have an established track record. Bear in mind, too, that while some benefits consultants charge on an hourly basis, others act as insurance brokers and get a commission (anywhere from 3 percent to 10 percent). If you're a good negotiator, you may persuade the broker to make price concessions.

✔ **Establish wellness programs.** Wellness programs that encourage employees not to get sick in the first place are a growing benefits trend. These initiatives can not only keep healthcare costs down for companies but also promote healthier behaviors that result in reduced absenteeism. Be aware, though, that having these programs in place can raise privacy and perceived discrimination issues, especially among people with hard-to-manage health issues such as obesity or smoking. If care is not taken in establishing them, workplace wellness programs can shift costs to those with the greatest healthcare needs and potentially violate federal antidiscrimination and privacy laws and other regulations.

One key step is to encourage employees to stay healthy. Conducting regularly scheduled seminars; distributing literature; and offering a wealth of information on your company's intranet on topics such as stress management, nutrition, sleep, and other health-related subjects can go a long way toward decreasing healthcare costs. Some large companies go farther, building on-site facilities that offer exercise equipment and even spa services. Some even provide financial incentives for employees who quit smoking, lose weight, or maintain a regular exercise schedule. Smaller firms can take many of these actions, perhaps including discounts on memberships at local health clubs.

This commitment to ensuring a healthy employee base fits in with much of what I cover in Chapter 13. HR can play an important role in creating and nurturing a culture where employees are urged to take good care of themselves. Be on the lookout, for example, for managers and employees who work themselves to the brink of exhaustion and end up getting sick. Although dedication is valued, rarely is a short-term productivity gain worth the long-term expense. (See the nearby sidebar, "Five ways to minimize healthcare costs.")

Retirement Plans

The business environment has changed radically in a single generation. Rarely do you see cases of one employee working at a single company for an entire career. In response, retirement plans have become much more flexible and portable. And because many companies no longer offer defined benefit (for example, corporate pension) plans, employees are seeking ways to personally remain in control of this important aspect of their careers and financial security.

Retirement plans that companies offer their employees generally fall into two categories:

- ✔ **Defined benefit plans:** In a defined benefit plan, employees know the amount they'll get out of it (the benefit). The company chooses how it will invest its employees' money and guarantees the amount they'll get at retirement. The most common type of defined benefit plan is a pension plan.

- ✔ **Defined contribution plans:** In a defined contribution plan, employees know how much they put in (the contribution) but do not know how much they'll eventually be able to take out. The employee chooses from a list of available investment vehicles, and the payout is dependent on how those vehicles have performed when the time comes to make withdrawals. The most common type of defined contribution plan is a 401(k) plan.

Companies can offer a hybrid of defined benefit and defined contribution plans. An example is a cash balance plan, which combines some of the elements of a 401(k) plan and a defined benefit plan, such as a pension. According to the U.S. Bureau of Labor Statistics, the individual account feature of a cash balance plan makes it resemble a defined contribution plan. From an employer perspective, however, these plans are defined benefit plans because the employer doesn't actually fund the individual accounts but rather keeps a common fund sufficient to pay all future benefits.

Defined benefit plans

Generally limited to large, established companies, defined benefit plans provide a fixed benefit after retirement, usually calculated by a formula that takes into account salary level and length of service. The employer can fully fund these plans *(noncontributory)* or require employee contributions *(contributory).*

Advantages: Employees can count on a fixed, set amount of retirement income. The plan encourages employee loyalty and retention. Employees generally can make pretax contributions.

Disadvantages: These plans aren't generally portable — employees can lose some or all benefits by changing jobs. The funding obligations for these plans vary depending on numerous factors and can fluctuate significantly over time. Administrative costs can be high, too, and pension liabilities can significantly affect a company's balance sheet.

Overall, defined benefit plans are becoming much less common than they used to be. According to consultant Towers Watson, defined contribution plans (see the next section) are becoming nearly universal among employers. In a 2012 report, Towers Watson cited reasons why companies are shifting away from defined benefit plans, including competition, cost reduction, and an intent to improve employee satisfaction. (See "Employer contributions to retirement plans," later in this chapter.)

Defined contribution plans

Defined contribution plans are the primary alternative to defined benefit plans and basically involve individual accounts for each participant. The 401(k) plan is the classic defined contribution plan, but others are profit-sharing plans and employee stock ownership plans (ESOPs).

Employees can contribute as much as 17 percent (as of 2012) of their income to a 401(k) fund, deferring taxes until they withdraw the income (when, presumably, they'll be in a lower tax bracket). Employees may borrow within certain limits against the investment account. Even if employed, withdrawal can start at age 59½. Some companies augment or match what their employees set aside in defined contribution plans. (See "Employer contributions to retirement plans," later in this chapter.)

Advantages: These plans are highly popular with employees; they also offer favorable tax treatment, lower administrative costs (usually), and portability — employees can take most or all funds with them when they change jobs.

Disadvantages: These plans offer no guaranteed payouts. Investment risks fall on employees. Employees face heavy tax penalties (10 percent) for early withdrawals unless for limited reasons, such as disability.

Employer contributions to retirement plans

As employers replace their defined benefit plans with defined contribution plans at only a portion of the cost — and only part of the benefit — many now make contributions to a profit-sharing or 401(k) plan. According to the Society for Human Resource Management, a company has a number of options in the way it goes about this: no contribution, nonelective contributions, or matching contributions. A nonelective contribution is one an employer makes regardless of whether the employee makes a contribution to the plan.

401(k) plans: Smart shopping tips for employers

These days, many financial institutions are aggressively marketing 401(k) plans to employers of all sizes. These organizations usually also handle virtually all administrative details for employers. Finding a 401(k) vendor isn't hard, but choosing the best one for your company can be a challenge. Here are some questions to ask any potential 401(k) provider:

✔ **Are the management fees reasonable?** Compare them with other plans and find out exactly what you're paying for.

✔ **Are the investment options all from the same family of funds, or can the employee choose individual funds from different companies?**

✔ **How easily and frequently can employees switch their investments — between an equity and a bond fund, for example?** If your employees can't change investments at least quarterly, they can't stay current with market trends.

✔ **How often do participants receive account statements?**

✔ **Does the plan offer a full range of investments, from conservative to moderately risky?** The more choices employees get and the broader the range of those choices,

the better the plan can meet employees' varied investment needs and goals.

✔ **What's the reputation of the 401(k) plan vendor?** How long has the vendor been offering and managing 401(k) plans? How have the investment options in the plan fared against similar options? Stack the plan's equity funds alongside similar equity funds to see how they compare.

✔ **How good is the vendor's documentation for your employees — its brochures, investment-option explanations, and so on?** Keep in mind that many employees require solid, easy-to-understand advice and guidance.

✔ **Can the vendor support IRS and Employee Retirement Income Security Act (ERISA) reporting?** See the upcoming section, "ERISA and other legal issues."

✔ **Does the provider offer self-service capabilities so that employees can access their accounts online to make changes?**

Because an employer's directors and officers face potential personal liability for mishandled 401(k) plans, smart employers establish investment committees and generally structure their mandate through a carefully drawn charter.

Ninety-eight percent of plan sponsors polled in a 2012 study by Towers Watson said they provide an employer contribution to their workers. Although 52 percent of companies in the survey still provide just a matching contribution, a very large minority (42 percent) said they now offer both matching and nonmatching contributions.

See the CD for a 401(k) plan summary called "A Look at 401(k) Plan Fees," one of many publications addressing retirement planning that is available from the U.S. Department of Labor's Employee Benefits Security Administration (www.dol.gov/ebsa/publications).

ERISA and other legal issues

Your company is under no legal obligation to provide a retirement plan for your employees. If you do offer a plan, however, you're subject to the regulations of ERISA — the Employee Retirement Income Security Act of 1974.

Since its passage, ERISA has created significant administrative requirements that small businesses often feel the most. Subsequent laws have modified some of ERISA's provisions. In general, these combined retirement regulation laws mandate that any pension or profit-sharing plan you offer meets the following requirements:

- ✔ The plan can't exclude most employees who are older than 21 or require an employee to complete more than one year of service.

- ✔ Employee contributions must be 100 percent vested at all times.

- ✔ Vesting for employer contributions must fall into one of the following two categories:

  - **Cliff vesting:** After five years, the employer's matching and other contributions become the complete (100 percent) property of the employee.

  - **Graded vesting:** The employer's matching and other contributions become the property of the employee *in increments* until the employee is fully vested. After three years, employees are permitted to own a certain percentage (20 percent is the minimum increment per years three through seven) until full vesting occurs.

- ✔ You must fund defined benefit pension plans annually, with funding requirements calculated on the basis of future obligations.

- ✔ Also in the case of a pension plan, your company must be part of and pay for ERISA's government insurance fund to protect employees from the possibility of the pension plan dissolving.

- ✔ No more than 10 percent of the assets in your defined benefit pension plan can be invested in your company stock, with 401(k) and other defined contribution plans being allowed to offer company stock as an investment alternative (but beware of significant personal liability risks to owners).

- ✔ You must meet ERISA standards for the people who administer the program. For example, persons convicted of certain crimes or violations of ERISA can't administer the program.

- ✔ Employers must report pension operations to the government and inform employees of their pension rights and the status of their pension plan.

The Rest of the Benefits Smorgasbord

Besides health-insurance and retirement plans, businesses frequently offer a number of other benefits. Here's a rundown of the most common benefits and what you should know about them.

Dental insurance

Dental insurance has become an increasingly popular employee benefit in recent years. More than 175 million Americans — 57 percent of the population — were covered by some form of dental benefits in 2010, according to the 2011 NADP/DDPA Joint Dental Benefits Enrollment Report. Companies sometimes offer dental care as part of a health-insurance package and occasionally as a separate policy or an add-on. Costs and deductibles vary widely by region and by extent of coverage.

Generally, these plans cover all or part of the cost of routine checkups, fillings, and other regular dental procedures. They also may cover orthodontics or extensive restorative dentistry (usually with stated limits). Most dental plans have deductibles and typically require the employee to pay at least part of the cost of each visit or procedure.

Vision care

Most benefit plans restrict vision coverage to routine eye exams. Most also impose a ceiling on how much is covered toward the purchase of lenses, frames, and contact lenses. (Your employees can forget the Armani frames unless they pay out of pocket.) These plans, moreover, don't cover serious eye diseases and other conditions that, in most cases, the employee's regular health-insurance policy covers.

Family assistance

The much documented increase in the number of two-income families, single working mothers, domestic partners, and employees who care for both children and aging parents has led to an accelerating demand for childcare and eldercare assistance from employers. You can expect the need to intensify in the years ahead. The following list describes some ways in which companies provide this benefit:

> ✔ **Childcare:** Beyond offering flexible schedules for employees with young children, some companies provide on-site childcare (daycare). This is a great idea in theory — the convenience to the working parent is

obvious — but only a handful of companies provide a daycare facility at the work location itself. The big problem is cost — liability insurance, in particular. Another obstacle is that state and county authorities extensively regulate on-site childcare centers, including the amount of play area required and the ratio of childcare workers to children.

✔ **Eldercare:** As people live longer, many employees must care for their aging parents or other relatives. As a result, some businesses are providing eldercare benefits to help employees met these obligations. Support ranges from partial reimbursement for eldercare specialists, emergency in-home care, and allowing employees to enroll adult family members in their healthcare plans.

✔ **Contracted daycare for children and seniors:** The company contracts with one or more outside providers to provide services for the children and parents of employees. This approach to healthcare is becoming more prevalent, but it also mandates a good deal of responsibility. When your company selects a particular provider, you vouch for that provider's quality of care and services.

✔ **Vouchers:** Vouchers are simply subsidies that you pay to employees to cover all or part of the cost of outside childcare. Voucher systems are the simplest form of childcare assistance to administer.

✔ **Dependent care reimbursement accounts:** These accounts enable an employee to use pretax dollars to pay for dependent care. They're subject to both IRS and ERISA regulations. (See the earlier section, "ERISA and other legal issues.")

Time off

Although many employees take the practice for granted, paying employees for days they don't work — whether for holidays, vacation, sick days, or personal days — is an important benefit that your employee handbook needs to spell out. Each company has its own philosophy, but the following list offers general observations about paid days off:

✔ Most companies provide employees with a fixed number of paid holidays per year, such as New Year's Day, Independence Day, Thanksgiving, Christmas, and so on.

✔ The average employed American worker gets 14 vacation days per year but only uses 12 of them, according to Expedia.com's 2011 Vacation Deprivation Study.

✔ Vacation accrual policies differ widely from one company to the next. Some companies enable their employees to bank vacation time. Others require employees to take all vacation time during the year in which they earn it. The more popular option is to enable employees to accrue vacation time, but be careful — this policy can leave you with huge liabilities for unused vacation time that you may need to pay in cash if the employee retires or leaves your company. Where lawful, hedge your bets by capping the maximum amount that can accrue.

✔ Some companies combine sick time, personal time, and vacation time into a single paid-time-off program.

The most important point here is that state authorities heavily regulate employee time off. In some states, for example, the law requires companies to allow employees who don't use accrued vacation time in a single calendar year to carry it over to the next year. In such states, vested vacation benefits are treated as a form of wages, so that a policy of "use it or (eventually) lose it" amounts to the failure to pay wages in violation of wage and hour mandates. In other states, this type of policy is permissible. Make sure to consult legal counsel regarding the lawfulness of your policy in the state(s) in which you operate.

Leaves of absence

A *leave of absence* is an arrangement whereby employees take an extended period of time off (usually without pay) but still maintain their employment status. They resume their normal duties when the leave is over. Employees either request or are granted leaves of absence for a variety of reasons: maternity, illness, education, travel, military obligations, and so on.

When a particular law does not apply to a leave of absence, then the specific policies you adopt regarding such leaves of absence are within your discretion. In such cases, it's up to you to determine how long employees can stay away from the job without jeopardizing their employment status. You decide what benefits will be maintained and what job, if any, will be guaranteed them when the leave is over. Most companies reserve the right to decide these questions on a case-by-case basis.

However, very often, a leave of absence is governed by law. For example, many leaves of absence related to certain military circumstances and family and health situations are covered by the federal Family and Medical Leave Act (FMLA) and, often, analogous state leave laws. The FMLA, passed in 1993 and amended in 2008, applies to companies with 50 or more employees. Eligible employees are entitled to take up to 12 weeks unpaid leave per year for any of the following reasons:

✔ To care for newly born or newly adopted children (note that this right extends to both parents)

✔ To care for a child, parent, or spouse with a serious health condition

✔ To attend to a serious health condition that makes the worker unable to perform his or her job

✔ Because of any qualifying exigency arising out of the fact that the spouse, son, daughter, or parent of the employee is on covered active duty (or has been notified of an impending call or order to covered active duty) in the armed forces

Also, the FMLA requires covered employers to grant an eligible employee who is a spouse, son, daughter, parent, or next of kin of a current member of the armed forces (including National Guard or Reserve) with a serious injury or illness up to 26 workweeks of unpaid leave during a single 12-month period to care for the service member.

Under FMLA regulations, you must maintain the employee's health coverage, at the same level, under any group health plan for the duration of the unpaid leave, and you must restore the employee to the same or equivalent job when she returns. The law also requires you to post and deliver notices advising workers of their rights under the law. Note that various states may have similar family and medical leave and/or pregnancy and/or baby-bonding leave requirements, while other states (California and Connecticut, for example) provide greater leave rights or benefits to eligible employees.

A leave of absence, with job restoration at the end of the leave, may be required as a form of reasonable accommodation to disabled employees under the Americans with Disabilities Act (ADA) and/or under equivalent state laws. Also, if an employee requests leave time in connection with a disability, and your company is covered by the ADA, you have a legal duty to engage, in good faith, in an interactive process (discussions and so on) with the employee. This process is aimed at identifying whether your company can provide a reasonable accommodation to enable the employee to perform her essential job functions — and that one accommodation could end up being a leave of absence. A lawyer can help you in this area, including on the related question of what, if any, benefits must be continued during the period of a leave that is provided as a reasonable accommodation. Also consult an experienced lawyer if you are unclear, in any given situation, if a particular leave of absence may implicate legal leave of absence protections.

See the CD for the following federal FMLA forms:

✔ Employee Rights and Responsibilities Under the Federal Family and Medical Leave Act

✔ Certification of Health Care Provider for Employee's Serious Health Condition (Federal Family and Medical Leave Act)

✔ Certification of Health Care Provider for Family Member's Serious Health Condition (Federal Family and Medical Leave Act)

✔ Certification of Qualifying Exigency for Military Family Leave (Federal Family and Medical Leave Act)

- ✔ Certification for Serious Injury or Illness of Covered Servicemember — for Military Family Leave (Federal Family and Medical Leave Act)

- ✔ Notice of Eligibility and Rights & Responsibilities (Federal Family and Medical Leave Act)

- ✔ Designation Notice (Federal Family and Medical Leave Act)

Sick days

Formal sick leave policies generally limit how many sick days the company is willing to pay for (anywhere from 6 to 12 days per year). In addition, companies usually impose a limit on the number of sick days that employees can take in succession (after which employees may be entitled to nonpaid leave of absences). Most companies have short-term disability plans that kick in either immediately following an accident or on the eighth calendar day after the onset of an illness. Short-term disability ends after a predefined interval (typically either three or six months after it has started), at which point long-term disability may begin.

Benefits for common-law and same-sex couples

Extending benefits to common-law couples, same-sex married persons, and domestic partners (either opposite-sex or same-sex nonmarried partners) has become a rapidly accepted practice at thousands of companies across the United States. This new benefit speaks powerfully to the ways corporations have become aware of the changing lifestyle arrangements of many of their employees.

The Human Rights Campaign Foundation's 2012 Corporate Equality Index shows that 60 percent of Fortune 500 businesses offer domestic-partner benefits, an increase of 76 percent since 2002.

Though no official, nationally recognized set of requirements determines eligibility for domestic-partner benefits, here are a few possible eligibility requirements to consider using if you decide to offer them:

- ✔ Both partners occupy a common residence, as proven by a lease or title deed, for at least six consecutive months.

- ✔ Both partners are at least 18 years of age and not related by blood.

- ✔ They have a joint bank account or joint credit cards or can provide other evidence of shared financial responsibility.

- ✔ They're registered as partners in a state or locality that permits registration of domestic-partner relationships.

Additionally, your business may be in a state where common-law or same-sex marriages are legal. As of this writing, ten states (Alabama, Colorado, Iowa, Kansas, Montana, Oklahoma, Rhode Island, South Carolina, Utah, and Texas) and the District of Columbia allow common-law marriages. Six states (Connecticut, Iowa, Massachusetts, New Hampshire, New York, and Vermont) and the District of Columbia allow same-sex marriages. Where those sorts of marriages are legal, both partners are afforded the same status — including employee benefits for spouses — that are provided "traditional" couples.

This is one area where it's prudent to talk with an attorney if you have any questions or concerns.

Sometimes companies offer a reward for employees who don't use their allot-ment of sick days — for example, a cash payment for a percentage (usually half) of an employee's unused sick leave at the end of the year or if he leaves the company. Many companies have choice-time-off (CTO) or personal-time-off (PTO) plans that combine vacation and sick days.

Failure to formulate and communicate to all employees a formal sick-day policy can be dangerous to the health of your company. If you have a loosely defined policy that sets no limits on paid sick days, for example, you may run into legal problems if you ever decide to discipline or fire an employee who's clearly abusing your guidelines. The employee may argue that you treated her more harshly because of a protected status (like her religion or national-ity) than you treated other employees who did not have that same protected status. Without a record of consistently administering a sick-day policy, you may have a more difficult time defending against such a discrimination claim.

Both the federal FMLA and the federal ADA (and/or similar state laws) may be implicated if employees who used paid sick days in connection with FMLA absences, or for reasons related to disabilities, are disqualified from a cash reward due to such absences. Also, some states require employers to allow employees to take a portion of their sick days to care for ill family members. An attorney can help you analyze these issues.

Employee Assistance Programs

Employee assistance programs (EAPs) originated in the early 1970s as a mechanism for helping employees deal with certain types of personal prob-lems (alcohol abuse, for example) that had on-the-job implications. In a way, EAPs were ahead of the curve in addressing employee well-being in a variety of areas that previously hadn't been covered by benefit programs. The fol-lowing list will likely look familiar to you, because a great many of the issues historically addressed by EAPs also have become the province of HR. Today, EAPs usually are presented as a benefit rather than included in work-environment programs.

Here's a sampling of areas in which EAP providers can assist employees:

- Stress management and conflict resolution
- Social, psychological, and family counseling
- Referral to legal services
- Preretirement planning
- Termination and career transition services (sometimes called *outplacement*)
- Alcohol and substance abuse

- Mental-health screening and referral
- Gambling addiction and other compulsive behaviors
- Marriage counseling
- Financial issues and credit counseling

Many large companies operate their own in-house EAPs, staffed with psychologists, social workers, counselors, and support staff. Smaller companies that have EAPs generally rely on outside sources, such as EAP providers. These providers range from fully staffed organizations to small groups of individuals who have arrangements with outside firms.

ON THE CD

Total rewards: Let employees know who's paying

With the smorgasbord of benefits offered by companies today, wouldn't it be great for your employee recruitment and retention efforts if everything could be grouped together in one easy-to-understand "basket"? That way, workers could readily see how much time, money, and other resources you're investing on their behalf.

Materials distributed to employees during the annual enrollment process likely already show part of the picture. A more comprehensive look could take into consideration compensation, benefits, work/life accommodations, and even taxes paid on behalf of employees.

This idea of holistically reporting to employees what their employer is doing on their behalf is sometimes referred to as *total rewards*. The goal is to ensure that staff understand what they're getting from the company and the associated costs.

If you decide to create a statement of the broader benefits you provide, make sure that you've gone through the thought processes I describe in this chapter to align your benefits with what employees actually value. If you haven't taken this step, a report you issue could have the opposite effect you intend: It could make your team aware that little you do for them has real meaning to them as individuals. In

short, a total rewards statement may be a good idea for your business; just be sure to approach it carefully and be realistic about what it actually portrays about your company.

A case could be made for including in your total rewards statement Social Security and unemployment insurance. These are so common that your employees probably don't consider these programs as "benefits." That means they may not realize how much your company is paying on their behalf. If you don't want to include this in your total rewards concept, you may want to list your company's contributions right on the employee's pay stub, next to deductions from the employee's gross pay. In some states, this and other categories of information may be required under applicable wage and hour laws. If you contract out your payroll, your contractor may already have the software to do so.

See the CD for a Total Rewards Statement. Keep in mind that the statement you prepare can be more comprehensive than the example on the CD. You also may use the total rewards statement to provide an explanation and amplification of how each benefit works and its value to the employee. Just be sure that the statement you prepare is an accurate reflection of your offerings and policies.

If your company has fewer than 3,000 employees, you probably can't justify the cost of an in-house professional counselor. Your best option is to find an outside source. You can obtain a list of EAP providers in your region by getting in touch with the Employee Assistance Professionals Association (`www.eapassn.org`). Another suggestion: Check with your local business associations, chambers of commerce, and other businesses in your area for referrals.

When the time comes to make a choice, here's what to do:

- **Check references.** As you would with any outside provider, carefully check references and make sure that the staff members of EAPs you're considering have the required training, certifications, and licenses. Companies normally do this during the request for proposal (RFP) process, comparing factors such as average call-center wait times and the level of medical and psychological education of staff before they sign up for a particular service. Ask providers to demonstrate the quality of their care through surveys or case studies.

- **Clarify fees.** EAP costs can vary widely, but in most situations, a basic per-employee fee can range anywhere from $12 to $20 per year, depending on the number of employees in your company. This fee is frequently adjusted on a yearly basis depending on how extensively your company actually uses the services. Ask about additional charges, such as referrals to therapists. The EAP's base fee should cover everything, including materials and administration.

- **Check with your health insurer.** Your health-insurance policy may not offer mental-health benefits or substance-abuse rehabilitation. You may want to upgrade your benefits to provide these services or find an alternate means of providing them.

If you offer an EAP, remember that confidentiality is essential for legal and practical reasons. Employees must have confidence that they can talk privately to a counselor without repercussions (information reported back to a supervisor, for example). The Americans with Disabilities Act (ADA) prohibits using information on employees' health problems in a way that would negatively impact their jobs. The Health Insurance Portability and Accountability Act (HIPAA) also protects health-related data from inappropriate intrusion. Your EAP contracts should provide for this confidentiality.

Five Ways to Make Your Life Easier

As this chapter emphasizes, benefits administration can get very complex. The good news is that five simple principles, if followed, can make the job of administering benefits in your company less stressful.

✔ **Remember that one size doesn't fit all.** With businesses more diversi-fied than ever, employees bring a wider range of values, desires, and expectations to their jobs. As a result, you need to constantly evaluate which mix of benefits works best for your company and its broad spec-trum of employees.

The point is that your benefits offerings need to be broad and flexible enough to appeal to a variety of diverse groups. However, your job isn't to make assumptions about which benefits will appeal to which people. The single most important thing that you can do to win employee sup-port for your program is to involve them as much as possible in all aspects of the plan, particularly as you're deciding which options to offer. If your company is small enough, you can keep your employees in the loop informally — simply by meeting with them regularly to discuss your benefits package and whether it's meeting their needs. If you have ten or more employees, however, a survey is a better option. Instead of asking employees to list benefit options that are important to them, pro-vide them with a list of options to rate on a scale of one to five.

✔ **Get to know your programs cold.** You and the people who work with you in benefits administration need to have a thorough knowledge of your benefits package and about the topic of benefits in general. Otherwise, you can't explain your offerings to employees, help employ-ees sort out problems, or make the best benefits choices for your com-pany. At the very least, you need to be able to write a brief description (in simple, clear language) in an employee handbook of all the programs that your company offers. And regardless of your level of experience in HR, you should make it a point to stay current. Be on the lookout for seminars and short courses that are offered nearby and make sure that you route important benefits articles that appear in HR journals or busi-ness publications to all those accountable for or interested in benefits administration.

✔ **Make benefits education a priority in your onboarding program.** Making sure that your employees have a thorough understanding of their benefits options should be one of the main priorities of your onboarding program. Take the time to develop an information package that spells out what you offer but that doesn't overload employees with overly detailed information. Make sure that the person who handles the benefits side of the onboarding program can answer the most frequently asked employee questions. (For more on onboarding, see Chapter 10.)

✔ **Monitor your program for problems and results.** Don't make the mis-take of waiting for resentment and dissatisfaction to build before you do something about aspects of your benefits package that aren't work-ing. Whether you do so informally through conversations or through some other means, such as a survey, make sure that you're attuned to employee attitudes, particularly about health insurance.

✔ **Provide feedback and problem-resolution procedures.** If you haven't already done so, establish formal mechanisms to receive employee comments and complaints and set up a system to resolve problems. Many problems aren't really problems at all but misunderstandings that stem from miscommunication. Try to develop some means of tracking problems through various stages of resolution. (One method is to use a form that lists the complaint and includes spaces for the various steps you need to take to resolve it.) The benefits complaints that employees voice most commonly today involve denial of health-insurance claims. Use employee feedback as a resource to periodically revise your communications about benefits.

The bottom line: Benefits let your employees know that you genuinely care about their well-being. Knowing that you care can help make them more productive and committed to the organization.

Chapter 13

Creating an Employee-Friendly Work Environment

In This Chapter

▶ Offering alternate work arrangements that boost employee flexibility

▶ Considering which perks to offer

▶ Investigating the value of being a good corporate citizen

▶ Using team-building exercises to promote collaboration

▶ Using employee surveys to gauge the mood of the organization

A wise man once said that the mark of an outstanding mind is the ability to hold two seemingly opposing ideas at the same time. Consider two aspects of contemporary business: On the one hand, in order to thrive, your organization must be diligent, competitive, and keenly focused on bottom-line results. But at the same time, most of the companies that earn both respect and profits know that nothing is more critical to attaining their goals than a workforce that feels not merely engaged but also valued. Companies that are appropriately attuned to creating a supportive, nurturing work environment stand the best chance for long-term growth. What appear to be opposite ideas — unwavering attention to business results, coupled with an employee-friendly environment — go together like bees and honey. Your skill in linking the two can go a long way toward building a first-rate organization.

Having an employee-friendly workplace doesn't mean that human concerns always take precedence over fundamental business principles. It simply means that there is a balance, and the welfare of employees is routinely taken into consideration when making bottom-line decisions.

Goodbye, 9 to 5: Alternate Work Arrangements

A company's ability to attract and retain employees with the expertise it requires relates increasingly to the human side of the day-to-day working experience — the general atmosphere that prevails in the workplace. This includes, in particular, the extent to which company practices help people balance the pressures they face at work with the pressures they have to deal with at home.

Benefits packages in employee-friendly companies often feature policies to help staff better balance work and personal priorities (see Chapter 12). These policies may include anything from allowances for childcare and eldercare to a sensitivity to simpler, occasional needs. Workers in employee-friendly companies can count on the support of their employers whenever a medical emergency occurs, for example, or, on a happier note, some special event takes place at their children's school. Permission to attend to these matters is granted almost implicitly.

One of the most popular ways to help employees improve their work/life balance in recent decades has been the scheduling concept known as *alternate work arrangements.* Broadly speaking, an alternate work arrangement is any scheduling pattern that deviates from the traditional Monday-through-Friday, 9-to-5 workweek.

Flexibility is the basic idea behind alternate work arrangements. You give employees some measure of control over their work schedules, thereby making it easier for them to manage non-job-related responsibilities. The business rationale behind the concept is that by making it easier for employees to deal with pressures on the home front, they'll be more productive when they're on the job — and less likely to jump ship if one of your competitors offers them a little more money.

However, before jumping into an alternate work arrangement, you must consider its legal impact.

Paying attention to legal implications

With certain groups of employees (hourly employees or unionized workers, in particular), flexible arrangements can easily run counter to existing agreements. You should check, for example, the laws on overtime pay before adopting a compressed schedule for any employee. In states like California, where overtime is calculated on a daily basis rather than on a weekly basis, a ten-hour workday will obligate the company to pay two hours of overtime for that workday. Some states permit compressed workweeks as long as they're created and administered according to strict regulations.

Also, the U.S. Department of Labor, Internal Revenue Service, and other federal or state authorities may challenge your classification of a former employee-turned-contractor, which could result from some phased retirement arrangements. If he returns to function in the same essential role, performing the same job duties, he may be deemed an employee by a government agency — potentially triggering numerous employment and tax consequences, including possible penalties — regardless of your characterization of him as a contractor.

Separately, one condition for employees to qualify as exempt from overtime and other wage and hour mandates is the receipt of a predetermined amount of pay (either per week or on a less frequent basis) that does not change because of variations in the quantity of hours worked. Employees otherwise classified as exempt could lose that status under a job sharing or phased retirement program if their pay drops below the statutory minimum.

Looking at alternate work arrangement options

Alternate work arrangements are generally grouped into the following basic categories:

- **Flextime:** Flextime is any arrangement that gives employees options on structuring their workday or workweek. In the most extreme (and rarest) form, employees decide for themselves not only when they work but also for how long. More typically, though, employees working under flextime arrangements are expected to be on the job during certain core hours of the workday. They're given the opportunity to choose (within certain parameters) their own starting and ending times — as long as they work the required number of hours each day.

  Here's an example: Say that you have a six-person customer service department, and the phones are answered from 9 a.m. to 7 p.m. The peak period — when the most calls come in — is between noon and 3 p.m. You can institute a flextime arrangement that obliges all six customer service representatives to be in the office from noon to 3 p.m. but also gives employees the latitude to work together to set up their own eight-hour days so that the department is never left unstaffed.

- **Compressed workweek:** Under this arrangement, employees work the normal number of hours but complete those hours in fewer than five days. The most common variation of the compressed work week is the so-called 4/10, in which employees work four ten-hour days rather than five eight-hour days.

- **Job sharing:** As the term implies, job sharing means that two part-time employees share the same full-time job. Salary and benefits may be prorated on the basis of what portion of the job each worker shares. Apart from the obvious consideration (both people need to be qualified for the job), a successful job sharing arrangement assumes that the employees can work together harmoniously to make the arrangement work.

✔ **Telecommuting:** Telecommuting is any work arrangement in which employees — on a regular, predetermined basis — spend all or a portion of their workweek working from home or from another noncompany site.

✔ **Permanent part-time arrangements:** The hours in these arrangements usually vary from 20 to 29 hours per week, with employees sometimes allowed to decide which days they work and how long they work on those days. The key attraction of this arrangement is that the employees may be entitled to company benefits, albeit on a prorated basis.

Making alternate arrangements work

In theory, alternate work arrangements offer a win-win situation. Many studies have shown that flexible scheduling policies improve morale and job satisfaction, reduce absenteeism, cut down on turnover and minimize burnout — and with no measurable decline in productivity.

That's the good news. The downside is that these arrangements don't work for every company or for every position. An effective alternate work arrangement is dependent on the company's commitment to support such an arrangement, in addition to the nature of the work and the employee. So, the practices may have to be carefully implemented with some legally sound ground rules. In addition, instituting a policy of alternate work arrangements involves a good deal more than simply giving your employees a broader selection of scheduling options. The process needs to be carefully thought out. It must be implemented with consistency, patience, and discipline because you can easily ruin a good thing. The following sections offer some guidelines if you're thinking of setting up a flexible scheduling policy in your company.

Be willing to rethink processes

Implementing a successful flexible work arrangement policy requires far more work than merely changing when jobs get done. More often than not, alternate work arrangement policies need to be accompanied by changes in how the work actually gets done and, in particular, how people are supervised.

So, when considering new work arrangements, think about this question first: How will the work itself be affected by the new scheduling? All subsequent decisions should be based on the answer to that question.

The ins and outs of telecommuting

Telecommuting is one of the fastest growing alternate work arrangements in corporate America. According to WorldatWork's Telework 2011 report, 26.2 million people worked from home or remotely at least once a month in 2010. That's nearly 20 percent of the working population. Several factors are fueling this trend:

- ✔ Increased demand from employees for this option

- ✔ Pressure on companies in certain parts of the country to alleviate commuter traffic and air pollution

- ✔ The growing availability of technology-based solutions — broadband and Wi-Fi access from remote locations, smartphones, videoconferencing, and, of course, access to information provided by the Internet — which has created the phenomenon generally known as the *virtual office*

Strictly speaking, telecommuters are employees of a company who regularly work out of their homes or other locations all or part of the workweek. The key word in the previous definition is *regularly*. The structured aspect of the arrangement is what differentiates telecommuters as a group from those employees who routinely take work home from the office.

Telecommuting arrangements vary. In some cases, employees never come into the office except for special events. More typically, though, a company's telecommuters spend part of the week — one or two days, usually — working out of their homes and the rest of the week in the office.

Establish guidelines

Flexible work arrangement policies don't have to be set in stone. At the very least, though, you need a set of guidelines that serve as the basis of the program. Some specifics:

- ✔ **Make sure that the flexible work arrangement policies your company develops are logically keyed to the nature and demands of your business.**

- ✔ **Be consistent.** Decisions regarding flexible scheduling should be based on the nature of the job as opposed to the needs of the individual. You can certainly be lenient and take into account the special needs of employees, but you can sabotage a formalized flexible work arrangement policy by making too many exceptions.

- ✔ **Make sure that managers and supervisors have some say in policy development.** Bear in mind that supervisors are always affected by the scheduling patterns of the people they manage.

✔ **Have clear employee eligibility guidelines in place, such as demonstrated work experience with little or no supervision, positive performance record, and tenure or experience in a job.** It's difficult to manage an employee remotely or working a flexible schedule who is not meeting performance expectations or needs constant supervision. Most new employees or those newer in their role need on-the-job training or mentoring to be able to fully perform. If they're working from home, it may be too difficult to learn from others.

Considering phased retirement options

One option that's become quite popular in recent years is the notion of a *phased retirement*, or allowing tenured employees to gradually ease their way out of the organization by reducing the number of hours they spend on the job. This plan has many positives. Phased retirement gives your company the ability to retain the valuable institutional knowledge of long-standing employees that would otherwise walk out the door with them. It also provides a better means of transitioning job responsibilities.

In many cases, phased retirement simply means lowering an employee's workload and training his replacement. But another approach is for the employee to technically retire and then continue to work for your firm on a contract or consulting basis. Given the numbers of the Baby Boomer generation expected to leave the workforce in coming years, a phased retirement option can be extremely productive for both employer and employee.

As I note earlier in this section, alternative arrangements can present new legal issues. Check with your legal counsel or state labor department to see whether flexible scheduling violates state or local laws and, in particular, how certain arrangements may affect overtime obligations. Also, employees who work at home for the majority of each workweek may need to receive notices and posters otherwise available only at the employer's offices.

Getting managerial buy-in

Regardless of how thrilled your employees may be with a flexible work arrangement, the policy itself will face rough sledding if it doesn't have the enthusiastic support and involvement of both senior management and line supervisors.

Popular Perks

A workplace that's designed to keep employees happy and productive helps pay for itself in many ways, such as greater retention and a sense that the company genuinely values the people it employs. Some larger companies go as far as creating in-house gyms complete with rock-climbing areas! Although the snazziest perks may be beyond the reach of many small and mid-size businesses, following are examples that a number of companies offer.

On-site exercise facilities

A healthy workforce is more energetic and productive. Healthy employees also have less downtime due to illness. Many companies promote employees' health and well-being by providing on-site exercise facilities. These can include weights, a variety of exercise machines, and locker rooms and showers. An unused portion of the company's building can make an ideal site for an in-house workout space. If that's not an option, many companies offer complimentary or subsidized memberships at nearby gyms.

On-site childcare

As I discuss in Chapter 12, some companies provide on-site childcare. Not only can this prove exceedingly convenient for working parents, but parents also have the opportunity to visit with their children, an option that's often impossible with other daycare arrangements. That can do wonders for employee morale. The downside is that childcare can be expensive, particularly with regard to liability insurance. Meeting any pertinent state and local childcare regulations also can be costly.

Tuition assistance or reimbursement

Most employees want to feel they're moving forward with both their lives and careers. A tuition assistance or reimbursement program can help make that happen. Here, you pay for part or all of your employees' tuition, covering anything from college and university classes to more specialized training and seminars. The employee feels valued, while you, in return, have a professional with a growing array of knowledge and skills.

Employee sabbaticals

Sabbaticals were once limited to scholars and college professors, but some companies now offer them to their employees. Encompassing both paid and unpaid forms of leave that can last several months, sabbaticals often are offered to employees who have been with a company for a number of years. Generally, employees on sabbatical can do pretty much what they want, including traveling, learning a new language, or reconnecting with family and friends.

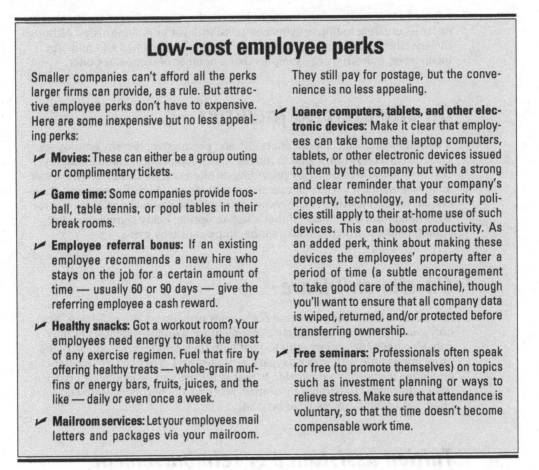

Low-cost employee perks

Smaller companies can't afford all the perks larger firms can provide, as a rule. But attractive employee perks don't have to expensive. Here are some inexpensive but no less appealing perks:

- **Movies:** These can either be a group outing or complimentary tickets.

- **Game time:** Some companies provide foosball, table tennis, or pool tables in their break rooms.

- **Employee referral bonus:** If an existing employee recommends a new hire who stays on the job for a certain amount of time — usually 60 or 90 days — give the referring employee a cash reward.

- **Healthy snacks:** Got a workout room? Your employees need energy to make the most of any exercise regimen. Fuel that fire by offering healthy treats — whole-grain muffins or energy bars, fruits, juices, and the like — daily or even once a week.

- **Mailroom services:** Let your employees mail letters and packages via your mailroom.

They still pay for postage, but the convenience is no less appealing.

- **Loaner computers, tablets, and other electronic devices:** Make it clear that employees can take home the laptop computers, tablets, or other electronic devices issued to them by the company but with a strong and clear reminder that your company's property, technology, and security policies still apply to their at-home use of such devices. This can boost productivity. As an added perk, think about making these devices the employees' property after a period of time (a subtle encouragement to take good care of the machine), though you'll want to ensure that all company data is wiped, returned, and/or protected before transferring ownership.

- **Free seminars:** Professionals often speak for free (to promote themselves) on topics such as investment planning or ways to relieve stress. Make sure that attendance is voluntary, so that the time doesn't become compensable work time.

On the plus side, a study in the *Journal of Applied Psychology* found that people who take sabbaticals not only experience a decline in stress during their sabbaticals but also have less overall stress after returning to work. On the other hand, you'll likely have to rearrange staffing or work responsibilities to pick up the slack for the absent employee. Of course, this could allow you to provide development opportunities to those employees who fill in for the person on sabbatical.

Note that some states severely restrict an employer's flexibility to offer sabbaticals by controlling their frequency, duration, and permissible uses.

Be careful to ensure that any perks you offer are deservedly distributed and don't violate any laws. When granting time off, for example, consult with an experienced lawyer about any impact on exempt employees of a partial-day absence; deducting an amount of salary because of a partial-day absence may compromise the employee's status as exempt from overtime laws and other wage protections. In addition, some employees may not see this as a perk.

Some state laws mandate that employees be afforded a certain amount of time away to attend their children's school-related activities. Finally, as I note earlier, some bonuses — including referral bonuses — may be required (by the U.S. Department of Labor) to be included in the wages used to calculate overtime.

Corporate Citizenship

Another aspect of your company's presence that can motivate some employees is knowing that the company they work for is a force for good. Put another way, many people want to work for businesses that are seen as good corporate citizens by the communities in which their employees live and work.

Businesses can act as good corporate citizens in many ways. Here are some examples:

- ✔ Putting ethics first in all interactions with customers and employees
- ✔ Providing safe, reliable products
- ✔ Demonstrating a commitment to fairness and diversity
- ✔ Supporting community causes financially, with employee volunteers or both
- ✔ Demonstrating environmental stewardship
- ✔ Being what employees consider an overall great place to work

Looking at a few of these a bit more closely, a good corporate citizen maintains an equitable, inclusive workplace made up of people of diverse backgrounds and interests. It provides its employees with salary and benefits that are administered fairly. A solid corporate citizen is also ethical in all its interactions with clients, customers, suppliers, and others.

A good corporate citizen also is keenly aware of the environment. That can translate to using energy-efficient equipment whenever possible, designing or refurbishing facilities along "green" environmental guidelines, and taking other steps to limit a company's carbon footprint.

Additionally, a good corporate citizen urges its employees to do their part by volunteering in their communities. Many companies go beyond mere encouragement by providing paid time off to allow employees to help causes or charities they deem worthwhile. Some companies even institute a "volunteer day," when staff from throughout the organization attend a philanthropic event as a group.

Volunteerism can be particularly meaningful for Millennial workers. According to the 2011 Deloitte Volunteer IMPACT Survey, Millennials who frequently participate in workplace volunteer activities are more likely to view their corporate culture as positive, be proud to work for the firm, and feel very loyal to it. They're also more likely to recommend their company to a friend.

Companies that are solid corporate citizens may enjoy greater employee productivity, higher morale, and longer employee retention. These companies are convinced that being a positive force in their local communities helps them attract the best employees, build closer relationships with customers, and build and reinforce a good reputation. That can make your business that much easier and more profitable to operate.

Team Opportunities

Not only is the use of employee teams a key approach to satisfying company goals, but it's also an element of a positive work environment for many employees. True, some people thrive working alone, but jobs where that's possible are fewer and farther between these days. *Collaboration* is the watchword of today's workforce. Even assembly lines are affected, as more employees are trained to address line breakdowns and more jobs become interdependent. Many people enjoy the intellectual stimulation and the chance to build their problem-solving skills that working on a team offers. Working in teams, for most people, makes a job more interesting.

Companies have long embraced team-building exercises as a way to promote collaboration — and at the same time bring a little fun into the workplace. Even activities that aren't purely for team building, such as group training, can have the added benefit of helping a team build camaraderie.

Employee Surveys: Keeping Tabs on Company Morale

In many cases, particularly if your company has fewer than 50 employees, you don't have a hard time getting a good read on the general atmosphere in the workplace. You're able to personally make your way around offices and work areas enough to observe how employees interact with one another, how they feel about the way they're treated by senior management, and whether morale is rising or falling.

But if your company is larger, periodically conducting a more rigorous employee survey can be exceedingly valuable. Not only can you gain a comprehensive sense of how employees feel about your company, but you also convey the message that you genuinely want their opinions and feedback. That can make employees feel valued and allow you to adjust policies and procedures based on your findings. In the long run, it can lead to greater employee loyalty and retention.

Here are some tips:

- ✔ **Watch your timing.** Don't conduct surveys during holidays, when many employees may be taking days off. Avoid exceptionally heavy workload periods.

- ✔ **Think carefully about your objectives before crafting your survey questions.** What do you want to find out? What do you intend to do with the information?

- ✔ **Share survey objectives with employees, but do so in language that's relevant to them.** In other words, instead of using HR terms such as "We want to assess employee engagement levels," tell them, "We want to hear your thoughts since we merged with Company X."

- ✔ **Before you unveil your survey to the entire company, test it out on a small group of employees to see whether your questions are appropriate and what you can refine.**

- ✔ **Assure employees that their comments are anonymous.**

- ✔ **Communicate to employees the results of the survey in a timely manner and take action, as appropriate, when employees make recommendations.** Let employees know how their input has affected company policy. It can be negatively impactful if you survey your employees, set their expectations that change will occur from their responses, and then take no action.

To get an idea of some of the questions you may want to ask on such a survey, see the Employee Opinion Survey on the CD.

Employee survey information may need to be disclosed during litigation. It's a good idea to consult with an attorney before initiating your own survey or the sample survey on the CD. Also, employers need to be prepared to address serious concerns raised in survey responses such as comments about perceived discrimination or harassment. The anonymous nature of surveys makes it difficult to respond, but inaction may be worse.

Taking the pulse of your workforce

Don't limit your use of employee surveys to those conducted every couple years of so. Pulse surveys also can provide valuable insight into employee attitudes and opinions.

True to its name, a pulse survey is designed to measure the "heartbeat" of a company by examining such issues as job satisfaction, support from management, and opinions regarding pay and benefits. Because pulse surveys can be given semi-annually, quarterly, or monthly, they allow you to keep an eye on any significant trends or developments.

Pulse surveys differ from conventional surveys in a number of ways. In addition to being conducted more frequently, they're often shorter and more focused on one or more particular issues. For instance, a pulse survey may include just five or ten numerically rated questions and one or two open-ended questions. Also, pulse surveys can be administered to one group of employees one time and another group another time. This offers a broad array of perspectives without the risk of burning out employees on too many surveys that are conducted too often.

Pulse surveys are valuable on several levels:

- They can offer an early warning system, bringing up issues that may develop into significant problems if left uncovered until a more comprehensive employee survey is conducted.

- Because they're more focused, pulse surveys also can encourage employees to think carefully about particular issues they may have never given much thought to.

- Conducting pulse surveys lets employees know that you consider these issues important and worthy of their feedback.

- They foster an ongoing sense of communication between you and your employees. You're conveying the message that you value what they think and are eager to regularly solicit their ideas.

Like a conventional survey, it's important that employees understand that pulse surveys are completely anonymous. That makes employees comfortable in being as candid and forthright as possible.

The CD includes a Sample Pulse Survey.

Exit interviews

When you're trying to take the temperature of the organization, some of the most candid employees are often those who are leaving your company. To gain valuable ideas about improving your working conditions and making the workplace more inviting, consider conducting exit interviews with employees who have resigned or are otherwise voluntarily leaving your company. (People you've had to fire — though potentially the most candid of all — are not good subjects for two reasons: They're unlikely to cooperate, and, if they do, their input will probably be overly negative rather than constructive.)

For an Exit Interview Questionnaire, see the CD.

Part IV
Developing Your Employees

The 5th Wave   By Rich Tennant

"A good employee never stops learning new skills."

In this part . . .

Your goal during the hiring process is to attract employees with the strongest functional and interpersonal abilities, but even the best and the brightest need to keep learning. In this part, I cover the ins and outs of employee training and career development. I also give you tips for assessing how your team members are handling their jobs.

Chapter 14

Back to School: Tying Training to Business Goals

In This Chapter

▶ Staying ahead of training demands

▶ Looking at training best practices

▶ Figuring out what kind of training you need

▶ Making sure that your training is tied to your strategic goals

▶ Looking at a variety of training methods

▶ Considering the factors that help a training program succeed

▶ Managing training with employee profiles

▶ Assessing training results

*I*n a perfect world, every employee you hire already would possess the combination of knowledge, skills, and background required to perform every facet of the job flawlessly. However, employees always can discover or nurture something that can help improve their performance. This simple, universally acknowledged principle underlies the HR function generally known as employee training and development.

Beyond retention and recruiting, supporting ongoing learning can help businesses grow, build employee commitment, and develop a more skilled workforce, an evolving need as jobs become more specialized (see Chapter 2). Companies benefit from developing a workforce that is equipped to meet evolving business needs.

Broadly speaking, employee training and development refers to a wide range of educational and learning-based tools. Activities aren't inherently built into job functions but generally produce some positive change in the way employees handle their work. These activities can include live seminars, CDs or podcasts that employees listen to while commuting, and online or DVD instructional sessions they participate in at home or at their desks. In taking on the HR role for your company, your responsibility is not only to determine the best training approaches but also to organize and run these programs in a cost-effective way that's in line with your organization's overall culture, business goals, and budget.

Note: Most HR professionals use the terms *training* and *development* together, but in this book I address them separately. Think of training as tactical and development as strategic. Training refers to activities a company offers employees to help them become more proficient at the tasks that are part of their jobs. Development is helping employees function better interpersonally and preparing them for future roles. I cover training in this chapter and development in Chapter 15.

The Changing Face of Training

The biggest change in training is the degree to which it has become intertwined with other HR functions (hiring, promotions, and so on) and the company's long-term business goals. For example, training departments used to operate as independent entities with their own budgets and objectives. Typically, every year the training department developed a curriculum of courses and seminars that employees enrolled in, either on their own or in conjunction with their managers. Rarely was any real thought given to whether this mix of courses was logically keyed to a company's business goals, nor was much attention paid to what happened to employees after they participated in the training course.

Today, some companies may still use this model of training administration. But those in an HR role responsible for training in a growth-oriented firm are working more closely than ever with senior managers, supervisors, and employees themselves. It's no longer sufficient to measure training success by the number of attendees. You need to make sure that a logical connection exists between the programs being offered and the skill sets necessary to keep their firms competitive. Here are the key factors fueling this shift:

✔ **The "learning" route to competitive advantage:** Profitable organizations recognize that in today's highly competitive and changeable business environment, it's not so much what employees currently know that shapes a company's future; it's what they must *eventually* know that's most important. That's why one major objective of training is to increase each employee's intellectual capacity for acquiring the knowledge and skills needed to thrive amid the increasing demands and pressures of a global marketplace.

✔ **The need to attract and keep talented employees:** The degree to which your company is genuinely committed to developing the skills of your employees is a critical factor in attracting and keeping high-performing employees. The only true job security people have today is largely a function of the skills and knowledge they can bring to an employer.

Workers understand this fact of business life, which is why companies that provide their employees with opportunities to learn and grow are more often seen as employers of choice and, therefore, have an edge when recruiting.

✔ **The competition for skilled labor:** Many companies have discovered the hard way that they can no longer solve performance and productivity problems by simply getting rid of subpar employees and quickly replacing them with others who are better equipped to meet performance standards. Forgetting for the moment the expense and disruption created by excess turnover, what compounds the problem is the reality that specialized workers are at a premium in many industries in both good and difficult economic times. Simply put, the shape-up-or-ship-out approach to managing is no longer feasible in most industries. In response to the realities of the workplace, companies are investing more time and money in training, mentoring, and developing employees.

✔ **The disappearance of hierarchies and the emergence of team play:** As more companies have moved away from the command-and-control approach to supervision, old-school managers have found themselves in workplace environments that require stronger interpersonal skills. That's a talent many of them were never called upon to develop. The ability to communicate effectively and build a spirit of teamwork, for example, is critical in today's workplace. Compare that with years past, when most communication between supervisors and their employees took the form of instructions that had to be followed or behaviors that needed to be corrected.

Creating the Right Environment for Training

It takes more than a curriculum of well-designed, well-delivered courses and workshops to make a training program successful. What's needed most of all is a corporate culture that values and supports continuous learning and development. There's no single formula for creating such an environment. Clearly, though, it's hardly a coincidence that companies frequently singled out for their commitment to employee training are headed by chief executives who are themselves strong advocates of employee education.

Here's a brief look at some of the best practices found in companies known for their outstanding training programs. You may want to use them as a checklist against what is currently going on in your company.

✔ **A mission statement** that incorporates continuous learning as a core value. Beyond this, there also should be a steady flow of communication from senior management that reinforces this commitment.

✔ **A systematic approach** to identifying the skills and knowledge needs of managers and employees that is explicitly connected to business objectives and goals.

✔ **An administrative support system** that makes it easy for employees to gather information about education and training programs, to relate them to their needs, and to arrange the time in their work schedules to take advantage of those offerings.

Principles of first-rate training

Some Fortune 100 companies spend large sums on training, which is largely related to their size. For smaller firms, what's important is to show your employees that you support their ongoing professional development. Here are just a few ways to "walk the walk":

✔ **A progressive tuition-reimbursement policy:** This may be an area where you can stand out from your competitors. Some studies suggest that companies are becoming less inclined to reimburse employees for training. Almost three-quarters of CFOs interviewed in a 2012 Robert Half survey said that they don't provide reimbursement for continuing education units, as compared to 50 percent who said this in a similar study in 2006.

✔ **A scheduling policy that doesn't oblige employees to attend training sessions during nonworking hours:** This policy is attractive not only to your team members, but also to you. Here's why: Nonexempt employees attending training outside their normal work schedule, such as during commute time or at home, may need to be compensated for their time. Depending on the hours worked and applicable laws, this could mean that after-hours training requires overtime pay.

✔ **Communicated learning maps:** Learning maps allow for a common reference for managers and employees when identifying relevant training. Skills are directly aligned to performance evaluation competencies, ensuring that all recommended learning options will enhance the skill in question. Individual employees also have access to this tool to so they can play a more hands-on role in their own development as it pertains to approved training options and activities to advance learning.

✔ **Excellent communication channels between HR professionals involved in training and line managers.**

✔ **Performance appraisal systems that take into account what managers have done to enhance the individual development of the employees they supervise.**

✔ **Ongoing feedback processes and 360 feedback tools (see Chapter 16) for developing training plans to address performance gaps.**

✔ **Access to books, periodicals, research studies, and self-administered courses on-site or through the company's intranet.**

All these efforts communicate to employees the importance that management places on their growth as individuals.

Assessing Your Training Needs

A growing number of consulting companies and individuals specialize in helping clients identify their training needs. If your company is large enough, and you don't have the time or resources to engage in this process yourself, it may well be in your best interest to hire one of these outside sources. If you do decide to manage this process yourself, consider exploring the following needs-assessment options.

Employee focus groups

Generally used in larger firms, employee focus groups often represent the ideal first step in a needs-assessment process. You pull together a group of employees from various departments or levels of your organization. If time permits, you spend a day or two (possibly off-site) discussing as a group what your company needs to do to achieve its strategic goals and what skills are required to meet this challenge.

If this time commitment isn't plausible, even a two- to three-hour session in a conference room at your company's offices can be illuminating.

No matter how much time you're able to take, two key factors ensure that this process is productive:

- ✔ **The makeup of the group:** The group should include representatives from a wide cross-section of departments and experience levels, as well as managers and staff-level employees.

- ✔ **The ability of the facilitator:** The facilitator can be you or someone else, but he needs to promote open discussion and keep the focus group from disintegrating into a gripe session.

Surveys and questionnaires

Surveys and questionnaires are standard tools in the needs-assessment process. Depending on the size of your company, surveys may represent the most cost-effective approach to needs assessment. In a typical needs-assessment questionnaire, employees are given a list of statements or open-ended and close-ended questions that focus on a specific skill. They're invited to indicate whether they think improvements in that area will enhance their ability to perform their jobs or advance in the company.

If you survey employees in this way, gathering feedback from supervisors is also a good idea. Each group may offer a unique perspective. Yet another way of enhancing the utility of questionnaires is to get some survey feedback from customers.

Observation

Simply observing how employees are performing on the job and taking note of the problems they're experiencing can often give you insight into their training needs. Here again, you should be careful about the conclusions you draw. It's tempting when observing employees who are struggling with some aspect of their jobs to attribute the difficulty to a single cause — some problem that you can solve by scheduling a training program or by sending them to a seminar. This assumption is dangerous. If you were to notice, for example, that your customer service reps aren't as courteous to customers as you would like, you may assume that what they need is training in phone skills. Phone training may indeed be called for, but other factors may be involved as well, such as inappropriate pressures from supervisors that are contributing to the negative behavior.

One way to avoid the common pitfall of jumping to conclusions is to speak directly with the employees you've observed and give them the opportunity to explain why their performance may be falling short.

Tying Training Needs to Strategic Goals

Whatever approach (or approaches) you take to evaluate your training requirements, the needs-assessment process should be strategically driven. A needs assessment will

✔ Determine how and if training will make a difference in productivity and the bottom line.

✔ Identify what specifically each employee needs to be trained on, as well as what will improve success and performance.

✔ Help identify the link between organizational issues and training.

After you've gathered the data — regardless of how you've collected it — you need to process it within the framework of the following questions:

✔ What are the strategic goals of this business — both long term and short term?

✔ What competencies do employees need to achieve these goals?

✔ What are the current strengths and weaknesses of the workforce relative to those competencies?

✔ How sound are our succession plans? Can training help promising employees reach a level where they might be able to take the reins from someone who eventually leaves the company?

✔ What improvements can training be expected to offer that differ from day-to-day supervision?

✔ What kind of a commitment — in money, time, and effort — is your company willing and able to make to provide necessary training?

Evaluating Training Methods

Figuring out which programs to offer employees used to be fairly cut and dried. Most corporate training was delivered the old-fashioned way: through instructor-led, classroom training. Today, more than ever, learning is a highly individual process. As a result, you must remain skeptical of taking the one-size-fits-all approach. Classroom training options still abound, but numerous other training delivery methods are available as well. What follows is a brief look at the range of approaches that are possible today, along with the pros and cons.

E-learning

The use of computer-based and online technology to deliver training content has become commonplace throughout corporate America. The concept of learning from sources based far away is, of course, hardly new. Correspondence courses were popular long before computers or the Internet entered the workplace. But the great payoff of e-learning is its flexibility and speed, delivering the real-time immediacy of classroom instruction without the need to actually be present in a classroom.

There's no question about it: E-learning is a big business. According to research firm Ambient Insight, worldwide revenues for self-paced e-learning products and services are expected to grow to $49.9 billion by 2015. If you decide to use an outside firm to help meet your organization's e-learning needs, you'll have to do some research on which company is best for you. Providers such as SkillSoft (www.skillsoft.com) and lynda.com (www.lynda.com), both of which offer learn-at-your-own-pace online training, are well suited to smaller companies. They allow you to simply provide your employees with a subscription to a library of ready-made tutorials so they can learn on their own, at their own pace.

A growing trend in the learning community is *gamification,* a subset of e-learning. Gamification involves the use of game mechanics to make learning activities more engaging. Through these types of activities, employees may earn "badges" for completing tasks or reaching certain milestones, track their progress against others on a leaderboard, or collect virtual currency to exchange for rewards. Numerous vendors are popping up to help companies implement game strategies to teach employees important skills in a fun, interactive way. Gartner, Inc., predicts that by 2014, more than 70 percent of the 2,000 largest global organizations will have at least one "gamified" application.

E-learning has a number of important benefits:

- ✔ It vastly increases the scope and reach of a corporate training effort.
- ✔ It eliminates, or greatly reduces, ancillary, nonlearning expenses of training, such as travel and lodging costs for participants.
- ✔ It enables students to work at their own pace and convenience so they avoid production downtime.
- ✔ It enables participants not only to experience training in real time but also to store and subsequently retrieve information transmitted through the course.
- ✔ It enables students to set up individualized objectives and to establish milestones to mark different levels of achievement.
- ✔ It allows for the use of video at the desktop to illustrate key points visually, which can aid in information retention.
- ✔ It liberates you or your training staff from classroom presentations, enabling more one-on-one consultations.
- ✔ It can be a particularly cost-effective learning tool for small businesses.

The downside of e-learning is the lack of human interaction and direct instructor involvement. These solutions tend to also eliminate the benefit of employees gaining insights from other employees through group discussions.

Here's a look at the ways e-learning is delivered by large, mid-size, and many small companies:

- ✔ **Internet:** By far the primary technology responsible for the growth of e-learning, the Internet is an online training mall, offering a rich and rapidly growing variety of workshops, courses, webinars, videos, blogs, discussion groups, and literature. Its impact increased tremendously when high-speed access became widely available.

  In addition to courses that employees can take at their own pace, some Internet training takes place in real time, where the instructor directs a course via chats and webcasts. Other courses are taught over a period of days, weeks, or months, with students turning in assignments, occasionally communicating in a group format, or intermittently checking in with the instructor. In some situations, these courses are conducted without any face-to-face contact. In others, the instructor employs a webcam, which can be quite useful when, for example, an instructor wants to provide a role-play scenario on a topic such as offering constructive criticism to a subordinate.

✔ **Intranets:** The biggest asset of a company's intranet is security. Businesses find intranets very useful in confidentially sharing information and resources with employees, including training. You often can work with a vendor to customize its courses to your company's specific needs and integrate them into your intranet.

Intranets engage learning and development by allowing for personalization. Users can quickly access knowledge sources that give them immediate answers to their questions and challenges, based on their job function and career and development aspirations.

✔ **Videoconferencing:** Though in many ways the Internet has absorbed videoconferencing as a training device, it still can be useful when you want to gather small teams of employees to receive a particular training. Much of your decision depends, of course, on the size of your company and number of employees. For mid-size to large companies, an orientation event, a critical part of the onboarding process, may be an ideal time for videoconferencing so that an entire group can hear one message and discuss it at the same time.

✔ **Mobile devices:** Using a portable device can be an easy way for an employee who missed a live session, lecture, or module to keep up. For those in travel-intensive jobs, mobile tools may be their only source of training. Smartphones and tablets can allow employees to conveniently access text, audio, or video files wherever they are. Another advantage is just-in-time learning: Many companies provide employees access to mobile instruction manuals, of particular use if a worker is on a customer's premises. Mobile devices also can be used as a gamification platform.

You need to determine which mix of e-learning approaches best matches your real needs. For example, the time and expenditures required to set up an effective system of intranet-based training makes sense only when you have a large population of potential students.

 Don't forget, you have to monitor and manage e-learning in order for it to succeed. If you simply upload a slew of training courses and tell employees to have at it, then you shouldn't expect your training to do much good. The good news is that e-learning is easy to monitor. In fact, one of the benefits of e-learning is that you can track its usage to make sure that employees are engaged and actively participating and completing the required workshops and courses. Quizzes and exams can be incorporated to assess comprehension. Encourage — and maybe even offer incentives — to employees who complete training. Set aside specific times for training so that employees feel comfortable temporarily stopping their day-to-day tasks to complete an online course.

In-house classroom training

With in-house classroom training, the traditional and most familiar form of training, employees gather in a classroom and are led through the program by an instructor. These sessions occur on- or off-site and can be facilitated by trainers who are either employees themselves or outside specialists.

Most companies have moved away from lecture-style sessions. Best practices for classroom training now include

✔ Using simulations and a hands-on approach that offer participants practical experience and practice

✔ Providing individuals with interactive exercises designed to better prepare them for their work when they return from the class

The main advantage to classroom training (apart from its familiarity) is that it provides ample opportunities for group interaction and social learning and gives instructors a chance to motivate the group and address the individual needs of students. Maximize the time in class together by building in as many hands-on exercises as possible. Consider providing background information or requiring prereading before the class meets so everyone is adequately prepared for the session.

In-house classroom training requires considerable administrative support (coordinating schedules, reserving training space, and so on). Also, in most cases, for larger companies with far-flung offices, this form of training can entail major expense (travel and lodging, for example), which isn't directly connected to the learning experience. A method that may circumvent this problem is to use videoconferencing to connect remote learners to the in-house training session. Remember, though, that videoconferencing entails expenses of its own.

Professional association conferences and public seminars

Professional association conferences and seminars can provide a wealth of information on a broad array of topics and professional issues. Often, associations rotate the location of such events from one city to another. That can make it more convenient for certain members to attend, depending on the proximity of the conference or seminar.

Associations are well aware of the issues that are most important to their members, and they tailor programs accordingly. Conferences and seminars also offer opportunities to meet other members to exchange insight and viewpoints.

Like other training options, however, the cost of travel and lodging can be a significant issue. Additionally, because some conferences can be quite large, one-on-one interaction with speakers and other people leading the program can be difficult if not impossible. Plus, topics may be more generic and not relevant to your organization or business goals.

To circumvent the travel expense issue, you may be able to identify local professional associations or user groups offering training that could benefit your employees. These may not be as comprehensive as an annual conference, but an after-work lecture or presentation could still be valuable.

You also can encourage employees to attend topic-specific workshops that are organized and run by training companies. These public seminars usually are held at a public site, such as a hotel or conference center. Companies that stage these seminars typically market them through direct mail or advertising. Recognize, however, that most public seminar offerings are, by necessity, generic. Similar to large industry conferences, the topics covered don't necessarily have direct relevance to your particular company. Another problem: inconsistent quality from one seminar to the next.

Executive education seminars

Seminars and workshops offered by universities and business schools are targeted, in most cases, to middle- and upper-level managers. Typically they cover a wide range of both theoretical ideas and practical pointers for putting these principles into practice.

Instructors are usually faculty members with a high level of expertise. These kinds of seminars are a good opportunity for attendees to network and share ideas.

However, courses at the more prestigious schools can take the executive away from the office for more days than desired. They're also expensive, in some cases as much as several thousands of dollars (including room and board) for a course lasting several days.

Choose these courses wisely. Make sure that events cover management concepts and techniques that are relevant or applicable to your firm's business focus and culture.

Mentoring

Some skills, such as interpersonal abilities, aren't easily taught in the classroom or through online courses. In fact, some skills aren't taught well in groups at all. Enter employee mentors. Just as appointing a more experienced employee to serve as a mentor for a new employee can help her acclimate to your work environment (see Chapter 10), well-chosen mentors can assist staff at any stage of their careers with longer-term developmental learning.

Common pitfalls of ineffective training

Your ability to put together a training program that achieves its desired results is often determined by the common mistakes you avoid. Here's a brief look at the most common pitfalls of training administration — and the consequences of those missteps.

Pitfall: Failing to incorporate business goals into the overall training effort.

Consequence: Because training efforts aren't aligned with business goals from the start, the results rarely have any impact on company operations, and the training initiative doesn't get any further support from senior management.

Pitfall: Not identifying clear, measurable objectives for your training initiatives.

Consequence: The organization devotes significant resources to training initiatives that do not produce a return on investment.

Pitfall: Not taking enough time to go through a systematic needs-assessment process.

Consequence: The offerings have little or no impact on the performance issues that have the most bearing on employee effectiveness and business results.

Pitfall: Inefficient process for evaluating training participants.

Consequence: Courses attract employees who, for any number of reasons, shouldn't be in the course to begin with, and whose presence can be disruptive to employees who badly need the training. An example is an employee who fails to meet the prerequisites for an advanced software course and spends the majority of the course getting up to speed on the basics.

Pitfall: Lack of a disciplined process for evaluating training programs brought in from the outside.

Consequence: Training initiative, in general, loses credibility among key constituents.

Pitfall: Failure to solicit feedback from supervisors during the needs-assessment process.

Consequence: Supervisors never really buy into the training initiative and fail to reinforce what participants learn.

Pitfall: A facilitator who is not engaging.

Consequence: A poor facilitator can reduce the credibility of both the course content and her own value to the organization even though she may be really smart and a very good performer.

Pitfall: Conducting the training in substandard facilities.

Consequence: Discomfort and inconvenience sends the wrong message to employees and inhibits their ability to absorb the training.

Pitfall: Trying to accomplish too much in a limited time frame.

Consequence: Employees who go through training feel more frustrated at the end of the course than they did when they first entered the class.

Pitfall: Lack of *experiential learning* (for example, simulations, hands-on exercises, and role playing).

Consequence: Employees like the ability to actually practice what they're learning during training sessions. Experiential learning ensures that they retain more of what they learn, and its popularity makes it a retention tool as well.

In a mentoring role, an employee who excels in a given area — customer service, for example — can help less-experienced employees discover how to smoothly interact with customers and colleagues or develop additional skills that require more long-term and individualized attention than a classroom or online course can offer. Mentoring also helps people build interpersonal, or people, skills.

Mentors also can serve as valuable training facilitators for high-potential employees you may want to groom to eventually take over key roles in your company. (I touch on this in Chapter 15.) This is no small advantage. As firms brace for significant turnover among their most experienced employees due to the eventual retirement of many Baby Boomers, such arrangements may become increasingly important as a means of passing on valuable expertise to less-experienced workers and preparing them to take on positions of greater responsibility.

In short, the opportunity to have a close confidant is a valuable — and appealing — form of training. I include a broader discussion of mentoring as a career development tool in Chapter 15.

Knowing What Makes for a Good Training Program

In this section, I cover some of the factors that most often influence the effectiveness of a program, regardless of which form it takes.

How receptive the students are

You should consider the extent to which participants are open and receptive to the concepts that are covered in the training.

Do your best to communicate to all potential participants the specific learning objectives of the course and how they'll benefit. Make sure that supervisors who've recommended that certain employees attend the program communicate to employees why that decision was made.

The applicability of the subject matter

The success of any program hinges largely on whether participants believe that what they're being taught has direct relevance to the day-to-day challenges they face in their jobs.

Take all reasonable steps to ensure that the workshop focuses on issues that are the most important to employees who are in the program. If you're using an outside training provider, make sure that the instructor is aware of those issues. Arrange to have examples and exercises customized, making ideas easy to relate to.

The overall learning experience

Consider how interesting or entertaining the training session is, content not-withstanding.

Bear in mind that adults aren't as accustomed as children to the passive nature of traditional classroom learning. Training sessions should be as inter-active and participant oriented as possible. The best courses use a variety of learning tools: lecture, simulation, discussion, and exercises.

Reinforcement of classroom concepts

Devise techniques to reinforce the skills learned in the seminar and apply them to the job or task at hand. Continuous learning is key in this regard. Instead of stand-alone sessions, many organizations create a *training series* where shorter sessions are conducted over a few months' time, during which participants handle projects in between sessions and assignments. This approach is particularly effective for emerging leaders or high-potential talent. Individuals are more likely to retain, apply, and improve if they learn through a series of activities and experiences.

Ask seminar participants to create follow-up plans during or at the end of a session. Alternatively, trainers can create a follow-up plan and send it to participants' managers with a request to integrate certain aspects of training into the job, if feasible. Class participants also can form a community postses-sion, sharing ways they've successfully applied what they learned in training courses in their day-to-day jobs.

Using Employee Profiles to Manage Training

One excellent way to match employees with appropriate training — and keep track of their progress — involves the use of employee profiles. These begin to take life when job seekers submit online candidate profiles (see Chapter 4), which typically include information pertaining to education, professional training, and other sorts of skills. When an applicant is hired, the data is carried over into an employee profile, now maintained by HR.

From there, you can add information to employee profiles as staff members accumulate other credentials and training, such as professional designations, advanced degrees, and participation in in-house education and other programs. Regular review of employee profiles allows managers to take stock of needs that have already been addressed and target other areas where employees may benefit from additional training. Not only does this help ensure that an employee's training is both systematic and thorough, but it also can aid in overall career development, a topic I address in Chapter 15.

The list of an employee's current skills within the employee profile is also very useful when you're evaluating internal candidates for promotion (see Chapter 4).

In addition, consider a learning management system (LMS), which I cover in Chapter 3. An LMS can not only help you manage, track, and deliver training, but also give you analytics on the impact of your training on the business so you can develop a comprehensive learning strategy.

But Is It Working? Measuring Results

As the person in your company responsible for the training effort, you can safely assume that you're going to be called upon at some point to answer a simple question: Is the money and time being invested in the program paying any real dividends?

If you aren't sure how to answer this question, join the club. HR professionals have long wrestled with the problem of quantifying the results of a process that doesn't readily lend itself to quantifiable measures. It's generally acknowledged, for example, that one of the primary benefits of employee training is that it enhances morale. But how do you measure the bottom-line benefits of morale? Not easily, to be sure.

To evaluate the value and effectiveness of a training program, you can use assessment and validation tools to provide you with data for the evaluation. The most common way to gather feedback from participants immediately following a training session is to distribute a questionnaire to each one at the end of the session.

E-mail has made it much easier to measure the effectiveness of training in a timely manner. You can quickly send surveys to large groups of employees. If you want, you can distribute them and ask for responses within a few days or even hours of the session's conclusion, though in many instances you may want your employees to reflect for a short time prior to providing feedback. You also can record survey responses online, with results organized into databases and available to HR team members and line managers.

Employees' answers to the following survey questions can help you gauge the effectiveness of your training sessions:

- ✔ Based on the course description, did the course meet your expectations?
- ✔ Were the topics covered in the course directly relevant to your job?
- ✔ Was the instructor sensitive and responsive to the needs of the group?
- ✔ Were the instructional materials easy to follow and logical?
- ✔ Would you recommend this program to other employees?
- ✔ Were the facilities adequate?

The feedback you receive is useful but limited. Post-training surveys measure initial reactions and offer little insight into the long-term value of the training. Because of this, it's important to observe the accomplishments or behavior of employees in the weeks and months after training, or to follow up with the individuals' supervisors for their assessment. Do those who had leadership training, for example, report lower attrition rates for their staff? Have employees who enrolled in a technical skills course shown noticeable improvement in their mastery of a certain software program? Do more trainees win promotions than the average employee base? Drawing a direct correlation between training and job performance isn't always possible, but this type of hard data can be invaluable when making the argument for additional training resources.

Chapter 15

Win-Win: Adding Value through Career Development

In This Chapter

▶ Grasping the importance of career development

▶ Using mentors to foster employee growth

▶ Helping your people to become leaders

▶ Boosting your organization's bench strength through succession planning

▶ Developing employee recognition programs

One of the chief responsibilities of your role as a HR generalist is finding and recruiting the best people. But, after they're onboard, it's every bit as important to help your staff keep growing professionally.

Companies that view career development as something employees should do on their own are missing valuable retention opportunities. Your team members — particularly your top performers — should be able to visualize their potential to advance and take on increasing responsibility within your organization. Employees clearly value this guidance from their organizations. In a 2012 Robert Half survey, 54 percent of workers interviewed said that knowing their career path is very important to their overall job satisfaction; another 31 percent said that they feel this feedback is at least somewhat important. The message isn't easy to miss: Employees want to know how to get to that next rung on the career ladder. You can help them by creating career development programs that show them how they can translate their professional interests, preferences, and strengths into long-term careers with your firm.

Note: Most HR professionals use the terms *training* and *development* together, but in this book I address them separately. Think of training as tactical and development as strategic. Training refers to activities a company offers employees to help them become more proficient at the tasks that are part of their jobs. Development is helping employees function better interpersonally and preparing them for future roles. I cover development in this chapter and training in Chapter 14.

Understanding Why Career Development Matters

Career development is a win-win for employee *and* employer. Employees acquire know-how that will benefit their careers both immediately and in the future. In the eyes of workers, this is no small advantage. In a Robert Half survey, employees were asked, "Aside from salary, which one of the following aspects of your job is most tied to your satisfaction?" "Work/life balance" and "opportunities to learn and grow" were in a virtual tie at the top.

Your support of employees' development shows them they're working for an organization that cares about their growth every bit as much as they do. That can do wonders for retention rates. A business case can also be made for investing in these processes. From the company's standpoint, career development enhances your staff's ability to contribute more fully, which in turn boosts your *bench strength* (the number and readiness of employees to fill vacant leadership and professional positions) and, ultimately, your competitiveness in the marketplace.

Although you may not be able to make promises to individuals about what the future will hold for them at your business, you and the company's line managers can work with employees to develop career maps that detail the steps required to achieve specific goals. An individual development plan (IDP) can be a useful tool in this process. An IDP is a document that outlines the employee's professional goals, as well as the steps the person must take to reach them. It allows you to consistently review, update, and discuss an employee's developmental goals. When someone is ready for the next level but no position is available, an IDP can be used to identify growth opportunities within the existing position so the worker remains challenged and motivated.

If an employee is planning to make a career change and wants to develop a skill set for this new role, make sure that her plans are in alignment with the goals of the business before the time and effort is invested.

The CD includes a sample Individual Development Plan Form for your reference.

One of the best ways to nurture career development is what I cover next — connecting staff with mentors.

Seeing Mentoring As a Tool for Growth

Elsewhere in this book, I discuss the value of mentoring in specific situations. For instance, in Chapter 10, I examine how it can help new employees acclimate and become comfortable with your work environment. Additionally, in Chapter 14, I look at mentoring in the context of a training tool to help employees develop skills and know-how that benefit your business. But perhaps the most valuable (and certainly the most broad) application of mentoring is its use in fostering overall career development for your staff. That differs from its other benefits in that it takes something of a longer view — an eye toward career development that can last a professional lifetime. That means using mentoring to build attributes that are effective today as well as farther down the road.

Why and how mentoring works

As I point out in Chapter 14, some abilities, such as people skills, are not easily taught in the classroom or through online courses. Still, these abilities are pivotal to your staff's ability to interact with customers and with each other in the office. Mentoring opportunities are ideally suited to this kind of skills and knowledge transfer.

One reason mentoring arrangements work is that topics discussed between mentor and mentee are typically kept confidential. If an employee is having difficulty working with some of her team members, for example, she can comfortably discuss these dynamics with her mentor in a way that's not possible in a structured setting or with an immediate supervisor.

Mentors must be trained to bring to HR's attention any mentee concerns that could amount to unlawful harassment or discrimination, or any other possible violation of company policy.

Mentors can prove to be especially valuable resources as their partners continue along their career development paths. For instance, a mentor can recommend ongoing learning and training programs that can best serve a mentee's career goals. If a company position opens up that represents a form of career advancement, mentors can suggest effective strategies to pursue that opportunity — or why it may not be a suitable fit.

Here are some more ways mentors can assist in your company's career development efforts:

- ✒ **Helping to identify an employee's long-term career goals:** Many people — those in the early stages of their work life in particular — often fail to take the time to consider how they want their careers to progress over time, and, for that matter, what that progress actually entails. A mentor can kick-start for an employee the process of beginning to think long term, not merely where he wants to be next year.

- ✒ **Acting as a dedicated role model:** Instead of an employee having to reinvent the career wheel, a mentor can serve as a living, breathing example. The mentee can emulate the behaviors and attributes of someone who's already taken a similar (and successful) career development path.

✔ **Unlocking the power of networking:** Career development doesn't exist in a vacuum. Mentors can introduce their protégés to others who can prove to be invaluable points of contact and perhaps become additional role models.

Think of it this way: Online courses give employees the black and white; mentors give them the shades of gray in between.

Much like career development, which it supports, mentoring is a win-win activity. The relationship benefits not just the mentee and the company but also the mentor. In addition to bolstering their supervisory competency and leadership abilities, mentors gain the inner satisfaction of knowing that they're facilitating someone's career growth and assisting the company in cultivating a future leader. Helping employees work and interact more effectively also brings some concrete, practical career benefits to mentors. Serving in this role adds value to the organization and increases the mentor's visibility and potential for advancement.

Setting parameters

Developing and implementing a mentoring program takes more than the best of intentions. First, pinpoint your specific goals and make sure that they align with the organization's goals and will benefit the employee in his current role. For example, you may want to increase staff retention rates, nurture employees who can help you introduce new product lines, or just make the onboarding process for new hires as stress free as possible.

With those objectives in mind, consider what sort of mentoring arrangement may be most helpful. Do you want formal relationships — with partners in regularly scheduled contact — or do you want to operate more on an as-needed basis? Do you want to pair mentors with protégés in the same department or mix things up a bit? Also consider how the mentee's manager will remain involved. There should be some type of communication process that helps all three parties (mentor, mentee, and mentee's manager) stay engaged. The manager needs to understand how she can help mentees in their day-to-day work.

Looking at the mentoring program as a whole, you need to decide who's going to have authority over it. Also, consider your budget and how you'll measure the success of the overall effort. Addressing such issues as these at the outset will better your results and keep thorny problems from cropping up along the way.

Choosing the right partners

The key to an effective mentoring program is to choose mentors who are temperamentally suited to the task. They don't necessarily need to be your most senior managers. Mentors should, however, be naturally empathetic and enjoy the role of helping, listening, and sharing information with others.

Among other attributes, ideal mentors should have

- Excellent communication and leadership skills
- Enthusiasm for working together as a team
- Patience and understanding, particularly with less-experienced protégés
- Solid connections within the organization
- A sense of how much involvement with a protégé is appropriate and what crosses the line to micromanaging
- A solid understanding of company policies and practices

Not coincidentally, these are some of the same traits I discuss later in this chapter as identifiers of promising leadership candidates.

Here are some other suggestions on how to identify people in the company — or, in certain instances, even outside the organization — best suited to fill a mentoring role:

- **Get recommendations.** Ask managers to recommend members of their staff who have the personality to act as effective mentors. Make sure that whoever they recommend has the time to devote to the task.
- **Choose good role models.** Select as mentors those whose attitudes you'd ideally want the new employee to emulate — flexible, agile, open minded, enthusiastic.
- **Talk to managers who have expressed that they're nearing retirement.** Sometimes people nearing retirement look for someone to mentor. This isn't always the case, of course, but it may be worth checking out.
- **Find common ground.** As you narrow down relationships to specific individuals, look for things (same schools, similar hobbies, past experience in certain industries) that can create a rapport between mentor and employee.

It's best if a mentor is not the mentee's direct supervisor. The mentee should feel comfortable asking questions of, discussing challenges with, and soliciting advice from a neutral party who has no control over his career advancement.

Mentors and coaches: What's the difference?

People sometimes (understandably) confuse mentoring and coaching. The rise of career coaches for higher-level managers has undoubtedly led to the issue coming up in the first place. Mentors, whether in a formal or informal capacity, focus on career growth and provide advice regarding professional development. A coaching program, by contrast, is more performance oriented and focuses on helping staff perform their jobs more efficiently and competently through specific skill improvement. In contrast to mentors, coaches don't focus on individual staff members' long-term professional development; instead, they focus on short-term performance improvement. A coach may be a supervisor on staff or an outside expert hired to oversee and guide the day-to-day activities of an employee according to specific, predetermined objectives and measurements.

Moving forward with the program

You should schedule an introductory training session for those who will serve as mentors. Even the most experienced employees will get a better handle on their mentoring responsibilities with some focused direction. For example, some managers may benefit from understanding the distinction between mentoring and managing. They also need to understand what you expect of them and what they can expect from the experience. Emphasize the fine line between being a valuable source of insight and hovering to the point where the employee feels smothered. Training is also helpful in terms of letting mentors know just what will be involved in terms of time commitment.

A meeting between you and each mentoring pair is the next step. Here, everyone can get on the same page regarding goals, expectations, and other elements of the program. Cover what's required of everyone involved and how they can best benefit from the arrangement. Address meeting frequency, goals, and how long the program will last. Solicit questions from participants to be sure that no one is left in the dark on any critical issues.

As the HR contact, it's best if you can conduct these trainings and meetings yourself.

If you check in at the outset to make sure that the mentoring relationship is on track, you'll be able to intervene early if there are any problems. Sometimes there's just a poor match, and people need to be reassigned. In other cases, there may be issues with time commitments or the level of mentoring being provided. If the mentor and newcomer clearly aren't hitting it off, end the relationship diplomatically but quickly. Without prejudging, try to get to the root of the problem.

You Can't Do It All Yourself: Developing Strong Leaders

Leadership development is a natural subset of career development. If you think about it, many employees who are good at attending to their overall career development would naturally like to segue that effort into a leadership capacity. Leaders are different from mentors because they lead entire teams of employees — the work of these teams, as well as their professional development.

Like any other element that's central to your business, you can always opt to rely on good fortune — in this case, that natural leaders will spontaneously spring up from among your employees. A choice, but not a sensible one. It's true that employees can develop leadership abilities entirely on their own initiative. But your business can greatly benefit from your involvement as well — specifically, in creating and developing a comprehensive leadership development program. Like career development itself, identifying and nurturing potential leaders can prove central to your business's success — and its future (as I discuss in "The Future Is Now: Succession Planning," later in this chapter). Many companies that don't use the term *leadership development* still have programs in place to nurture high-potential workers. These firms recognize that identifying employees who are most likely to eventually assume greater responsibility is a key component of developing a pool of strong leaders.

Defining leadership qualities that will move your business forward

Being (or developing) a great leader is not a simple proposition. Every business is unique, so a leader who's effective in one setting may prove utterly ineffective in another.

For instance, if your business is more inclusive by nature, a leader who invites input and consensus would be a very suitable fit. Similarly, a leader in your sales group may have as her top qualities charisma and an eagerness to engage with others.

Focus on developing the leadership qualities your business needs most. When you have a sense of the tailored-to-your-business leadership qualities you'd like to develop, you're well on your way to identifying people with the greatest promise. But there are additional personal characteristics and attributes that any business should look for that are good predictors of real leadership potential. These include

✔ **An interest in, well, leading:** It's so obvious that it doesn't hit some people as a "quality of leadership." But the people you want are those who are passionate about taking on new opportunities and genuinely want to lead others. Here, you're also looking for a person willing to accept additional time commitments and comfortable with taking charge.

✔ **Integrity:** The last thing you want are people who'll lead others into actions that don't reflect a commitment to being honest and forthright. *Remember:* Your leaders will set the tone for others within the organization.

✔ **A knack for motivating others:** The ability to spur others into action is a key sign of someone who can lead effectively.

✔ **Ability to collaborate across groups and build consensus:** A person who can't convince people to work together under his leadership won't ever be much of a leader.

✔ **Excellent communication skills:** As we increasingly become a service economy, it would be nice if all of a firm's employees could be good communicators. But for leaders, it's a must. Great communicators can adapt to their audience, don't waste the other person's time with small talk or a lengthy buildup to their point, are diplomatic with requests, use straightforward language when talking and writing, are good listeners who don't jump to conclusions before another speaker is finished, and are always trying to improve their communication style.

✔ **True adaptability:** Leaders are willing to change as circumstances dictate and are comfortable with feedback — both positive and negative. This includes dealing with ambiguity, a critical skill for good leaders.

✔ **Willingness to admit shortcomings:** Real leaders are not arrogant know-it-alls. They understand where their strengths lie and where they don't (and are comfortable relying on others to fill those gaps in skill and experience).

To help you identify potential candidates, look for outstanding performance reviews that may suggest leadership potential. It also can be helpful to ask others — managers, employees, and even vendors — for insight into what qualities may make for an effective leader in the company.

Starting your program: Factors to consider

To begin building a leadership development plan, consider the following questions:

✔ **Do you have or anticipate any leadership gaps?** Consider what may be (or will be) missing within your organization in terms of leadership attributes and characteristics. In other words, what kind of traits does it take to keep your organization humming? A big factor could be the retirement of Baby Boomers, which may cause a gap between middle-level and senior-level managers because the next group of workers, Generation X, is smaller. This could result in a shortage of leadership talent at your business. Some companies create "leadership tracks" that address different leadership gaps, assigning executive-level sponsors with expertise in each area to help design, socialize, and champion each track. Tracks may include such areas as leading and motivating teams, clarity in communication, or business development.

✔ **How will the program link to organizational goals and strategic objectives?** How will leadership development assist your organization in meeting your goals? For instance, are you looking to grow financially, structurally, or in some other fashion? Sync your leadership development program to those priorities.

✔ **Are you thinking long term?** Be sure to address both short- and long-term goals. Too often, companies think about filling a particular role and overlook longer-term needs. Focus instead on developing a "bench" of talent versus grooming people for specific roles only.

Program options

There's a reason I decided to cover leadership development in the same chapter as mentoring and succession planning: They're all linked. Most leadership development programs include some kind of mentoring, training, and organizational future planning. Individual activities can include coaching, rotational assignments, job shadowing, project leadership, classroom training (such as MBA programs, executive education, and online courses), and other options. External coaches and business school programs can be helpful (especially for larger organizations with commensurate budgets), but most successful companies don't outsource leadership development. And even internally, HR shouldn't run the whole show. Internal programs can be created to combine structural elements built by HR with the active participation of senior managers who are considered leadership role models as coaches and mentors. To offer hands-on experience, allow leadership candidates to head up meetings and direct the office when other leaders are away.

Leaders can come from a variety of sources, including staff-level employees, as well as current leaders who want to move up even farther or improve at the job they're in. Make all employees aware that the opportunity is there if they have the potential and the desire to pursue it.

REMEMBER

Not everyone is suited to be a leader — or has the interest

Be careful to avoid tunnel vision when looking for leadership candidates. There are many superior performers who are great at supervising themselves but who can't manage anyone else. It's natural to think current superstars, such as a top salesperson or marketing whiz, would make terrific leaders. Trouble is, no matter how gifted they may be in one particular area, that doesn't mean they'll be great leaders.

In a similar vein, it's nice when employees have big ambitions, but you have to help them remain realistic. If the top job at a law firm requires a law degree and the employee in question works in the accounting department, it may require a trip to law school to gain the right qualifications. It's not insurmountable, but neither is it something that will happen overnight and without considerable dedication on the part of the aspiring accountant/law firm CEO.

At the same time, many people don't even have a desire to advance and are satisfied in their current jobs: More than three-quarters of employees polled in a Robert Half survey, for example, said they have no interest in having their manager's position. A key to retaining these people is to make sure that they know that moving into a supervisory role is not the only way to advance in your company.

The bottom line: Keep your perspective broad, look beyond the most obvious suspects and set realistic expectations for leadership prospects.

Measuring progress and success

Of course, you'll want to know whether your leadership development efforts are paying off. Here are some questions to help with that critical measurement:

- ✔ **Do participants feel they're progressing?** Ask people in the leadership program if they're enjoying the process. Do they feel they're learning and growing? How are they putting what they've learned into practice?

- ✔ **Are their leadership activities and responsibilities increasing?** If so, how are they handling them? Do the people or departments they're managing have higher levels of productivity, customer satisfaction, and so on?

- ✔ **What do others say?** Solicit feedback from employees who have worked with those in leadership programs. Do they feel the candidates are developing into effective leaders? If so, in what fashion? Taking employee comments in aggregate, try to measure leaders' success in terms of retention and employee engagement within their respective teams.

- ✔ **Are your development efforts positively affecting overall business goals?** For instance, if one objective is to open additional branches, have beneficiaries of your leadership development efforts contributed to designing, implementing, or staffing new locations that are up and running?

✔ **Is there a ripple effect?** A strong leader will also develop other leaders. Are individuals in your program reaching out to develop further talent?

✔ **Are you doing enough to keep the leaders you're grooming?** Don't forget to develop and update incentives to keep candidates with the greatest leadership promise onboard. The last thing you want to happen is to invest time and resources in a promising individual, only to have that person jump ship because a more attractive opportunity surfaces elsewhere. Make sure that compensation and opportunity are sufficient to ward off advances from rival businesses. Consider creating a mentoring group to bring developing peers together from time to time so they can share experiences and progress toward their goals.

The Future Is Now: Succession Planning

In a way, succession planning is the culmination of career and leadership development. It's where you identify — from among your developing leaders — individuals who have the most potential and whose movement toward key positions, either laterally or upwardly, you want to accelerate.

Succession planning is not just for big companies. A mistake some smaller organizations make is feeling that they aren't big enough to need to boost their bench strength. Many vacancies can be anticipated and planned for, but not all talent gaps can be foreseen. No matter what your size, you can't run a business without good people ready to fill potential gaps if they occur.

If you're not currently thinking about who will fill your shoes (or the shoes of any of your senior managers), then you're leaving a critical HR responsibility unattended. No one has an infallible crystal ball, but your organization should ponder contingencies if a key role in the organization were to be vacated.

For an entire book on succession planning, check out *Business Succession Planning For Dummies,* by Arnold Dahlke (Wiley).

Don't put it off!

When is the best time to begin succession planning? Yesterday.

Unfortunately, many companies don't see the urgency. They still view succession planning as a task they'll undertake when a clear need presents itself. A Robert Half survey bore this out. Eighty-three percent of financial executives interviewed said that they had not identified a successor for their position. Of these individuals, 81 percent said their primary reason for not identifying a successor was that they had no plans to leave their present companies in the near future.

What they're missing is that having a succession plan in place can head off confusion and uncertainty, particularly if the timing of succession is abrupt, such as a sudden resignation or death. Just as important, succession planning imbues confidence throughout a business. It provides a sense that, no matter what may occur, plans are in place to keep the company moving forward and operations going. Speak to senior managers about the importance of having a plan in place for key positions in all areas of your company — whether people are planning to leave or not.

Putting together the plan

Businesses manage succession in different ways based on their individual cultures. Plans cover a wide range in terms of complexity and degree of formality. But most agree that the primary goal is to create a pipeline of talent by offering top performers extra support along their developmental paths.

Smaller businesses can learn a lot from the formal policies put in place at large companies, where establishing a management succession plan is a recommended practice. Some corporations have a centralized succession planning function, whereas others empower people or teams throughout the organization to manage the function on their own.

Begin your succession plan by identifying jobs whose role in the overall function of the business are too important to remain in limbo while a search is on for a replacement of some sort. Choices should be driven with an eye on your near-, mid-, and long-term business strategies. President, chief executive officer, chief financial officer, chief operating officer, and other similar positions are the likeliest candidates. In the largest companies, the board of directors plays a key role in selecting C-level succession candidates, especially for a CEO transition. (The *C* in *C-level* refers to "chief," as in *chief executive officer, chief financial officer,* and *chief information officer* — in other words, top-ranking executives within an organization.)

But it's not all about these C-level executives. Succession in all business-critical roles should be included in your planning. For instance, if your company leans heavily on technology (and, these days, most businesses do), you may want to add the chief information officer or other IT executive to the list. If you market your products around the world, the chief marketing officer may be another. And don't limit the field to managers only, but apply your business-critical eye to all levels in the organization. For instance, an accounting firm may need to plan just as diligently for replacing a tax specialist with in-demand expertise as it does someone in a management position. When compiling your list, talk to others throughout the company to solicit their feedback and ideas. They may suggest a job you inadvertently overlooked — a potentially costly oversight.

Pinpointing succession candidates

After you've selected key positions in which you want to ensure continuity, it's time to select the individuals from your leadership development efforts who can best fill these roles. This step involves holding discussions with protégées to explain that they're being singled out for positions of increasing importance (see "Creating a flexible understanding with succession candidates," later in this chapter), gauging their interest, and getting their buy-in.

When selecting succession candidates, take into account not only skills but also how well individuals work with others throughout the company, particularly when they've transitioned into a position of some authority.

Three of the most common missteps in succession planning are understandable byproducts of human nature:

- **Selecting a successor who is a mirror image of his predecessor:** Of course, there's a line of reasoning that suggests that, because the outgoing person was successful in his job, it only makes sense that a similar individual will carry on that history of achievement. It may seem reasonable, but the constancy of change dictates that what made one person successful in a job doesn't necessarily carry over to someone else. Instead, look at the position as it exists today. From there, match the requirements and challenges to the best-qualified candidate.

- **Choosing a successor because her predecessor likes him:** Of course, it's never entirely misdirected to select someone with whom you and others get along, but likeability shouldn't be the sole factor in a succession decision. Qualifications and potential are the most important attributes to consider. Again, match job function to the person best suited to that role. Allow the reality of the job requirements to direct the decision and put feelings and friendships aside.

- **Identifying only one successor:** Avoid "anointing" someone for a role. Consider multiple candidates.

Companies sometimes discover that high-potential employees aren't eager to assume senior management roles. This is understandable, as many aspects of management involve making difficult, sometimes unpopular decisions that not everyone is comfortable with. There may also be concerns about work/life balance, travel, office politics, and general stress associated with moving up the ladder. Even top performers may not see themselves as potential leaders. By addressing possible barriers, you may be able to encourage reluctant candidates to step forward.

Selecting candidates outside the company

It may seem strange at first to consider succession candidates external to the business. Often, timing is what makes the difference. If you think you have enough time, you may be able to develop an existing employee's skills. But if your time horizon is shorter, you may need to look for an external candidate who is already somewhat prepared for the role. Still, keep in mind that there's no guarantee that person will be able to hit the ground running, and he may not be an immediate solution. He doesn't already know your business and may need time to mesh with the team and become acquainted with your operations.

With your existing staff, there are potential morale and retention issues to address if you bring someone onboard from the outside. What will existing employees' reactions be to being passed over for a promotion? The more open line managers are with their teams in performance and development discussions, the easier staff can accept being passed over at that particular time. If an employee is somehow convinced she's in line for the next step, finding out that this isn't true could come as a hard blow. Make sure that existing employees have strong development plans to prepare them for the next opportunity, whether it arrives now or sometime in the future. You also want to make sure that you thoroughly vet the incoming outside leadership candidate. You could encounter morale issues if the identified person is less of a standout than you had assumed, or if he doesn't exhibit leadership qualities immediately when he comes onboard.

Creating a flexible understanding with succession candidates

Companies handle their interaction with succession candidates in different ways. Some hire and promote people with the message that they're being groomed either for a specific position or for a more senior but unspecified leadership role; other companies hire and promote less specifically for succession and place candidates into a *high-potential pool* (a designated group of people who are being groomed generally for higher leadership or critical executive roles).

Exactly who succession candidates are supposed to eventually replace or what positions they're preparing for may not be known to them — the choice to share this information is yours. If you do decide to reveal this, make sure that you establish an understanding that there are no guarantees, and the situation can change due to circumstances encountered by either the company or the succession candidates themselves. In addition, note that after succession takes place, either party may decide the fit is not right and reserves the right to back out. This arrangement also reduces the likelihood that the "heir apparent" will become frustrated if the person he's supposed to replace doesn't leave or retire when expected.

An approach many companies prefer today is to place emphasis not on individual positions, but on developing high potentials and letting them know that the longer they stay with the company, the more likely they are to be promoted when someone leaves. The company benefits as it maintains greater flexibility than if the preparation and investments made in individuals were designed specifically to back up a particular role or, worse, a particular person. The high-potential person benefits because he doesn't have to wait for just one or a finite group of people to leave. And the person who needs the backup isn't threatened that someone will be ready to succeed her before she's ready to leave.

The bottom line: Because they may eventually find that initial assumptions were too aggressive or unrealistic, many companies are reluctant to be specific with high potentials about any more than a general course of development.

Developing succession candidates

In addition to your general leadership development efforts, you should take the follow steps with succession candidates:

- ✔ **Expose them to other parts of the company.** For instance, an IT person who spends a month or two learning the ropes from a finance manager will come to understand and appreciate the importance of reducing costs and improving the efficiency of processes, many of which fall under IT's purview. That broadened perspective makes for a better leader.

- ✔ **Offer other training and development.** Although you want to offer every employee appropriate training and development opportunities, this is even more critical for succession candidates so they can achieve their full potential. It can include varied work experience, job rotation, specific projects, and other challenging assignments. You should monitor progress carefully by evaluating how succession candidates perform in those activities. That way, you know that they'll be ready when the time comes to move up. International experience or knowledge is among the most difficult to impart. In these cases, an expatriate assignment, wherever practical, may give the best view to nondomestic operations.

✔ **Consider the next person in line.** Succession planning means drawing up plans for more than just the next person up to bat. What if he strikes out? Be clear on success criteria for the future position, and keep things moving by continuing to train others farther down the pipeline. If some people seem discouraged that they weren't selected as heir apparent, encourage them with reminders that they're still in line for upcoming leadership opportunities. Point out that leadership openings often come out of the blue, so they need to be ready.

✔ **Make it as much of a nonevent as possible.** Succession shouldn't be viewed as a coup d'état or power grab. When planned well, succession occurs smoothly and systematically. To an outside observer, in fact, it will appear seamless. That is the goal of succession planning — to ensure that the business moves forward without missing a beat, despite a change at the top.

✔ **Utilize the IDP process.** Individual development plans (see "Understanding Why Career Development Matters," earlier in this chapter) can be particularly useful in succession programs because they're customized to the individual, allowing you to work with the candidate to set specific goals and the steps needed to reach them.

✔ **Consider succession planning technology.** As with most things in business today, "there's an app for that." Succession planning software applications can automate many of the tasks involved in creating a succession plan. In a nutshell, these programs allow you to readily identify upcoming succession requirements and develop necessary training and programs to address those needs. (For a full discussion of HR technology systems, refer to Chapter 3.)

Assessing succession outcomes

A succession plan is important, but it's not enough. That's because a plan doesn't develop people. They need experience, advice, mentorship, and feedback from you.

Your reviews, check-ins, and performance metrics are essential to tracking progress and keeping everyone accountable. Here are a number of barometers that can prove helpful in determining what works and what may warrant reconsideration in your succession planning efforts:

✔ **Are your new leaders successful?** Are succession candidates who have been newly installed as leaders meeting objectives and goals in their new jobs? Besides asking for a self-evaluation from the new leader himself, also talk to the people he works with to gauge their confidence level in his direction. Again, if you identify gaps or problems in the performance in new leadership, revisit your succession process to pinpoint the source of the shortfall. Was he ill prepared for the role, or did you over-estimate his leadership potential?

✔ **What do participants themselves think?** Consider making succession participants part of your evaluation process. What worked well for them? What was most impactful? What was least useful?

✔ **Are new leaders staying on?** As I discuss earlier in this chapter, it's just as important to retain talented new leadership as it is to develop it. Track leadership retention rates. If your best people are leaving for other companies, determine whether your compensation package is adequate by benchmarking against similar companies in similar indus-tries and markets. Also, consider if the responsibilities of the new posi-tion are sufficient to engage highly talented leaders. Boredom or a lack of opportunity will send your best and brightest out the door.

✔ **Is the flow of candidates consistent?** Succession planning should be an ongoing process. Are your efforts providing the business with a reli-able supply of candidates, or are there occasional gaps that could pose a problem if an important position suddenly became available? Review your program to see if you can make it more consistent across the board.

✔ **Make evaluation a habit.** Just as succession planning shouldn't be an every-so-often consideration, so, too, should your evaluation be an ongoing responsibility. Not only does that allow you to maintain close touch with the results of your program, but it also lets you identify issues that may be impeding overall success. That gives you the oppor-tunity to change and tweak elements of the program before they grow into more significant problems.

Even if replacing a top job seems too far down the road to be important today, don't neglect succession planning. Life happens — and you need to expect the unexpected.

Saying Thank-You: Focusing on Employee Recognition

One key to career development is keeping people motivated. It's not always easy for busy prospective leaders to take time out to acquire new skills as part of a formal professional development plan. They need to be recognized for their hard work at their "regular" jobs, as well as efforts they're making down the career development path. One reinforces the other.

Employee recognition includes a varied group of offerings and incentives that, taken as a whole, are designed to celebrate all sorts of employee achievements. In some ways, you might see them as feel-good measures, but the benefits of recognition go beyond simply inspiring good will. Letting employees know that you value their contributions also increases productivity and innovative thinking.

But recognition can't be a rare event. It has to be a positive feedback loop woven into each and every day.

Employee recognition programs defined

An employee recognition program is an acknowledgment — either formal or informal — of an employee's or team's behavior, effort, or business result that supports the organization's goals in ways that went beyond normal expectations. Examples include

- ✔ Exceeding expected sales levels
- ✔ Obtaining new contracts or business
- ✔ Going beyond productivity quotients
- ✔ Solving a particularly problematic issue or situation
- ✔ Reaching certain lengths of service

Just how employees are rewarded or recognized for outstanding performance will vary from one company to another. Some companies continue to use something as simple (and inexpensive) as a certificate or plaque marking the achievement, but cash and gift certificates are also popular. Registration for a helpful seminar or a paid membership to an association are also good choices.

A payment that qualifies as a gift is not included in determining an employee's regular rate of pay — the basis for calculating overtime pay. Generally, a payment is in the nature of a gift if its amount is not measured by or dependent on hours worked, production, or efficiency. A lawyer experienced in wage and hour law can help you to determine when an extra payment to an employee should, or should not, be included in the regular rate of pay, as well as other complex compensation issues.

Your employees benefit — how do you?

Your employees benefit in the following ways:

✔ **Greater motivation:** Employees who know they stand to be rewarded for outstanding performance approach their jobs with greater enthusiasm and creativity. The opposite is unfortunately also true: Not being appreciated is a common reason departing employees cite when deciding to move on to a business where they feel that their efforts are more likely to be recognized.

✔ **Peer acknowledgment:** Chances are, employees who get word of a co-worker's achievement will take the time to offer their own congratulations. It's hard to imagine an employee who wouldn't welcome the acknowledgment.

✔ **Empowerment and inclusion:** Employee recognition programs can make staff members feel a greater part of a company rather than just the recipient of a regular paycheck. That moves loyalty beyond just a financial appeal.

Employee recognition programs also benefit the business owner by

✔ **Reinforcing positive behavior:** If employees excel, others will notice. That can help others raise their performance in the hopes of being recognized as well.

✔ **Lowering stress levels:** If the emphasis is on the positive rather than an overriding concern about snafus, employees are likely to feel less overwhelmed about their job responsibilities.

✔ **Increasing customer retention:** Higher employee motivation levels typically carry over to satisfied customers and clients. Those you do business with inevitably notice employees who bring a commitment and enthusiasm to what they do. Unfortunately, a disgruntled or frustrated employee can stand out to customers just as much.

Getting the fundamentals in place

Now's the time to put an employee recognition program in place. How do you want to run it? Even the best program doesn't run itself. You need to make sure that you have a workable foundation. Here's a checklist to get you started:

✔ **Make sure that people know about it.** One of the key duties of the person managing a recognition program is to publicize it. Mention it in your employee communications, such as an employee magazine or company intranet.

✔ **Set up a budget.** How much do you want to spend? You'll need to ensure that your programs are affordable to the business. In considering this question, don't forget that money and tangible rewards aren't everything to employees. It's a good idea to set up a formal program, while also encouraging managers to informally recognize employees when and how they see fit. Some managers may overlook doing this if they know the company has an official program in place.

✔ **Make your recognition efforts an investment, not an expense.** Any program you set up shouldn't be a line item like a company retreat, but rather part of your operating costs that can't be cut. It's that important.

✔ **Make sure that it's aligned with your overall business strategy.** For instance, if your goal is to cut expenses, reward people who suggest and implement money-saving ideas.

✔ **Encourage line managers to weave it into their regular schedules.** They should be encouraged to make recognition a habit rather than the exception. Even simple thank-yous can work wonders. You don't have to hand out goodies left and right to recognize employees.

✔ **Make it fair.** If only a few select employees are regularly singled out, that can breed resentment and jealousy among others. Spread the recognition as equitably as possible.

✔ **Make it mean something.** Bonuses, raises, and other financial rewards are always welcome, but they're not the only forms of recognition that carry real weight. Extra time off, a complimentary meal, and other means of saying "thanks" or "job well done" can mean just as much. The bottom line: Whatever you do to recognize performance, be sure that the recipient will genuinely appreciate it. It's all too easy to see through recognition that's cosmetic and little more.

✔ **Make recognition go beyond a slap on the back.** However rewarding your words may be, sometimes it's nice to spice them up a bit. Picture the employee going home and telling her spouse: "Virginia stopped by to say thanks for the great job on the contract. And, check it out — dinner for two at that new Thai restaurant!" Powerful stuff.

✔ **Reward only exceptional achievements.** An employee who's always willing and available to make a fresh pot of coffee is one thing; a salesperson who sets a record for deals in a given month is something else entirely. Offering recognition for every little thing dilutes the impact of the reward. Establish guidelines that truly separate the exceptional from other activities that don't necessarily warrant special attention.

✔ **Solicit employee feedback.** Ask staff whether they value your recognition program. If they want changes, what would they be? For instance, what sorts of rewards do they feel really mean something? The greater the connection people feel with the program, the more involved they'll become.

✔ **Connect recognition to professional growth.** A form of recognition I shouldn't leave out is promoting existing employees. No, this isn't always possible, but when it is, it demonstrates your long-term commitment to employee growth and development.

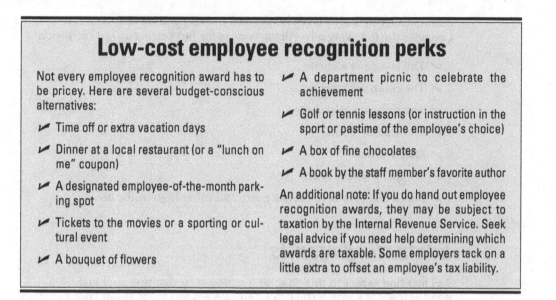

Low-cost employee recognition perks

Not every employee recognition award has to be pricey. Here are several budget-conscious alternatives:

🖊 Time off or extra vacation days

🖊 Dinner at a local restaurant (or a "lunch on me" coupon)

🖊 A designated employee-of-the-month parking spot

🖊 Tickets to the movies or a sporting or cultural event

🖊 A bouquet of flowers

🖊 A department picnic to celebrate the achievement

🖊 Golf or tennis lessons (or instruction in the sport or pastime of the employee's choice)

🖊 A box of fine chocolates

🖊 A book by the staff member's favorite author

An additional note: If you do hand out employee recognition awards, they may be subject to taxation by the Internal Revenue Service. Seek legal advice if you need help determining which awards are taxable. Some employers tack on a little extra to offset an employee's tax liability.

Administration and communication

Even an established recognition program doesn't run itself. You need a capable administrator. If you're handling your company's HR function, that point person may well be you. If not, it's helpful to have one person charged with the administrative and technical duties of running the program. That makes overall administration and troubleshooting that much easier.

One of the key components of sound program administration is communication. Don't let yours exist in a vacuum. Even the most appealing employee recognition program will prove ineffective if employees don't know that it's available. Make sure that your staff members know which programs are in place and what the criteria are for who receives awards. Many firms use company intranets for such news. The initiative will be more successful if it has support from all levels of management — and employees are made aware of this. Senior management buy-in and joint ownership ensures that the effort doesn't sit solely — and potentially languish — on one person's (or department's) shoulders.

Handing out awards: The importance of publicity

Although recognition can be handled in a personal one-on-one setting, it's often more effective to make the event public — in a variety of ways. That can help maintain enthusiasm and high levels of participation.

Publicly offering kudos gives employees the recognition they deserve.
Consider the following advertising venues for publicizing award recipients:

- ✔ The company website
- ✔ The company intranet
- ✔ The company newsletter
- ✔ The annual report
- ✔ Staff meetings
- ✔ Company-wide e-mails
- ✔ Photo displays in the break room and other high-traffic areas

Evaluating results

As I mention earlier in this chapter, employee recognition isn't just a feel-good activity. It's wonderful if your employees feel great about your program, but you also need to make sure that you're getting the results you want from it. Measure productivity, retention, and other barometers alongside the implementation of employee recognition programs. If those numbers are up and can be correlated, the plan is paying off.

Chapter 16

Assessing Employee Performance

In This Chapter

▶ Identifying the benefits of performance appraisals

▶ Creating a performance appraisal process

▶ Introducing the program

▶ Maximizing difficulties

▶ Following up

*F*ew management practices are more basic or prevalent than performance appraisals — the mechanism managers or supervisors use to evaluate employee job performance. Yet, as common as the practice may be, nearly one in three workers polled in a 2012 Robert Half survey said appraisals are either somewhat or very ineffective in helping them improve their performance. In the same survey, 94 percent of executives interviewed said formal evaluations are either somewhat or very effective.

Despite this dichotomy of opinion, performance appraisals are a vital management function. Supervisors have to monitor the performance of direct reports, note which areas of job performance need to be improved, and then communicate assessments to them in a positive and constructive way. If these steps aren't taken, it would be very difficult to determine how people get promoted, if they deserve salary increases, and how much they should be making (not to mention if and how a particular employee may warrant certain types of professional development opportunities).

It's up to you to help your company implement a structured and systematic program that takes into account the realities of today's workplace — and the nuances of your firm's unique culture. As I point out in Chapter 11, raises, bonuses, and other types of rewards should always be pegged to your performance evaluation system.

The information in this chapter is legally sensitive. As it has with this entire book, the firm of Paul Hastings LLP generously helped with this chapter. I strongly recommend that you consult with an attorney before adopting an official appraisal system or converting to a new system. The policies you set in place can make or break your company in a potential lawsuit. So, do yourself a favor: Hire a lawyer *before* you need one.

Reaping the Benefits of Performance Appraisals

Creating and implementing a structured performance appraisal process is by no means a modest challenge. For one thing, performance appraisals invariably create additional work for supervisors. The process also puts pressure on employees by forcing everyone involved in the process to establish specific goals and identify the behaviors necessary to achieve those goals — dismissed by many as needless "busy work." What's more, the very nature of appraisal systems puts both employees and supervisors into situations that most people find uncomfortable. Being, in effect, "graded" makes many employees feel as though they're back in school. And most managers, even those who've been involved with an evaluation process for many years, find it difficult to be both candid and constructive when they're conducting an appraisal session that has to incorporate negative feedback, no matter how gently phrased.

Why, then, should you put in the time and effort needed to create and implement this process? The answer, simply put, is that the long-term benefits of an effectively structured and administered performance appraisal process far outweigh the time and effort the process requires. Here's what a well-designed, well-implemented performance appraisal system can do for your company:

✔ Create criteria for determining how well employees are truly performing — and, to that end, make it clear how their responsibilities fit in with company and departmental priorities.

✔ Provide an objective — and legally supported — basis for key human resources decisions, including merit pay increases, promotions, and changes in job responsibilities.

✔ Verify that reward mechanisms are logically tied to outstanding performance (see Chapter 11).

✔ Motivate employees to improve their job performance.

✔ Enhance the impact of coaching that is already taking place between employees and their managers.

✔ Establish a reasonably uniform set of performance standards that are in sync with company values.

✔ Confirm that employees have the skills or attributes needed to successfully fulfill a particular job.

✔ Iron out difficulties in the supervisor-employee relationship.

✔ Give underperforming employees guidance that can lead to better performance.

✔ Provide real-time feedback to keep employees focused on business goals and objectives.

✔ Help employees clarify career goals.

✔ Validate hiring strategies and practices.

✔ Reinforce company values.

✔ Assess training and staff development needs.

✔ Motivate employees to upgrade their skills and job knowledge so they can make a more meaningful contribution to the company's success.

Deciding on a Performance Appraisal System

The first step you need to take after you've decided either to introduce a performance appraisal system in your company or to change your current one is to determine which kind of system is best. All performance appraisal systems are driven by the same objective: to establish a systematic way of evaluating performance, provide constructive feedback, and enable employees to continually improve their performance.

The basic ingredients in all systems are pretty much the same: setting performance criteria, developing tracking and documenting procedures, determining which areas should be measured quantitatively, and deciding how the information is to be communicated to employees. Where different methods vary is in the following areas:

✔ The degree to which employees are involved in establishing performance evaluation criteria.

✔ How employee performance is tracked and documented.

✔ How performance is rated and how it aligns with corporate priorities, goals, and objectives.

✔ The specific types of appraisal tools used. In some cases, for example, certain approaches are more appropriate for evaluating managers and professionals than for other employees.

✔ The amount of time and effort required to implement the process.

✔ How the results of the appraisal are integrated into other management or HR functions.

✔ How the actual appraisal session is conducted.

There is no one "right" way to determine which specific evaluation method will work best in your company. Here are factors to take into account:

- ✔ **The level of employees being appraised:** Some methods, such as MBO appraisals (discussed in the next section), are more suited to managers and professionals than to other workers. The degree of an employee's autonomy is one key variable that can help shape your range of evaluation techniques.

- ✔ **The degree of training needed to implement the program:** Some systems, such as MBO and critical incidents (described later in this chapter) require more training than others to implement effectively. Make sure that you take into consideration the current workload of your supervisors before you introduce a program that requires extensive training.

- ✔ **Availability of development resources:** The more complex the appraisal system, the more time and effort you'll need to develop it. So, if you decide to launch a system that involves extensive research into how jobs are performed and what constitutes outstanding performance, make sure that you have the appropriate time and resources available. Remember, too, that as job requirements change, the evaluation forms also must change, which can mean additional work down the road. Don't bite off more than you can chew.

This section offers a brief description of performance appraisal systems most commonly used today.

Devising an appropriate employee appraisal system doesn't have to occur solely from square one with a keyboard or pen and paper in hand. The overall growth of HR technology also has led to the development and greater availability of performance appraisal software applications. Look back to Chapter 3 for a primer on this option.

Goal setting, or management by objectives

First created by influential business thinker Peter Drucker in 1954, *management by objectives* (MBO) is still an extremely popular appraisal system because of its focus on results and the activities and skills that truly define an employee's job. Even more recent forms of appraisal that require reciprocal feedback, such as the increasingly popular multirater assessment I describe later in this section, are in large part based on the principles of MBO.

In a typical MBO scenario, an employee and manager sit down together at the start of an appraisal period and formulate a set of statements that represent specific job goals, targets, or *deliverables* (milestones that comprise a project or process).

What makes MBO so powerful is its direct link to organizational objectives and priorities. Goals, targets, and deliverables should be as specific and measurable as possible. For example, rather than "improve customer service," a more effective and understandable goal would be "reduce the number of customer complaints by 5 percent." And instead of "increase number of sales calls," "increase the number of sales calls by 10 percent without changing current criteria for prospects" would be both specific and quantifiable.

This list of targets becomes the basis for an action plan that spells out what steps need to be taken to achieve each goal. At a later date — six months or a year later — the employee and the manager sit down again and measure employee performance on the basis of how many of those goals were met.

Advantages:

✔ Has been used for decades and provides a sharp focus for evaluating employee performance

✔ Enlists the employee in the appraisal process

✔ Can be easily integrated into companywide performance and improvement initiatives

✔ Gives employee a blueprint for successful performance

✔ Emphasizes action and results

Downsides:

✔ Takes time and involves considerable documentation

✔ Works effectively only if supervisors are trained in the process

✔ Can lack sufficient specificity of goals

✔ Doesn't work well for employees who have little discretion as to how their jobs are performed

Behaviorally anchored rating scale

Behaviorally anchored rating scale (BARS) systems are designed to emphasize behaviors, traits, and skills needed to successfully perform a job. A typical BARS form has two columns: The left column has a rating scale, usually in stages from Very Poor to Excellent, and the right column contains behavioral anchors that reflect those ratings.

If the scale were being used, for example, to evaluate a telephone order taker, the statement in the left column may read "2-Poor" and the statement in the right column may read, "Does the employee behave courteously to callers even in challenging circumstances?" followed by your observations, such as "Occasionally rude or abrupt to customer."

Advantages:

- ✔ Reduces the potential for biased responses
- ✔ Focuses on specific, observable behaviors
- ✔ Provides specific and standardized comments on job performance

Downsides:

- ✔ Can be time consuming and complicated to develop
- ✔ Depends on accuracy and appropriateness of "anchor statements"
- ✔ Must be updated as job requirements change
- ✔ Impractical for jobs with frequently changing requirements

Critical incidents

The *critical incidents* method of performance appraisal is built around a list of specific behaviors, generally known as *critical behaviors,* that are deemed necessary to perform a particular job competently. Managers, the HR department, or outside consultants can draw up the list. Performance evaluators use a critical incident report to record actual incidents of behavior that illustrate when employees either carried out or didn't carry out these behaviors. You can use these logs to document a wide variety of job behaviors, such as interpersonal skills, initiative, and leadership ability.

Advantages:

- ✔ Records employee performance as it happens
- ✔ Always links employee behavior to job performance
- ✔ Provides a documented record of behaviors over time
- ✔ Identifies the most important dimensions of a job
- ✔ Offers more insight into job descriptions and core competencies

Downsides:

- ✔ Requires disciplined and regular attention
- ✔ Can often compromise objectivity of recorded incidents because of the evaluator's emotional state when the incident is recorded
- ✔ Depends on a clear definition of critical behaviors

Multirater assessments

Multirater assessments are also called *360-degree assessments* or, more simply, *360 reviews.* The employee's supervisors, co-workers, subordinates, and, in some cases, customers are asked to complete detailed questionnaires on the employee. The employee fills out the same questionnaire. The results are tabulated, and the employee then compares her assessment with the other results.

Advantages:

- ✔ Draws assessments from a wide variety of sources
- ✔ Gives maximum feedback to employee

Downsides:

- ✔ Must be professionally developed
- ✔ Relies on people outside the employee's immediate work circle, which may cause resentment

Launching an Appraisal Program in Your Company

When you set up a new performance appraisal system, you need to gather input from both senior management and employees. You also need to make sure that the program is workable and well communicated throughout the organization. The success or failure of an appraisal system hinges on factors that are based more on company issues than on the system itself. The following sections list successful guidelines.

Enlist the support of senior management

Because appraisals can be a difficult sell to both employees and managers in some organizations (especially in companies that have never formalized the process), you have to make sure early in your development process that senior management is willing to give the initiative strong support. Explain how the particular approach you're recommending is tailored to the company's business and culture and how this process will support them in driving to a higher-performing company.

Choose performance measures with care

The cornerstone of a successful performance appraisal process is the criteria used as the basis of evaluation. Here are some of the key factors to bear in mind when formulating criteria, along with questions you should ask yourself with respect to each factor:

- ✔ **Core values:** Do your criteria reinforce the core values and behaviors that you want your employees to exhibit?

- ✔ **Job relevancy:** Are the criteria connected to strategic business goals? How are these big-picture goals linked to successful work performance?

- ✔ **Feasibility:** Do employees have the resources, the training, or the autonomy required to meet the goals?

- ✔ **Measurability:** Can the behaviors that underlie each performance be observed, measured, and documented?

Develop a fair and practical tracking mechanism

In small companies, when supervisors and employees are working closely together, following day-to-day behavior isn't much of a problem. In larger companies, though, tracking can become a key issue. Essentially, you need a reliable and fair mechanism to ensure that the results of the appraisal are an accurate reflection of day-to-day employee performance.

Here are some questions to ask yourself when confronting this issue:

- ✔ What specific procedures will be used to track and monitor behavior?

- ✔ During what specific periods is behavior going to be tracked and observed?

- ✔ What training, if any, do managers need to carry out these procedures without placing undue pressure on themselves?

- ✔ To what extent will employees be made aware that their behavior is being observed and measured?

- ✔ What recording mechanism will be used to document performance?

- ✔ Where is the documentation going to be kept and what assurances of confidentiality, if any, will be given to employees about the tracking procedure?

Resist the temptation to create the perfect system. Keep in mind that no matter how hard you try to quantify the measuring of any performance criterion, you can never remove the human element. It's not a science. Don't shoot yourself in the foot by creating a system so complicated that no one will take the time or effort to learn it.

Develop a communication game plan

Most appraisal processes live or die on the basis of how clearly and openly you communicate the aims and mechanics of the system to employees. At the very least, everyone involved in the process should be aware of the following information before you actually launch the program:

- ✔ The overall goals of the initiative

- ✔ How employees themselves will benefit

- ✔ How performance criteria will be developed

- ✔ The length of the appraisal periods

- ✔ The degree to which appraisal results will be linked to bonuses, merit pay increases, and other HR-related activities

- ✔ What recourse employees have if they disagree with the results

- ✔ What training, if any, will be made available to managers designated to implement the program

You can communicate this information in any number of ways. The important thing is to have a communications strategy. Make sure that everyone has a clear understanding of how the program will work and their roles in ensuring the program's success.

Getting the Most Out of the Performance Appraisal Meeting

At one point or another in the process of creating a performance appraisal process, you have to address the "people" component — what should happen when managers and employees sit down together or otherwise meet for the purpose of discussing the employees' actual performance review.

The one thing you can't afford to do is assume that this aspect of the process will simply take care of itself. The truth is, very few managers have ever been trained to conduct an effective performance appraisal session. So, although your managers may be responsible for what happens during the session, you and your HR colleagues are responsible for making sure that they're prepared for the challenge.

Preparing for the meeting

Managers should be thoroughly briefed on what they need to do prior to holding a performance appraisal session. The key point to emphasize is to be ready — don't wait until the last minute before thinking about how the meeting will be handled. Managers should have a clear idea before the meeting begins of what specific behaviors will be the focal point of the session. Other points to stress include the following:

- ✔ Give employees enough time to prepare for the session.

- ✔ Allot enough time to conduct a productive session.

- ✔ Have all documentation ready prior to the meeting and thoroughly review it.

- ✔ Choose a suitable place for the meeting. It should be private, quiet, and relaxing, and allow you to meet with no interruptions.

- ✔ Recognize that the goal of the meeting is not to just review the written appraisal with employees but also to engage in a two-way dialogue with them on their performance so it can be either sustained or improved.

Also, you may want to role-play how to respond to difficult or hostile questions with the manager or supervisor who will be conducting performance evaluations. Ensure that she has a phrase or message to fall back on if an employee question is difficult to answer (for example, "I want to respond to your question, but I don't want to give you inaccurate information, so I'll look into that and get back to you promptly after our meeting ends").

Conducting the session

If more than a handful of managers will be involved in your performance appraisal process, think about setting up training sessions for them on how to conduct an effective appraisal session. Whether you conduct this training yourself or bring in an outside company, here are the points that should be stressed:

- ✔ The appraisal meeting should always be a two-way conversation, not a one-way lecture. Feedback should be honest and genuine.

✔ Positives should always be emphasized before negatives are discussed.

✔ Emphasis should be on what needs to be done to improve and not what was done wrong.

✔ Employees should be encouraged to comment on any observation managers share with them.

✔ Managers should know how to explain to employees the difference between *effort* (how hard employees are working) and *quality results* (whether the results of those efforts are contributing significantly to business objectives).

Giving constructive feedback

If your company is like most, the toughest thing for your managers to do during the appraisal meeting will be to talk about where an employee's performance is lacking. Here, again, it's in your best interest to work in advance with your managers so they're prepared to handle this undeniably tricky aspect of the process. Here are the points to emphasize:

✔ **Focus on why candor is important.** Managers who, when the need arises, fail to focus on the negative aspects of employee performance are not only doing the employee a disservice but also can be harming your company. The employee can't improve if the manager doesn't communicate the need. Additionally, if it becomes necessary to fire an employee, a manager's failure to mention the employee's weakness in a performance appraisal can jeopardize the company's ability to defend the firing decision.

✔ **Stress the importance of documentation.** Managers should always be prepared to back up critical comments with specific, job-related examples. The documentation for these examples should be gathered prior to the meeting.

✔ **Highlight the importance of careful wording.** Managers should be made aware that the wording of criticism is every bit as important as what behavior is being described. Remind managers to focus on the behavior itself and not on the personality quality that may have led to the behavior. For example, instead of saying, "You've been irresponsible," describe the specific event that reflects the irresponsibility, as in "For the past few weeks, you've missed these deadlines."

✔ **Encourage employee feedback.** After managers have issued any piece of criticism, employees should be given the opportunity to comment. Given a chance, employees often will admit to their shortcomings and may even ask for help.

✔ **End on a positive note.** No matter how negative the feedback may be, performance appraisal meetings should end on a positive note and with a substantive, detailed plan for improvement.

The legal aspects of appraisal

Depending upon how you develop and conduct it, an appraisal system can do one of two things with respect to your company's legal exposure:

✔ Unnecessarily expose your company to the danger of discrimination or other employment-related lawsuits.

✔ Provide your company with a strong defense if an employee or former employee threatens a legal claim based on an unfavorable personnel action.

The best defense when an adverse employment action is taken for performance reasons and the employee claims wrongful dismissal, demotion, failure to promote, or similar action is a carefully documented record of unfavorable performance evaluations, coupled with an employee's inability or refusal to carry out suggestions to correct poor work or on-the-job behavior.

At the same time, you need to be sure that your appraisal system is defensible if challenged as violative of local, state, or federal antidiscrimination laws.

Preparing for a negative reaction

In a well-managed company, most employees are probably performing adequately or better. However, some people simply don't take criticism well, no matter how minimal or appropriately delivered. In any performance appraisal meeting, an employee whose work is being critiqued may very well become agitated, confrontational, verbally abusive, and, in very rare instances, violent. Managers should be alerted to this possibility and be prepared with a strategy for response. Here's some advice to share with them:

✔ **Within reason, let the employee blow off steam.** Don't respond, comment, or challenge the employee while he's agitated or angry. In certain situations, a calm, nonthreatening demeanor can defuse a situation. Give the employee adequate time to get past the initial reaction and cool off.

✔ **Don't feign agreement.** The worst thing you can say in this sort of situation is "I can see why you're upset." It can very well set the employee off again ("You're not the one who was just told you're doing a lousy job!"). Even more important, the supervisor or manager conducting the meeting *is* the company for all practical purposes; it's inappropriate, and possibly legally risky, for the supervisor or manager to communicate a personal viewpoint at odds with the substantive content of the review.

✔ **When the storm passes, continue the meeting.** A lack of response usually ends most outbursts, and the employee quickly realizes that he's made a serious mistake. Accept any apology and move on. If the employee simply cannot or does not move on, take a break or end the meeting and arrange to reconvene later in the day or in the next few days.

✔ **If there's any hint that the employee may become violent, leave the room immediately and seek help.** Contact an in-house security guard and 911. Also, prior to the meeting, the supervisor or manager conducting the meeting should be familiar with your company's workplace violence policy, if one exists.

Choosing areas for further development

What's most important following the delivery of any constructive criticism is a mutual effort between employees and managers to begin the process of making changes to help staff perform at a higher level. As part of the appraisal meeting, supervisors should identify areas for improvement and, together with their employees, build a set of workable performance development activities.

To prepare, supervisors should take time prior to the meeting to create a concise, one-page list of potential developmental activities for the employee. The list can include

✔ Recommended readings, both current and ongoing, devoted to the topics where development is suggested

✔ Possible classroom or online courses

✔ People within the company who may offer useful input ("John became a supervisor last year, so you can talk with him about the challenges of managing people.")

✔ Potential on-the-job experiences to help develop skills in an area that has a gap or needs to be more fully developed to move to the next level

Employee development isn't just for underperformers, of course. Even the very best employees have room to improve and further develop themselves. For any professional, appraisal time is the ideal opportunity to look back, as well as constructively plan for the future.

Performance development activities are a way to help employees better achieve the job objectives set at the start of the appraisal period (see "Goal setting, or management by objectives," earlier in this chapter). As a result, the employee and manager should revisit these objectives during this phase of the appraisal meeting to ensure that they're still on target. Many companies require an annual goal-setting meeting. The appraisal meeting may be a good time to tackle that task. You certainly don't want to establish developmental activities around goals that will soon be changing.

Following Up on Performance Appraisals

Some managers may feel that the performance appraisal meeting is the conclusion of the appraisal process. The truth is, the days following this session are also extremely important. You need to explain to managers or supervisors that providing adequate follow-up, including regular monitoring of employee progress toward performance development goals, is key. Without sustained follow-up — both formal and informal — any input an employee receives is unlikely to be long lasting.

The employee and supervisor should have both short- and long-term methods to review progress on the areas of improvement discussed. They also should schedule specific dates to do so. Many companies advise managers to conduct interim meetings after six months, but the interval can be shorter or longer depending on the situation. Between these sessions, supervisors should be encouraged to remain easily accessible so employees can share thoughts, concerns, or suggestions on any of the topics covered during the appraisal. Managers should understand the benefits of providing input to staff throughout the year. If feedback is ongoing, nothing in the performance appraisal should come as a surprise to employees.

Part V
Law and Order

The 5th Wave   By Rich Tennant

"I've never been good at this part of the job, which is why I've asked 'Buddy' to join us. As you know, business has been bad lately, and, well, Buddy has some bad news for you..."

In this part . . .

1 highlight the major laws and regulations governing the employer-employee relationship, including in the areas of recruiting, hiring, and managing employees. I help you understand how these issues affect you in your HR role and, ultimately, your organization. I also give you some tips on handling the unfortunate but inevitable problems in job performance and workplace conduct that can quickly damage productivity, accelerate turnover, deplete employee morale, and expose your organization to risks of legal claims.

Chapter 17

Navigating the Legal Minefield of Hiring and Managing

In This Chapter

▶ Getting the big picture

▶ Determining your role in labor relations

▶ Guarding against discrimination

▶ Knowing what disparate impact means

▶ Understanding EEOC requirements

▶ Putting employment laws under the microscope

The legal aspects of HR are complicated, and, yes, they can be more than a bit daunting — especially when you first encounter them. Laws affect virtually everything you do in the field of HR: hiring, determining compensation, choosing how to evaluate employee performance, and many more tasks. All these activities carry significant legal implications. Failing to fully understand the law can prove costly.

You're not alone if you find this topic intimidating. However, with ample preparation (and frequent contact with legal counsel when it's called for), you should do just fine.

In this chapter, I cite what I believe to be the most up-to-date and legally sound information available, largely based on the assistance and recommendations of the prestigious law firm Paul Hastings LLP. But, just like heart surgery, the practice of law is not something you should do yourself. Consult an attorney. The information contained in this chapter gives you an overview, but it is no substitute for the specific and tailored advice that your own legal counsel can provide about your company and workforce.

Legal Matters: The Big Picture

The legal issues covered in this chapter require careful deliberation for the following reasons:

- ✔ **Daily changes:** I'm not kidding. Every day, federal and state governments pass new statutes; new regulations are adopted by federal and state agencies; new ordinances are adopted by local governments; and courts are ruling on existing statutes, regulations, and ordinances and developing case law. The discussions in this book help make you aware of these topics, but you still need to be familiar with the laws that apply in the states and cities where you have operations and have your own lawyer review your forms, policies, and procedures.

- ✔ **Vague definitions:** It would be nice if all laws were as clear as the posted speed limit. If the sign says the speed limit is 65, you're safe if you're driving 64 and know that you can get a ticket if you're driving 66. Many employment laws aren't so clear. For example, many laws specifically require you to do what is "reasonable." But what is reasonable in a specific situation? The law doesn't tell you. Just because you think you're acting reasonably doesn't mean that the courts, the administrative agencies, or your employees will agree. If a dispute arises between you and one of your employees over whether you've acted reasonably, don't expect it to be resolved quickly by some easy-to-reach arbiter. You may instead face a long and expensive process of finding out whether your actions were reasonable. And if the court or agency eventually decides that you *didn't* act reasonably, your organization, and sometimes its individual supervisors, may be liable for large sums of money or subject to injunctive remedies, like implementing a proper policy or rehiring a terminated worker.

- ✔ **Inconsistencies:** If only one level of government were involved, and all the laws involving HR practices were adopted at the same time, you might have an easier time. But the federal government, states, counties, cities, and so on adopt laws and regulations, and they might not consult with one another. The laws of one government or agency may contradict the laws of another. In addition, each law is adopted at a different time, and efforts aren't always made to be consistent. In fact, new laws can conflict with old laws that are not repealed.

My advice to you is simple: Don't be your own lawyer. Most laws are defined, refined, and clarified by agency regulations and court rulings that cover areas that the average person wouldn't anticipate. For example, if a law applies only to businesses with 25 or more employees, does it apply to your business? That depends on how the law defines *employee.* Do owners count? Do part-time employees count? Do temporary or supplemental employees count? Do independent contractors count? What if you never had more than 23 people at a time, but because of turnover, 40 different people worked for you at various times during the last year? The answer to questions like this may depend on which law you're analyzing, and courts in different parts of the country may answer similar questions in different ways.

It sounds confusing, but keep in mind that lots of companies are surviving and thriving in this environment. You can, too. This chapter gives you common-sense guidance. However, this information is no substitute for legal advice. Get a lawyer and talk to that lawyer often.

Keeping the Peace

The extent to which you need to concern yourself with labor relations in your company, both formally and informally, depends on many factors, but two are key: the number of people in your company (because often, employment laws are triggered based on an employer's size) and whether the company is unionized.

If your company is unionized, chances are, you may spend a considerable amount of your time negotiating and administering labor agreements. What's more, you're likely to be the person union representatives approach whenever they have grievances.

If you're in a nonunion company, you can't take anything for granted. People are people, and this being the case, occasional disputes will arise between employees and their managers, as well as among employees. You may have never thought of yourself as a peacemaker. Get used to the idea.

Discrimination

Many federal, state, and local laws make it illegal to discriminate on the basis of a number of factors, including, but not limited to, race, color, religion, sex, national origin, ancestry, citizenship, age, physical or mental disability, genetic information, military service or obligation, veteran status, pregnancy, marital status, and domestic partner status. Some states, counties, and cities prohibit discrimination on the basis of sexual orientation. But the laws don't stop there.

Take employee appearance, for example. Section 12947.5 of the California Government Code makes it unlawful for an employer to refuse to permit an employee to wear pants on the basis of sex. Hairstyles, tattoos, and body piercings also have been issues in lawsuits. Of course, discrimination laws cover many areas besides employee appearance. My point here is that, no matter how trivial an issue may seem to you, *numerous forms of discrimination are unacceptable,* and it's your responsibility to be familiar with federal, state, and local laws that address discrimination.

So, how should you deal with these laws? The answer is simple: Make all your hiring, promotion, and other decisions solely on the basis of ability to perform the job, and you should generally be okay. I say "generally" because of a type of discrimination known as disparate impact (see the next section).

Disparate Impact

The laws against discrimination not only extend to intentional acts by you (called *disparate treatment*), but also may cover actions that aren't intended to discriminate but have the effect of doing so, which is called *disparate impact*.

For example, assume that you own a trucking company. If you decide that you won't employ people of a certain race, sex, or religion, you're practicing disparate treatment, which is illegal from the standpoint of federal, state, and many local laws. Even the 2001 Patriot Act, which is primarily focused on matters of national security, takes this form of discrimination very seriously. It condemns discrimination against Arab and Muslim Americans and Americans from South Asia on the basis of religious, ethnic, or racial background.

On the other hand, suppose that you don't intentionally discriminate, but you require all your truck drivers to speak French. If it turns out that this requirement results in limited hiring of members of a certain race, sex, or religion because, for whatever reason, few members of that particular race, sex, or religion speak French, you may be found to have violated discrimination laws because your policy created an unlawful disparate impact on the basis of a protected group. You haven't intentionally adopted a policy against a protected group, but an apparently neutral policy has had that adverse impact.

What happens if you're challenged on this policy and a disparate impact is shown? If you can then demonstrate that speaking French is a *bona fide occupational qualification* (BFOQ) for the job, then you may not be found liable for discrimination. For example, if your trucking company is based in Vermont, and all your drivers, as part of their routes, have to drive across the border into Quebec (the part of Canada where French, and not English, is the official language and appears on all signs), you may be able to establish that the ability to speak French is a BFOQ. However, if your trucking company is located in Arizona, and the drivers drive only between Arizona and Mexico, speaking French may not be considered to be a BFOQ, and you could be found liable for disparate-impact discrimination because Spanish-speaking applicants may lack French fluency.

BFOQ has a special meaning under the law, and it may or may not match with your determination of what is a BFOQ. Your good-faith belief isn't enough to guarantee that your BFOQ will stand up if challenged. A court or administrative agency reviewing the situation doesn't have to agree with you. Seek legal advice to help you analyze if a neutral policy or practice may adversely impact a protected category and whether your reason for that policy or practice will likely qualify as a BFOQ.

The Equal Employment Opportunity Commission

The Equal Employment Opportunity Commission (EEOC) is the federal agency responsible for enforcing federal antidiscrimination laws in employment.

Regardless of how disciplined you are in your company about following equal employment opportunity (EEO) principles, there are some important steps you must or should take in this area:

✔ Post all mandatory federal, state, and/or local EEO-related posters.

The CD includes a poster from the EEOC entitled Equal Employment Opportunity Is the Law. It describes the federal laws prohibiting job discrimination based on race, color, sex, national origin, religion, age, equal pay, disability, and genetic information. Every employer covered by the nondiscrimination and EEO laws is required to post this notice on its premises. The notice must be posted prominently, where employees and applicants for employment can readily see it.

✔ Depending on the size of your company (and its affiliation with or ownership by another company with enough employees to meet the 100-employee threshold) and type of organization, or whether you qualify as a federal contractor not exempt from the requirement, you may be required to prepare and file with the EEOC an annual report (known as the Employer Information Report, or EEO-1). This report sets forth certain demographic data related to your workforce, broken out into specific job categories.

✔ Retain copies of personnel and employment documents (job applications, payroll records, records related to discharges, and so on), including those that may conceivably become relevant if your company is involved in a discrimination suit. The recommended minimum period for maintaining these records is three years, though particular laws may impose their own retention periods for such documents. Certain records, such as payroll records, should be kept for longer (even for seven to ten years or longer) to enable your organization to defend against claims of discriminatory pay practices originating years earlier. Modern-day technology may make electronic storage of such records much less burdensome than in years past. Also, keep on file records of hiring practices, identifying total hires within a particular job classification and the percentage of minority and female applicants hired.

Hopefully, it'll never happen, but in the event that an employee or group of employees, applicant, or group of applicants, or an administrative agency like the EEOC decides to file a discrimination complaint against your company, you should at least have a basic idea of what to expect.

As a preliminary matter, an individual may not file a lawsuit in court claiming discrimination under certain federal laws unless he has first filed an administrative charge with the EEOC and, in most situations, received from the EEOC a notice expressly affording him the right to proceed in court. This is true for most claims of discrimination under federal law (for example, race, sex, national origin), though not for claims under the Equal Pay Act (see "The Equal Pay Act of 1963," later in this chapter), which may be asserted in court in the first instance.

According to the EEOC, employees filed almost 100,000 charges of discrimination with the EEOC in fiscal year 2011. Though EEOC research indicates that the vast majority of these cases result in no benefit to the individual filing the charge, you need to understand the steps involved in case you need to interact with the EEOC. What follows is a rough description of the sequence of events that typically takes place after a claim is registered with the EEOC.

1. **The EEOC receives the charges.**

    The EEOC will, in nearly every case, accept a charge for filing. It will not do so when, for example, the EEOC simply doesn't have jurisdiction.

2. **The EEOC notifies the respondent (the employer) of the charges.**

    The EEOC promptly notifies you that a charge has been filed and provides a copy of the charge. The EEOC generally requests information about your organization and about the allegations in the charge, including a statement of the company's position in response. That notice may include an invitation to participate in an early mediation/conciliation to try to resolve the charge immediately, before a full investigation is undertaken.

    If you choose not to participate in an early mediation/conciliation, skip to Step 4.

3. **The parties may try to resolve the charge early in a conciliation/mediation facilitated by the EEOC.**

    If you choose to participate in early mediation/conciliation, then generally someone from your company (probably you) meets with the person who filed the charge and an EEOC staff member. The charging party gets a chance to tell her side of the story — that is, why the person feels that she is the victim of discrimination. Your company's representative then gives the company's side of the story — why, in your view, your company acted based solely on legitimate business reasons and did not unlawfully discriminate. The EEOC staff member will likely try his best to resolve the issue and accomplish a satisfactory settlement of the charge. (Note that the resolution may involve, for example, giving a dismissed employee another chance or additional severance pay.)

4. **If the parties do not resolve the charge early, the investigation begins.**

    If Step 3 is unsuccessful (or you choose not to participate), the EEOC requests that you provide the information and the position statement requested in Step 2. The EEOC may follow up this step with requests for more information, which can include telephone or in-person interviews of witnesses, a review of documents, and/or a visit to your facility.

5. **The EEOC makes a determination.**

Generally, on the basis of the allegations in the charge, the parties' other written submissions and its investigation, the EEOC will issue a finding on the merits of the charge and notify both parties of its finding — either of "reasonable cause" to believe that your company unlawfully discriminated against the individual or "no reasonable cause" to believe that your company unlawfully discriminated.

In the event of a "reasonable cause" finding, the EEOC will once again solicit you to participate in a conciliation process aimed at resolving the charge (as in Steps 2 and 3). If the conciliation process fails (or you choose not to participate), the EEOC is authorized to enforce violations of federal antidiscrimination statutes by filing a lawsuit in federal court itself. If the agency elects not to litigate, it will issue to the charging party a Notice of Right to Sue, triggering the charging party's right to bring a lawsuit on the discrimination claims within 90 days.

If the EEOC issues a "no reasonable cause" finding, the agency will issue to the charging party a letter dismissing the charge and describing information regarding the charging party's right to pursue the claim in federal court within 90 days.

In the event that the complaint leads to EEOC action, you may find yourself with a difficult choice: You have to either go along with EEOC proposals or gird yourself for a legal fight that may take years and cost your company thousands (or more) in court costs, damages, and, possibly, negative publicity.

If the EEOC doesn't take the case, the individual claimant can proceed on his own, and you may find yourself in litigation.

When a right-to-sue notice is required, the individual can — and often does, when already represented by an attorney — short-circuit the administrative process by requesting an immediate right-to-sue notice, even before the EEOC has concluded its investigation. The EEOC is obligated to furnish the notice only if more than 180 days have passed since the charge was filed, but it may furnish the notice earlier.

Importantly, separate and apart from the federal EEOC are state equal employment opportunity agencies that are charged with very similar authority and responsibility for enforcing state antidiscrimination laws. Employees or former employees may file charges of discrimination with these agencies, just as they may with the EEOC offices, and such state agencies may investigate and act on such charges in accordance with their statutory powers — again, in a manner often quite similar to the EEOC. In fact, many states have "work-share" arrangements with the EEOC, where a charge may be deemed dually filed at both the EEOC and state agency level, but one agency agrees to lead the investigation, the results of which are accepted by the other agency. Employers must be careful to respond to state agency charges just as they would to an EEOC charge. You should consult with a knowledgeable and experienced attorney if your business becomes the subject of these investigations.

The Discrimination Fact Sheets included on the CD detail discrimination guidelines.

The Family of EEO and Other Employment Laws: A Closer Look

More than a dozen pieces of major, HR-related federal legislation have been enacted since 1963, all relating in some way to the area of equal employment opportunity. Local, county, and state government bodies have enacted hundreds of statutes and regulations as well.

The focus of this legislation and the type of employer covered by each piece of legislation vary, and a good deal of overlap occurs. The following sections offer a quick glimpse of the key federal laws in this area.

Some statutes impose posting requirements on employers, some impose requirements about specific notices that must be given to employees, and some impose both types of duties. Be sure to consult an attorney so you're aware of the notice and posting requirements applicable to your locations.

ADEA: The Age Discrimination in Employment Act of 1967

What the legislation does: Prohibits discrimination against applicants for employment and employees who are age 40 or older. Also prohibits retaliation against individuals who oppose unlawful employment practices based on age or who participate in proceedings or hearings under the ADEA. This law was amended in 1990 by the Older Workers Benefit Protection Act of 1990 (discussed later in this chapter).

Who the legislation applies to: Almost any private-sector employer with 20 or more employees who worked 20 or more weeks in the current or preceding calendar year. Includes labor unions (25 or more members), employment agencies, and state and local governments.

OWBA: Older Workers Benefit Protection Act (1990)

What the legislation does: Prohibits age-based discrimination in early retirement and other benefit plans of employees who are age 40 or older and establishes a statutory regime for assessing the effect of waivers of claims under the Age Discrimination in Employment Act, separate and apart from contract law.

Who the legislation applies to: All individuals, partnerships, associations, labor organizations, corporations, business trusts, legal representatives or organized groups of persons engaged in an industry affecting commerce and that have 20 or more employees for each working day in each of 20 or more calendar weeks in the current or preceding year.

Additional details: One provision of this law requires that employers give an individual employee at least 21 days to consider a release or waiver of claims presented by the employer (that is, a company's offer that includes a promise not to sue the company for age discrimination). This time period increases to a 45-day mandatory consideration period for employees terminated as part of an employment termination program. In either situation, this law also requires that employees be given seven days after signing the release/waiver to change their minds and revoke their agreement.

AC-21: American Competitiveness in the 21st Century Act (2000)

What the legislation does: Seeks to help the U.S. economy in both the short and long run by a combination of temporary visa increases issued for highly skilled labor, as well as training and education initiatives.

The act benefits both job seekers and employers. It allows individuals whose employers are trying to get them an extension on their visas to stay in the United States until a decision is made on their cases instead of forcing these people to leave the country. The act also includes training and educational opportunities for U.S. citizens. In addition, it exempts from the cap on visa allotments those visas obtained by universities, research facilities, and graduate-degree recipients to help keep top graduates and educators in the country.

Who the legislation applies to: Any company.

ADA: Americans with Disabilities Act of 1990, as amended by the Americans with Disabilities Act Amendments Act of 2008

What the legislation does: Among other things, ensures that people with physical or mental disabilities have access to public places and public services. Also requires employers to provide reasonable accommodation for applicants and employees with disabilities and prohibits employment discrimination on the basis of disability.

Who the legislation applies to: Almost any private-sector employer that has employed 15 or more employees for 20 or more weeks in the current or preceding calendar year, as well as state and local governments, employment agencies, and labor unions.

Additional details: Employers in recent years have taken major steps to accommodate otherwise qualified disabled employees by outfitting the workplace with certain features (for example, wheelchair ramps) specially designed for disabled people or modifying schedules or training programs with an eye toward the special needs of disabled people. The Americans with Disabilities Act Amendments Act (ADAAA) of 2008 amended the ADA to greatly increase the coverage of the statute, including by determining disability without regard to mitigating measures (such as eyeglasses and medication) and counting impairments that are in remission if they would substantially limit a major life activity when active (for example, epilepsy).

See Facts about the Americans with Disabilities Act on the CD for details about major provisions of the ADA and ADAAA.

COBRA: Consolidated Omnibus Budget Reconciliation Act (1986)

What the legislation does: Provides certain former employees, retirees, spouses, former spouses, and children the right to temporary continuation of health coverage at group rates.

Who the legislation applies to: Employers with 20 or more employees are usually required to offer COBRA coverage and to notify their employees of the availability of such coverage. COBRA applies to plans maintained by private-sector employers and sponsored by most state and local governments.

Unquestionably, healthcare is an extremely important part of the world of human resources. I cover the topic more extensively in Chapter 12.

The Equal Pay Act of 1963

What the legislation does: Generally prohibits discrimination in pay between men and women on the basis of sex for work requiring equal skill, effort, and responsibility and that is performed under similar working conditions.

Who the legislation applies to: All employers covered by the Fair Labor Standards Act (covered later in this section) and, thus, all enterprises with employees who engage in interstate commerce; produce goods for interstate commerce; or handle, sell, or work on goods or materials that have been moved in or produced for interstate commerce.

FMLA: Family and Medical Leave Act (1993)

What the legislation does: Grants to eligible employees the right to take up to 12 week of unpaid leave per year for one or more of the following reasons:

- Because of the birth of a child.
- Because of the adoption of a child or placement of a foster child.
- To care for a spouse, parent, or child with a serious health condition.
- Because of an employee's own serious health condition that makes the employee unable to perform the functions of his or her position.
- Because of any qualifying exigency arising out of the fact that the spouse or a son, daughter, or parent of the employee is on covered active duty (or has been notified of an impending call or order to covered active duty) in the armed forces. In addition, a qualified employee who is the spouse, son, daughter, parent, or next of kin of a covered servicemember is entitled to a total of 26 weeks in a single 12-month period to care for a seriously ill or injured servicemember.

Who the legislation applies to: Generally, the FMLA covers any individual or entity "engaged in commerce or in any industry or activity affecting commerce," employing 50 or more employees for each working day during each of 20 or more calendar workweeks in the current or preceding calendar year. Public agencies also are covered regardless of the number of employees they employ.

Additional details: Under the FMLA, employers have posting obligations and a series of notice obligations to give to employees at various points. The content and timing of these notices are complicated. A lawyer can assist in this area.

For details of the major requirements of the FMLA, see the Family and Medical Leave Act Fact Sheets on the CD.

FLSA: Fair Labor Standards Act (1938)

What the legislation does: Generally, establishes minimum wage and overtime pay standards, restricts and regulates the employment of minors, and requires certain forms of record keeping.

Who the legislation applies to: Most private and public employers.

The CD includes the FLSA minimum-wage poster, titled Employee Rights under the Fair Labor Standards Act. Every employer of employees subject to the FLSA's minimum wage provisions must post, and keep posted, a notice explaining the act in a conspicuous place in all its establishments. Visit the Department of Labor's website at www.dol.gov/whd/regs/compliance/posters/flsa.htm to download other versions of the poster.

FUTA: Federal Unemployment Tax Act (1939)

What the legislation does: Stipulates that employers must contribute to a government tax program that offers temporary benefits to employees who have lost their jobs. In most cases, includes both a federal and a state tax.

Wage-theft prevention laws

Some states have enacted, or are considering enacting, wage-theft prevention laws. Among other things, these laws require employers to provide a notice containing specific wage information (for example, rate of pay, designated payday) to new nonexempt employees at the time of hiring, and possibly to existing nonexempt employees under certain circumstances.

California and New York are two states that have enacted these kinds of laws. Forms addressing California's law can be accessed on the California Department of Industrial Relations website. The California Notice to Employee is available in several languages and

can be downloaded at www.dir.ca.gov/dlse/Governor_signs_Wage_Theft_Protection_Act_of_2011.html. The same web page contains a link to an FAQ sheet addressing the California law.

Forms addressing New York's law can be accessed on the New York Department of Labor website. For example, the Pay Notice for Hourly Rate Employees, which is available in several languages, can be downloaded from the following website, along with many other forms related to the New York law: www.labor.ny.gov/formsdocs/wp/ellsformsandpublications.shtm.

Who the legislation applies to: Generally, companies that paid wages of $1,500 or more in any calendar quarter.

Additional details: The current maximum tax imposed is at a rate of 6.2 percent on the first $7,000 paid annually by employers to each employee.

HIPAA: Health Insurance Portability and Accountability Act (1996)

What the legislation does: Establishes rights and protections for participants and beneficiaries in group health plans, including protections for coverage under group health plans that limit exclusions for preexisting conditions; prohibits discrimination against employees and dependents based on their health status; and allows a special opportunity to enroll in a new plan to individuals in certain circumstances. HIPAA is commonly known for its privacy rule. The law established, for the first time, a set of national standards for the protection of individuals' health information, including standards for individuals to understand and control how their health information is used.

Who the legislation applies to: Covered entities include all employers, employers' health plans, healthcare providers, and healthcare clearinghouses.

Again, more information on healthcare is provided in Chapter 12.

IRCA: Immigration Reform and Control Act of 1986

What the legislation does: Among other things, requires that employers attest to the immigration status of their employees and bans employers from knowingly hiring illegal aliens — and establishes penalties for such behavior.

Who the legislation applies to: Any individual or company, regardless of size or industry.

Determining the legality of the employee's status is the employer's responsibility. Indeed, the IRCA introduced the Employment Eligibility Verification Form (Form I-9). Matters related to immigration and security are even more important since 2001, when the Department of Homeland Security was established, and the Patriot Act (covered later in this chapter) was passed.

Pregnancy Discrimination Act of 1978

What the legislation does: Prohibits employers from refusing to hire a woman because of pregnancy and requires that pregnant women are given the same work modifications and medical-leave benefits that are available for employees with disabilities.

Who the legislation applies to: Employers with 15 or more employees who work 20 or more weeks a year, including privately or publicly held companies; employment agencies; labor unions; and local, state, and federal governments.

Additional details: The act covers both married and unmarried women. Also, both female employees and pregnant spouses of male employees can receive pregnancy benefits. (The spouse receives benefits if she is covered by the husband's health plan, but the employer isn't required to pay for a spouse's leave of absence, which is the duty of the spouse's employer if she is working.)

The Rehabilitation Act of 1973

What the legislation does: Certain employment-related provisions of this law impose an affirmative-action obligation on federal government employers to seek out disabled individuals for employment, require federal contractors to take affirmative action in employing and advancing the employment of qualified individuals with disabilities, and prohibit discrimination on the basis of disability by private and governmental recipients of federal financial assistance. In 1998, Congress amended the Rehabilitation Act to require access to electronic and information technology that is provided by the federal government for people with disabilities. The law applies to all federal agencies when they develop, procure, maintain, or use electronic and information technology.

Who the legislation applies to: Entities that possess a certain connection to the federal government (for example, those that contract with the federal government or those that receive federal financial assistance).

Additional details: In general, requires written affirmative-action programs from employers of 50 or more people that have supply or service (nonconstruction) federal contracts worth $50,000 or more.

Sarbanes-Oxley Act (2002)

What the legislation does: Requires publicly held companies to be more straightforward in reporting their financial results and how they were calculated. Also requires more stringent company controls to ensure the ethical behavior of all employees.

Who the legislation applies to: Publicly held companies and private firms that are considering becoming public companies through an initial public offering of their stock.

Additional details: Sarbanes-Oxley requires the establishment of a company code of ethics for its senior financial officers. By extension, many companies seek to uphold the spirit of the law by requesting that their HR teams update and communicate the firm's code of conduct for all employees.

Title VII of the Civil Rights Act (1964)

What the legislation does: Prohibits employers from discriminating against employees and applicants for employment on the basis of race, color, religion, sex, or national origin.

Who the legislation applies to: Employers with 15 or more employees for each working day in each of at least 20 calendar weeks in the current or preceding calendar year, as well as employment agencies and labor organizations, but excluding the federal government.

Additional details: The Civil Rights Act of 1991 amended Title VII and provided for the right to trial by jury on Title VII discrimination claims and authorized recovery of a broader range of remedies, including emotional distress and punitive damages (while imposing caps on such relief under Title VII).

USA PATRIOT ACT (2001)

What the legislation does: Among its provisions, the law expands the federal government's ability to conduct investigative and surveillance activities.

Who the legislation applies to: All employers.

Additional details: The Patriot Act requires employers to provide the government access to business and employee communications and, thus, requires vigilance in two areas. On the one hand, you need to maintain your employees' privacy rights. On the other, you must comply as requested by the government and allow scrutiny of employee communications, including telephonic and electronic — without any mandatory prior notice to employees. Meeting these two demands requires thoughtful discussions with attorneys who can help you clarify and articulate the Patriot Act's legal implications for your employees. You also should work with computer, telecommunications, and security experts who can assist with everything from ensuring a safe internal communications environment to creating proper, secure means for employees to enter and exit your offices.

The WARN Act: Worker Adjustment and Retraining Notification Act (1988)

What the legislation does: Requires 60 days' advance written notice to affected employees (or their bargaining unit), as well as state and local rapid response/dislocated worker agencies, of mass layoffs or plant closings that will result in employment losses.

Who the legislation applies to: Employers with 100 or more employees.

Chapter 18

Handling Difficult Situations

In This Chapter

▶ Creating an ethical culture

▶ Understanding at-will employment

▶ Safeguarding your company against wrongful discharge action

▶ Dealing with discipline

▶ Handling employee grievances

▶ Settling disputes

▶ Giving employees the boot

▶ Handling layoffs

▶ Keeping your employees safe and healthy

▶ Eliminating sexual harassment

▶ Coping with workplace violence

Regardless of how good a job you've done in organizing the human resources function in your company, and regardless of how diligently you handle your day-to-day challenges, it's wishful thinking to expect your organization to be entirely free of personnel-related concerns. Even your best employees will make mistakes from time to time. So will your best supervisors.

As unpleasant as the prospect may seem, inevitably, you or the managers in your company will be obliged at some point to take some sort of corrective action — including termination — against an employee whose job performance or conduct falls short of company expectations.

Of course, at least with respect to job performance issues, you're rarely the one responding directly to the problem — the ultimate responsibility for evaluating job performance normally lies with the employee's immediate supervisor or manager. Nevertheless, as the person responsible for HR in your company, you still have a crucial role to play. It's up to you to make sure that job performance and workplace conduct issues are handled promptly, intelligently, and fairly — and in a way that doesn't diminish productivity, accelerate turnover, or deplete employee morale. And most important perhaps, you (more than likely) have to make sure that your company's disciplinary and termination policies minimize your company's exposure to wrongful discharge and other lawsuits.

In this chapter, I look at a more challenging aspect of HR management — but with an upbeat message. Most human resources problems are preventable and/or solvable, as long as you're alert to the early danger signs and you respond promptly with a clear sense of purpose.

This chapter provides you with a significant amount of legally sensitive information, prepared with the assistance of the law firm Paul Hastings LLP. But this area is not one where you can afford to be your own lawyer. Employee disciplinary action, termination, and layoffs are matters that require advice tailored to your particular company, location, and situation. My advice: Hire an attorney.

Establishing an Ethical Culture

The best overall way to reduce the number of difficult situations you have to deal with is to prevent them from happening in the first place. You can never hope to avert all employee improprieties and poor judgment, of course. But establishing a culture based on ethical behavior can go a long way toward diminishing these situations in your organization.

From the "tone at the top" on down, become a company that emphasizes the critical importance of employees' ethical behavior in all their interactions. People will always find ways and excuses to commit wrongdoing, just as they'll always be capable of making honest mistakes. But including integrity and consideration of others among your organization's core values not only prevents many unpleasant situations from occurring but also helps you develop a reputation as a business people want to work for.

It's very important that managers be every bit as accountable as employees. Your company should have a formal code of conduct that isn't buried on a shelf but is actively reinforced by all your managers. When employees hear one set of values but see another enforced — or, for that matter, neglected — by managers, the inconsistent messages can confuse them or cause them to question your commitment to your basic principles.

Fleshing Out the Meaning of At-Will Employment

Ever since horse-and-buggy times, employers in the United States have operated under a doctrine generally known as employment-at-will. *Employment-at-will* (sometimes referred to as *termination-at-will*) means that, in the absence of any contractual agreement that guarantees employees certain job protections, you (as an employer in the private sector) have the right to fire any of your employees at any time and for any (or no) reason — so long as the reason is not improperly related to an employee's protected status. In other words, you may terminate an employee with or without cause, with or without first exhausting all progressive discipline steps (if they exist), and with or without notice. At the same time, your employees have the right to leave at any time, for any (or no) reason, even without giving notice.

The concept of employment-at-will is specific to the United States. Other countries have their own sets of requirements concerning termination.

Employment-at-will is, however, subject to a number of significant limitations. If your company is unionized, for example, your employees' jobs are likely subject to contractual constraints.

Courts recognize and uphold the employment-at-will doctrine in particular cases so long as the employer's actions do not violate certain public policies and so long as the parties have not agreed otherwise (for example, by agreeing that employment is for a specified term, that employment can be terminated only for good cause, or that an employee can be discharged only after all progressive discipline steps have been exhausted). You can't terminate an employee for refusing to forge reports to the government or to violate antitrust laws, for instance. So, yes, your company still has the right to set behavioral standards, take corrective action when those standards aren't met, and fire employees who don't perform their job duties. However, you must be sure that in the process of carrying out these practices, you're not impinging on public policies.

Staying Out of Court

Wrongful discharge cases remain a mainstay of litigation against employers. Even more sobering is the fact that plaintiffs win most wrongful discharge suits that reach a jury trial largely because juries tend to favor employees over employers. How does a company protect itself? In short, protection comes from preventive action. Here are some key principles to bear in mind:

  ✔ **Review all company recruiting and orientation literature to ensure that no statements, implicitly or explicitly, "guarantee" employment.** Be especially careful about using terminology in employee literature and in conversations with employees (especially prior to hiring) that suggests an increased level of job security beyond employment-at-will, such as words like *permanent*. Courts have held that terms like this, which relate to duration of employment, can create an implied contract of employment through normal retirement age. If you need to differentiate between classes of employees, *regular* or *full time* are better terms. The term *probationary* should be used with caution for similar reasons;

some courts have concluded that, after an employee is no longer on probation, the employee has moved into a more secure employment relationship such that the employer must have good cause to terminate the employee (and can no longer terminate at will).

✔ **Train managers to maintain careful, detailed records of all performance problems and the disciplinary actions that have been taken in response to those problems.** Keep in mind that the verdict in many wrongful discharge suits hinges on whether the jury believes that the discharged employee was given "fair warning." Juries don't like it when they think an employee was surprised when terminated.

✔ **Make sure that all disciplinary and dismissal procedures are handled "by the book."** This means in a manner consistent with your company's stated disciplinary and termination policy. To be safe, your disciplinary and dismissal procedures should include a clause permitting the company to skip disciplinary steps or to impose more severe discipline or termination as circumstances warrant.

✔ **Make sure that all the managers and supervisors in your company are well versed in your company's disciplinary and termination procedures.** Train them and confer with them on a regular basis to ensure that they're following procedures. If you discover that they aren't, talk with them immediately, letting them know emphatically that failure to follow proper disciplinary and termination procedures is unacceptable and can prove extremely costly. Seek legal advice whenever you're uncertain about any aspects of your company's disciplinary or legal policy.

✔ **Be aware of how your actions may be misconstrued.** Be sensitive to the possibility that an employee who leaves your company voluntarily as a result of a change in assignment or work practices may be able to convince a jury that the change in assignment or work practices was a deliberate attempt on your company's part to force the employee to quit.

Developing Progressive Disciplinary Procedures

Some companies like a formalized disciplinary process, one that reasonably and systematically warns employees when performance falls short of expectations. A *progressive discipline system* is one in which problematic employee behavior is addressed through a series of increasingly serious disciplinary steps.

A formal progressive disciplinary procedure tends to work best in companies that are highly centralized, where personnel decisions for the entire company are made within one department (most likely HR), which makes sure that each step of the disciplinary process is implemented properly. The advantage is that the rules and regulations of job performance are consistently communicated to everyone. The disadvantage, however, is that you may be restricted to adhering, lockstep, to your established disciplinary system, even in a situation when you would prefer to immediately terminate an employee. If your company doesn't abide by these self-imposed rules, it could be found to have breached an employment contract.

On the other hand, some companies don't like such a process. A formalized disciplinary process doesn't work as well for organizations that are decentralized, where personnel decisions are made within each office or department on a case-by-case basis in accordance with a company's general expectations. In these situations, ensuring that each office or department follows the same disciplinary procedure can be difficult.

If your company is not required to have a progressive discipline system (for example, under a collective bargaining agreement) but elects to implement one, the policy should be very carefully written and administered. If not, the company may find itself having established a contractual arrangement where the company is required to exhaust each progressive step of discipline before it may terminate an employee. In this situation, a decision to jump immediately to employment termination or harsh discipline can amount to a breach of the contract, and expose the company to damages to the affected employee. You may want to consult with legal counsel to create or review your company's policy.

If your company elects to adopt a formal disciplinary process, you may want to create some or all of the following phases:

1. **Initial notification:** The first step in a typical progressive disciplinary process is informing the employee that his job performance or workplace conduct isn't measuring up to the company's expectations and standards. The employee's manager typically delivers this initial communication verbally in a one-on-one meeting. Details from this and all later conversations should be documented. The report doesn't have to be lengthy; a few bullet points highlighting the main topics are perfectly acceptable.

2. **Second warning:** This phase applies if the performance or conduct problems raised in the initial phase worsen or fail to improve, generally by an established time frame. The recommended practice is for the manager to hold another one-on-one meeting with the employee and accompany this oral warning with a memo that spells out job performance areas that need improvement. At this stage in the process, the manager needs to make the employee aware of how her behavior is affecting the business and what the consequences are for failing to improve or correct the problem. The manager needs to work with the employee to come up with a plan of action (written, if possible) that gives the employee concrete, quantifiable goals and a timeline for achieving them.

3. **Last-chance warning:** The penultimate phase of discipline, sometimes documented in a performance improvement plan (PIP), usually takes the form of a written disciplinary communication from a senior manager. The document informs the employee that if the job performance or workplace conduct problems continue, the employee will be subject to termination. Particularly with a PIP, very specific performance correction steps are laid out, along with specific deadlines by which the steps must be accomplished. What you're doing here is using the PIP as a tool to assist the employee in gaining (or regaining) an acceptable level of performance — and notifying the employee that his failure to meet this standard will lead to termination.

   If a union contract applies, this step also may involve a suspension, a mandatory leave, or, possibly, a demotion.

4. **Termination:** Termination is the last phase in the process — the step taken when all other corrective or disciplinary actions have failed to resolve the problem.

This description of progressive disciplinary steps is a general guideline and is not intended as a substitute for legal counsel.

Cause for termination

In the absence of a collective bargaining agreement or written employment agreement stating otherwise, certain employee infractions and misdeeds are so egregious that they justify immediate termination — even without going through the normal disciplinary steps that you otherwise may follow. Your orientation literature and employee policies should provide examples of offenses that may lead to immediate dismissal (but also should expressly state that the company reserves the right to take any disciplinary action, including termination, at any time it chooses, regardless of whether the offense is listed). Here's a list to get you started:

✔ Stealing from the company or from other employees

✔ Possessing, using, distributing, or selling illegal drugs

✔ Exhibiting blatant negligence that results in the damage to or loss of company machinery or equipment

✔ Falsifying employment-related or company records

✔ Violating confidentiality, trade secrets, and similar agreements

✔ Misappropriating or misusing company assets

✔ Making threatening remarks to other employees or managers

✔ Engaging in activities that represent a clear case of conflict of interest

✔ Misrepresenting or lying about job credentials

However you decide to structure your disciplinary plan, the process itself — apart from being fair — should meet the following criteria:

✔ **Clearly defined expectations and consequences:** Every employee in your company should be aware of the expectations and standards that apply companywide and to her particular job. These expectations and consequences should be introduced during the onboarding process (see Chapter 10) and then reinforced in one-on-one meetings between the manager and the employee. Your standards should be attainable and, to the extent feasible, measurable. Employees also need to know how not meeting these standards and expectations affects the company's operations. Your company needs to communicate standards and expectations early on in the employee's tenure. The same principle applies to workplace rules. Where an employer has imposed upon itself binding progressive disciplinary procedures, some courts may hold that the employer can't fire employees for violating rules of which they were unaware.

✔ **Early intervention:** This nip-the-problem-in-the-bud principle is that an employer steps in as early as possible when an employee's job performance or workplace conduct isn't satisfactory. Failing to provide pointed performance feedback early on can hurt you in two ways:

   • Employees can interpret the lack of any intervention as an implicit sign that they're doing just fine.

   • If you take action against another employee who is having similar problems, you leave yourself open to charges of favoritism or discrimination.

The discipline needs to be appropriate for the offense. Or, more specifically, the discipline needs to seem fair to employees and, possibly, to a jury. If your company is ever called upon to defend its actions, one issue that has a profound bearing on the final ruling is the relationship between the severity of the offense and the type of discipline. The general principle here is that you need to draw a clear distinction between those offenses or performance issues that warrant lower-level disciplinary action and those that are sufficiently serious to warrant immediate dismissal. You also need to factor into all disciplinary decisions — termination, in particular — the overall performance and discipline record of the employee and whether other employees in similar situations have been subjected to similar discipline.

✔ **Consistency:** You need to apply your company's policies and practices consistently — no favoritism or bending of the rules allowed! Solid, legitimate, nondiscriminatory reasons are the only justification for deviation.

✔ **Rigorous documentation:** The phrase *get it in writing* takes on extraordinary importance in any disciplinary process. Cumbersome though it may be, the supervisors and managers in your company must get into the habit of recording all significant infractions and problems, along with the steps taken to remedy those problems. Lacking detailed documentation of what the company has done throughout the disciplinary process seriously weakens its case, regardless of whether the firing was justified. When deciding whether to terminate an employee, review evaluations, warning notices (if any), personnel policies or work rules, witness statements, *witness evaluation notes* (notes by the employer representative conducting an internal investigation in which she is documenting her impressions of the credibility of the witness being interviewed), and other relevant documents, such as customer complaints, production reports, and timecards. If the documentation is not deemed sufficient, ask the manager for more information and hold off on taking action until you've determined that you have a sufficient record to support the action you've decided to take.

Four questions to consider in employee discipline

Whether the format of employee counseling is oral or written, effective and defensible employee discipline should address four subjects:

✔ **What's wrong?** This is the most critical and difficult portion of any disciplinary communication to develop. Here's where you clearly and concisely tell the employee about the defects in his performance. Beware of three pitfalls: First, determine whether there are other employees who share the same deficiency but who are not subject to the same discipline. Selective discipline for "sins" that others also commit (but for which they are not disciplined) is difficult to sustain. Second, avoid jargon and confusing acronyms (for example, "Numerous late and defective GST forms and FFR reports"). Third, avoid conclusory statements where the employee cannot understand the precise problem (for example, "Your performance undermined our productivity goals"); instead be specific, explaining the cause-and-effect relationship between the unacceptable behavior and the unacceptable consequence of that behavior.

✔ **What does it take to correct it?** This is the second most critical portion of any disciplinary communication. Don't leave the employee with only an explanation of the defects in her performance. Provide an equally clear explanation of what it takes to correct the deficiencies. Again, beware of three pitfalls: First, the corrective steps may not require training. For example, an employee may understand her duties well but perform them carelessly. If so, you may be able to say nothing more than that she must adhere to known policies and procedures. Second, if the corrective steps require training, be sure that the employee receives it. Third, if the corrective steps involve close monitoring by a supervisor or manager, make sure that the supervisor or manager is available to provide it. Otherwise, the employee may claim later that "no one helped me during the entire period of my PIP."

✔ **How long does the employee have to correct it?** This section may be short. It may be no longer than "You must demonstrate immediate and sustained correction of the deficiencies that we have identified." Do not use the word *improvement* in place of the word *correction;* there is bound to be improvement, but your expectation is correction. If discipline is linked to improvement, the employee will assert that he satisfied your expectations. Also, if you specify a period of correction, such as 30 or 60 days, always make it clear that you, as the employer, may shorten or eliminate this period. If the communication is in writing, be sure to insert the phrase: "The company reserves the right to shorten or eliminate this review period, if there are repeat or additional performance deficiencies."

✔ **What are the consequences of failure to correct it?** Clearly communicate the specific consequences that the employee will face if she fails to correct the problem. If written, this portion of the disciplinary communication also may be short (for example, "Failure to [immediately] correct these deficiencies may result in more severe discipline, including discharge, without further progressive counseling").

Defusing Grievances

An effective, well-balanced disciplinary process does more than provide a means for dealing with employees' problem behavior. It also gives them an opportunity to speak up (and be heard) when they're not happy with the way things are going in the workplace. Their complaints are technically known as grievances. Here are suggestions on how to implement a grievance procedure:

✔ **Offer complaint-reporting options.** As a general rule, instruct employees to bring their complaints to the attention of their immediate supervisors. If the complaint involves the supervisor, however, employees should have the right to address the matter with someone outside the established chain of command. In many circumstances, directing complaints through a different channel, such as a trained and designated member of the human resources department, may be appropriate.

✔ **Stress the importance of prompt response.** Everyone in the company who's responsible for receiving employee complaints should make it a point to address the complaint as promptly as possible. Ideally, an employee should know within 24 hours that you've received his complaint and you're handling it. Don't worry — that doesn't mean you have to provide a complete answer in a day. But a swift initial response demonstrates your concern and commitment to resolving the issue. Of course, determining how long a problem takes to resolve depends on how complicated the issue is.

How swiftly your company responds is critical when the complaint involves alleged sexual harassment or discrimination. In such cases, all supervisors and/or managers should be trained immediately to notify you or others in an HR role. They should likewise be trained to promptly escalate complaints of serious workplace safety or health violations or criminal activity. Ignoring any complaint that deals with serious issues greatly increases your company's exposure to legal action.

✔ **Report back to the employee.** Whether the complaint is substantiated or not, you need to keep the employee who registered it informed of what you're doing to deal with the situation. If you ultimately find that the complaint isn't substantiated ("We have no evidence to suggest that someone is poisoning our water supply"), explain why you feel that more action isn't warranted.

If the complaint is justified, indicate that corrective action is being taken. Depending on the circumstances, such as workplace safety, you may even want to communicate the nature of the action to the complainant. On the other hand, given privacy considerations, you may want to be careful in terms of communicating the nature of the disciplinary action taken against another employee.

✔ **Protect the employee from reprisals.** Ensure employees that if they follow the company's recommended procedure for filing complaints, they won't be penalized for doing so — regardless of the nature of the complaint, as long as it's offered in good faith. When handling a complaint, remind all parties involved of your company's antiretaliation policy. And if you need to resolve a dispute between an employee and a supervisor, caution supervisors about taking any actions that may be perceived as retaliatory — such as unfavorable work assignments, an inappropriate transfer, or a demotion — while an investigation is underway or shortly after its completion.

It is critical that your company distinguish between complaints of alleged unlawful harassment or discrimination and complaints of other, day-to-day workplace issues. In this section, I address the latter — the day-to-day personnel problems and workplace issues that may arise. In contrast, for complaints of sexual harassment or harassment based on another protected characteristic, or of discrimination, your company needs to have a separate antiharassment/antidiscrimination policy and an established procedure for raising complaints under such policy. Also, there are specific features that must be embedded in such a policy in order to ensure that it complies with applicable federal and, possibly, state or local laws.

Settling Disputes: Alternative Dispute Resolution Programs

Left unresolved, conflicts often escalate into major disruptions. But if you can resolve these disputes, you can create the kind of atmosphere that fosters open communication and innovative thinking. The key is to settle any workplace dispute fairly, dispassionately, and quickly.

Whenever possible, settle disagreements or disputes at the local level. Some organizations establish an open-door policy, where employees are encouraged to raise concerns or disputes with their supervisors or HR or other company leaders who are trained on how to handle these issues and are sensitive to when a reported concern must be escalated for higher-level attention.

There may be times when it is not possible to resolve matters internally, and an employee's legal claim against your organization is threatened or initiated. For many companies, alternative dispute resolution (ADR) is an appealing alternative to the costly and unpredictable court action in wrongful discharge suits. ADR involves the same options as traditional conflict resolution strategies: mediation or arbitration. Both mediators and arbitrators typically have legal backgrounds, a vital skill given the extremely sensitive and potentially expensive implications of the termination process.

Mediation and arbitration programs also can be created and implemented in-house by an organization's own management team or ombuds office. Even then, however, the actual mediation or arbitration meeting or hearing is processed best by an outside firm or professional who specializes in these areas.

If you elect to try mediation or arbitration, you should consult a knowledgeable and experienced attorney.

Firing Employees: It's Never Easy

Even when you have ample cause for doing so, firing employees is difficult — not only for the employees losing their jobs and the supervisors making the decision, but for co-workers as well.

You can do only so much to ease the pain and disruption that firings create. You can do a great deal, however, to help ensure that your company's approach to firing meets two criteria:

✔ Protects the dignity and the rights of the employee being terminated

✔ Protects your company from legal and/or retaliatory action by a disgruntled former employee

The standard (and recommended) practice in most companies is for the immediate supervisor to deliver the termination notice. The message should be delivered in person and in a private location. Depending on the circumstances, it's generally beneficial for the company to have a third person also attend the meeting, such as another supervisor or member of the HR department.

This person can serve as something of a neutral presence, as well as a witness, provide moral support for the company representative, and, if necessary, help manage the situation if it becomes emotionally charged. Do not involve co-workers. (*Note:* Some union contracts require the presence of a third person, such as a union official.)

Regardless of why an employee is leaving your company, keep the termination meeting as conclusive as possible. It's not subject to negotiation. This is a meeting that is, in essence, a one-way meeting, in which a conclusion about the employee's termination is communicated and not up for challenge or reconsideration. All this means that you need to prepare prior to the meeting. The following list covers some issues to consider:

- ✔ **Legal notices that must be given to terminating employees:** Some states impose obligations on employers to furnish certain information to employees upon their termination, such as written notice of the change in the employment relationship, information related to unemployment benefits, and conversion rights related to group insurance policies. You'll need to check applicable laws before the termination meeting.

- ✔ **Final payment:** Ideally, any employee being dismissed should walk out of the termination meeting with a check that covers everything he is entitled to, including severance if your organization has a policy allowing for an unconditional severance payment under the circumstances (see "Easing the burden," later in this chapter). Some states, such as California, impose penalties for failing to pay an employee all wages (including accrued, unused vacation benefits) due at the time of termination.

- ✔ **Security issues:** Think about company security, including keys, building or facility access cards, and company credit cards. Prepare your IT department in advance as to when to deactivate the employee's logins and passwords and access to company systems and files.

- ✔ **Company-owned equipment:** Be prepared to ask the employee to return any company-owned equipment immediately. If the equipment is off-site (a computer in the employee's home, for example), arrange for its pickup or for it to be sent back to the company in prepaid packaging to make it easy for the former employee to send you back your valuables.

- ✔ **Workplace violence or aggravated behavior:** You may want to contact your building's security services, if such services exist, to inform them that a termination is occurring and that you'll let them know if you need assistance.

- ✔ **Extended benefits information:** If your company is subject to COBRA regulations (see Chapter 17), you're generally obligated to extend the employee's medical coverage — with no changes — for 18 months. Who pays for the benefits — your company or the employee — is your call; you're under no legal obligation to pick up the tab. Make sure, though, that you provide all the information the employee needs to keep the coverage going. Often, this simply means contacting your insurance carrier and advising it of the upcoming termination and ensuring that the employee will receive all legally required COBRA notices and information. Also, prepare in advance so you can resolve all questions regarding an employee's 401(k), pension, or stock plan during the meeting, providing up-to-date information on what options, if any, the employee has regarding those benefits. Otherwise, advise the employee of the name and contact information of your benefits representative so he can obtain this information after the meeting.

✔ **Notification of outplacement or other support mechanisms:** If your company has set up outplacement arrangements (or any other services designed to help terminated employees find another job), provide all the relevant information, including company brochures and the level of services the company does (and does not) provide. Some companies arrange for an outplacement counselor to be on-site to serve as the first person the terminated employee talks to following the termination meeting.

Avoiding common firing mistakes

The following guidelines can help you avoid some common mistakes in connection with employee terminations:

✔ **Is there a rule, policy, practice, or performance standard?** Be sure to identify a rule, policy, practice, or performance standard that an employee violated that warrants his discharge. Sometimes what seems to be an obvious standard just doesn't exist. For example, although an employee may have "stolen" parts from a distribution center, there may be no express policy regarding the parts that the employee "stole" if, for example, he took them out of the dumpster in the parking lot.

✔ **Did the employee know the rule, policy, practice, or performance standard?** An employer may have a policy on a particular subject, but the company never disseminated it or it was never disseminated to the particular employee. It is not true that only policies or standards that are distributed to employees in writing will support an employee discharge, but you should explore the possibility that the employee legitimately did not know of (or understand) the policy or standard at issue. At the same time, some behavior is so outrageous that an employee can't legitimately claim that she didn't know she was doing something wrong (though these situations are not the norm).

✔ **Did the employee break the rule, policy, or practice or fail to meet a performance standard?** Be sure to carefully analyze the situation. Think objectively about whether the circumstances are convincing. Also consider a related issue: Is there a plausible excuse? For example, an employee late to work five times in one month may explain that on two of these days, he stopped to talk to a supervisor in the parking lot before heading to his desk.

✔ **Is termination appropriate?** In deciding to fire an employee, you need to consider whether other employees who have engaged in similar behavior were terminated. Often, there are nuances that seem to justify a termination in this instance, even if termination has never (or seldom) occurred previously. Think critically about whether the nuances may be difficult to rely on if the person sues. On the flip side, there also can be instances in which an employee has committed a terminable offense for which others have been terminated, but for which termination in this specific case may be too harsh or appear too callous (for example, the employee was distracted by a close family member's illness). This isn't to say that termination may not still be appropriate — you just need to think about how the termination "plays" to an outsider and how you can show that the punishment was justified, despite the excuse.

Delivering the news

No perfect script lets employees know that they're being discharged, but the news should be delivered as soon as the termination meeting starts, immediately after opening greetings are exchanged.

Employees being discharged have the right to be told why the decision was made, even if you've had a previous discussion about problems and infractions. Tact and sensitivity are important, but so is honesty. Keep the conversation short and to the point. Don't try to fill in awkward silences, and don't apologize for taking this step.

Remind managers that whatever they say during the termination interview (for example, "It wasn't my idea — management is just trying to cut back") can come back to haunt your company in a wrongful discharge or similar lawsuit. Managers should be trained to state the specific reason for the company's termination decision and not offer additional explanation. If the manager doesn't feel confident about how the discussion is to be handled, he can conduct the termination discussion with you, the HR professional, in the room.

Keep any discussion of the employee's shortcomings brief — one or two sentences at most. The termination meeting is not the time to engage in a lengthy discussion of the employee's faults, even if the employee challenges the basis for the decision and tries to engage in extended discussion about the merits of the decision. So much has occurred prior to this stage that it's best to let the decision speak for itself.

Putting in place a post-termination protocol

If your company hasn't developed one, work with your management to develop a disciplined, clearly defined procedure for what happens after you discharge an employee. Make the break as clean as possible — albeit with respect to the feelings and dignity of the person being fired. Harsh and humiliating though the practice may seem, accompany the dismissed employee back to her workstation, give the employee a chance to collect her personal belongings, and escort the employee out the door. If the company has confidentiality agreements, remind employees — in writing — of their legal obligations, ideally by handing them a copy of such agreements. Also, advise employees that they're no longer authorized to access the company's computer systems and any online accounts.

Generally speaking, holding the meeting early in the week and at the end of the workday is best. If you conduct the termination meeting on Monday or Tuesday, you make it easier for the dismissed employee to get started immediately on a job search and for you to begin searching for another employee. By delivering the news as late in the day as possible, you spare the employee the embarrassment of clearing out his or her office in front of co-workers.

Asking the employee to sign a waiver of rights

Some companies ask a discharged employee to sign a written waiver or release of legal claims in exchange for a financial payment or other extra consideration. Often called a *severance agreement,* some employers require employees to sign this document and return it by a specified date as a condition for receiving severance payments. Note that this payout is separate from any wage-related compensation regulated by state or federal law, such as accrued benefits or regular compensation. Due to the differences in the time requirements between when final pay must be given to the terminated employee and when payment under a severance agreement may be due, it is quite possible that there will be two separate checks involved.

Although some people believe that employers who present waivers of rights while terminating employees can communicate — merely by presenting the waiver — that they're worried about the legality of their actions, it's quite common practice in many companies and a useful business tool. Keep in mind, though, that your legal counsel should closely review such a document and that, typically, the employee should be encouraged to consult legal counsel as well. In fact, it's a good practice to discourage employees from signing the document during the termination meeting — if she does, she may argue later that she signed the document while under duress, a legal doctrine that could justify setting it aside as invalid.

If your company asks an employee to release claims of age discrimination under federal law, Congress has established a series of requirements that must be met, including certain language within the document itself and certain time requirements. Otherwise, the release will be considered an invalid waiver — even if the employee accepts the financial payment for the release. Also, the federal Fair Labor Standards Act and some state laws impose limitations on the release of wage claims. Consult legal counsel for help in these technical areas.

Easing the Trauma of Layoffs

Layoffs differ from firings in a variety of ways, but one critical aspect comes to mind: The people being let go haven't necessarily done anything to warrant losing their jobs. Layoffs occur for a number of reasons, which can include

- ✔ Seasonal shifts in the demand for the company's products or services
- ✔ An unexpected business downturn that requires the company to make drastic cost reductions
- ✔ A plant or company closure
- ✔ An initiative that restructures work practices, leaving fewer jobs
- ✔ A merger or acquisition that produces redundancy in certain positions

Generally, in a nonunion, private work environment, when someone is laid off, there is no expectation that she will be returning to work. Some companies use the term in a different sense, however. When business is slow and they don't need the entire current workforce, some firms (particularly those operating in a unionized environment) notify workers that they'll be placed on *furlough* for a period of time and will be offered the opportunity to return to work on a certain date or in stages. Some companies (especially seasonal businesses and those for which losing a major project creates a significant worker surplus) call this arrangement a "layoff" or "seasonal layoff" even though they plan to bring people back to work if and when conditions allow. Depending on the nature of the business — and its affiliation with unions or public- versus private-sector obligations — many companies today avoid suggesting that a layoff is temporary because it can be difficult to determine with certainty whether or when employees will be recalled to work. Layoffs (sometimes called *reductions in force, position eliminations, restructuring, downsizing,* or *rightsizing*) are far more common when they refer to employee terminations that are final. One thing that all these approaches have in common, however, is that they're involuntary and generally are considered to be no fault of the people affected.

I say employees *generally* are laid off through no fault of their own because sometimes a business must eliminate a certain number of positions in a department or business line, and the decisions about who will be selected may be based on evaluations of the employees' relative work performance. In such cases, employees with weaker job performances may be placed at the top of a layoff list, whereas those with stronger job performances may be protected from layoff.

Whatever the reason for a layoff, the pressure on the HR function is the same. You need to help your company navigate this difficult turn of events with as few long-term repercussions as possible. The following sections guide you through the process.

Analyzing whether layoffs are the right strategy

Carefully consider whether layoffs will be effective in achieving your business objectives — whether your goals are to reorganize operations, reduce operations, or eliminate unprofitable business units or lines. When weighing the possibility of layoffs, make sure that the management team is considering more than the bottom-line implications and is thinking about the impact on customers and remaining staff members. Layoffs may turn out to be inevitable, but management should be aware that the short-term, cost-cutting benefits of layoffs may well be offset by the following factors:

- ✔ Severance and outplacement costs for the laid-off employees (including accrued vacation and sick pay)
- ✔ The impact on your company's future unemployment compensation obligation
- ✔ The effect on morale and productivity
- ✔ The impact on future recruiting and new employee training efforts

Knowing the federal and state law

If the number of full-time employees in your company meets or exceeds 100, your layoff strategy needs to consider the federal Worker Adjustment and Retraining Notification (WARN) Act. As I explain in Chapter 17, the WARN Act requires that covered employers give 60 days' advance written notice of a mass layoff or plant closing. A *mass layoff* is a reduction in force that is not a plant closing and that results in employment losses within any 30-day period for 500 or more employees or 50 or more employees if they represent at least 33 percent of the active, full-time employees at that single site of employment. For this purpose, an *employment loss* includes a reduction in hours of work of more than 50 percent during each month for six months or more.

Employers covered by the WARN Act don't have to give 60 days' advance written notice in the event of smaller layoffs. Beware, though, that multiple, related layoffs occurring within a 90-day period may be aggregated to reach the threshold number required to trigger WARN Act obligations. Also, more than one-third of states have their own WARN-like laws.

Congress has repeatedly considered proposed laws to amend the WARN Act to require, for example, notice farther in advance (for example, 90 days). These matters can be tricky, so consult your legal counsel.

Be prepared to defend the rationale behind your layoff criteria. Be careful, too, that in the process of carrying out this more strategically driven approach, you're not laying off a disproportionately high number of employees who are in any group protected by equal employment opportunity legislation. (For more details on such laws, see Chapter 17.)

Easing the burden

Moral considerations notwithstanding, it is in your company's long-term best interests to do whatever is reasonably possible and fiscally responsible to ease both the financial and psychological pain that layoffs invariably create. You may want to consider offering severance packages (and indeed, you may have a written policy or practice obligating you to do so). If so, most employers offering severance benefits require a release of legal claims from the employee in exchange for the separation benefits. But you can take additional steps — for example, help in résumé writing, financial planning, networking, and so on — that won't cost you much money but will, nonetheless, help employees get back on their feet again.

Hiring outplacement specialists

Outplacement firms are companies that specialize in helping dismissed employees (usually middle managers and above) move through the transition and find new employment. In a typical outplacement program, managers who've been let go get an opportunity to attend seminars or one-on-one sessions in such areas as career counseling, professional goal setting, and job-hunting basics (preparing effective résumés, networking, interviewing, and so on). Among the services offered by outplacement firms to job seekers are office space, access to a phone and voicemail, Internet access, assistance in developing or revising résumés and crafting cover letters and online job inquiries, and administrative help for a predetermined period of time.

Outplacement, which is paid for by the former employer, can get expensive, particularly if your company is dealing with large numbers of dismissed managers. But it's one of the best ways to help those managers who've been with your company a long time and need the support. In major companies that conduct large-scale layoffs, outplacement services tend to be the rule, not the exception. Also, outplacement firms offer varying levels of services. It may be beneficial to offer at least a basic set of services to displaced employees versus none at all.

Alternatives to layoffs

If the purpose of the layoff is to cut down on costs (as opposed to reduce redundancy), you may want to explore options that, at the very least, can reduce the number of people who need to be terminated:

✔ **Temporary pay cuts:** Reducing salary costs is probably the simplest and most direct way to cut staffing costs without cutting staff. The key to this strategy is to ensure that everyone — including senior managers — shares the pain. Many companies, in their efforts to ensure equality, vary the percentage of reduction according to the amount of salary an employee is earning, with higher salaried workers surrendering a higher percentage of their regular paychecks than their lower-salaried counterparts.

Downside: No matter how justified the cuts and how many jobs you save, some workers will resent losing pay — and the decision to cut back on pay may induce some workers to quit. Keep in mind, too, that employees who agree to pay cuts will expect the salary to be restored — and then some — when the business turns around.

✔ **Work schedule reductions:** This option is worth exploring for companies that have large numbers of hourly workers. You maintain the same hourly rates, but employees work fewer hours per shift or per week. As an inducement to accept the lower take-home pay, most companies pledge to maintain benefits at full-time levels (so long as insurance carriers allow it).

Downside: Reduction of hours per shift or per week doesn't achieve financial savings for exempt salaried employees and managers who aren't paid by the hour. You may be able to reduce exempt employees' hours and pay by eliminating entire workweeks. If you want to reduce exempt employee work hours and salary by eliminating less than a full workweek — for example, one day per week — you should consult an attorney.

✔ **Short-term compensation programs:** Depending on the state laws under which your organization is operating, there may be legislation to help reduce hours (and, thus, costs) but avoid layoffs. Nineteen states have implemented some version of short-term compensation (STC) programs, authorized by federal legislation passed in 1982. In temporary economic downturns, STC programs allow employers that otherwise may be forced to lay off a portion of their workforce instead to apportion work reductions across the broader workforce. Affected employees receive unemployment insurance benefits on a prorated basis commensurate with the extent of their partial layoff. For example, rather than lay off 30 percent of employees, an employer might reduce the work hours of all employees by 30 percent; generally, the employees could then receive 30 percent of the unemployment benefits to which they would otherwise be entitled.

Downside: All 50 states participate in the unemployment insurance system, but only approximately one-third have STC programs, and until relatively recently, STC programs were rarely used — at least partly because employers were unfamiliar with them. However, such programs are garnering increased attention, even at the federal level, with more states moving toward establishing them.

✔ **Exit incentives:** An often-used method of reducing payroll costs is to offer voluntary

(continued)

(continued)

exit incentives, such as special early-retirement benefits. Because senior employees often are the most highly paid, trimming their ranks can result in significant savings.

Downside: Senior employees often are your most valued, and losing too many of them at one time can significantly weaken the leadership of your firm. Remember, too, that under the Age Discrimination in Employment Act, it is illegal, with rare exceptions, to force anyone to retire.

Addressing the concerns of those who remain

Layoffs are traumatic not only for the people who are laid off but also for those who remain. Apart from the sympathy they may feel for colleagues, remaining workers must generally take on increased workloads. Regrouping after layoffs as quickly and effectively as possible and giving your new, smaller staff a renewed sense of purpose and opportunity is key to your future.

If, at some point, your company finds it necessary to conduct layoffs, keep the following pointers in mind:

- ✔ **Honest, open communication is critical.** Bear in mind that what you don't say to employees can be as disconcerting and worrisome as what you do say. It's important for managers to have team meetings very soon after layoffs have occurred, not merely to explain what's taken place but also to set goals, clarify roles, and, most of all, genuinely listen to concerns.

- ✔ **Treat employees as professionals.** Explain why the layoffs were necessary, why current staff members were chosen to stay on, and what you're expecting from them in the future. Make employees aware that their contributions are now more essential to the company's continued success than ever before.

- ✔ **Focus on the future.** You'll need to clearly explain why downsizing was an unavoidable move for your company. But instead of focusing too much on what employees have *lost* in terms of colleagues, focus on what they're *gaining* in terms of a stronger, more stable company.

- ✔ **Consult a staffing firm.** Just as staffing services can help your displaced employees find new work, they also can help you bring in skilled supplemental workers to maintain continuity and prevent burnout on the part of remaining full-time staff.

Protecting the Safety and Health of Your Employees

U.S. employers are legally obligated to provide a workplace in which neither the environment nor the work practices subject employees to any unreasonable risk in safety or health. Safety- and health-related regulations vary considerably within an industry and according to state or federal regulations. (A good resource is the Occupational Safety & Health Administration, also known as OSHA.) Although the federal Occupational Safety and Health Act law applies throughout the United States, it permits states to implement their own plans with requirements above and beyond the federal regulations. More than 20 states have adopted their own plans. Consequently, no one single standard or list of safety- and health-related regulations applies across the board to every company. At the very least, though, it's your responsibility as your company's HR specialist to make sure of two things:

- ✔ Your company is in compliance with the federal and/or state safety and health regulations that apply to your company.

- ✔ Your company is doing everything that is reasonably possible (independent of your legal obligations) to protect the safety and health of your employees.

The safety and health area is a complicated one. When in doubt, consult an attorney.

The CD includes several documents that can help you ensure a safe workplace, including the following:

- ✔ Employee Emergency Notification Form

- ✔ OSHA Information Posting

- ✔ Work-Related Injury and Illness Report Form

Sexual Harassment: Keeping Your Workplace Free of It

The definition of *sexual harassment,* on the surface, seems fairly straightforward. Broadly, it is imposing an unwanted condition on a person's employment because of that person's sex. Then again, maybe not. At issue is the connection between the behavior and the working circumstances and conditions of the person who is being harassed and the role of the alleged harasser. Often, sexual harassment is really about power — abuse of power — in the workplace.

Generally speaking, sexual harassment falls into one of two categories:

✔ *Quid pro quo* **harassment:** The *quid pro quo* theory rests on the notion that an individual has relied on his or her actual or apparent authority to extort sexual favors from an employee.

✔ **Hostile environment harassment:** Hostile environment sexual harassment, in contrast, is when an individual has been required to endure a work environment that substantially affects a term or condition of employment.

The Equal Employment Opportunity Commission's guidelines describe sexual harassment as follows: "Unwelcome sexual advances, requests for sexual favors, and other verbal or physical conduct of a sexual nature." The guidelines go on to add additional requirements:

✔ Submission to such conduct is made either explicitly or implicitly a term or condition of an individual's employment.

✔ Submission to or rejection of such conduct by an individual is used as the basis for employment decisions affecting such individuals.

✔ Such conduct has the purpose or effect of unreasonably interfering with an individual's work performance or creating an intimidating, hostile, or offensive working environment.

You don't have to be a linguistic scholar to figure out that these guidelines are loaded with terms that are highly dependent on perceptions and interpretations. People (courts included) have varying ideas of what is implicit and different perceptions about what factors make a workplace intimidating or hostile. Nevertheless, these are important concepts that you should at least have a basic understanding of in order to address this important area in your work environment.

I can make one statement with certainty: No company today can afford to ignore this issue, and no one with HR responsibility can afford to forget that what one person may view as a harmless joke may well be perceived by another as an aggressive and unwelcome sexual advance. Sexual harassment is one area of HR management in which you can never be too careful. To point you in the right direction, this section offers guidelines that may help you develop a proactive — and effective — sexual harassment policy in your organization.

Spreading the word

It's no longer enough to simply declare in writing your company's commitment to prevent sexual harassment. You need a written policy that spells it out clearly, and you need to state, in no uncertain terms, the penalties for violating the policy. In fact, under the law, an employer may be found not liable for certain forms of sexual harassment if the employer can show that it exercised reasonable care to prevent and correct promptly any harassment and that the employee complainant unreasonably failed to take advantage of preventive or corrective opportunities provided by the employer. Establishing and enforcing an antiharassment policy is an important part of showing that your organization exercised reasonable care in addressing any harassment. The Equal Employment Opportunity Commission (EEOC) has identified key elements to include in such a policy, such as a clear explanation of prohibited conduct, assurances that complainants will be protected from retaliation, and a process for reporting complaints of sexual harassment (see the next section), among others.

The CD includes a Sample Policy Statement on Harassment and Retaliation. You should consult an attorney for assistance in preparing your own policy.

Your company is responsible for making sure that everyone in the organization — supervisors, managers, and employees — recognizes that sexual harassment is wrong and will not be tolerated in the workplace. Some laws require employers to display posters setting forth information about the law and employee rights in this area, other laws require employers to distribute notices directly to employees containing similar information, and still other laws require that employers conduct training of employees in this area. For example, in California and Connecticut, covered employers must provide at least two hours of sexual harassment training on certain topics and at certain time frames. You may want to talk to an attorney or obtain information from your state equal employment opportunity agency, regarding your legal obligations in this area.

What the court was saying, in other words, is that it's not enough to simply adopt and publish a sexual harassment policy. It's also the company's responsibility to effectively communicate the philosophy and procedures associated with it to everyone in the company.

Publicizing your policy on sexual harassment can be accomplished yearly. Set a date during the same month each year and send copies of your policies to every employee. You also may consider developing an online sexual harassment policy manual and training course that you can deliver to every employee annually.

Creating a reporting process

Employees are not required by law to report sexual harassment to their employers in order to file a sexual harassment claim with the EEOC or a court. However, it's in your best interest that they do so — and it's critical that your organization establish a reporting procedure for complaints of sexual harassment, generally as part of a broader antiharassment policy. The complaint process must be understandable. It needs to identify accessible people, hot lines, or anonymous toll-free phone numbers to which complaints can be reported (and alternative people in the event that the alleged harasser is one of the designated company representatives who would otherwise receive sexual harassment complaints). There must be assurance that the employer will protect — to the extent possible — the confidentiality of harassment complaints. Aside from its legal significance in helping your organization defend against a claim of sexual harassment, the existence of an internal complaint procedure likely will help you to address, and hopefully resolve, alleged sexual-harassment-type issues without "help" from the government.

Investigating complaints

Regardless of how frivolous you may consider a sexual harassment complaint, you must take it seriously and investigate it in accordance with your policy. If an incident ultimately spirals into a court case, and it's revealed in testimony that management was aware of the complaint but didn't act on it, you may, as a result, have to pay more in damages.

Every sexual harassment complaint should be documented, and your organization must undertake a prompt, thorough, and impartial investigation into the alleged harassment. When management or HR learns of alleged harassment, it should decide if a detailed fact-finding investigation is needed (obviously not the case if the alleged harasser doesn't deny the accusation) and, if so, undertake it immediately. As part of the investigation, getting detailed statements from the person making the harassment charges, as well as from the accused and any witnesses, is paramount. Don't view paperwork as a burden. It can be your company's best defense. Documentation of discipline demonstrates that your company is serious about the problem and the solution.

Taking decisive action

If you determine that harassment has occurred in violation of your policy, undertake immediate and appropriate corrective action, including discipline. The type of remedial measures you take should be designed to stop the harassment, correct its effects on the employee, and ensure that the harassment doesn't happen again. These measures don't have to be those that the employee requests or prefers, as long as they're effective.

Doing nothing or being too lenient can put your firm at great risk and, at the very least, create the impression that you're condoning the behavior. This impression won't do much to help your company recruit or retain good employees and will expose the company (and possibly individual supervisors) to monetary damages.

Dealing with Workplace Violence

Violence in the workplace is an issue that no company — regardless of how large or small the company or where it's located — can afford to ignore.

What steps can your company take to provide reasonable protection for your employees? Your best source of information on this matter is your local police department. Most police departments have specialists in crime prevention who can survey your business and make recommendations. Other good sources for crime prevention strategies are your state occupational safety and health agency, which may have guidelines and recommendations on employee safety measures. Also, look to violence prevention experts, insurance companies, or private security consultants.

You need to take a twofold approach of both protecting your employees from the violent acts of outsiders and protecting your employees from the violent acts of fellow employees.

As much as you don't want to dwell on the unpleasant, it's better to be prepared for both external and internal threats. You can put in place specific policies that can lessen the possibility of emergency situations. To address external threats, consider the following:

- ✔ **Pay your employees by check, not cash.** Better still, encourage direct deposit of pay into employee bank accounts (with appropriate employee consent, of course).

- ✔ **Keep building perimeters and parking lots well lit.**

- ✔ **Limit access to strangers.** Consider implementing an access card system for employees. If appropriate for your business, ask visitors to wait in the reception area until an employee is available to escort them. Identify visitors with a special badge and escort them at all times. Instruct employees to notify the security office about strangers with no identification.

- ✔ **Provide lockers, desk drawers, or other safe areas where employees can secure valuables.**

To address internal threats, take these steps:

✔ **Establish and communicate to employees a strong, unequivocal policy of zero tolerance for violence.** Include as causes for immediate dismissal threatening gestures, fighting words, and physical actions. This policy should be included in your company's workplace violence policy and employee code of conduct.

✔ **Consider providing counseling and other assistance — possibly through an employee assistance program — for troubled employees or those with personal, financial or substance abuse problems.** Bear in mind your various legal obligations relative to disabled employees.

✔ **Be constantly aware that certain workplace situations, such as disciplinary meetings and termination interviews, have a potential for violence.** Take precautions accordingly.

Part VI
The Part of Tens

The 5th Wave   By Rich Tennant

"The next part of your employment test is designed to determine your sense of humor."

In this part . . .

Every book ends with top-ten lists, and this one is no exception. In this part, I offer ten keys to HR success in the future, ten ways to become a great HR professional, and ten HR-related websites worth exploring.

Chapter 19

Ten Keys to HR Success in the Future

In This Chapter

▶ Maximizing staffing

▶ Creating a healthy culture

▶ Understanding regulatory compliance

▶ Considering tech security

Your skill at building human resource strategies and policies that reinforce strategic objectives helps ensure your company's long-term success. In this chapter, I offer you ten ways you can positively affect your organization's future.

Adopt a Strategic Approach to Staffing

Hiring smart today means hiring *strategically* — taking the time and effort to make sure that each staffing decision matches the goals and operational needs of your company. The traditional approach to hiring — finding the one person who best fits the specs of a particular job — is losing ground in contemporary companies. Taking its place is a much more fluid and flexible model in which the goal is to determine what the job really requires and what combination of resources best meets that requirement.

If you follow this model, you begin the process by developing a clear picture of your company's strategic goals. You then focus on the skills and competencies that you need to accomplish them. Armed with this knowledge, you can target your search for the "right" people far more efficiently, and your search is more likely to produce the business results you want.

Understand the Strength of Traditional and New Strategies in Recruiting

Good people are always in demand. No company can afford to take a laid-back, business-as-usual approach to recruiting. The value of thoughtful and proactive recruiting has only grown in recent years. One reason is the Internet (see Chapter 6). Everything from online job boards to social media has made it possible to identify a wider range of prospective employees than ever before.

But recruiting has changed in other ways as well. In a sense, highly qualified job candidates seem to know more than ever just how much their skills and services are in demand and what companies are willing to do to attract them. (Again, the Internet has played a key role.) That makes the challenge of effective recruiting all the more significant. To get the best, you need to be at your own best when it comes to devising and implementing a successful recruiting strategy.

New advances have only supplemented — not replaced — traditional recruiting methods, such as personal referral networks. The point is, you need to constantly explore and experiment with new ways to find superb candidates. Job fairs, staffing firms, and campus recruiting all are valuable strategies. The key is to be as broad based as possible in your overall approach. No single recruiting strategy works for all situations. In the future, you'll need to become increasingly innovative in your practices.

Seek to Create a Healthy Culture

Every company has a *culture,* a working style and general environment that influence how it carries out its business and how employees relate to one another. The big question is whether the culture that prevails in your company is healthy — and whether senior management has a clear idea of the kind of culture it wants to create.

Healthy, dynamic company cultures — those seen at firms that rate high with employees, such as Intuit, Nordstrom, and Whole Foods — don't evolve overnight. Nor can you create them with a single all-employee e-mail or the introduction of one or two policies. Clearly, however, such cultures, whether you're a Fortune 500 company or a small business, take their cues from senior management.

As the HR practitioner in your organization, an essential first step to creating a positive cultural change in your company is to get senior management's vision of the ideal environment. (If you're a business owner, this is, of course, *you* — plus your top-ranking managers.) Only then can you develop the values necessary to create such a workplace. After management identifies those values, you and others within the company can examine individual practices to evaluate whether they reflect the company's desired "personality." This task isn't easy, but the long-term dividends are well worth the time and effort.

Get the Most out of Contingent Staffing

The astonishing growth in the last two decades of the contingent workforce (see Chapter 4) has given companies of every size and in every industry staffing flexibility and options that weren't previously available. (The opportunity to hire a former CFO on a project basis to help you take your company public is one such option.)

But if you want to take full advantage of the benefits these workers provide, you need to incorporate them into your overall human resources strategy. The most effective way to access the contingent talent you need is to work with a specialized staffing firm. A key advantage for you is that contingent staffing companies handle all compensation, payroll taxes, and, in many cases, benefits for their own employees.

Take a Proactive Approach to Regulatory Compliance

The legal ins and outs of the human resources function are becoming more confusing — and more restrictive — by the day. And all signs point to a trend that's only going to intensify in the future. Your challenge is twofold: Not only must you keep pace with changes in employment law, but you also must make sure that you're constantly bringing other key people in your organization up to speed as well.

Court rulings in recent years make clear that companies not taking an aggressive and proactive approach to communicating employment-related laws and regulations to their teams may still be held accountable for violations by individual employees. In addition, your frontline supervisors and your managers often are the first (and possibly only) company representatives with whom employment-law-related matters are raised (for example, when an employee calls in an absence that could trigger a Family and Medical Leave Act leave or Americans with Disabilities Act accommodation issue). Their ability to respond in a way that carries out your company's legal responsibilities is, in effect, your *company's* response. A failure to respond appropriately because of ignorance of the law could mean significant problems — and legal exposure — for your company. The moral is that, in keeping people in your organization informed about employment law, there is no such thing as overkill.

Make Work/Life Balance a Priority

Creating family-friendly policies is more than a simple act of company altruism. A smart policy covering work and family has become a bottom-line-driven best practice among some of today's most successful and respected companies. Policies enabling perks such as flextime, childcare support, and telecommuting can produce improvements in employee morale, employee satisfaction, and productivity while reducing turnover and absenteeism.

Even if some industries lend themselves more than others to these practices, your company needs to explore any workable options available to you. Top candidates in any economy can largely dictate which companies they want to work for, and lifestyle factors often play a key role in their decisions.

Keep Pace with Changing Demographics

As you take on the HR function, you become, in one sense, the psychologist of your workplace. Understanding what makes people tick and seeing how individuals can work together productively are key parts of your job.

But I urge you to borrow from another social science discipline, too: demographics. To be effective, you must also — at least to some degree — be attuned not just to individuals but to the broader, shifting demographics of our society. For the first time in history, the current workforce includes four distinct generations, each with its own set of desires, strengths, and work styles. They range from the Silent Generation (born before World War II) and the Baby Boomers to Generation X and the most recent addition to the workforce, Generation Y (also known as the Millennial Generation or Millennials). You need to understand how these groups differ from each other in terms of workplace approaches and preferences and how you can help them most effectively interact. Make knowledge sharing a priority to take advantage of your staff's variety of viewpoints, creativity, and talents.

Although awareness of these trends can be helpful in designing management policies and approaches (your benefits package, for example), be careful not to fall into the stereotype trap when considering generational differences. You and company line managers should develop individual relationships with staff to get an accurate picture of the attributes of each.

Demographic shifts are producing another challenge for the HR function. Although many Baby Boomers say they plan to work beyond the traditional retirement age of 65, large numbers of this group will inevitably leave the workforce each year for the foreseeable future. Companies, therefore, face the loss of some of their most experienced workers. Many companies are recognizing this potential knowledge drain and are taking steps to compensate for the departure of Baby Boomer–age workers. In your HR role, you'll have to boost recruitment efforts to attract new talent, but you also need to capture as much of the institutional knowledge of the Boomers as possible before they leave. The time to begin identifying your company's next generation of leaders and transferring critical wisdom is now. Organizations that do the best job of preparing for the anticipated exodus put in place well-thought-out programs and policies for knowledge exchange.

I'm not saying that you need to create new programs for every societal change you read about. But you, as a business owner, or the managers you work for will want to keep up with shifts in the composition of the workforce in your area that may affect employee concerns and priorities. That kind of big-picture understanding is precisely the kind of thinking that's making the HR profession so dynamic these days.

Play It Safe When It Comes to HR Technology

As HR professionals work to maximize the benefits of information technology, security is another key factor to keep in mind. With so many people in the organization now having access to more information, any system you use must be properly safeguarded against intrusion. This security is especially important in human resources, which houses such sensitive information as employee compensation, performance reviews, health records, and other important data.

Your second priority: the ability to consistently, smoothly, and affordably upgrade and integrate technology. It's not stop-the-presses news that technology is constantly changing and — at least in theory — improving. Not only do you want any new technology to be easy to master, but it also should integrate itself seamlessly into existing systems and applications. Cutting-edge technology is of little value when it can't be used to its fullest. As an HR professional, you're charged with balancing the appeal of new technology with how readily it can be incorporated into your business.

View Training As an Ongoing Investment

Training in progressive companies has a new face. It's no longer an event — a group of employees filing into a classroom to attend a one- or two-day workshop that they signed up for months earlier. Training is now an ongoing process, fueled by the notion that the one skill employees need to develop today, above all, is the ability to learn. Employees' ability to learn enables the companies they work for to keep pace with the relentless demands of a competitive, rapidly shifting economy.

The good news is that the Internet has made this ongoing learning process far easier. You can download engaging, interactive, often video-based training courses and materials to help more employees take advantage of new programs you and your colleagues create. For more on this and other aspects of training, see Chapter 14.

Handle Discipline and Dismissal Carefully

Bad things can happen to even the best companies. Regardless of how innovative and leading edge you want to be in your HR policies, don't lose sight of the basics, especially involving disciplinary action and dismissals. Wrongful termination suits remain common — with juries frequently showing a penchant for favoring the dismissed employee (see Chapter 18). When handling these difficult situations, apply fair and consistent practices and show respect for the dignity of the individuals involved. The manner in which disciplined or dismissed employees are treated can make a difference when it comes to whether they bring legal claims against you and/or your company. It also provides a message to the remaining workforce that can directly affect employee motivation, morale, and commitment.

Chapter 20

Ten Ways to Become a Great HR Professional

*L*ike virtually every field, human resources is not a static profession. You need to stay on top of trends and new developments, but that's not easy to do when your hands are full just carrying out your day-to-day responsibilities.

Amid the changes and challenges, which are likely only to accelerate in the coming years, you need to keep certain principles in mind. This chapter covers ten signposts for success as an HR professional.

Develop a Business Orientation to HR Initiatives

Leading HR professionals are keenly aware of the ways in which their work fits into their organization's overall business. They do this by understanding the complexities and operating challenges that set their companies apart from their competitors.

A basic understanding of business finance is helpful. (Quick test: Can you read a P&L statement?) Even more important, you need an in-depth understanding of your company's products and services, the competitive challenges it faces, and the strategic initiatives that are underway to meet those challenges. The best way to gain this knowledge is to participate in as many meetings and discussions involving these initiatives as possible. Set up meetings with line managers or other colleagues to find out about their strategic goals.

Position Initiatives As Bottom-Line Benefits

Human resources departments are traditionally viewed as cost centers. In more recent years, though, a growing appreciation for the bottom-line benefits of sound, innovative HR practices has emerged. You can reinforce this by providing more insight into the bottom-line implications of any HR initiative that you plan to recommend — everything from training programs to hiring practices and, difficult as it often is, employee termination procedures. Work with the financial analysts in your company to establish some concrete ways to attach a dollar value to the contributions your HR efforts are making to the company's bottom line.

Develop a Marketing Mindset

Typically, you need to aggressively market and make a case for new HR initiatives to all segments of your internal customer base: senior management, supervisors, and staff-level employees. The key is to focus your communication efforts on the benefits these projects deliver. As you're selling HR initiatives to senior management, stress competitive advantage. If your audience is made up of supervisors, stress the operational advantages — how a program can ease their day-to-day burdens.

As with any marketing initiative, you need to know your audience and base your approach on their needs and concerns. *Remember:* Whenever you're introducing a new initiative to a group of employees who are already under tremendous time pressures, anticipate resistance — even though the new program may be designed to ease those pressures in the long run.

Share Your Expertise

Your background and training has helped you develop skills you may take for granted — skills many managers in your company may lack. Chief among these are the ability to conduct an effective selection interview, resolve disputes, and facilitate team meetings. A small company may not have the time or budget to provide formal training in these areas, but you can accomplish a great deal through one-on-one coaching of employees to help them develop these skills. The bottom line: Don't sell yourself short as a resource.

Serve As the Model

One of the best and most easily controlled ways to increase your leverage and credibility in your company is for your own actions — and the actions of your staff members if you're not a one-person shop — to be a model for others. If you're trying to get line managers to adopt a less authoritarian, more collaborative management style, for example, demonstrate the benefits of that approach by managing your own people in a similar fashion.

Be particularly careful about the quality of the people you hire to assist you with your HR responsibilities. Make sure that your own staff recognizes that all employees in the company are internal customers, understands that all HR team members must be the model for your HR policies and procedures, and exhibits professionalism in day-to-day work activities.

Develop Your Communication Skills

Any measures you can take to enhance your communication skills — courses, seminars, personal coaching — will pay enormous dividends for you in almost every aspect of your job. Remember that, as an HR professional, you want to contribute to the growth of the company. To be truly effective in that role requires constantly earning acceptance for the initiatives you create. Your own skills as an effective speaker and writer greatly influence your ability to generate support for your initiatives.

Move Quickly — But Not Too Quickly

Regardless of the pressure you may be under to solve pressing problems, resist the tendency to rush (except when the law and individual circumstances require that you do so, such as by swiftly responding to and investigating a report of sexual harassment). Others may ask for something by yesterday, but a hurriedly assembled presentation to explain a fundamental change in benefits policy will come back to bite you. Do your best to prioritize the initiatives you'll undertake, and make sure that they're well thought out and enjoy the enthusiastic backing of key managers.

If you establish a pattern of introducing HR programs that lack follow-through or don't positively impact the bottom line, you lose credibility with the workforce and make acceptance of future programs all the more difficult for yourself. You're better off tackling a few programs that succeed than spreading yourself too thin.

Create and Maintain a Flexible Workforce

Part of the art of being an HR professional is knowing how to achieve a balance between understaffing and overstaffing as workloads ebb and flow. On the one hand, you don't want your company to be caught understaffed and unable to take advantage of growth opportunities. At the same time, you don't want to overhire. The answer is somewhere in between. Strive to adopt a flexible staffing strategy as your permanent business model. By augmenting the efforts of full-time employees with contingent professionals when workloads peak, you can better manage expenses, reduce the possibility of future layoffs (because you haven't added full-time employees beyond your core team), and gain the flexibility to easily staff up or down as demand for your company's services fluctuates.

Whether you seek to add staff on a temporary or permanent basis, consider using a staffing firm that specializes in the kinds of positions you're looking to fill. A specialized staffing firm can locate hard-to-find talent, and the individuals it provides also are more likely to make strong candidates for becoming full-time employees for positions you may have, or will soon have, open.

Be Sensitive to the Needs and Agendas of Line Managers

Even if HR programs have the blessing of senior management, never assume that your line managers will support them simply because doing so is "their job." Timing is everything. To get the most support from the company's managers when you need them to focus on HR initiatives, make a point of understanding their prior commitments and what's going on in their day-to-day jobs. You won't get much buy-in, for example, if you try to roll out a new program to the accounting team when they're approaching quarter or year-end deadlines.

One reason many initiatives get bogged down isn't for lack of a blessing from senior management, but because line managers haven't been shown the value of these ideas. Anticipate resistance and be patient. Be sure that you cascade communication around the value of specific HR initiatives from senior management to line managers and, ultimately, to all employees. Any HR initiative that you need to force on people is doomed to fail.

Stay on the Leading Edge

Dedicate a portion of your workweek — *every* week — to remaining current on new developments in the field. Here are some ideas on how to stay ahead of the curve:

- ✔ Read major HR publications and regularly read online articles, blogs, and social media postings for information that's relevant to your field, your company, and the overall business environment. Keep a current folder of new ideas and trends for ready access.

- ✔ Join your local HR group and actively involve yourself in programs and committees relevant to your work.

- ✔ Attend seminars and conferences geared specifically for HR practitioners.

- ✔ Stay informed about legal issues that can affect your policies through Internet research, through occasional conversations with lawyers, and by monitoring news stories and legal cases that will likely have HR implications. But don't go too far — be sure to consult an attorney when you're unclear on particular areas or when you're making important employment decisions that may involve legal risk to the company.

- ✔ Pay close attention to your competitors' HR practices — compensation and benefits, in particular. *Remember:* These differences may be giving them an edge in attracting high-performing employees.

Chapter 21

Ten HR-Related Websites Worth Exploring

. . . .

In This Chapter

▶ Websites on laws affecting the practice of HR

▶ Websites for HR information and professional guidance

▶ Websites to help you continue your HR education

. . . .

*P*lenty of websites address various aspects of the human resources function. Here, I list ten "desert island" sites. If I were forced to whittle them
down to just ten, these sites are the ones every HR professional should know
about and use.

American Society for Training & Development

www.astd.org

Access to most of the American Society for Training & Development (ASTD)
website is limited to members, but nonmembers can browse through the
library and get useful information on a variety of training-related topics.
Members have access to current and past articles from *Training and
Development*, ASTD's monthly magazine, as well as the usual features of a
professional organization website, including information on conferences,
education, job-related data, and certification.

Americans with Disabilities Act Document Center

www.ada.gov

As the name implies, this website devotes itself exclusively to information relating to the Americans with Disabilities Act (ADA) of 1990. In addition to a full text of the ADA, you get access to technical assistance documents and manuals prepared by the U.S. Equal Employment Opportunity Commission (EEOC), Department of Justice (DOJ), National Institute on Disability and Rehabilitation Research (NIDRR), and Department of Labor (DOL). The site provides you with links to other sources of information concerning workplace disability issues. Another great feature is information on proposed and new regulations.

Bureau of Labor Statistics

www.bls.gov

The website of the Bureau of Labor Statistics (BLS) is *the* place to go for numbers on all aspects of work in the United States. It contains a ton of information on specific industries, regions of the country, economic figures throughout the country, business costs, demographics, and more. Other elements include a steady flow of news releases, research papers, and online access to the DOL's publication, *Monthly Labor Review*. The data is well organized — the site groups news releases, for example, according to major BLS statistical categories, such as "Employment and Unemployment," "Inflation & Prices," and so on — and most of the statistical data comes with concise explanations provided by the BLS economic staff.

The elaws Advisors

www.dol.gov/elaws

Employment Laws Assistance for Workers and Small Businesses (elaws) was developed by the DOL and enables employers and employees alike to interact with online "advisors" about employment issues. The elaws Advisors simulate the interaction you might have with a DOL employment law expert. They ask questions, provide information, and direct you to the appropriate resolution based on your responses. Also available is a handy employment law guide that outlines major statutes and regulations affecting business and workers.

Human Capital Institute

www.hci.org

Human Capital Institute (HCI) is a global association for talent management on leadership, as well a clearinghouse for best practices and new ideas. Practitioners, Fortune 1000, and Global 2000 corporations; government agencies; global consultants; and business schools all contribute information, which is available through HCI communities, research, education, and events. The material is timely and consistently informative.

Occupational Safety & Health Administration

www.osha.gov

Given the scope of the Occupational Safety & Health Administration (OSHA) mission, the fact that this government-operated website is unusually large and varied is no surprise. Departments include an OSHA newsroom; sections on laws, regulations, and compliance; a reading room; outreach material; and easy links to the DOL website. The categories are voluminous — everything from asbestos to hazardous waste to workplace violence. A typical entry consists of a summary of the topic, along with an extensive list of links to other information sources. In some cases, you can download entire slide presentations. Some information on this website comes from sources other than the government, but you can download and copy nearly all of it without restriction. The library gives you online access to most OSHA documents.

Society for Human Resource Management

www.shrm.org

The Society for Human Resource Management (SHRM) provides much of its information to nonmembers, although you need to join to gain access to all articles and sections. The various departments include an "HR Talk" discussion forum (with a highlight feature that identifies recent topics of interest), a robust "Research" section, and a "Templates and Tools" section that allows members to access testing resources, how-to guides, and other materials.

SHRM provides a broad swath of timely information from a number of resources. In addition to news and information, the site also offers a comprehensive advocacy guide that addresses governmental regulations, public policy, and other important topics.

U.S. Equal Employment Opportunity Commission

www.eeoc.gov

Categories on this site include background on the commission, facts about employment discrimination and enforcement, litigation information, and areas that summarize Equal Employment Opportunity Commission (EEOC) policies for small businesses. You can access the full text of EEOC legislation and a manual offering an overview of compliance. A news feature provides information and updates related to employment discrimination.

WorldatWork

www.worldatwork.org

WorldatWork is a superb resource for news, research, educational resources, networking opportunities, and many more human resources topics. You may find that the cost of joining is well worth it, because the site covers a wide range of valuable publications and materials. As an HR professional, you may be particularly interested in WorldatWork's professional certification program, which includes certified compensation professional, certified benefits professional, global remuneration professional, and work-life certified professional. An online community allows members to connect with other professionals.

Workforce Online

www.workforceonline.com

Workforce Online was created and is run by the editors of *Workforce Management* magazine and takes a broad-based approach to its subject matter. Although you must register to access the information on this site (registration is free), after you log in, you can find a great deal to explore. The information database, for example, includes hundreds of easy-to-find articles covering every aspect of the HR function. Other departments include a technology directory, a buyer's guide, and job postings. A number of blogs provide analysis and up-to-date news and information.

Appendix

About the CD

In This Appendix
▶ Getting the lowdown on the system requirements
▶ Using the CD with Windows and Mac
▶ Exploring the CD contents
▶ Troubleshooting if something goes wrong

*H*ere's what you'll find on the *Human Resources Kit For Dummies* CD:

✔ More than 50 documents, including policies, forms, and contracts
✔ Adobe Reader, for viewing the PDF documents
✔ OpenOffice, for viewing the Word documents

If you're reading this in an electronic format, please go to `http://book support.wiley.com` for access to the additional content.

System Requirements

Make sure that your computer meets the following minimum system requirements:

✔ A PC running Microsoft Windows or a Mac running OS X
✔ A CD-ROM drive

If your computer doesn't meet these requirements, you may have problems using the software and files on the CD.

Using the CD

To install the items from the CD to your hard drive, follow these steps.

1. **Insert the CD into your computer's CD-ROM drive.**

   The license agreement appears.

   Note to Windows users: The interface won't launch if you have autorun disabled. In that case, choose Start⇨Run. In the dialog box that appears, type *D*:**Start.exe**. (Replace *D* with the proper letter if your CD drive uses a different letter. If you don't know the letter, see how your CD drive is listed under My Computer.) Click OK.

   Notes to Mac users: When the CD icon appears on your desktop, double-click the icon to open the CD and double-click the Start icon. Also, note that the content menus may not function as expected in newer versions of Safari and Firefox; however, the documents are available by navigating to the Documents folder.

2. **Read through the license agreement and then click the Accept button if you want to use the CD.**

   The CD interface appears. The interface allows you to browse the contents and install the programs with just a click of a button (or two).

What You'll Find on the CD

The following sections are arranged by category and provide a summary of the software and other goodies you'll find on the CD. If you need help with installing the items provided on the CD, refer to the installation instructions in the preceding section.

Software

The CD contains the following two programs:

- ✔ **Adobe Reader, from Adobe:** Adobe Reader allows you to view the PDF documents on the CD. For information about all the features and controls in Adobe Reader, be sure to check out the Adobe Reader Help file or visit www.adobe.com/products/reader.html.

- ✔ **OpenOffice, from Apache:** Use OpenOffice to view the Word files on the CD (if you don't already have Microsoft Word installed on your computer — if you already have Word, you don't need to download OpenOffice). You can find more about OpenOffice by reading the Help file or visiting www.openoffice.org.

Both of these programs are *freeware* (free, copyrighted applications); you can copy them to as many computers as you like — for free — but they offer no technical support. They work on Windows and Mac.

Documents

I've organized the forms and documents on the CD by the chapter in which they're mentioned. I briefly describe each document in this appendix, but refer to the actual document for more information.

Note: As is often indicated in the chapters, the forms and draft policies provided are only samples. Different state and local laws may impose different legal obligations, including with regard to the content of the documents and how you use them. An attorney can explain the particular laws that apply to your organization and employees.

Chapter 4

Blank Skills Inventory Form and Sample Skills Inventory Form: The form can serve as a model for an employee skills inventory.

Staffing Firm Evaluation Checklist: You can use this checklist to evaluate staffing firms.

Worker Classification Quick Reference Table: This document provides an at-a-glance summary of the differences among worker classifications.

Chapter 5

Blank Job Description Form and Sample Job Descriptions: This document includes a blank job description form so that you can develop your own job descriptions, as well as three sample job descriptions.

Chapter 6

Acknowledgement of Receipt of Résumé or Job Application: This form acknowledges that the company has received a candidate's résumé or job application.

Sample Job Ads: This document includes three sample job ads you can use as a reference when preparing your own.

Chapter 7

Applicant Self-Identification Form: This form is for use only by federal government contractors or subcontractors. It should be given to job applicants. The data collected are compiled in the EEO-1 Report, which is a report that private employers with 100 or more employees and certain federal contractors are required to submit to the Equal Employment Opportunity Commission (EEOC) annually.

Rejection Letter: This is an example of a "thanks, but no thanks" letter to an unsuccessful applicant.

Sample Employment Application: This document is a sample employment application you can make available to job candidates.

Sample Phone Interview Questions for Hiring Managers: This form lists a number of sample questions to consider when conducting a job interview over the phone.

Sample Résumés: This document includes examples of well-written résumés and a résumé that could cause you to question the qualifications of the applicant. Keep these in mind when reviewing the résumés you receive for open positions with your firm.

Chapter 8

Candidate Interview Evaluation Form: Use this form to record your general impressions of a job candidate.

Employment Inquiries Fact Sheet: This fact sheet contains suggested guidelines for managers involved in the hiring process. The information is specific to California and may be different for other states.

Nondiscriminatory Interview Question Reference Sheet: You can use this reference sheet to avoid interview questions that could pose legal problems.

Interview Q&A Form: Use this form to write down questions you want to ask a job candidate during an employment interview, to record the candidate's answers, and to jot down any of your own comments.

Pre-Interview Checklist for Hiring Managers: This form lists issues to take into account when preparing to interview a job applicant.

Chapter 9

Background Check Permission (Comprehensive) for Prospective Employee: This is a sample form in which a prospective employee grants the employer permission to do a comprehensive background check on the prospective employee.

Confirmation of Receipt of the Summary of Your Rights Under the Fair Credit Reporting Act and the Copy of Consumer or Investigative Report: Under the federal Fair Credit Reporting Act (FCRA), an employer must provide a prospective employee with a copy of the official summary of rights under the act issued by the Federal Trade Commission (FTC), and with a copy of the consumer report or investigative consumer report, prior to taking any adverse employment action based in whole or in part on information in a report.

Consent to Criminal Background Check: With this form, a prospective employee grants the employer permission to do a criminal background check on the prospective employee.

Disclosure and Authorization Regarding Procurement of Consumer Report for Employment Purposes: Under the federal FCRA, an employer must disclose and obtain the individual's authorization regarding the procurement of a consumer report from a consumer reporting agency.

Disclosure and Authorization Regarding Procurement of Investigative Consumer Report for Employment Purposes: Under the federal FCRA, an employer must disclose and obtain the individual's authorization regarding the procurement of an investigative consumer report from a consumer reporting agency.

Disclosure of the Adverse Action Based on Information in a Consumer or Investigative Report: Under the federal FCRA, an employer must disclose if it has taken any adverse action based in whole or in part on information in a consumer report or an investigative consumer report.

Employee Self-Identification Form (for Federal Contractors and Subcontractors): This form is for use only by federal government contractors or subcontractors. It should be given to new hires after they've been offered the job. The data collected are compiled in the EEO-1 Report, submitted to the EEOC annually.

Employee Self-Identification Form (for Non-Contractors): This form is for use by non-contractor employers with 100 or more employees that are required to file an annual EEO-1 Report.

Employment Agreement: This form is a sample draft employment agreement, stating the level of compensation and other benefits the employee will receive in exchange for specific work performed and establishing other terms and conditions of employment.

Employment Inquiry Release: With this form, a prospective employee grants the employer permission to make investigative inquiries on the background of the prospective employee.

Letter Giving Notice of Planned Adverse Action Based on Information in Consumer Report or Investigative Consumer Report (Fair Credit Reporting Act): Under the federal FCRA, when an employer has obtained a consumer report or investigative consumer report and intends to take an adverse employment action on the basis of information contained in such a report, the employer must give the applicant a copy of the report, as well as a written description of the individual's FCRA rights before taking such action. As a practical matter, employers usually send a letter, similar to this sample letter, in which they provide the report and rights information.

Offer Letter to a Prospective Employee: This sample letter offers a job to a prospective employee.

Sample Reference Check Questions: This document lists several questions you should consider asking when checking an applicant's references.

A Summary of Your Rights Under the Fair Credit Reporting Act: Under the federal FCRA, an employer is required to provide the individual with a copy of the official description of individual rights under the act issued by the FTC at various stages in the decision-making process.

Chapter 10

Employee Handbook Table of Contents: This document is a sample table of contents for an employee handbook. You'll want to customize it to reflect those policies applicable to your company or organization.

Employee Handbook and At-Will Employee Status Acknowledgment: This document is a sample form in which a new employee acknowledges receiving and agreeing to the matters contained in the company's employee handbook. The form also requires the employee to acknowledge that he is an at-will employee.

Onboarding Checklist: This document lists criteria to consider when evaluating the effectiveness of your onboarding process.

Chapter 12

Certificate of Group Health Plan Coverage: This form helps employees document their prior health coverage when enrolling in a new employer's health plan.

Certification for Serious Injury or Illness of Covered Servicemember — for Military Family Leave (Federal Family and Medical Leave Act): Employers are entitled to require that an employee's request for leave under the federal Family and Medical Leave Act (FMLA) to care for a covered servicemember with a serious injury or illness is supported by a healthcare provider's certification. The employer may use this optional form for this purpose.

Certification of Health Care Provider for Employee's Serious Health Condition (Federal Family and Medical Leave Act): Employers are entitled to require that an employee's request for leave under the FMLA due to the employee's own serious health condition is supported by a healthcare provider's certification. The employer may use this optional form for this purpose.

Certification of Health Care Provider for Family Member's Serious Health Condition (Federal Family and Medical Leave Act): Employers are entitled to require that an employee's request for leave under the FMLA due to a serious health condition affecting a covered family member is supported by a healthcare provider's certification. The employer may use this optional form for this purpose.

Certification of Qualifying Exigency for Military Family Leave (Federal Family and Medical Leave Act): Employers are entitled to require that an employee's request for military family leave under the FMLA due to a qualifying exigency is supported by a healthcare provider's certification. The employer may use this optional form for this purpose.

Designation Notice (Federal Family and Medical Leave Act): When an employer covered by the FMLA has sufficient information to determine if an employee's leave is FMLA qualifying, the employer must provide the employee with notice stating that the leave has been designated as FMLA leave (or that additional information is needed to determine whether the leave is FMLA qualifying) within five business days, absent extenuating circumstances. The employer may use this optional form for this purpose.

Employee Rights and Responsibilities Under the Federal Family and Medical Leave Act: Employers covered by the FMLA must provide employees with written notice detailing the specific expectations and obligations of the employee under the law and explaining any consequences of a failure to meet such obligations. The employer may use this optional form for this purpose.

A Look at 401(k) Plan Fees: This document answers common questions that employees have about 401(k) plans.

Notice of Eligibility and Rights & Responsibilities (Federal Family and Medical Leave Act): After an employee notifies her employer (who is covered by the FMLA) of a need for leave, or when the employer acquires knowledge that an employee's leave may be for an FMLA-qualifying reason, the employer must notify the employee of her eligibility to take FMLA leave within five business days, absent extenuating circumstances. The employer may use this optional form for this purpose.

Total Rewards Statement: This form lists all the compensation and benefits that an employer provides to an employee.

Chapter 13

Employee Opinion Survey: This document is an example of a simple opinion survey an organization can distribute to employees to gauge worker satisfaction and determine areas of needed improvement.

Exit Interview Questionnaire: This form lists questions a company representative can ask when an employee voluntarily leaves the company.

Sample Pulse Survey: This document includes a number of sample questions to ask when conducting a pulse survey of your employees.

Chapter 15

Individual Development Plan Form: Employees can use this form to work with their managers in setting learning objectives and career goals.

Chapter 17

Discrimination Fact Sheets: This document includes fact sheets from the EEOC and Department of Labor (DOL) that detail discrimination guidelines.

Employee Rights Under the Fair Labor Standards Act: This document includes the Fair Labor Standards Act (FLSA) minimum-wage poster, titled Employee Rights Under the Fair Labor Standards Act. Every employer of employees subject to the FLSA's minimum-wage provisions must post, and keep posted, a notice explaining the act in a conspicuous place in all its establishments.

Equal Employment Opportunity Is the Law: This poster describes the federal laws prohibiting job discrimination based on race, color, sex, national origin, religion, age, equal pay, disability, and genetic information. Every employer covered by the nondiscrimination and equal employment opportunity laws is required to post this notice in a conspicuous location on its premises.

Facts about the Americans with Disabilities Act: This document includes a fact sheet from the EEOC detailing major provisions of the federal Americans with Disabilities Act (ADA).

Family and Medical Leave Act Fact Sheets: This document includes fact sheets from the DOL detailing major provisions of the FMLA.

Chapter 18

Employee Emergency Notification Form: This is a form the employee fills out, advising the employer as to whom to notify in the event of an emergency.

OSHA Information Posting: This document lists the major provisions under the federal Occupational Safety and Health Act (OSHA).

Sample Policy Statement on Harassment and Retaliation: This form is meant to be a sample policy prohibiting harassment of the type your organization should issue to its employee workforce.

Work-Related Injury and Illness Report Form: This form is used for reporting accidents or hazards in the workplace.

Troubleshooting

I tried my best to compile programs that work on most computers with the minimum system requirements. Alas, your computer may differ, and some programs may not work properly for some reason.

If you get an error message, try one or more of the following suggestions and then try using the software again:

- ✔ **Restart your computer.** Sometimes a simple reboot is all it takes to get everything working again.

- ✔ **Turn off any antivirus software running on your computer.** Installation programs sometimes mimic virus activity and may make your computer incorrectly believe that it's being infected by a virus. Just remember to turn the antivirus software back on again after you've installed the software.

- ✔ **Close all running programs.** The more programs you have running, the less memory is available to other programs. Installation programs typically update files and programs, so if you keep other programs running, installation may not work properly.

Customer Care

If you have trouble with the CD, please call Wiley Product Technical Support at 800-762-2974. Outside the United States, call 317-572-3994. You also can contact Wiley Product Technical Support at http://support.wiley.com. John Wiley & Sons, Inc., will provide technical support only for installation and other general quality-control items. For technical support on the applications themselves, consult the program's vendor or author.

To place additional orders or to request information about other Wiley products, please call 877-762-2974.

Index

• Numerics •

360-degree assessments, 266
401(k) plans, 195–196

• A •

AC-21 (American Competitiveness in 21st
    Century Act of 2000), 285
acceptance of job offers, 140–141
ADA (Americans with Disabilities Act), 59, 67,
    176, 201, 205, 286
ADAAA (Americans with Disabilities Act
    Amendments Act), 286
adaptability in leaders, 246
addresses, interview questions about, 116
ADEA (Age Discrimination in Employment
    Act), 67, 175–176, 284–285
administrative support system, 226
Adobe Reader, on CD, 338
ADR (alternative dispute resolution), 302–303
affiliations, including in employee skills
    inventory, 43
age, interview questions about, 116–117
age discrimination, 115
Age Discrimination in Employment Act
    (ADEA), 67, 175–176, 284–285
agendas, orientation, 153
aggregators, 67, 69
alignment. See onboarding
alternate work arrangements
    guidelines for, 213–214
    legal implications, 210–211
    options for, 211–212
    overview, 210
    rethinking processes, 212–213
alternative dispute resolution (ADR), 302–303
American Competitiveness in 21st Century
    Act of 2000 (AC-21), 285
American Society for Training & Development
    (ASTD) website, 333
Americans with Disabilities Act (ADA), 59, 67,
    176, 201, 205, 286
Americans with Disabilities Act Amendments
    Act of 2008 (ADAAA), 286

Americans with Disabilities Act Document
    Center website, 334
analytics, 24
annual bonuses, 178
antiharassment policies, 315
Anti-Kickback Act of 1948, 176
appearance of employees, antidiscrimination
    laws regarding, 279
applicability of subject matter in training
    programs, 235–236
applicant tracking systems (ATSs), 24, 26, 96
applications, job, 92–94
aptitude and ability tests, 99
arbitration programs, 303
armed forces, unpaid leave related to, 201
assessments of contingent workers, sending
    to staffing firms, 53–54
assimilation. See onboarding
ASTD (American Society for Training &
    Development) website, 333
ATSs (applicant tracking systems), 24, 26, 96
audiovisual presentations for orientation
    events, 153
award recipients, publicizing, 259–260

• B •

Baby Boomers, 19, 20, 325
background checks, 134–138
bargaining for pay levels, 168
BARS (behaviorally anchored rating scale),
    265–266
base wages, 164–165
behavioral interview questions, 113
behaviorally anchored rating scale (BARS),
    265–266
BeKnown, 69
bench strength, 240
benefits. See also health insurance
    cost containment, 185
    defined, 165
    demographic changes, effect on, 184–185
    dental insurance, 198
    diversity, effect on, 19
    domestic-partner, 202

benefits *(continued)*
  EAPs, 203–205
  family assistance, 198–199
  five principles for, 205–207
  government regulation, 186
  for home-based employees, 185–186
  leaves of absence, 200–202
  Medicare, 186–187
  overview, 10, 183–184
  retirement plans, 193–197
  sick days, 202–203
  Social Security, 186–187
  time off, 199–200
  total rewards, 204
  unemployment insurance, 187
  vision care, 198
  workers' compensation, 188
benefits administration systems, 27–28
benefits consultants, 192–193
BFOQ (bona fide occupational qualification), 60, 280
biannual bonuses, 178
blind ads, 72
BLS (Bureau of Labor Statistics) website, 334
bona fide occupational qualification (BFOQ), 60, 280
bonuses
  defined, 165
  employee referral, 216
  general discussion, 178
  signing, 141
bottom-line benefits, position initiatives as, 328
BranchOut, 69, 86
broadbanding, 169–170
Bureau of Labor Statistics (BLS) website, 334
business orientation to HR initiatives, developing, 327
business school seminars, 233

• *C* •

cafeteria-style benefits, 19, 185
campus recruiting, 75–77
candidates, succession
  assessing outcomes, 254–255
  creating flexible understanding with, 252–253
  developing, 253–254
  pinpointing, 251
  selecting outside company, 252

career development. *See also* employee recognition programs; succession planning
  general discussion, 13
  importance of, 240
  leadership development, 245–249
  mentoring, 240–244
  overview, 10, 239
career transition services, 203
CareerBuilder website, 66
cascading goals, 155
cash balance plans, 194
cash profit-sharing plans, 179
CD
  documents included on, 339–345
  installing files, 338
  overview, 337
  software, 338–339
  system requirements, 337
  technical support, 346
  troubleshooting, 345
CDHPs (consumer-directed health plans), 192
Census Bureau website, 172
certification, verifying, 135–136
checklists
  for employee recognition programs, 257–259
  for new employees, 156
  for staffing firms, 49–50
childcare, 198–199, 214–215
choice-time-off (CTO) plans, 203
chronological gaps in résumés, 90
chronological résumés, 89
citizenship, corporate, 217–218
citizenship status, interview questions about, 116
Civil Rights Acts of 1964 (Title VII), 67, 175, 291
classified ads, 72
classroom training, in-house, 232
C-level succession candidates, 250
cliff vesting, 197
cloning effect, 130
closed-ended interview questions, 113
cloud computing, 25
coaching versus mentoring, 157–158, 244
COBRA (Consolidated Omnibus Budget Reconciliation Act of 1986), 286, 304–305
cognitive tests, 99
collaboration, 218, 246
collective bargaining for pay levels, 168
college campus recruiting, 75–77

comfortable atmosphere, creating during interviews, 109–110
commission, 165
common-law couples, benefits for, 202
communication
  about company to recruits, 63–64
  about compensation policies, 181–182
  about performance appraisal systems, 269
  in employee recognition programs, 259
  with job candidates, 139, 141–142
  leadership skill, 246
  skills, developing, 329
companies
  basing job descriptions on objectives of, 58
  communicating to recruits about, 63–64
  hiring from outside of, 43–44
  hiring from within, 40–43
  information in job postings about, 65
  rules and policies, providing, 151
  websites for, 68
compensation
  bonuses, 178
  broadbanding, 169–170
  communication about policies, 181–182
  competency-based pay systems, 170
  defined, 165
  exempt and nonexempt employees, 173–176
  flexibility in job offers, 140
  guidelines for, 181
  HR role in, 164
  overview, 10, 12, 163, 168
  pay levels, setting, 167–168
  payroll/sales ratio, 172
  people factors, 170–171
  profit-sharing plans, 179
  raises, 177–178
  skill-based pay systems, 170
  state wage and hour laws, 172–173
  stock, 179–180
  terminology, 164–165
  variable pay systems, 169
competency models, 62
competency-based pay systems, 170
complaints, filing, 301–302
compressed work weeks, 211
computers, loaning to employees, 216
conferences, professional association, 232–233
conflict resolution, 302–303
Consolidated Omnibus Budget Reconciliation Act (COBRA), 286, 304–305

consumer-directed health plans (CDHPs), 192
contingent workers
  defined, 45
  feedback for staffing firm about, 53–54
  in flexible staffing approach, 18–19
  fliers with basic information, creating for, 53
  general discussion, 46
  incorporating into team, 50–53
  legal responsibility, 54
  overview, 47–48, 323
  staffing firms, 49–50
contracted daycare, 199
contractors, independent, 18–19, 45, 46
contracts, employment, 142
Copeland Act of 1934, 176
corporate citizenship, 217–218
costs
  of benefits, 185
  of healthcare, 190–193
  of HR technology, 25
cover letters, 90
creativity, measuring in job candidates, 129
credentials, including in employee skills inventory, 43
credit checks, 135–136
criminal background checks, 135–136
critical behaviors, 266
critical incidents, 266
cross-training, 18
cross-verifying job candidates, 131
CTO (choice-time-off) plans, 203
culture, creating healthy, 322–323
current information, staying up on, 331
customers, discovering soft skills needed through, 62

• D •

Davis-Bacon Act of 1931, 176
daycare, 199, 215
deadlines for job offers, 139
decision-making stage of hiring
  background checks, 134–138
  cross-verifying, 131
  hiring criteria, 130
  influencing factors, 124–126
  input from others, 131
  making offers, 138–142
  not forcing issue, 131
  overview, 123–124
  reference checking, 132–135

decision-making stage of hiring *(continued)*
 systems for selecting candidates, 126–130
 taking time during, 130–131
 "top of mind" syndrome, 131–132
deductibles on health insurance, 192
deferred profit-sharing plans, 179
defined benefit plans, 194–195
defined contribution plans, 194, 195
deliverables, 264
demographics, workplace, 184–185, 324–325
dental insurance, 198
dependent care reimbursement accounts, 199
Dice website, 66–67
difficult situations, managing. *See* problem
 management
digital footprints, 134
direct applications, 80
disability discrimination, 59
disciplinary procedures, 296–302, 326
discrimination. *See also* nondiscriminatory
 questioning
 age, 115
 against contingent workers, 54
 disability, 59
 disparate impact, 280
 during interviews, 106
 in job applications, 92–93
 in job descriptions, 60
 legal consequences, 279–280
 online job boards, 67
 reverse, 82
dishonest information in résumés, 26
dismissal procedures, 296, 326
disparate impact, 280
dispute resolution programs, 302–303
diversity in workforce
 benefit of recruiting outside of company, 44
 general discussion, 19–20
 recruiting, 81–82
documentation in disciplinary process, 299–300
domestic-partner benefits, 202
downsizing. *See* layoffs
driving histories, 135–136
drug benefits, 192
drug tests, 101, 135–136

● *E* ●

EAPs (employee assistance programs), 203–205
education
 as factor in pay scales, 171
 including in employee skills inventory, 42

requirements for job candidates, 59
tuition reimbursement, 215
verification of records, 135–136
EEOC. *See* Equal Employment Opportunity
 Commission
eFinancialCareers website, 67
elaws Advisors website, 334
eldercare, 20, 199
e-learning, 229–231
electronic devices, loaning to employees, 216
electronic résumés, 86–87
e-mail, evaluating training through, 237–238
empathy for new employees, 149
Employee Assistance Professionals
 Association, 205
employee assistance programs (EAPs),
 203–205
employee focus groups, 227
employee handbooks, 159–161
Employee Polygraph Protection Act of 1988,
 102
employee profile systems, 27, 236–237
employee recognition programs
 administration and communication, 259
 benefits of, 256–257
 checklist for, 257–259
 defined, 256
 evaluating results, 259–260
 low cost, 259
 overview, 255–256
 publicizing award recipients, 259–260
employee referral programs, 78–79, 216
Employee Retirement Income Security Act of
 1974 (ERISA), 197
employee sabbaticals, 215–217
employee skills inventory, developing, 41–43
employee stock ownership plans
 (ESOPs), 195
employee surveys, 218–220
employee-friendly workplaces
 alternate work arrangements, 210–214
 corporate citizenship, 217–218
 employee surveys, 218–220
 managerial involvement, 214
 on-site childcare, 214–215
 on-site exercise facilities, 214–215
 overview, 12–13, 20, 210
 phased retirement options, 214
 sabbaticals, 215–217
 team opportunities, 218
 tuition assistance or reimbursement,
 214–215

employees
  appearance, antidiscrimination laws
    regarding, 279
  cascading goals, 155
  defined, 45
  firing, 303–307
  layoffs, 308–312
  placing job candidates based on skills, 131
  self-service software, 28–29
  sexual harassment, 313–317
  worker classification, 45
employer contributions to retirement plans,
    195–196
employment agencies, 73
employment contracts, 142
employment laws
  AC-21, 285
  ADA, 286
  ADEA, 67, 175–176, 284–285
  COBRA, 286, 304–305
  compliance with, 323–324
  Equal Pay Act of 1963, 287
  FLSA, 173, 288
  FMLA, 200–201, 287–288
  FUTA, 288–289
  HIPAA, 191, 205, 289
  IRCA, 289
  layoff-related, 309–310
  overview, 284
  OWBA, 285
  Pregnancy Discrimination Act of 1978, 290
  Rehabilitation Act of 1973, 290
  Sarbanes-Oxley Act, 290–291
  Title VII of Civil Rights Act, 67, 175, 291
  USA PATRIOT ACT, 291
  WARN Act, 292, 309–310
employment loss, 309
employment-at-will doctrine, 294–295
ending interviews, 122
enthusiasm of candidates in interviews, 112
environment for training, 225–226
environmentally conscious companies, 217
Equal Employment Opportunity Commission
    (EEOC)
  antiharassment policy regulations, 315
  compliance with, 26
  disability discrimination, 59
  employment testing, 98
  general discussion, 281–284
  job applications, 92
  rights of contingent workers, 54
  website, 336

Equal Pay Act of 1963, 175, 287
e-recruiting systems, 26
ERISA (Employee Retirement Income Security
    Act of 1974), 197
ESOPs (employee stock ownership
    plans), 195
ethical culture, establishing, 14, 294
ethnic minorities, 81
evaluating applicants. *See also* pre-
    employment testing; résumés
  criteria for, 94–97
  job applications, 92–94
  overview, 85
  phone interviews, 104
executive education seminars, 233
executive search firms, 73–74
exempt workers
  defined, 165
  including information in job description, 58
  other legal considerations, 175–176
  overtime, 175
  overview, 173
  reasons for exemption, 173–174
exercise facilities, on-site, 214–215
exit incentives, 311–312
exit interviews, 220
experience, as factor in pay scales, 171
experience rating, 187
experiential learning, 234
expertise, sharing, 328

• F •

Facebook, 32, 69–70, 86, 88, 134
facilitators, focus group, 227
failure to hire claims, protection against, 25
Fair Labor Standards Act (FLSA), 173, 288
Family and Medical Leave Act (FMLA),
    200–201, 287–288
family assistance, 198–199
family status, interview questions about, 117
federal contractors, 94
Federal Unemployment Tax Act (FUTA),
    288–289
feedback
  on benefits, 207
  on contingent workers, sending to staffing
    firms, 53–54
  on onboarding program, 158
  in performance appraisal sessions, 271–272
  on recognition programs, 258
  on training, 237–238

fee-for-service plans, 189
files, CD
    documents, 339–345
    installing, 338
firing employees
    avoiding mistakes, 305–306
    care in handling, 326
    delivering news, 306
    overview, 303–305
    post-termination protocol, 306–307
    technology as legal protection, 25
    waivers of rights, 307–308
firms. *See* companies
firms, staffing. *See* staffing firms
first day welcome for new employees,
    149–150
flexible workforce, 18–19, 330
flextime, 211
flow sheets, 96
FLSA (Fair Labor Standards Act), 173, 288
FMLA (Family and Medical Leave Act),
    200–201, 287–288
focus, during interviews, 111
focus groups, employee, 227
following up
    on new employees, 156–158
    on performance appraisals, 274
foreign languages, 118, 161
formal orientation sessions, 152–153
free seminars, 216
friendly atmosphere, creating for contingent
    workers, 52
full-time employees, 18
functional résumés, 89
furlough, 308
FUTA (Federal Unemployment Tax Act of
    1939), 288–289

• G •

game time as employee perk, 216
gamification, 229–230
gatekeepers, 189
Gen Xers, 19
Generation Y, 19
generations in workplace, 19–20, 324–325
Genetic Information Nondiscrimination
    Act, 81
gifts for employees, 256
Glassdoor, 70

goals
    cascading, 155
    clarification during onboarding, 154–155
    for incentive programs, 181
    long-term employee, 241
    in MBO appraisals, 264–265
    relating training to strategic, 228–229
Googling job candidates, 103
government employment services, 80–81
government regulation. *See* regulatory
    compliance
graded vesting, 197
green companies, 217
grievances, 301–302
group presentations during onboarding,
    152–153

• H •

halo effect, 108, 130
handbooks, employee, 159–161
HCI (Human Capital Institute) website, 335
headhunters, 73–74
headlines, job postings, 65
health
    of employees, promoting, 193
    of employees, protecting, 313
    interview questions about, 117
health insurance
    fee-for-service plans, 189
    general discussion, 21
    healthcare reforms, 185
    HMOs, 189
    minimizing costs of, 192–193
    options, 190–191
    overview, 188
    PPOs, 189–190
    rising costs of, 191–193
Health Insurance Portability and
    Accountability Act (HIPAA), 191, 205, 289
health maintenance organizations
    (HMOs), 189
health savings accounts (HSAs), 192
healthy snacks as employee perk, 216
helicopter parents, 82–84
high-potential pool, 252
HIPAA (Health Insurance Portability and
    Accountability Act), 191, 205, 289

hiring. *See also* evaluating applicants; job descriptions; recruiting stage of hiring process
criteria for, 65, 130
failure to hire claims, protection against, 25
internal, 40–43
job titles, 61
from outside of company, 43–44
overview, 39, 55
qualities and attributes, 61–62
HMOs (health maintenance organizations), 189
hobbies in résumés, 90
holidays, 199
home-based work arrangements, 20–21, 27, 185–186, 212, 213
hostile environment sexual harassment, 314
hour laws, state, 172–173
HRISs. *See* human resources information systems
HSAs (health savings accounts), 192
Human Capital Institute (HCI) website, 335
human resources information systems (HRISs)
ATSs, 26
benefits administration systems, 27–28
employee profile systems, 27
employee self-service features, 28–29
overview, 25
payroll administration systems, 28
time management systems, 27
hypothetical interview questions, 113–114

• I •

icons, explained, 6
Identified website, 86
IDPs (individual development plans), 240, 254
IHRIM (International Association for Human Resource Information Management), 31
Immigration Reform and Control Act of 1986 (IRCA), 289
inbreeding, organizational, 44
incentives, 165, 311–312
Indeed website, 67
independent contractors, 18–19, 45, 46
individual development plans (IDPs), 240, 254
industriousness, measuring in job candidates, 129
infographic résumés, 87

in-house classroom training, 232
initial notifications in disciplinary process, 297
injuries, workplace, 54
installing CD files, 338
insurance. *See also* health insurance
dental, 198
unemployment, 187
workers' compensation, 188
intangible attributes, 128–130
integration. *See* onboarding
integration of technology, 31
integrity in leaders, 246
integrity tests, 101–102
intelligence, measuring in job candidates, 129
interactivity in training classes, 236
intergenerational workforce, 19–20, 324–325
International Association for Human Resource Information Management (IHRIM), 31
Internet. *See also* social media
hiring policies, 94
job boards, 66–68
networking, sourcing through, 69–71
reference checking, 134
searches for information on candidates, 103
training via, 230–231
Internet Applicant Final Rule of 2006, 81, 94
interpersonal abilities, 61–62
interviews
comfortable atmosphere, creating, 109–110
ending, 122
focus, 111
giving candidates time to respond, 112
halo effect, 108
impressions of candidates, 125
inconsistencies between, 107
making every question count, 111
nondiscriminatory questioning, 115–118
notes, 112
overview, 105–106, 107, 110–111
panel, 110
paying attention, 111
preparing for, 108–109
probing, 111–112
psychoanalyzing candidates, 108
questions to ask, 118–121
recording, 114
scheduling, 109
styles of questions, 113–114

interviews *(continued)*
  suspending judgments, 112
  talking too much, 107–108
  time devoted to, 107
  video, 110
intranet training, 231
investigating sexual harassment
    complaints, 316
IRCA (Immigration Reform and Control Act of
    1986), 289

• J •

job applications, 92–94
job boards, online, 66–68
job demands, ability to cope with, 129
job descriptions
  basing on company objectives, 58
  educational requirements and
      qualifications, 59
  elements included in, 57
  language in, 60
  overview, 55–58
  purposes of, 56
  realistic jobs, 59–60
  salary ranges, 61
  setting priorities, 58–59
job duties
  accurate descriptions of, 60
  prioritizing in job descriptions, 58–59
job fairs, 77–78
job history in company, including in
    employee skills inventory, 42
job hopping, 90
job offer letters, 138
job postings, writing, 64–66
job ranking, basing pay levels on, 167
job sharing, 211–212
job titles, 61
"just follow Joe around" approach to
    onboarding, 147–148

• L •

language in job descriptions, 60
languages, foreign, 118, 161
laptops, loaning to employees, 216
last-chance warnings in disciplinary
    process, 298
LawCrossing website, 67
laws, employment. *See* employment laws

layoffs
  addressing concerns of remaining
      employees, 312
  alternatives to, 311–312
  easing burden of, 310
  effectiveness of, 309
  federal and state laws, 309–310
  outplacement firms, hiring, 310–312
  overview, 308–309
leadership development, 245–249
leadership tracks, 247
leading interview questions, 114
learning management systems (LMSs),
    29–30, 237
learning maps, 226
leaves of absence, 200–202
legal issues. *See also* employment laws
  with alternate work arrangements, 210–211
  with background checks, 136
  with benefit packages, 186
  compliance with laws, 323–324
  contingent workers, 54
  discrimination, 279–280
  disparate impact, 280
  EEOC, 281–284
  employee handbooks, 159
  exempt and nonexempt employees, 175–176
  general discussion, 13–14
  importance of understanding, 278–279
  in job descriptions, 58
  overview, 277
  peacemaking in organizations, 279
  with performance appraisal systems, 272
  records retention, 27
  retirement plans, 198
  staying informed of, 331
  technology as protection, 25
  with time off, 200
licenses
  including in employee skills inventory, 43
  verification of, 135–136
lie-detector tests, 102–103
lifestyle benefits, 185
line managers
  matching employee tasks to talents, 38–39
  role in employee-friendly work
      environment, 214
  sensitivity to needs and agendas of, 330
LinkedIn, 32, 69, 70, 134
LMSs (learning management systems),
    29–30, 237
lynda.com, 229

• M •

mailroom use as employee perk, 216
managed-care programs, 189–190
management by objectives (MBO), 264–265
managers
  control of pay levels, 168
  matching employee tasks to talents, 38–39
  role in employee-friendly work
    environment, 214
  sensitivity to needs and agendas of, 330
  of staffing firms, visits from, 50
market data, basing pay levels on, 167–168
marketing mindset, developing, 328
mass layoff, 309
MBO (management by objectives), 264–265
mediation programs, 303
medical examinations, 99–100
medical exams, checking, 135–136
medicare, 186–187
mentoring
  in career development, 240–244
  during onboarding, 157–158
  training by, 233–235
mentors, 242–244
merit raises, 177–178
Microsoft SharePoint, 32
minimum wage standards, 173
minorities, ethnic, 81
mission statements, 225
misspellings in résumés, 90
mobile devices, used as training devices, 231
model behavior, 329
monitoring recruiting process, 84
Monster website, 66
motivation
  measuring in job candidates, 129
  motivational ability in leaders, 246
movies as employee perk, 216
multirater assessments, 267

• N •

names, interview questions about, 117
national origin, interview questions about, 116
needs-assessment options for training,
    227–228
negative reactions, during performance
    appraisal sessions, 272–273
negotiating salary, 139–140
networks, checking references on, 133–134

new employees, orientation of. *See*
    onboarding
nondiscriminatory questioning
  addresses, 116
  age, 116–117
  citizenship status, 116
  family status, 117
  health and physical condition, 117
  language, 118
  name, 117
  national origin, 116
  overview, 115–116
  religion, 117
nonexempt workers
  defined, 165
  including information in job description, 58
  other legal considerations, 175–176
  overtime, 175
  overview, 173
  reasons for exemption, 173–174
notebooks, loaning to employees, 216
note-taking for interviews, 112, 122

• O •

observation
  of job candidates, 125–126
  need for training based on, 228
Occupational Safety & Health Administration
    (OSHA), 313, 335
offer letters, 138
offers for job candidates
  acceptance details, 140–141
  communication with candidates,
    139, 141–142
  deadlines for, 139
  knowing when to draw line, 140
  negotiating salary, 139–140
  overview, 138–139
  urgency in, 138
off-site work arrangements, 20–21, 27,
    185–186, 212, 213
off-the-wall interview questions, 114
Older Workers Benefit Protection Act of 1990
    (OWBA), 285
On the CD icon, 6
onboarding
  benefits education, 206
  clarification of tasks and goals, 154–155
  company rules and policies, providing, 151
  empathy for new employees, 149

onboarding *(continued)*
  employee handbooks, 159–161
  first-day welcome, 149–150
  follow-up meetings, 156–158
  formal sessions, 152
  group presentations, making user-friendly,
    152–153
  involving senior management, 152
  large-group sessions in suitable locations,
    152
  overview, 12, 145–147
  procedures manual, 159–161
  spacing of events during, 154
  unproductive approaches, 147–148
  written orientation agendas, providing, 153
online job boards, 66–68
online networking, sourcing through, 69–71
online reference checking, 134
on-site childcare, 214–215
on-site exercise facilities, 214–215
open houses, 79–80
open-ended interview questions, 113
OpenOffice, on CD, 338
organizational inbreeding, 44
organizations. *See* companies
Orkut, 71
OSHA (Occupational Safety & Health
    Administration), 313, 335
osmosis approach to onboarding, 147
outplacement, 203, 305
outplacement firms, hiring, 310–312
overtime, 173, 175
OWBA (Older Workers Benefit Protection Act
    of 1990), 285

• *P* •

panel interviews, 110
part-time employees, 212
passive job candidates, 70
past experience of job candidates, 124–125
past job performance, as factor in pay
    scales, 171
Patient Protection and Affordable Care Act,
    21, 185
pay
  broadbanding, 169–170
  competency-based pay systems, 170
  cuts in, temporary, 311
  frequency, 172
  levels, setting, 167–168

overview, 168
raises, 177–178
skill-based pay systems, 170
timeliness, 172
variable pay systems, 169
paying attention during interviews, 111
payroll administration systems, 28
payroll/sales ratio, 172
peacemaking in organizations, 279
performance appraisal systems
  BARS, 265–266
  benefits of, 262–263
  communication about systems, 269
  critical incidents, 266
  following up on, 274
  MBO, 264–265
  multirater assessments, 267
  overview, 13, 29, 261, 267
  performance measures, 268
  sessions with employees, 269–273
  support of senior management, 267
  tracking mechanisms, 268–269
performance improvement plan (PIP), 298
personal referral networks, 322
personality tests, 100–101
personal-time-off (PTO) plans, 203
phased retirement options, 214
phone calls
  interviews, 104
  to references, 133
physical ability tests, 99–100
physical condition, interview questions
    about, 117
Pinterest, 71
PIP (performance improvement plan), 298
policies, workplace
  antiharassment, 315
  employee handbooks, 159–161
  explaining to new employees, 151
  Internet hiring, 94
  overview, 10
  violence, 317–318
polygraph tests, 102–103
position eliminations. *See* layoffs
post-termination protocol, 306–307
post-training surveys, 237–238
potential of employees
  developing in existing staff, 38–39
  as factor in pay scales, 171
PPOs (preferred provider organizations),
    189–190

pre-employment testing
  aptitude and ability tests, 99
  drug tests, 101
  integrity tests, 101–102
  overview, 97–99
  personality tests, 100–101
  physical ability, 99–100
  polygraph tests, 102–103
  precautions, 103–104
  proficiency tests, 99
  psychological tests, 100–101
preferred provider organizations (PPOs),
    189–190
Pregnancy Discrimination Act of 1978, 290
pregnancy leave, 200–201
previous job history, including in employee
    skills inventory, 42
priorities, setting for job descriptions, 58–59
probationary periods, 126
probing during interviews, 111–112
problem management
  dispute resolution programs, 302–303
  employment-at-will doctrine, 294–295
  ethical culture, establishing, 294
  firing employees, 303–307
  grievances, 301–302
  layoffs, 308–312
  legal issues, 295–296
  overview, 293–294
  progressive discipline systems, 296–301
  safety and health of employees,
    protecting, 313
  sexual harassment, 313–317
  violence in workplace, 317–318
problem-solving ability, measuring in job
    candidates, 129
procedures manual, 159–161
productivity increases, 177
professional association conferences,
    80, 232–233
proficiency tests, 99
profit-sharing plans, 179
progressive discipline systems, 296–301
psychoanalyzing candidates during
    interviews, 108
psychological tests, 100–101
PTO (personal-time-off) plans, 203
public seminars, 232–233
publicizing award recipients, 259–260
pulse surveys, 219–220

• Q •

QR code links on résumés, 87
qualifications, in job postings, 65
qualities and attributes, 61–62
quality of medical services, 190
questionnaires, needs-assessment, 227–228
questions in interviews. *See* interviews
quid pro quo harassment, 314

• R •

raises, pay, 165, 177–178
realistic job descriptions, 59–60
receptivity of students in training
    programs, 235
recognition, employee. *See* employee
    recognition programs
recording interviews, 114
records retention, 27, 94, 281
recruiters
  choosing, 74–75
  employment agencies, 73
  executive search firms, 73–74
  headhunters, 73–74
  overview, 72–73
  reasons for using, 74
  staffing firms, 73
recruiting stage of hiring process. *See also*
    sourcing
  communicating about company, 63–64
  diversity recruiting, 81–82
  helicopter parents, 82–84
  kicking off process, 64
  monitoring progress, 84
  as ongoing process, 84
  overview, 63, 322
  specialization and, 18
  writing job postings, 64–66
reductions in force. *See* layoffs
reductions in work schedules, 311
references, checking, 132–135
referrals from employees, 78–79
regulatory compliance. *See also* legal issues
  benefit packages, 186
  importance of, 323–324
  overview, 10
Rehabilitation Act of 1973, 290
rehiring former staff members, 41

reimbursement of tuition, 214–215, 226
reinforcement of training concepts, 236
religion, interview questions about, 117
Remember icon, 6
remote work arrangements, 20–21, 27, 185–186, 212, 213
replacement guarantees from recruiters, 75
reporting process for sexual harassment, 316
resourcefulness, measuring in job candidates, 129
response method, in job postings, 65
response time during interviews, 112
responsibilities of HR
  legal, 13–14
  overview, 9–10
  retaining employees, 12–13
  strategic staffing, 11–12
  training and developing employees, 13
restricted stock, 180
restructuring. *See* layoffs
résumés
  basics of, 88–89
  dishonest information in, 26
  evaluating, 95–96
  evolution of, 86–88
  overview, 85
  reading between lines, 89–90
  red flags, 90–91
résumé-scanning applications, 88
retaining employees, 10, 12–13
retention bonuses, 178
retirement, early, 311–312
retirement plans
  defined benefit plans, 194–195
  defined contribution plans, 195
  employer contributions to, 195–196
  ERISA and other legal issues, 197
  overview, 193–194
reverse discrimination, 82
review services, online, 70–71
Re.vu, 87
rightsizing. *See* layoffs

● **S** ●

SaaS (software as a service), 25
sabbaticals, 215–217
safety of employees, protecting, 313

salary. *See also* pay
  defined, 164–165
  in job descriptions, 61
  negotiating with job candidates, 139–140
  temporary pay cuts, 311
salary guides, 167
same-sex married persons, benefits for, 202
Sarbanes-Oxley Act (2002), 290–291
scheduling job interviews, 109
search engine optimization (SEO), 66
second warnings in disciplinary process, 297
second-language skills, including in employee skills inventory, 42
security, technology-related, 325–326
selecting job candidates, systems for, 126–130
self-service software for employees, 28–29
seminars
  executive education, 233
  free, 216
  public, 232–233
senior management
  cascading goals, 155
  involving in onboarding program, 152
  support for performance appraisal systems, 267
seniority
  as factor in pay scales, 171
  step-ups, 177
SEO (search engine optimization), 66
sessions, performance appraisal
  choosing areas for further development, 273
  conducting, 270–271
  constructive feedback, 271–272
  negative reactions during, 272–273
  overview, 269–270
  preparing for, 270
severance agreements, 307
severance benefits, 310
sexual harassment
  investigating complaints, 316
  overview, 313–314
  reporting process, creating, 316
  taking decisive action, 316–317
  written policies about, 315
SharePoint, Microsoft, 32
short-term compensation (STC) programs, 311
short-term disability plans, 202

SHRM (Society for Human Resource Management) website, 335–336
sick days, 202–203
signing bonuses, 141
signing job offer letters, 141
Silent Generation, 19
Simply Hired website, 67
skill-based pay systems, 170
skills of employees
  employee skills inventory, developing, 41–43
  intangible attributes, 128–130
  placing job candidates in other positions based on, 131
  qualities and attributes, 61–62
SkillSoft, 229
SlideShare, 87
slideshow résumés, 87
social media
  accessing personal accounts, 88
  checking references, 134
  general discussion, 30–31
  international, 71
  sourcing through, 69–71
social-network-enabled services for résumés, 86
Social Security, 186–187
Social Security number verification, 135–136
Society for Human Resource Management (SHRM) website, 335–336
soft skills, 61–62
software as a service (SaaS), 25
software on CD, 338–339
sourcing
  blind and classified ads, 72
  campus recruiting, 75–77
  company website, 68
  direct applications, 80
  employee referrals, 78–79
  government employment services, 80–81
  job fairs, 77–78
  online job boards, 66–68
  open houses, 79–80
  overview, 66
  professional associations, 80
  recruiters, 72–75
  social media and online networking, 69–71
spacing of events during onboarding, 154
special preferences, including in employee skills inventory, 42

specialization, 17–18
spot bonuses, 178
staffing. *See* strategic staffing
staffing firms
  asking managers to visit businesses, 50
  checklist for, 49–50
  feedback on contingent workers, sending to, 53–54
  general discussion, 73
  overview, 49
state employment agencies, 80–81
state laws regarding wages and hours, 172–173
STC (short-term compensation) programs, 311
stock option plans, 179–180
strategic staffing. *See also* contingent workers
  developing potential of existing staff, 38–39
  general discussion, 16–17
  hiring employees, 39–44
  overview, 10, 35, 321
  syncing with business needs, 36–38
  when to begin, 39
  worker classifications, 44–46
students in training programs, receptivity of, 235
subject matter in training programs, applicability of, 235–236
subjective criteria in job descriptions, 62
success drivers, 62
success of company, factors affecting
  contingent staffing, 323
  culture, creating healthy, 322–323
  demographics, keeping pace with changing, 324–325
  disciplinary action, 326
  dismissals, 326
  overview, 321
  recruiting, 322
  regulatory compliance, 323–324
  strategic staffing, 321
  technology-related security, 325–326
  training, viewing as investment, 326
  work/life balance, prioritizing, 324
success of HR professionals
  business orientation to HR initiatives, developing, 327
  communication skills, developing, 329
  expertise, sharing, 328
  flexible workforce, maintaining, 330

success of HR professionals *(continued)*
  line managers, sensitivity to needs and agendas of, 330
  marketing mindset, developing, 328
  model behavior, 329
  overview, 327
  position initiatives as bottom-line benefits, 328
  staying on leading edge, 331
  tendency to rush, avoiding, 329
SuccessFactors, 25
succession management systems, 29–30
succession planning
  assessing outcomes, 254–255
  creating plans, 250
  developing candidates, 253–254
  flexible understanding with candidates, 252–253
  overview, 249
  pinpointing candidates, 251
  selecting candidates outside company, 252
  technology in, 254
  urgency of, 249–250
supervision of contingent workers, 52
surveys
  employee, 218–220
  needs-assessment, 227–228
  post-training, 237–238
system requirements, CD, 337

• T •

tablets, loaning to employees, 216
talent management systems (TMSs)
  LMSs, 29–30
  overview, 29
  performance appraisal systems, 29
  succession management systems, 29–30
talent of employees, placement according to, 38–39
tasks
  clarification during onboarding, 154–155
  instructions for contingent workers, 52
teams
  bonuses, 178
  capacity for teamwork, measuring in job candidates, 129
  incorporating contingent workers into, 50–53
  opportunities, 218
Technical Stuff icon, 6

technical support, CD, 346
technology. *See also* social media
  choosing systems, 30–31
  general discussion, 17
  growth of HR-related, 24–25
  HRISs, 25–29
  for off-site work arrangements, 21
  overview, 16, 23
  résumé-scanning applications, 88
  security, 325–326
  succession planning, 254
  TMSs, 29–30
telecommuting, 20–21, 27, 185–186, 212, 213
telephone calls
  interviews, 104
  to references, 133
temperament, measuring in job candidates, 129
temporary pay cuts, 311
tenure, raises linked to, 177
termination
  avoiding mistakes, 305–306
  care in handling, 326
  cause for, 298
  delivering news, 306
  for just cause, 161
  overview, 303–305
  post-termination protocol, 306–307
  technology as legal protection, 25
  waivers of rights, 307–308
termination-at-will doctrine, 294–295
testing
  aptitude and ability tests, 99
  drug tests, 101
  impressions of candidates, 125
  including in employee skills inventory, 43
  integrity tests, 101–102
  overview, 97–99
  personality tests, 100–101
  physical ability, 99–100
  polygraph tests, 102–103
  precautions, 103–104
  proficiency tests, 99
  psychological tests, 100–101
time management systems, 27
time off, 199–200
Tip icon, 6
Title VII of Civil Rights Act (1964), 67, 175, 291
TMSs. *See* talent management systems
"top of mind" syndrome, 131–132
topic-specific workshops, 233

total rewards, 204
tracking mechanisms, in performance
    appraisal systems, 268–269
training
    changing face of, 224–225
    effectiveness of programs, 235–236
    e-learning, 229–231
    employee profiles, using to manage, 236–237
    employee skills inventory, including in, 42
    environment for, 225–226
    executive education seminars, 233
    general discussion, 13
    improving efficiency with, 39
    in-house classroom, 232
    LMS technology, 29–30
    measuring results, 237–238
    mentoring, 233–235
    needs-assessment options, 227–228
    overview, 10, 223–224, 229
    pitfalls of, 234
    professional association conferences, 232–233
    public seminars, 232–233
    relating to strategic goals, 228–229
    for succession candidates, 253
    viewing as investment, 326
training series, 236
transition. *See* onboarding
trends in HR
    benefit-related, 184–186
    diversity, 19–20
    flexible workforce, 18–19
    healthcare, 21
    overview, 15–16
    specialization, 17–18
    strategic thinking, 16–17
    technology, 17
    work/life initiatives, 20–21
troubleshooting CDs, 345
tuition assistance or reimbursement,
    214–215, 226
TweetMyJobs, 69
twesumes, 87
Twitter, 32, 69, 70, 88, 134
Twitter résumés, 87
typos in résumés, 90

• *U* •

unemployment insurance, 187
Uniform Guidelines on Employee Selection
    Procedures, 98

unionized companies, negotiations in,
    168, 279
university campus recruiting, 75–77
university seminars, 233
U.S. Census Bureau website, 172
USA Patriot Act (2001), 280, 291

• *V* •

vacation days, 199–200
values and best practices, emphasizing to
    new employees, 156
variable pay systems, 169
vesting for employer contributions, 197
Viadeo, 71
video approach to onboarding, 148
video interviews, 110
video résumés, 86
videoconferencing as training device, 231
violence in workplace, 273, 317–318
virtual offices, 213
vision care, 198
Vizualize.me, 87
volunteerism, 217
voucher systems, 199

• *W* •

wage and hour claims, protection against, 25
Wage Garnishment Law, 176
wage laws, state, 172–173
wages, base, 164–165
wage-theft prevention laws, 288
waivers of rights, 307–308
walk-ins, 80
Walsh-Healey Act of 1936, 176
WARN (Worker Adjustment and Retraining
    Notification) Act, 292, 309–310
Warning icon, 6
websites
    Americans with Disabilities Act Document
        Center, 334
    ASTD, 333
    BLS, 334
    company, sourcing through, 68
    EEOC, 336
    elaws Advisors, 334
    HCI, 335
    job boards, 66–68
    OSHA, 335
    overview, 333

websites *(continued)*
  SHRM, 335–336
  U.S. Census Bureau, 172
  Workforce Online, 336
  WorldatWork, 336
weighted application forms, 96–97
weighted evaluation systems, 126, 127–128
wellness programs, 193
witness evaluation notes, 300
Worker Adjustment and Retraining
    Notification (WARN) Act, 292, 309–310
worker classifications
  contingent workers, 46
  employees, 45
  independent contractors, 46
  overview, 44–45
workers' compensation, 135–136, 188
Workforce Online website, 336

work/life balance, 20–21, 324
WorldatWork website, 336
writing job postings, 64–66
written documentation for orientation
    events, 153
written orientation agendas, providing, 153
written policies about sexual harassment, 315
wrongful discharge, 295–296

● *X* ●

Xing, 71

● *Y* ●

Yelp, 70

John Wiley & Sons, Inc.
End-User License Agreement

READ THIS. You should carefully read these terms and conditions before opening the software packet(s) included with this book "Book". This is a license agreement "Agreement" between you and John Wiley & Sons, Inc. "WILEY". By opening the accompanying software packet(s), you acknowledge that you have read and accept the following terms and conditions. If you do not agree and do not want to be bound by such terms and conditions, promptly return the Book and the unopened software packet(s) to the place you obtained them for a full refund.

1. **License Grant.** WILEY grants to you (either an individual or entity) a nonexclusive license to use one copy of the enclosed software program(s) (collectively, the "Software") solely for your own personal or business purposes on a single computer (whether a standard computer or a workstation component of a multi-user network). The Software is in use on a computer when it is loaded into temporary memory (RAM) or installed into permanent memory (hard disk, CD-ROM, or other storage device). WILEY reserves all rights not expressly granted herein.

2. **Ownership.** WILEY is the owner of all right, title, and interest, including copyright, in and to the compilation of the Software recorded on the physical packet included with this Book "Software Media". Copyright to the individual programs recorded on the Software Media is owned by the author or other authorized copyright owner of each program. Ownership of the Software and all proprietary rights relating thereto remain with WILEY and its licensers.

3. **Restrictions on Use and Transfer.**

   (a) You may only (i) make one copy of the Software for backup or archival purposes, or (ii) transfer the Software to a single hard disk, provided that you keep the original for backup or archival purposes. You may not (i) rent or lease the Software, (ii) copy or reproduce the Software through a LAN or other network system or through any computer subscriber system or bulletin-board system, or (iii) modify, adapt, or create derivative works based on the Software.

   (b) You may not reverse engineer, decompile, or disassemble the Software. You may transfer the Software and user documentation on a permanent basis, provided that the transferee agrees to accept the terms and conditions of this Agreement and you retain no copies. If the Software is an update or has been updated, any transfer must include the most recent update and all prior versions.

4. **Restrictions on Use of Individual Programs.** You must follow the individual requirements and restrictions detailed for each individual program in the "About the CD" appendix of this Book or on the Software Media. These limitations are also contained in the individual license agreements recorded on the Software Media. These limitations may include a requirement that after using the program for a specified period of time, the user must pay a registration fee or discontinue use. By opening the Software packet(s), you agree to abide by the licenses and restrictions for these individual programs that are detailed in the "About the CD" appendix and/or on the Software Media. None of the material on this Software Media or listed in this Book may ever be redistributed, in original or modified form, for commercial purposes.

5. **Limited Warranty.**

    (a) WILEY warrants that the Software and Software Media are free from defects in materials and workmanship under normal use for a period of sixty (60) days from the date of purchase of this Book. If WILEY receives notification within the warranty period of defects in materials or workmanship, WILEY will replace the defective Software Media.

    (b) WILEY AND THE AUTHOR(S) OF THE BOOK DISCLAIM ALL OTHER WARRANTIES, EXPRESS OR IMPLIED, INCLUDING WITHOUT LIMITATION IMPLIED WARRANTIES OF MERCHANTABILITY AND FITNESS FOR A PARTICULAR PURPOSE, WITH RESPECT TO THE SOFTWARE, THE PROGRAMS, THE SOURCE CODE CONTAINED THEREIN, AND/OR THE TECHNIQUES DESCRIBED IN THIS BOOK. WILEY DOES NOT WARRANT THAT THE FUNCTIONS CONTAINED IN THE SOFTWARE WILL MEET YOUR REQUIREMENTS OR THAT THE OPERATION OF THE SOFTWARE WILL BE ERROR FREE.

    (c) This limited warranty gives you specific legal rights, and you may have other rights that vary from jurisdiction to jurisdiction.

6. **Remedies.**

    (a) WILEY's entire liability and your exclusive remedy for defects in materials and workmanship shall be limited to replacement of the Software Media, which may be returned to WILEY with a copy of your receipt at the following address: Software Media Fulfillment Department, Attn.: *Human Resources Kit For Dummies,* 3rd Edition, John Wiley & Sons, Inc., 10475 Crosspoint Blvd., Indianapolis, IN 46256, or call 1-800-762-2974. Please allow four to six weeks for delivery. This Limited Warranty is void if failure of the Software Media has resulted from accident, abuse, or misapplication. Any replacement Software Media will be warranted for the remainder of the original warranty period or thirty (30) days, whichever is longer.

    (b) In no event shall WILEY or the author be liable for any damages whatsoever (including without limitation damages for loss of business profits, business interruption, loss of business information, or any other pecuniary loss) arising from the use of or inability to use the Book or the Software, even if WILEY has been advised of the possibility of such damages.

    (c) Because some jurisdictions do not allow the exclusion or limitation of liability for consequential or incidental damages, the above limitation or exclusion may not apply to you.

7. **U.S. Government Restricted Rights.** Use, duplication, or disclosure of the Software for or on behalf of the United States of America, its agencies and/or instrumentalities "U.S. Government" is subject to restrictions as stated in paragraph (c)(1)(ii) of the Rights in Technical Data and Computer Software clause of DFARS 252.227-7013, or subparagraphs (c) (1) and (2) of the Commercial Computer Software - Restricted Rights clause at FAR 52.227-19, and in similar clauses in the NASA FAR supplement, as applicable.

8. **General.** This Agreement constitutes the entire understanding of the parties and revokes and supersedes all prior agreements, oral or written, between them and may not be modified or amended except in a writing signed by both parties hereto that specifically refers to this Agreement. This Agreement shall take precedence over any other documents that may be in conflict herewith. If any one or more provisions contained in this Agreement are held by any court or tribunal to be invalid, illegal, or otherwise unenforceable, each and every other provision shall remain in full force and effect.

Apple & Mac

iPad 2 For Dummies,
3rd Edition
978-1-118-17679-5

iPhone 4S For Dummies,
5th Edition
978-1-118-03671-6

iPod touch For Dummies,
3rd Edition
978-1-118-12960-9

Mac OS X Lion
For Dummies
978-1-118-02205-4

Blogging & Social Media

CityVille For Dummies
978-1-118-08337-6

Facebook For Dummies,
4th Edition
978-1-118-09562-1

Mom Blogging
For Dummies
978-1-118-03843-7

Twitter For Dummies,
2nd Edition
978-0-470-76879-2

WordPress For Dummies,
4th Edition
978-1-118-07342-1

Business

Cash Flow For Dummies
978-1-118-01850-7

Investing For Dummies,
6th Edition
978-0-470-90545-6

Job Searching with Social
Media For Dummies
978-0-470-93072-4

QuickBooks 2012
For Dummies
978-1-118-09120-3

Resumes For Dummies,
6th Edition
978-0-470-87361-8

Starting an Etsy Business
For Dummies
978-0-470-93067-0

Cooking & Entertaining

Cooking Basics
For Dummies, 4th Edition
978-0-470-91388-8

Wine For Dummies,
4th Edition
978-0-470-04579-4

Diet & Nutrition

Kettlebells For Dummies
978-0-470-59929-7

Nutrition For Dummies,
5th Edition
978-0-470-93231-5

Restaurant Calorie Counter
For Dummies,
2nd Edition
978-0-470-64405-8

Digital Photography

Digital SLR Cameras &
Photography For Dummies,
4th Edition
978-1-118-14489-3

Digital SLR Settings
& Shortcuts
For Dummies
978-0-470-91763-3

Photoshop Elements 10
For Dummies
978-1-118-10742-3

Gardening

Gardening Basics
For Dummies
978-0-470-03749-2

Vegetable Gardening
For Dummies,
2nd Edition
978-0-470-49870-5

Green/Sustainable

Raising Chickens
For Dummies
978-0-470-46544-8

Green Cleaning
For Dummies
978-0-470-39106-8

Health

Diabetes For Dummies,
3rd Edition
978-0-470-27086-8

Food Allergies
For Dummies
978-0-470-09584-3

Living Gluten-Free
For Dummies,
2nd Edition
978-0-470-58589-4

Hobbies

Beekeeping
For Dummies,
2nd Edition
978-0-470-43065-1

Chess For Dummies,
3rd Edition
978-1-118-01695-4

Drawing For Dummies,
2nd Edition
978-0-470-61842-4

eBay For Dummies,
7th Edition
978-1-118-09806-6

Knitting For Dummies,
2nd Edition
978-0-470-28747-7

Language &
Foreign Language

English Grammar
For Dummies,
2nd Edition
978-0-470-54664-2

French For Dummies,
2nd Edition
978-1-118-00464-7

German For Dummies,
2nd Edition
978-0-470-90101-4

Spanish Essentials
For Dummies
978-0-470-63751-7

Spanish For Dummies,
2nd Edition
978-0-470-87855-2

Available wherever books are sold. For more information or to order direct: U.S. customers visit www.dummies.com or call 1-877-762-2974.
U.K. customers visit www.wileyeurope.com or call (0) 1243 843291. Canadian customers visit www.wiley.ca or call 1-800-567-4797.
Connect with us online at www.facebook.com/fordummies or @fordummies

Math & Science

Algebra I For Dummies,
2nd Edition
978-0-470-55964-2

Biology For Dummies,
2nd Edition
978-0-470-59875-7

Chemistry For Dummies,
2nd Edition
978-1-1180-0730-3

Geometry For Dummies,
2nd Edition
978-0-470-08946-0

Pre-Algebra Essentials
For Dummies
978-0-470-61838-7

Microsoft Office

Excel 2010 For Dummies
978-0-470-48953-6

Office 2010 All-in-One
For Dummies
978-0-470-49748-7

Office 2011 for Mac
For Dummies
978-0-470-87869-9

Word 2010
For Dummies
978-0-470-48772-3

Music

Guitar For Dummies,
2nd Edition
978-0-7645-9904-0

Clarinet For Dummies
978-0-470-58477-4

iPod & iTunes
For Dummies,
9th Edition
978-1-118-13060-5

Pets

Cats For Dummies,
2nd Edition
978-0-7645-5275-5

Dogs All-in One
For Dummies
978-0470-52978-2

Saltwater Aquariums
For Dummies
978-0-470-06805-2

Religion & Inspiration

The Bible For Dummies
978-0-7645-5296-0

Catholicism For Dummies,
2nd Edition
978-1-118-07778-8

Spirituality For Dummies,
2nd Edition
978-0-470-19142-2

Self-Help & Relationships

Happiness For Dummies
978-0-470-28171-0

Overcoming Anxiety
For Dummies,
2nd Edition
978-0-470-57441-6

Seniors

Crosswords For Seniors
For Dummies
978-0-470-49157-7

iPad 2 For Seniors
For Dummies, 3rd Edition
978-1-118-17678-8

Laptops & Tablets
For Seniors For Dummies,
2nd Edition
978-1-118-09596-6

Smartphones & Tablets

BlackBerry For Dummies,
5th Edition
978-1-118-10035-6

Droid X2 For Dummies
978-1-118-14864-8

HTC ThunderBolt
For Dummies
978-1-118-07601-9

MOTOROLA XOOM
For Dummies
978-1-118-08835-7

Sports

Basketball For Dummies,
3rd Edition
978-1-118-07374-2

Football For Dummies,
2nd Edition
978-1-118-01261-1

Golf For Dummies,
4th Edition
978-0-470-88279-5

Test Prep

ACT For Dummies,
5th Edition
978-1-118-01259-8

ASVAB For Dummies,
3rd Edition
978-0-470-63760-9

The GRE Test For
Dummies, 7th Edition
978-0-470-00919-2

Police Officer Exam
For Dummies
978-0-470-88724-0

Series 7 Exam
For Dummies
978-0-470-09932-2

Web Development

HTML, CSS, & XHTML
For Dummies, 7th Edition
978-0-470-91659-9

Drupal For Dummies,
2nd Edition
978-1-118-08348-2

Windows 7

Windows 7
For Dummies
978-0-470-49743-2

Windows 7
For Dummies,
Book + DVD Bundle
978-0-470-52398-8

Windows 7 All-in-One
For Dummies
978-0-470-48763-1